Following Jesus

———

What He Said to Do,

and What He Did

Nelson P. Miller

Following Jesus: what he said to do, and what he did.

Miller, Nelson P.

Published by:

Crown Management LLC – August 2015

1527 Pineridge Drive
Grand Haven, MI 49417
USA

ISBN: 978-0-9905553-7-7

c/o 111 Commerce Avenue S.W.
Grand Rapids, MI 49503
(616) 301-6800 ext. 6963

For those seeking the greater realm.

Summary Table of Contents

Detailed Table of Contents

iv

ix

Entering the Realm

This book is a love affair. Everyone knows love affairs. For the young, they might start with sports stars, action figures, or television characters. Many, though not all, of us move on to film stars, musicians, and book characters, and some to politicians, professionals, activists, and business leaders. And of course, we have romantic love affairs, first with childhood infatuations, then teen heart throbs and beyond to dating and marriage. Sprinkled throughout are deep friendships whether in childhood, middle and secondary school, college, graduate school, the workplace, community, church, and retirement.

For some the subject of love affairs is painful. Actually, the subject is probably painful not just for some but for all of us. Who passes through life without the ups and downs of relationships? In the best of situations, love can be irregular and conditional, and most of us are not in the best of situations. Ignorance leads to insensitivity and beyond to coldness, insult, betrayal, abuse, and abandonment. Let's face it, too: we all have bigger needs for love than any mortal can fill. We blame our love-starved condition on the other's incapacity, but the truth is that we each have a love-need too large for the other to fill.

The creed is that the one relationship that does not change, not at least on the side of the other, is our relationship with Jesus Christ. No matter the size of our love-need and the rude ways in which we take to expressing it, Jesus remains steadfast, willing, and true. We

1

trust and know that creed, taking its belief as a faith fundamental. Yet without attention even belief, like a love affair, can grow cold. Both love affairs and belief require feeding. They require attention, thought, structure, inquiry, evidence, proof, and beyond to creativity and imagination. Our proximity to and intimacy with Jesus are not primarily matters of imagination, although consciousness of his presence and activity certainly helps. When we welcome him, his Spirit acts in and through us. The riches that we experience moment to moment and day to day are his riches, blessing us. Yet we must still remember him, see him, recognize him, and know him in those blessings.

How then do we think and feel more deeply of Christ? The stories that we know of him, the historical events at which he was the center, compel us. Every crystal recollection of manger, wine, fish, loaves, storm, cross, and empty tomb draw us back to him, bring us to love him anew. Yet true love, Jesus says repeatedly, requires more than interest and admiration. Love requires obedience. We are not simply acquaintances, fellows, and friends, even intimate friends, of Jesus. We are also disciples, students, followers of Jesus, each of which imply submission and obedience. How then do we obey? Whom do we obey? We know to obey *him*, but *who is he*, and *what does he tell us to do* that we should construe as his command? Do as he did, the bracelet slogans tell us, but what did he do that we should repeat or imitate?

The four gospels are a rich record of exactly that guidance that we need from him. We should have no doubt of the abundance and clarity of Jesus's guidance from such momentous and carefully recorded events as the Sermon on the Mount and Last Supper. Still, their story or account form, the unsurpassably profound and immeasurably significant history that they describe, can sometimes mask for us the pragmatic instruction and example that Jesus gives us through them. The frequent gospel reader grows hungry to draw that instruction and example out, in order to develop and sustain the Christ-like character and activity that feeds the moment-to-moment love-need. We wish to follow and adhere to our lover, and so we parse his every action and word to prove our love both to ourselves and him, and to feed our hunger.

Of course, in pursuing him through his words and actions, we only do as Jesus invited, encouraged, and exhorted us to do. Jesus spoke a consistent message of his wanting us to join him not just in the future eternally but in the present limited now. The future part we get intellectually and sometimes even emotionally, even if the frightening curtain of death colors our contemplating it. Yet our inquiry here is not about that future, a reward that we instead leave to resurrection evidence and soul-felt faith. The inquiry here is his present presence. If as he says Jesus occupies a realm of greater dimension that is nonetheless inclusive of our own realm, and we have present access to him, then give us more and more of that access. Nothing should have greater value to us, nothing occupy more of our thought and time.

The concept of a realm or *kingdom,* if you prefer, is not as foreign, spiritual, dogmatic, or mysterious as to you it may have long seemed. Like Jesus, we each also occupy realms where we are in a sense lords or masters, although in our case very little lords and masters. Our realms can be quite small, sometimes barely influencing even so many more than one. Yet we are certainly capable of being our own masters, even though we too often and too quickly give away to others even that. We direct the activity of our limbs, going where we wish when we wish, to do as we wish. And in doing so, in directing our own actions, we inevitably influence others or at least influence conditions. Fortunately or unfortunately, we live in a cause-and-effect universe. Sometimes, we get to be the cause, while other times, we feel the effects. In fact, we are constantly causes, unavoidably causes, when often we would rather only feel the effects.

Jesus likely meant us to understand this *influence* sense of a realm or kingdom, although his direct hearers would have had a stronger sense of that meaning, living in actual earthly kingdoms. They knew what obeying Caesar or Herod meant and, having served such bizarre and hard rulers, would undoubtedly have understood and embraced Jesus' invitation to pursue, serve, and obey instead a loving King. They did embrace him, following him into the fields and hills in droves. Yet even as he invited all to his own realm, Jesus also constantly spoke to our own choices, influences, and realms. Indeed, how does one enter his realm other than to align one's own? My kingdom and your kingdom should look more like his realm if

3

we can credibly claim to be members of his own. And for our kingdoms to be aligned within his, to be member-states of his grand association, we must pursue actions he would pursue and maintain relationships he would form and value.

So read carefully and closely of his actions. Read the gospels for what he told us to do and for what he did, as patterns for our actions. When you do so, you will see dozens and dozens of things that he said to do and things that he did. Those actions that he instructed and demonstrated, while in specific context important to understanding them, nonetheless have a generality and timelessness to them. Yes, he acted in an ancient agrarian society, but the instruction he gave and actions he took work just as well in an industrial, post-industrial, information, or even post-information society. The world works as it works. Human character continues as it once did within natural laws and social opportunities and responsibilities that very little change. Jesus was and is the master of this universe.

Read here then of the things that Jesus said to do and things that he did. Every one of his couple-hundred admonitions that head the following sections is from his own words and actions reflected throughout the four gospels. The admonitions divide reasonably well into a Part 1 on actions and Part 2 on relationships. Each of those two parts further divides naturally into major sections. Major actions around each of which Jesus stated many admonitions include believing, praying, learning, teaching, serving, persevering, receiving, and giving. Major relationships around each of which Jesus stated many admonitions include God, Jesus, the Holy Spirit, yourself, your family, children, others, and enemies.

If the divisions and headings don't help you, then ignore them, but read of what Jesus said to do and did. Then pursue those admonitions just as you pursue him. Love is obedience. Align your realm with his realm, your influence with his influence. Live in and through him. Set aside anything that you value more than you value him, so that you can pursue him. When you do so, he will give it all back to you, everything that you desired, in the manner he designed you to receive and enjoy it. Your direct pursuit of love and happiness will fail. You must instead pursue him to have the love and

4

happiness for which he made you. Life is like that. You don't always get what you want, but you do get what you deserve, and often what you want, what you truly deep-down value, is what you deserve. Want him. Pursue him. Deserve him. Do what he said to do and what he did.

1

Actions

Jesus said a lot about actions, even as he acted decisively, demonstrably, and profoundly.

The myth may be that Jesus had a lot to say about attitude but not much about action. Culture today portrays him as a sentimental rather than active figure, as if his primary concern was with our peculiarly post-modern, self-involved, disengaged form of love. He was not and is not a post-modern. He is instead the Ancient of Days, the complete trajectory of history brought to life in the most active and engaged of personalities. His life was movement, and within that movement he anticipated, modeled, and justified the movement of all others. His statements described and demanded actions. Indeed, his words themselves were living and active, transforming and redirecting those who heard and embraced them, literally and figuratively feeding the masses who flocked to him. See in this Part 1 the actions that Jesus urged and actions that he took in their demonstration.

1.1 Believing

Believe. _{John 11:15.} *Do not doubt.* _{Matthew 14:31.} *Do not doubt Jesus's resurrection.* _{Luke 24:38.} *Believe the prophets.* _{Luke 24:25.} *Stop doubting and believe.* _{John 20:27.} *Have faith.* _{Matthew 17:20.} *Have faith and believe.* _{Matthew 21:21.} *Just believe.* _{Mark 5:36.}

Jesus spoke frequently and clearly about believing. Some readers would protest that belief is not action. Starting this part on action with a study of Jesus's statements about belief might undermine Jesus's admonitions to other actions. Those readers have this apology and explanation. Belief is forerunner to action, even as belief entails a mental action of its own. By speaking frequently about belief, Jesus gave us the impetus for action. We first believe, then we act. Or to put it another way, the kind of action about which Jesus spoke so frequently was *willful* action, action to which we commit based on belief about action we know to be fruitful and due. We act unconsciously or subconsciously all of the time, satisfying primal functions like to breathe, eat, and digest. By contrast, the kind of action to which Jesus exhorts is *committed* action, *chosen* action, *alternative* and *valued* action, all of which depend on belief. Listen carefully to what Jesus says about belief. Do as he says, and do as he does, in belief.

Believe. _{John 11:15.}

What Jesus would have us believe is obviously just as important as his having us believe at all. Belief is itself important, that we must recognize and know that we choose to believe this or that. Yet the subject of belief is just as important. Jesus had a particular concern over beliefs *about him*, about who he was, what he could do, and whom he represented in God his father. We perceive Lazarus's resurrection as a miracle, wonder, and phenomenon, so out of the natural order as to command a response. We must either believe that Jesus had the power to give new life to the dead, or believe that Lazarus was not dead and only temporarily rotting, or reject the account as unreliable, or (what most do) ignore the question entirely. In another sense, though, Jesus did not so much alter the natural order as correct our perception of it. One need not and indeed should not see any of Jesus's life-giving acts as unnatural disturbances of natural order, as if he had mysterious power apart from that order. Rather, the natural order of conception, birth, life, and death are his order. Nothing that he wills is out of order. He could and in fact did utterly reverse that natural order. Out of his death he brought life, gushing into new birth, leading to new conception, a perfect reversal of what we believe to be natural order. He permanently redefined for us what death itself had long meant. He can and in fact does bring new birth in the middle or even near the end of life. He gave new meaning to birth itself, offering birth again. He even gave new meaning to conception, showing that God conceives, knitting together in the womb whom he wishes how he wishes, while bringing about his own immaculate conception.

Jesus's friend Lazarus lay sick, so sick that his two sisters Mary and Martha sent word to Jesus who had a special love for the three of them. Instead though of rushing to heal Lazarus before he should die, Jesus remained where he was for two more days specifically in order that Lazarus *would* die, Jesus could then bring him back to life, and many more would thus believe. "So that you may believe," Jesus explained. Believe. He wants us to believe. He gives us evidence for belief, but whether we witness or others witness the evidence, he wants us to believe. Belief is critical to joining him. Belief is critical to knowing who he is, what he can do, what he has done, and what he will do. Jesus acted specifically to engender belief, give life to belief, sustain belief, and justify belief.

A dear woman, long in severe back pain, made her way to a particularly vital church comprised of members who above all believed. They surrounded her at the altar praying earnestly for relief of her back pain, knowing that God could heal it through

10

skilled surgeons or instantly that night just as they then prayed. The moment of intense prayer passed seemingly without incident, the disconsolate woman turning from the altar to return quietly to her seat. Then she shrieked in discovery that her back pain was gone. "I can't believe it," she said over and over, jumping up and down while hugging her intercessors. Believe it, dear woman. He healed you. He has healed many and has many more to heal. Believe. Base all actions on belief, a particular belief in God's power to give life through Jesus Christ. He has that power and wishes to share it with you in his realm right now.

Do not doubt. Matthew 14:31.

The flip side, antithesis, or opposite of belief is doubt. To know our friend, we must know our enemy. To believe, we must recognize and dispel disbelief. Doubt though is not simply the other side of belief. One can, as Peter plainly did, believe at times and yet disbelieve and doubt at other times. When fear creeps in, as it did for Peter, we must turn again to belief, as Peter turned to Jesus crying out, "Lord, save me!" Even while we believe, we must not in-between times disbelieve and doubt. While building belief, we must separately and consistently banish doubt. Doubt undermines belief. The one who doubts is like a wind-tossed wave, as Jesus's brother James wrote in what could easily have been reference to Peter's water-walking experience. Doubt carries one up and down in turbulent mind producing inconsistent action. Doubt indeed undermines action. Doubters stand on the sidelines, hands in pockets. When the moment requires action, doubters first hesitate, then question, and then before long scoff and mock. Doubt is simply the first step in the wrong direction.

Jesus had just healed the sick among a large crowd that had followed him to a solitary place. There, he had fed five thousand from five loaves and two fish. Needing solitude, he dismissed the crowd, sent his disciples ahead of him across the lake, and went up a mountainside to pray through the night. Knowing that the disciples

11

had struggled through the night to propel the boat across the lake against the wind, Jesus walked out to them on the water just before dawn. They were terrified by the apparition until they recognized his voice, and Jesus invited Peter to walk to him on the water. Peter began to do so until fear again took hold, sinking him down into the water until he cried for Jesus, who caught his hand, admonishing, "You of little faith, why did you doubt?"

The good-hearted and bright-minded pastor invited his congregation to bring their doubts to church and share them for investigation and inquiry. The invitation was a proper one when construed consistent with its intention. We are inquirers, explorers, adventurers, and investigators. We have restless minds that ask restless questions. Smart pastors, elders, and deacons can answer those questions. Yet we ought not to practice doubt. The faith is not a debating society. Jesus answers doubt with a command not to. Do not doubt. When fears arise, put them off, while reaching for Jesus. Listen for the voice and reach for the hand of Jesus. Doubt, and sink. Believe, and walk on water. He wants you to share the power of his realm.

Do not doubt Jesus's resurrection. Luke 24:38.

Life beyond death, life after death, life despite death do seem too good to be true, even when hundreds of others confirm what one personally witnesses. The mind is a powerful thing. We believe what we choose to believe even when doing so requires disbelieving direct observation and substantial other evidence. Custom and convention are powerful influences. We perceive what we expect even when our eyes, ears, and touch prove to us something different. We take natural laws as such, immutable, unchangeable, subject to no exception or extension. When we see only so far, we believe that we have no farther to see. Our minds close to half or more of what we might perceive if we only had the courage to open momentarily our fixed and puny minds and the sensitivity to accept direct report and observation. Yet the world continues to supply contrary evidence, finally evidence so powerful that we must accept it. We learn that what we thought was everything was barely anything. We learn that reality has a vaguely foretold but spectacular new dimension. In his resurrection, Jesus gave us a portal to the ultimate dimension to enter the creator's realm. In living beyond death, he did the unthinkable, even if that unthinkable has been everyone's ultimate thought. Who has not thought of, desired, and hoped for relief from death and yet simultaneously doubted the thought? That gift he decidedly gave that we could do more than hope and shudder. Jesus wants us not to doubt that gift, having given us the reason and reality not to doubt.

One thing that Jesus most instructs that we not doubt is his power over death, specifically that he came back to life, and not merely spiritual life but authentic physical life. The women who had accompanied and cared for Jesus during his ministry had seen the empty tomb. They told the apostles that two gleaming messengers had told them that Jesus had risen, but the apostles were slow to believe. Two men who had walked, talked, and eaten with the risen Jesus confirmed the women's reports. Jesus then stood among the apostles and spoke to them. His sudden appearance so unnerved them that they thought they were seeing a ghost. He had them look him over head to toe and touch him, trying to convince them that he was real. "Don't let doubting questions take over," Jesus admonished as he showed them his scarred hands and feet, and asked for something to eat. The apostles remained in half disbelief, the realization of his return simply being too good to seem true.

He was a good man, husband, and father, even if one who, though raised within sight of the faith, never let it take hold. He nevertheless occupied himself well throughout life, busying himself primarily with artistry and career. Few could doubt his professional accomplishments. He was intelligent, aware of developments in the world particularly in design and technology, and generally well read in all but the Bible. About things of faith he was moderately though inconsistently respectful, just not interested. And so in the deep things of life and love, though well intentioned, he nonetheless fell just short of wise. More than doubting, he simply did not believe that Jesus had returned to life. Thus in the encounter that Jesus has with each of us, he fell decidedly short, up until his very last. He struggled mightily in his relatively swift and steady demise that he and everyone around him could see coming. Somehow, at the very end of that struggle, perhaps on the wings of his child's prayer, he saw the risen Lord, his last words, "Jesus, my God, my God, my God." Why should one doubt his resurrection on such clear evidence and with so great a reward?

Believe the prophets. Luke 24:25.

Jesus wants us to believe not only on evidence but also on reliable things that trusted others have said will occur in the future. Believing on evidence is what anyone would do. The sky has dark clouds, the air is still and heavy, and lightning rumbles, that evidence suggesting oncoming rain. Or the traffic thickens on the drive into the city at a morning rush hour, that evidence suggesting slowing traffic and likely the usual traffic jam. Yet many persons to whom we listen also predict things that we are often ready to believe. Those authorities might include the weather reporter or the traffic reporter. If they predict bad weather or traffic, then we listen and dress, drive, or otherwise plan and act accordingly. Whether for good or for ill, we listen and to some degree follow the predictions of economists, financial advisors, sportscasters, political commentators, travel agents, friends, and neighbors. Jesus simply asks that we also believe reliable authorities whose expertise is spiritual discernment.

The two men whom Jesus met along the road after his resurrection did not immediately recognize him, although they knew him well enough that they should have. Instead, they walked along the road telling him things that they knew, heard, believed, and had hoped about Jesus, right up to the report just that morning from women whom they knew that angels at the empty tomb had told them that Jesus had risen. Their companions even went to the tomb to confirm the women's report. Jesus's response to them, indeed his rebuke, was that they should have believed the prophets. "How foolish you are," he said, "and how slow to believe all that the prophets have spoken! Did not the Messiah have to suffer these things and then enter his glory!" Jesus then explained the prophecies to the two men who still did not recognize Jesus until he broke bread with them and their spiritual eyes for him opened. Jesus then disappeared, leaving the two men to bolt back to the waiting disciples to tell them the Good News that the Lord of hosts had indeed risen.

She had first read the Bible as literature in a college class in which faith was not the goal or subject. The Bible version that the professor had chosen omitted several books and included critical introductions to several others. The message was clear that while the Bible had certain merits (and demerits) as literature, it was not the Good Book or even a holy book but instead simply a prominent example of interesting but nonetheless misguided religious writings. Yet the Bible somehow resonated with her like nothing else she had ever encountered — not in literature, art, history, or life. The Bible had not just majesty, unprecedented historical span, and mind-altering insight but also inexplicable other-worldliness. And so long after the college class, she resumed reading it, and not the secular-literary version that the professor had mandated but a real version with all of its books and without the denigrating commentary. The Spirit of Christ whom she had long felt and welcomed but only recently openly and formally received, and the many fellow-travelers whom she met along the way, showed her how to hear, understand, and believe the prophets in the Bible and in her own life.

Stop doubting and believe. John 20:27.

So we are to believe. And we are not to doubt. Doubt and belief are clearly not independent of one another. They are instead like opposite sides of the same coin. Indeed, Jesus expressly connects the two for us, doubt and its antithesis belief. One cannot doubt while believing. One cannot believe while doubting. Both are actions. Doubt takes commitment and energy, spawning negative expression, just as belief takes commitment and energy but spawning positive expression. Oh yes, the positive expression of belief may bring negative response. Expect it. That negative response to positive

15

belief may be part of why Jesus connects for us doubt with belief. One fights the other. More doubt means less belief. More belief means less doubt. Doubt feeds doubt, while belief feeds belief. Everyone doubts at some point. Jesus's advice, his command, invitation, and beseeching, is that we *stop* doubting so that we may believe. Evidence is a modern person's demand, and naturally so, living as modern persons do in an age of reason. Because we want, to some degree need, and in some measure even *deserve* evidence, Jesus gives us all the evidence that we would demand from anyone to believe any other proposition. He gives us a millennia-spanning Old Testament predicting his advent, then gives us the precise advent predicted. He gives us multiple written eyewitness and second-hand accounts of his life from persons inside, alongside, and outside the faith community into which he came and in which (even against which) he acted. These accounts come from persons transformed in the cases of Matthew, Mark, and John, indifferent in the case of Josephus, and in the case of Luke convinced to the point of certainty but yet investigatory. Jesus gives us the greatest account ever told, words whose life-giving meaning uncounted scholars have yet to exhaust, and both ancient and modern miracles. Jesus gives us the witness of hundreds, and yet more thousands, and not even that but billions of believers. Yet skepticism is a post-modern person's disease. Turn to Jesus, letting him heal your disease. Stop doubting and believe.

Thomas is the disciple whom we know as *Doubting* Thomas. The skepticism within our culture today for anything other than our own right to judge what is true probably makes Thomas more like us than any of the other disciples. Thomas entered too late the locked room in which the hidden disciples had just seen Jesus. Jesus, having stood among them, shown them his pierced hands and side, breathed on them, and blessed them, had already left. The excited disciples told Thomas that they had seen their Lord. Scoffing, Thomas declared that he *would not believe* unless he too saw the nail marks, and not only that, but put his hands into those nail marks in Jesus's hands and sides. Thomas would continue to doubt until he could see and touch the living Christ. And so Thomas continued to doubt for another week until Jesus appeared again to them, saying to Thomas, "Put your finger here; see my hands. Reach out your hand and put it into my side. Stop doubting and believe." Having instantly transformed the skeptical Thomas from a doubter into a believer forever, Jesus added, "Blessed are those who have not seen and yet have believed."

He recognized that the things that he was coming to believe about and around Jesus were improbable, although their improbability bothered him less and less until they disturbed him not at all. Lots of things that he witnessed about the world were improbable, he had learned, new things that he was learning all the time. Nothing much surprised him anymore, and in thinking so, he was not using that phrase in the weary sense that one usually hears it. Nothing *spectacular*, nothing *amazing*, nothing *wondrous* surprised him anymore. Instead, he would just smile at those things, whether they were new extraordinarily improbable deep-sea creatures, or new microscopic organisms of fantastic shape and powers, or new marvelously complex and whimsical features discovered about the human cell. Nothing surprised him because he increasingly held the wonder of God. Doubt was no longer his lens. Belief was now his marvelous perspective, one that God fulfilled with new wonders daily. He knew finally how to receive with full grace the little evidence, the just-enough evidence, that God offers each of us to stop doubting and believe.

Have faith. Matthew 17:20.

Jesus then directs us to take the next step beyond belief to faith. As Jesus's brother James wrote, even demons believe in God, yet all they do is shudder. Belief is not enough. Belief is only a beginning. Jesus wants our belief to involve more than fear of consequences. The intentional wrongdoer knows how wrongs affect adversely the wrongdoer's soul and yet continues. Belief is present but has not changed the believer. Faith is the next step after belief. Faith requires relying on the belief for the good things that will follow. Faith broadens and deepens belief. Faith connects one belief to another into meaning on which one can rely for commitments that guide action. Although he demonstrated the ability and foreshadowed the event by breathing life back into other dead several times, Jesus's rising after death was the single most remarkable event in history. Yet somehow, we must form that belief into an abiding faith that affects our lives in actions. Jesus tells us to do so, tells us to have faith.

The disciples had failed. A believing man had brought his seizure-ridden son to the disciples for healing prayer, but the disciples' prayer had failed to heal him. The disciples believed. They had seen and would see Jesus turn water into wine, multiply fish and bread to feed thousands, walk on water, and even raise the dead. They believed that Jesus had brought about these events because their own eyes had seen them. Their hands had touched the living evidence of them. They could not disbelieve. To do so would require closing their eyes, withdrawing their hands, and closing their minds to the most concrete of evidence. Yet they lacked the next thing, which was faith. They had not yet broadened their belief into a reliable faith. They asked Jesus why they had failed to heal the man's seizure-ridden son. Jesus replied, "Because you have so little faith." Faith as small as the smallest seed enables one to move mountains. Jesus urges us to have faith.

She did not know if the growing seed of her ambition was possible. Oh, the steps toward it were plain enough, even if they were also many, long in duration, challenging beyond anything that she had yet attempted, and complex. Her greatest obstacle though in even thinking about this goal was that she had no real confidence that she could accomplish what it would require. Who was *she* to think that she could possibly achieve and become *that*, the many contrary voices in her head said repeatedly and clearly? She did not even know how badly she wanted it, whether it was indeed her dream or someone else's dream. Yet it nonetheless beckoned to her, called to her, even if only still remotely, but yet the call was present, pressing, growing. She had no doubt of the value of its accomplishment. It would open opportunities for her to grow, acquire substantial new skills with which she could serve others, and assume an identity of effectiveness and maybe also of influence that she had always respected in others even while not imagining it possible in herself. Her pursuing this vague dream required only that she have faith. And now she had a Lord who waited eagerly to lend that faith to her. Yes, she would try it, and he would accomplish it for her. Then together, they would celebrate.

Have faith and do not doubt. Matthew 21:21.

While faith extends belief into commitment and action, faith nonetheless faces the same challenge that belief faces. Simply because we acquire faith, or perhaps more accurately learn to rely on the Lord's faith, does not mean that doubt disappears. Doubt remains the nagging cohort not only of belief but of faith. When Jesus tells us not only to have faith but to have faith *and not doubt*, he is telling us something important, just as everything that he says is important. Even as doubt undermines belief, so too does doubt undermine faith. We may believe the basics that form the foundation of faith and yet allow doubt to undermine the faith that such belief would gladly produce. Instead, we must remove doubt not only from belief but from faith itself. Factual contradiction is the kind of doubt that undermines belief, like saying that Jesus did not heal, did not die willingly, and did not rise, indeed did not even exist. Factual contradiction though is not the kind of doubt that undermines faith. Instead, the kind of doubt that undermines faith is disbelieving in outcomes, what is possible, what is likely to happen in the future. Jesus says then to have faith *and not doubt*.

What a week it had been, traveling back and forth into the city with Jesus. They had first entered triumphantly. Crowds had lain cloaks and branches on the road ahead of Jesus's donkey while children shouted hosannas to Jesus who had healed everyone whom the crowds brought to him. Jesus had also driven the dishonest money changers from the great temple, his actions and the crowd's joyous response mortifying the chief priests and religious instructors. Jesus and the disciples had spent the night outside the city once again. The next morning on their return to the city, Jesus had approached a fig tree for fruit to satisfy his hunger. Finding no figs, he had admonished the tree, the leaves of which quickly withered.

19

The astonished disciples asked Jesus how the tree had responded so quickly. Jesus answered, "Truly I tell you, if you have faith and do not doubt, not only can you do what was done to the fig tree, but also you can say to this mountain, 'Go, throw yourself into the sea,' and it will be done." So great is the faith that Jesus invites us to have, free from doubt.

He did not know whether what he hoped for would happen, but he knew that now was not the time to doubt. He needed to produce. He needed some *good* things to happen and happen quickly. Things had not been going so well lately. He sensed that everyone around him, especially those most important to him and to his own future success, were looking to him for something good, helpful, positive, even just sustainable, at a time when too many things seemed to be shifting, crumbling, failing. Indeed, things were changing so quickly and so out of control that a part of him wanted to just give up, to believe that under the present circumstances positive things simply could not happen. Why even try? Now was a time to hunker down, self-protect, withdraw, and conserve, not venture, plow forward, initiate, and believe. Yet exactly here faith confronted him. He must continue, must plow forward in faith while banishing the doubt. When everyone was saying that they could not see the way, he decided to push aside that doubt. If Jesus commanded it, then he was going to so act.

Just believe. Mark 5:36.

The final act, our final act, anyone's first and final act, is to just believe. Jesus said each of the above things about belief, instructing about belief in several different ways. Yet he also said in another context recounted below to *just* believe. When the question turns to the big matters, to the really important matters including especially the matters of life and death, we are to *just believe*. We might find many other good things to do, many things that fall within Jesus's instructions, things that would please and serve God, things even that would gain God's favor. But when the problem is a big problem, when the goal is a big goal, when the question is the big question,

20

Jesus's exhortation is to *just believe*. Sometimes, we must examine the physical evidence in order to believe. Other times, we must hear from more authority in order to believe. At still other times, we must have another witness confirm the matter in order to believe. Then, the time comes simply to believe. We each face times when the only thing to do is to just believe. One might wish belief were otherwise, always a matter for proof, but why so? Why wouldn't God bring us to a point that we simply trust him, that we put aside our queries and questions simply to believe him, that we lay down our defenses simply to accept him? We should be glad that God at some point gives us the opportunity to make our confidence in him a matter of belief, faith, trust, and love. Love believes. Just believe.

The large crowd had pressed in around Jesus as he tried to make his way to the house of the synagogue leader to heal his daughter. Someone in the crowd had deliberately touched Jesus's clothes, he said, because he had felt power flow out from him. He kept asking who had touched him for that power. The disciples thought he couldn't be serious because of all the people pressing in on him. Yet finally the woman who had touched Jesus for healing came forward in fear to confess that she had indeed received that healing. Jesus blessed her. As he was about to proceed on to the religious leader's house to heal the leader's daughter, some people arrived from the house telling him not to bother because she had already died. Jesus told them not to be afraid and then added, "Just believe." He would now not heal but raise the leader's daughter. Like the woman who had touched his clothes for his healing power, they just needed to believe.

He finally felt that the point for simple belief had come. He had suspected that it would. Indeed, he had hoped that it would come. His heart had long anticipated it, long welcomed it, even though his mind had not yet reached it. His mind had insisted, in precisely the way the world had trained it, to not believe God without proof. And so he had for years studied God's word, listened to sound preachers, read credible personal accounts, and turned to the authoritative scholars. He slowly convinced his mind in the way that the world held that evidence must but could not convince. While the world said God had no proof, he found instead many reliable forms of proof, things that God himself had said through Jesus and others would be his proof. Yet even as he did so, even as he slowly convinced his mind, he knew from the outset of this journey that it would reach a turn, reach a fork in the path, where he must no longer rely on proof. He had looked forward to reaching that point because he knew that God regarded it as critical to his welcome into the kingdom. Indeed, he suspected that he would not fully enter the kingdom until he had reached the path's fork. And then it came, and he stepped confidently and gladly forward on faith.

1.2 Praying

Be always ready to pray. Luke 21:36. *Watch and pray.* Matthew 26:41. *Do not sleep but wake and pray.* Luke 22:46. *Pray in secret.* Matthew 6:6. *Do not pray babbling.* Matthew 6:7. *Pray for those whom God gives you.* John 17:9. *Pray for those who mistreat you.* Luke 6:28. *Pray forgiveness of others.* Luke 23:34. *Pray for God to have mercy on you.* Luke 18:13. *Pray that Jesus remembers you.* Luke 23:43. *Ask Jesus for healing.* John 4:49. *Pray not to be tempted.* Luke 22:40. *Pray as Jesus taught you.* Matthew 6:9. *Persist in prayer to God.* Luke 18:5. *Ask.* John 16:24. *Ask, seek, and knock.* Luke 11:9. *Ask in Jesus's name.* John 14:13. *Believe Jesus is able.* Matthew 9:28.

After believing, Jesus also spoke frequently and clearly about prayer. While readers may question whether *believing* is really an appropriate subject for this book's first part on Jesus's actions, by contrast *praying* looks at least a little more like an action than does *believing*. Praying may not involve much action but at least requires some action beyond mere belief. Certainly, belief precedes prayer because without belief one prays to no one and nothing. Jesus makes quite clear that prayer without belief is perfectly ineffective. One may as well mutter to one's self as pray without faith. Yet belief alone, faith alone, is only a beginning when it comes to effective actions, when it comes to choosing how to live one's life in a way that most fully engages reality and possibility. You want a full, meaningful, even joyous life? Then yes, believe, but beyond your belief, *pray.* Pray often. Pray passionately. Pray persistently. Pray believing. Do not mutter to yourself. Speak instead to the available King. Listen now to the words of Jesus about praying. Hear what he says about prayer, watch what he does in prayer, and follow. Enter now the great realm available to you that you may enter most confidently and fully later.

23

Be always ready to pray. Luke 21:36.

The first thing about prayer that one realizes is that it is has no constraint. You may pray at any time, in any place, under any circumstance, with or without others knowing. God knows your heart. He knows your mind. He knows your every thought. Prayer can thus be silent and inward, known only to you and God who hears it. Prayer is a conversation with God that need not be vocal or outward but may instead be interior. You choose whether to share your prayer with others. You may certainly pray openly for and with others. They may deeply appreciate it. We probably vastly underestimate the willingness of others to hear, receive, and participate and share in our prayers. We probably keep our prayers too silent too often. Yet we may pray at any moment even without others knowing it. We may also pray with others half knowing or even mistaking it, as Hannah prayed for a son in the temple, the priest thinking her a mumbling drunk. We choose whether to pray privately or to share our prayers. The priority of prayer though is that we should be constantly ready to pray when we and others most need it. Indeed, appreciate this truth that if God knows our every thought, then our every thought is to some extent a conversation with God, and so we ought to recognize and appeal to the omniscient Conversant.

Jesus taught constantly, especially among his disciples. When some of them remarked to him about the great temple's grandeur, he cautioned them that it would not last a generation, although his words would last forever. He cautioned them not to let their hearts get weighed down in dissipation or anxieties, especially as the end of earthly life approaches, as it approaches for all of us. He urged them to be ready, watch constantly for those things that would rob their souls, and then when those things come, as they come for all of us, to pray to escape them so that we might have him forever. "Be always on the watch, and pray that you may be able to escape all that is about to happen, and that you may be able to stand before the Son of Man." We need to communicate with him. Our outlook must always be for the things that he would have us see, particularly the things

24

that would draw us away from him. And when those things come, as they come for all of us, we must call for him, pray to him, that he would save us.

She could feel the darkness so close to her, indeed inside her, draining her life away. That darkness seemed to stalk her. As much as she feared and hated it, and wished that it would leave her, she never felt rid of it. It seemed to cling to her, making her constantly anxious. It seemed to affect everything that she did, everything that she said, everything that she thought. She could do little right and instead seemed to do much wrong. Things looked hopeless. Yet at the same time, she had a seed of faith within her. It seemed at first too small to do anything at all against the great darkness that daily grew around and inside her. Still, the seed was always there. And gradually, just little bit by little bit, she learned to recall it, learned to coax it, learned to appeal to it especially in her darkest moments. It soon seemed as if the darkness no longer faced her but faced the tiny seed within her. Before too much longer, the seed had grown into something powerful enough to vanquish at least temporarily the darkness. Before too much longer, the darkness had receded, and light grew within her. In retrospect, it had been years, but the seed of faith too whom she appealed had always been with her. She had finally learned to watch for the darkness constantly and appeal to the seed for escape as soon as she saw it. The darkness had finally disappeared in a great light that daily lifted and carried her. She prayed joyfully and often, even as she watched constantly.

Watch and pray. Matthew 26:41.

The next thing that we need to realize about prayer is that we are its fair subject. So often, we tend to think of prayer as an opportunity to intercede on behalf of others, which is appropriate, even wonderful. We should think often and deeply of others, and should call on God to help them in their need. Yet who is most needy of all? We know our own condition better than we know the condition of anyone else. Anyone who is frank about their own condition knows their own need of prayer, particularly around temptation. Tempting is our one constant, whether to sloth, despair, anxiety, suspicion, hate, violence, bias, greed, lust, pride, vanity, or indulgence. We live and breathe in temptation, surrounded by invitations to pursue things that distract us from him and destroy us. We must know our need for his help to avoid these dissipations, offenses, and transgressions. We need to see these things first, to discern them first, and then to have the strength to resist them. We must watch for things that lure us in wrong directions and then pray for his strength to move in the opposite direction. Our spirits want to rise but to do so must overcome weaknesses.

Jesus was so distraught that he took three disciples into a corner of the garden to keep watch with him as the night deepened. There, Jesus prayed that his Father would relieve him of his awful burden. Turning after an hour back to the three disciples, he found them sleeping. He asked again, this time more specifically, that they watch *and pray*. "Watch and pray," Jesus said, "so that you will not fall into temptation. The spirit is willing, but the flesh is weak." Jesus returned to prayer, but when he checked again, the disciples had gone back to sleep. So alone, he turned once again to prayer until the moment of his great challenge had come. His flesh would be weak, but his Father's Spirit would be with him so that he would not fail in his life's great moment.

The aging man felt defeated whenever he measured his spiritual condition directly. He could never quite take any satisfaction in his spiritual progress. When he had first begun the light and happy disciplines of faith reading the Bible, getting together with others of faith whether at or outside church, praying, tithing, and even fasting, he had expected to feel differently about himself. Yet candidly, he knew that he never did. He was the same old self, which disappointed him, even tore at him. He wanted to be *free* of desire, pride, anger, and coarseness, when all of those things still nagged and wounded him. He wanted to forget who he was and what he had done in all of his interminable failings. Yet gradually he came to realize that he was who he was and that God had not intended to make him any different. If things tempted Jesus, then why should he of all people not also expect continuing temptations? He had expected those nagging tendencies and desires to disappear

26

gradually, and he supposed that they had receded (he was certainly behaving a little better now and then), but they had not disappeared. Finally, he was alright with temptations, realizing that in resourceful prayer, temptation had little or no power over him. He just needed to watch and pray, finding that power in God through Jesus rather than his own corruptible condition.

Do not sleep but wake and pray. Luke 22:46.

We have such a tendency to let days slip away in spiritual sleep, ignoring the power of the realm Jesus invites us to enter. We are alive to every stimulus, awake to every temptation, and yet asleep to Jesus's presence. Odd to say that he planned it that way. Love is funny that way. Love is jealous. It wants us to look away from the many other things that attract us, to pull our attention away in order to gaze upon it in devotion and wonder. If nothing else were there, if the world were empty of stimuli other than the One who desires devotion, then we would hardly be showing devotion by turning our attention to him. Rather, Jesus knows that we have temptations with which we could toy but wants us to turn away from them to him. He wants us to wake up and pray with him, speak with him, let him draw us away from those dissipations.

The disciples who had accompanied Jesus to the garden's corner were the same ones on whom Jesus had counted most during his brief public ministry. The vocal and irascible Peter had been the most prominent of his followers, the first to declare Jesus's divinity, while John had been Jesus's closest companion, his brother James also not far from his side. The three disciples had followed Jesus up the mount to witness his transfiguration. Yet now, at the moment of his greatest need, when they too should have been watching and praying as he had asked, they were instead sleeping. Sleeping, as he poured his heart out to his Father to save him from his imminent crucifixion. Sleeping, as the soldiers climbed the hill to arrest him. Sleeping, as they should have been strengthening themselves through prayer. "Why are you sleeping?" he asked, adding, "Get up and pray so that you will not fall into temptation." But it was too late. The soldiers had arrived. The disciples had failed in prayer, and so Peter would fail in his greatest challenge.

She knew that her spirit slept often. She regarded that new awareness as precious. She wanted to know that she had a soul, had a spirit, and had a future with the King, even if she also knew that she often slept on that knowledge. At least she was aware of this other dimension to her life that was in some ways so obvious and in other ways so hidden. Such an extraordinary thing as life, with all of the miracles that anyone could see in it, had to have more meaning, cause, and destination. Jesus's long premonition, sudden advent, multiple miracles, and crowning achievement in resurrection, not to mention the witness of millions through the ages, certainly explained it. Yet she slept. Even as she slept, though, she heard his call to sleep less often, instead to wake and speak with him that he would draw her away from slumber in distractions. Wake and pray, she would, more and more often, as she remembered and meditated on Jesus's request of his disciples in the corner of the garden.

Pray in secret. Matthew 6:6.

Repeatedly, the way of faith is distinct. The world's way is to do your good works in public. If you have a prayer, then pray openly, especially where the person for whom you pray will hear it. Then, the thinking goes, you will have your reward immediately in the good regard that the person for whom you pray will hold you. "He is always praying" and "she is always praying," they will say about you, in which you can then take instant satisfaction. Yet open prayer, as encouraging as it can be to yourself and others, is not the only way that prayer works or even the primary way. The satisfaction that you and others draw from public prayer is not prayer's purpose. Prayer's purpose has much more to do with moving God than moving persons. That purpose may be why God regards secret prayer with special favor, and favor not just for the one for whom you pray but also favor for you, the one praying. While pride seizes on public prayer to corrupt you, secret prayer has special power to reward you. Secret prayer is safe prayer, effective prayer, when only the Father hears you.

Jesus had seen the hypocrites standing in the synagogues and on the street corners praying loudly and openly where all could hear them. He knew why they prayed so publicly, which was for the reputation and regard it would bring them. That twisted purpose was why he called them *hypocrites*. They were actors more so than intercessors. God knew their hearts and motivations even before they opened their mouths in public prayer. Prayer is a heart thing. If the heart is right, then God rewards it. If the heart is wrong, then God rejects it to discipline and change it. Even as Jesus explained this God principle, the crowd gathered around him on the mountainside knew it. They had seen the public prayers and perceived the prideful intentions. So Jesus gave the crowd the solution, saying, "When you pray, go into your room, close the door, and pray to your Father, who is unseen. Then your Father, who sees what is done in secret, will reward you."

Public prayers still unnerved her, which was fine. She felt it better to leave those prayers to others who had a stronger sense of themselves and their public voice. She always felt awkward and self-conscious when praying aloud with others. Her first words were fine because she was able to plan them, but as soon as she got more than a sentence into her open prayer, her words began to sound hollow, like she didn't really mean them and was only saying them for others to hear rather than for God to hear them. That echo effect was precisely her problem in that she started listening to herself and thinking about what others might be thinking of *her* rather than her thinking about *him*. So she just felt better when praying alone, to herself and him. That happy result in her private prayer was another good part of public prayers by others. They reminded her to pray in secret when only he could hear her. She didn't mind telling others once in a while that she had been praying for them, although she took care even with those small disclosures. She wanted her prayer to be private. After all, she needed an audience of only One.

✞

Do not pray babbling. Matthew 6:7.

Who is not a babbler? Oh, sure, some of us don't speak aloud much, but aren't the words still running through our heads? To realize that God knows our every thought should give us pause. Maybe we should slow the torrent of words, even those silent words that we only think and do not express. Care in speech is especially important when praying, meaning when we speak directly to God, whether aloud or silently, and with others listening or alone. Sometimes, saying the same thing several different ways can help others understand us. God doesn't need that repetition. He understands the first time. Persistent prayer is fine. Bring things back to God repeatedly. He appreciates earnestness and commitment, passion and purpose. Yet don't feel the need for incantations, for multiplying meaningless words. Sounds don't impress him. He concerns himself with intentions. Babblers he does not need. No need to be high mindedly articulate, either. Fancy language won't impress him. Earnest men and women of pure heart using simple words in constant devotion are sufficient. Prayer's effect is not in its quantity but quality.

Jesus spoke at length to the crowd on the mountainside, longer than most of the crowd had expected. Much of what he had to say then, as at other times when he taught, was about prayer. Given all that he said about prayer, how we should speak to the Father must have concerned Jesus deeply. How one speaks to another says a lot about the quality of the relationship, when the quality of our relationship to God is more consequential than anything else. To speak properly to another requires knowing enough of the other's power and character. Our prayer in a sense defines and judges us. How we speak to God determines how he will regard us, when nothing means more. Are we to be to him like non-believers who hardly know anything of his character, or are we to be familiar to him and with him as one is familiar with close friends and companions? And so Jesus taught, "When you pray, do not keep on babbling like the pagans who think their many words will get them a hearing, for your Father knows what you need before you ask him."

30

He liked putting his simple prayers into words even though he sensed that his doing so was ultimately unnecessary. He had long ago learned to trust that God was acting in and around him consistent with what his heart was pursuing whether he formed those desires into the words of a prayer or not. He had seen too many times in his own life and the lives of others how God rewards the heart even when the mind misses the heart's appeal to him. Yet the words meant something to him, even if God hardly needed them having already known his heart's intention. His prayers became for him like signposts pointing him toward his heart's better intentions. For he knew that his heart, while often inclined in good directions, was nonetheless incapable of curing its natural deception. Forming the words of prayers forced his heart and mind to agree on those better intentions. As he prayed briefly, simply, and quietly for others, he knew that God was healing his own soul, just as he expected God to heal the souls of those others. He had no patience for babble, especially his own, but the few words that he spoke often in prayer he trusted made the difference.

Pray for those whom God gives you. John 17:9.

God must love it when we pray for world peace, for the stranger, for those about whom we hear on the news. We have many for whom to pray because the world holds many needs that only God can fulfill. Yet God places us in special relationship to a few whom he gives us, just as he gives us to those few. Only certain people follow us, have proximity to us, surround us with their interest, needs, and love. Only certain people are closer to us than they are to the busy things of the world. Only certain people stop to listen to us, care for us, and rely on us outside of what they seek and receive from the world. We should pray earnestly for those spiritual sisters and brothers. Of course we pray for family members, neighbors, and friends. Yet we have others close to us within the family of faith for whom our prayers should be most earnest and responsible. We hold a sacred trust in those whom God gives us to encourage, perhaps to

31

guide or even teach. Even as we spread our prayers widely, our prayers ought also to reach those trusted few.

Jesus had finished his last supper with the disciples and was now sharing his final precious words with them. No longer did he speak in the parables that required the disciples to search for his meaning. Now, he spoke plainly, and for the first time the disciples understood him clearly. Jesus was leaving them to return to his Father. They would grieve deeply for a time over his loss, and they would face much trouble in the world during that time, but he would leave them with the power to ask the Father for anything in his name, and the Father would grant it to them. Jesus told them these and other things clearly before turning to pray to the Father for them. As he began to pray, he acknowledged that the Father had given him these men for whom he would now pray, saying, "I pray for them. I am not praying for the world but for those you have given me, for they are yours."

The elderly man realized from his Bible studies that he had a circle of younger men whom God had entrusted to him. The elderly man was not being prideful in thinking so. He was not falsely imagining himself a person of unusual insight or influence. No, he actually knew that these several younger men listened to him, looked to him, and even sought him out from time to time especially when most in need. Those instances were often enough and clear enough that he could not avoid their recognition. He had in every instance regarded his influence as amusing because he thought himself no better than any of these other men, indeed thought himself less than several or all of them. Yet they still looked to him, not out of admiration or to imitate, for he was little to admire and nothing to imitate, but out of confidence and trust. He supposed that they knew that he had one thing that they also sought, which was confident and close relationship with the full-provider Lord. And so he did the one thing that he knew would carry the most influence for them, which was to pray for them out of the world. Never mind what they might face and suffer, all of which they were tough enough to withstand. He prayed instead that God would protect their souls that he would lose not one of them.

Pray for those who mistreat you. Luke 6:28.

Jesus also wants us to pray especially for those for whom we would otherwise be least likely to pray, those who mistreat us. Everyone has an occasional antagonist, someone who interferes with what we think is best for us. Some of us have more than an occasional antagonist, someone who constantly and directly opposes us in what we think is essential for us. That person may be a supervisor, co-worker, neighbor, or even a family member or fellow church member. We may in our worst moments attribute all kinds of evil to those persons, and indeed, they may in some respects be acting maliciously, although much more often they are likely to believe that they act only for the better of one or both. We certainly believe the same thing about ourselves that we act for our own good and perhaps also the good of the other, when we oppose and in rare cases antagonize others, even though from an objective standpoint our actions could in very rare cases look malicious. Their good even if misguided intentions may be part of why Jesus tells us to pray for our enemies. We may simply misperceive their motives as evil when their motives are instead neutral or good. Jesus wants our hearts right toward others. One of the worst things that one can do in a relationship is attribute bad intentions to someone who does not hold them. We properly call that misattribution *demonizing*, to turn others into demons when they are not demons. Even more sadly, we usually demonize others for the purpose of diminishing their influence with others, to destroy their goodwill and reputation. Praying *for* them instead of speaking *against* them could change our hearts and correct our misperceptions. Yet even if not, even if instead we correctly perceive that our enemies are demonizing us to destroy unfairly our own reputation, then Jesus would still have us pray for them. Jesus's heart is that big because after all he prayed for us when we were the broken, corrupted, and faithless ones. If our antagonist is corrupted, then they need our prayer more than others. Jesus seeks the lost. We should, too. As we move through life, we should in some respects hope that the corruption of others catches us, sticks to

33

us, grinds us to the point that we turn and pray for them. They have more need of Jesus than do our good friends and fellow faith travelers. We should be lightning rods for the sick, and when we find them, we should pray for them. Prayer for enemies is a powerful ministry.

Jesus had just prayed through the night on a mountainside until morning came, when he appointed his twelve disciples. They then went down the mountain to a level place where a large crowd from all over the region gathered to hear Jesus and have him heal the sick whom they brought to him. Such power flowed from Jesus, and he was healing so many, that everyone was trying to touch him. And so Jesus began to speak and teach in order that when he and his power had moved on, the people might carry away his words holding his power within them. He spoke of the rich, and he spoke of the poor, knowing that wealth isolates and divides us. Then Jesus spoke directly to the issue of division, of cursing, hatred, and enemies, saying simply, "Love your enemies, do good to those who hate you, bless those who curse you, pray for those who mistreat you." Yes, pray for your friends and family members, but pray even and especially for your enemies.

He did not really feel that he had enemies, but he knew that certain people, fortunately a very few people but some people nonetheless, seemed to work against him, speak against him, oppose and undermine him. He knew because his friends told him so, as if they expected him to do something about it. But he knew that he could do nothing about it. Whenever he tried to fix things with those so-called enemies, those who seemed to want to be enemies even if he did not feel the same way, things just stayed the same or got worse. Sometimes he even felt like *he* was the one who was fueling their divide, antagonizing the other, which made him even more upset, disappointed, and despondent as he thought about them, nearly to the point of obsession. So he did what he knew quite well Jesus said to do for them, which was to pray for them. He did not pray that they would go away or even that they would grow up or change. He simply prayed for their healing and welfare. He prayed for their growth and blessing. He prayed for their peace. And as he did so, each time Jesus healed his own heart toward them just enough to help him move on to other tasks and other relationships where his attention seemed to do more good. Prayer for enemies became one of his first and best prayers.

Pray forgiveness of others. Luke 23:34.

Sometimes enemies leave their wounds, deep wounds, even mortal wounds. Jesus does not want us praying for enemies only when they annoy us. He and his most-devoted followers have prayed for enemies even as they crucified, stoned, and murdered them. Prayer for enemies should not only be for their growth, comfort, healing, and blessing but also for their forgiveness. It is one thing to pray that an enemy prosper in other areas while ignoring the offense to the one praying. It is another thing to pray that God forgive the offense to the one praying. Praying that God forgive one's enemy for the very offense that made the person an enemy must be the harder prayer to make, harder certainly than praying for their general blessing, but that prayer is what Jesus and his closest followers have made and so is a prayer that we should also make. Identify the very thing that the person did that made them your antagonist, and then ask God to disregard that offense, to allow you to take that offense on yourself for your own payment as Christ took your offense and paid for you. Pray the difficult prayer of forgiveness.

With the prisoners dragging their own crosses as far as they were still able, the group finally reached the hill, known as the Skull, on which the government executed criminals. Only a few, mostly women, had the courage and strength to follow the little group that included the one whom many had called the Messiah. The crowds who had followed him and whom he had fed and healed were gone, even the band of his disciples. The soldiers stripped him and the two criminals who would die alongside him before nailing each to a cross and raising each cross skyward. As the soldiers divided Jesus's clothing among them by casting lots, Jesus spoke from the cross only, "Father, forgive them, for they do not know what they are doing," a prayer that the martyr Stephen would soon repeat for the religious officials who stoned him for his witness to Jesus.

She hurt so badly over what he had said that she could not seem to ignore it, never mind forgetting it. He never should have said it. He had admitted that while apologizing for it, even if to her his apology had looked like it was only grudging. She should be getting over it, getting on with it, moving on as she had so many times before, and indeed as he had gotten over her own harsh words so many times before, too. But these words hurt her more deeply to the point it seemed of killing something inside her. She wasn't sure that she would ever get over it, which scared her because she knew that she wanted to get over it. She did not like feeling the way she did and wanted to feel better, and to act better, too. Finally, she did as she knew to do, which was to pray that God would forgive him for what he had said. Let me just take that wrong for him, she told God, and not just once but repeatedly. You have forgiven me so many times, Father, she prayed, that I beg you to forgive him again. And sure enough, relief came to her, just as she knew that God was forgiving him.

Pray for God to have mercy on you. Luke 18:13.

Mercy is the lifeblood of those who follow Jesus, who know that they rely for their closeness to him on *his* purity, not their own. Many think that they are not good enough to be spiritual, to become close to Jesus, when the opposite is true that belief in one's own goodness leads one away from Jesus. One has instead to see one's own corruption, the constant errancy in which each of us lives that so distorts our better intentions, which themselves are not always that good. Jesus has no heart for the self-righteous because the self-righteous have no need for him. Jesus lived a mercy mission to provide his perfect path for us back to the Father when our corruption gave us no other path. Jesus not only lived out that mercy mission but also said that we ought to pray humbly to his Father for that mercy. God grants us entry into his realm when we ask him to do so out of mercy, not because we earned or deserve it. We haven't earned it and don't deserve it. We have no standing before God. Our only standing is the mercy that God grants us in his Son.

Jesus found himself among some people whom he knew were confident of their own righteousness. Knowing that they looked down on everyone else in their self-righteousness, Jesus set them straight by telling them a parable about a very religious man and a very un-religious tax collector. The religious man took special pride that he fasted and tithed regularly, Jesus explained. Indeed, the religious man prayed thanking God that he was not unrighteous like so many others. "But the tax collector stood at a distance," Jesus told his self-righteous listeners, continuing, "He would not even look up to heaven but beat his breast and said, 'God, have mercy on me, a sinner.' I tell you that this man, rather than the other, went home justified before God." Jesus has no patience for self-righteousness. He knows that we all need God's mercy, none of us having sufficient righteousness.

He had always doubted his merit. Lately, he was sure that he had none. He knew at every turn that he came up short of what God would have him do and be, not even to mention what others would have him do and be. He knew that he failed at virtually everything he did, at least when one judged on God's standard so far above human standards. Even on human standards, he was no great shakes, nothing to write home about, no one whom to emulate. Yet it wasn't meeting standards, whether God's or human standards, that really mattered to him. What mattered to him was nearness to God, proximity to God, closeness to and acceptance by God. He wanted to come home to that divine home that he knew must somehow lie within his grasp, or God would not have put the sense of that home there for him to perceive. And he knew the path to that home through Jesus. The gospel was so clear, available, and profound that he almost shuddered to think that he might somehow miss it, miss his entry into God's realm through Jesus. So he prayed, prayed humbly, prayed quaking, prayed for forgiveness. With every breath of his walk, he moaned for more of the mercy earned for him by Jesus.

Pray that Jesus remembers you. Luke 23:43.

Odd it may seem, but simple familiarity is the prayer that Jesus seems most ready to answer. He wants to know us while also wanting us to want him to know us. He wants us to desire his notice. Has history ever known a God like him, one whose great desire is not only to have *we* know *him*, that we would love him, as one supposes that other gods have been jealous for attention, but moreover to have us know that *he* wants to know *us,* that inexplicable desire of his that we acknowledge how much he loves us? This extraordinary God whom Jesus revealed in his own person is a loving God, meaning that he wants to care for us, indeed wants us to ask him to care for us. God is the Father who wants us to call him Daddy, just as we would want him to give us good things, particularly himself, as daddies give good things, particularly themselves. He wants us to pray that he remember us, particularly as we breathe our last breath, so that he can fully and finally draw us to him so that he can care most intimately for us. Give me the opportunity to love you, he asks, by praying that I know and remember you.

What an epic scene, history's most dramatic ever, on the hill called the Skull outside Jerusalem. The soldiers had paraded Jesus out to the hill dragging his own cross until he could no longer do so, having a man drag it the rest of the way for him. The soldiers then crucified two others next to Jesus, except the other two were common criminals, not the celebrated one whom so many called the Messiah. The first criminal hurled insults at Jesus to save himself and the two criminals hanging on crosses next to him. The other criminal though told the first criminal to stop it, to fear God at this last moment to do so. They deserved their death sentences, the second criminal added, while Jesus had done nothing wrong. Then the second criminal turned to Jesus and said simply, "Jesus, remember me when you come into your kingdom." Jesus answered, "Truly I tell you, today you will be with me in paradise."

38

She had never needed the limelight, never really sought attention. She felt fine most of the time being ignored and overlooked. She could enjoy it almost just as much when others got attention. Indeed, she liked to give others attention and usually took pains to avoid notice from others so that she would not keep others from getting that attention that they seemed to need. She saw that so many others wanted the attention more than she wanted or needed it. Yet she felt at the same time that she did want attention, only not the attention of others. The realization came slowly to her. It felt like one of the last great parts of her new maturity. But at last the realization was fully present to her. She knew what she wanted, indeed what she craved. She wanted God's attention. As crazy as the thought at first seemed, she wanted God to know and remember her. How though would he do so? She would pray. She would pray that God remember her. And she danced inside, basking in his attention.

Ask Jesus for healing. John 4:49.

Prayers for healing are the bread and butter of faith. Sickness comes to all, and it isn't pretty. Our family members, friends, and acquaintances face many physical and mental challenges, some slight, others serious. Illness can have huge impact on a person, family, and community. In the worst cases, illness leads to death, and not only of the aged or middle aged but also of the young. Everyone is subject to illness. None are immune. Illness has its own timetable, never convenient to ours. It strikes not just at the body but at the mind and spirit. When illness comes, depression and loss of faith can easily come with it. In good health, we are cheerful and ready to trust and believe. In ill health, we are downcast and too ready to give up and disbelieve. While medical care can help, illness must often take its course beyond our control or even our influence. Prayer changes the equation. To pray for another's healing is to pray for something more personal and important than a new job, car, friendship, or home. God wants to heal us. He also wants us to ask for healing. Pray the prayer of healing, particularly for family members while also for friends and acquaintances.

A royal official heard that Jesus had returned to the town where he had turned water into wine, the first of Jesus's public miracles. The official's son was very sick, so sick as to be about to die. Knowing Jesus's power, the official traveled to meet Jesus, begging him to come heal his son. Jesus at first rebuffed the official that persons of his station needed miracles to believe. The official pressed ahead with his request. So Jesus relented, saying simply, "Go, your son will live." Taking Jesus at his word, the official headed off toward home, met along the way with the news that his son had recovered at the exact moment that Jesus had said so. The official had asked for healing, and because he had asked persistently and believed, he had received the healing for which he asked. The official and his whole household believed.

His position was such that he often heard of illnesses, too many of them serious illnesses. Sometimes they were illnesses of those whom he knew and served, while other times they were illnesses of people for whom those individuals cared, like the illness of a spouse, parent, or child. He generally heard about the illnesses only when they were serious enough to require his attention to their consequences, when illness or caring for the ill kept those with whom he dealt from performing. Sadly, some of the illnesses resulted in death. On each report of illness, he would give the counsel and take the administrative steps that his position required. He would also routinely share words of encouragement and, with the most serious illnesses and with deaths, would often pull a get-well or condolence card from his drawer to sign and convey. Yet he also prayed, earnestly, even with tears. He never knew whether his prayers made a difference, but he believed that they did, and that belief was enough.

Pray not to be tempted. Luke 22:40.

Moved by prayer, God will correct things that have already happened. He will heal sickness that has already begun, comfort the grieving, mend broken hearts, and restore body, mind and soul. He will forgive for wrongs already propagated. Yet prayer will also move God to help us not fall into things in which we never should have engaged in the first place. That God will help us avoid temptation must be one of the most mysterious of the powers of prayer. Temptation involves the senses. Situations and stimuli alert us to opportunities to do as we should not do. As we see, hear, and sense things, the thought occurs that we might find ease, security, or satisfaction in doing as we should not do. Prayer enlists God to interrupt that sensing. Prayer involves the Holy Spirit in our own spiritual sensing. Prayer shifts the mind's eye from pursuit after the senses to pursuit after the spirit. Temptation, often only a small voice, can nonetheless have great power in some situations, but prayer makes avoiding temptation possible in every situation.

The garden was going to be a difficult place, the late night a very difficult time. Jesus wanted his closest disciples with him but knew that the night would challenge them, too. He knew that they needed to prepare with prayer for what was surely to come, just as he needed to prepare through prayer. So before praying himself, Jesus told the disciples, "Pray that you will not fall into temptation." The disciples though were exhausted with sorrow after the long last supper at which Jesus had revealed his impending departure. Returning from prayer, Jesus rousted them from sleep, repeating the admonition, "Get up and pray so that you will not fall into temptation." He wanted his disciples prepared and ready for the things that were surely to come.

She was nothing if not circumspect. She had always been thoughtful, always been prudent. She often wondered why others didn't think before they acted, especially when she could see the unhappy consequences of their actions. She knew that we live in a cause-and-effect world in which actions bring consequences. Indeed, she had suffered consequences just as others suffered them, even if she seemed more ready to at least try to avoid them than others seemed ready to do so. Better to avoid things in advance than to deal with them later, she always thought. Yet she also felt the power of the pull toward wrong things, just as she saw others succumb more

41

often than she to that same power. She wondered about that awful power and how one best resists it. But she knew the answer in prayer. God, not man, defeats temptation. She would not put her own little power up against temptation. She would put God's infinite power up against it, and God would keep her from pursuing those things that, although attractive, would burden and destroy her.

Pray as Jesus taught you. Matthew 6:9.

Among the many things that Jesus said about prayer, he also gave us a specific prayer to pray as a model prayer and told us to pray it. Jesus prayed that model prayer. Yet just before he did so, he said to pray that prayer. When we pray the prayer that Jesus taught us to pray, we are both imitating Jesus who prayed that prayer and also following his instructions when he told us to pray it. Jesus could have been no clearer than that. Scholars have written books about that prayer. Its profound structure enables us to accomplish in a few clear words what any prayer should. We do not need to guess at how Jesus intended for us to pray. We need only follow his model, do as he said about prayer and do as he did in prayer. When he placed his model prayer in the middle of his greatest teaching and then told us to pray it, Jesus was being as clear as he could be about his expectations for our prayers. Why would we pray in any other way than the way that he taught us so clearly and profoundly? Prayer is creative and personal. We have many ways in which to pray. We should also pray as Jesus taught us to pray.

He surely knew that people would pray the prayer he taught us for generations, down centuries, for millennia. As faith spread around the globe, the prayer he taught us to pray would echo over and over, from every corner of the world, filling the air at every moment, in every language, from every inspiration, in every need. Legions of earnest believers would meditate on the prayer hour after hour, across lives spanning many decades, until they had discerned and prayed the prayer's every nuance. And yet the prayer revealed new nuance to new believers, finding its way into new regions of new hearts, connecting each heart in its own unique way with the Father to whom Jesus taught us to pray. Jesus stood that day on the mount in the midst of a great crowd. He taught and taught as the people had grown accustomed to his teaching. Then, right in the middle of his one greatest teaching that believers down the ages would come to know as his Sermon on the Mount, Jesus turned his listeners to the subject of prayer and instructed, "Pray like this, then: Our Father in heaven, hallowed be your name...."

He had silently recited the prayer so many times that it had become less a thought than a pattern, indeed a structure within his mind, nearly his mind itself. The prayer was more like his anatomy or physiology than an ephemeral thought or wisp of unspoken words. Perhaps, he realized, that intimate familiarity is what Jesus had meant when speaking about knowing his Father's mind. To become one with the Father might be to have more of the Father's mind, to think more like the Father thinks, although we are not the Father and so must instead think *of* the Father as he would have us think. And so he repeated the prayer that Jesus had taught him to pray, again and again. As he repeated the prayer, though, he did not let it become a dead thought, a dead thing, but continued to listen to it, draw from it, and let it shape his other thoughts. He wondered how many times one could say the prayer, meditate on the prayer, explore words, phrases, and emotions within the prayer. Let us find out, he thought.

Persist in prayer to God. Luke 18:5.

Why would we have to persist in prayer to God, especially if God is loving, listening, and almighty? The idea of persisting in prayer is a strange one, in the impersonal way that too many of us think of God too often. God created a world of natural laws that respond promptly and reliably to our actions. We don't have to coax gravity or urge the sun to come up in the morning. And so God must be someone who responds rather automatically or mechanically to the correct form of request made with just the right intention at just the right moment, right? Jesus teaches and shows us otherwise that God is highly personal and relational, caring how we regard and relate to him. No vending machine, God instead desires to deepen our relationship with him, granting us things in justice especially when we reach the point of persistently imploring him. He clearly wants us to ask him for things but sometimes also wants us to ask more than once, repeatedly, to show him our desire. Indeed, he would be stranger to us, more foreign and impersonal, if instead he preferred form over relationship. Do not hesitate to persist in prayer. Do not too quickly believe that he is not listening or does not care about your request. He may just want you to persist in prayer.

Jesus had one set of words for the religious leaders but different words for his disciples. After rebuking the religious leaders for their errors, he would turn to his disciples to teach. Those who persist in error receive rebuke, while those who follow Jesus receive teaching. On one such occasion, after the religious leaders had once again missed Jesus's divinity to ask when God would come, he had told the religious leaders that God's kingdom was already among them. He had then turned to his disciples to teach that within the kingdom they should always pray without giving up. His instruction included a story about an unjust judge who kept refusing a widow's just request. Yet the widow kept bothering the judge with her request until he finally relented and granted her justice. Jesus concluded the parable saying, "And will not God bring about justice for his chosen ones who cry out to him day and night? He will see that they get justice and quickly."

He had already blessed her far beyond her imagination. She knew that was true. Oh sure, her life still had challenges. Every life does. She wouldn't have it any other way. She probably feared the absence of challenge much more than its frequent presence. She needed reasons to get up, stand up, and struggle. But when she stepped back and looked at all that had come her way, all of the circumstances that seemed to have conspired in the best of ways to give her unearned and bountiful blessings, she was certain that God had every intention to bless her far beyond anything she could have dreamed. And yet she still had needs and desires, just needs and desires, things that she could quite reasonably have expected would come her way and should come her way, not that she deserved them more than others deserved them, but just things that should happen for her. These were things for which she had long prayed. She would persist in these prayers. She would not give up until God gave her what he knew was in her heart. She even felt that God wanted her to keep asking him for these same things, felt that if she gave up asking, then God would think less of her in her relationship with him. So she kept asking and asking, while believing that they too would come her way.

Ask. John 16:24.

If prayer is anything, then it is to ask. Prayer is supplication. Prayer is request. Prayer would be begging, but because we pray to a God who holds all things without limit, prayer is hardly like expecting only sustaining crumbs as a beggar might expect while remaining a beggar. Prayer is more like asking for gifts from the extravagant Giver who offers us transformation, who invites us into a realm in which joy is the expected condition. God wants us to ask him for things that we know would be good for us and others as we move through life within his realm. His realm is one in which to ask is to receive. We do not receive because we do not ask. If we were only to get in the habit of asking, then we would get in the condition of receiving. In prayer, having a long list is nothing offensive. God seems to welcome lists of prayer. He wants us relying on him more so than others. Asking involves communication, while communication requires relationship, and the most-effective communication requires confidence, closeness, and commitment. We should pray asking for responses that God especially can give. Go big or go home is the saying in prayer as it is elsewhere. God wants us to ask, and so we should ask richly, deeply, and often.

The long last supper had included so much instruction, so many things that Jesus had so long wanted to say and now poured out to his disciples. His instruction, as was so often the case, included analogy. In this instance, he said that the disciples were like a woman in labor. The labor and delivery involved pain, just as the disciples would be at loss and would grieve. But the labor ended in the great joy of a new child. And so too would the disciples' grief in losing Jesus for a time end in great joy in having him back permanently. The Father would answer their prayers, if only they prayed in Jesus's name. Jesus ended the analogy saying, "Until now you have not asked for anything in my name. Ask and you will receive, and your joy will be complete."

He needed that reminder to pray for results. Often, he simply trusted that God knew his needs and the needs of his family, friends, and acquaintances, and that God would provide for those needs. Yet he knew that God desired him to ask. And he always felt better about asking. Things even worked that way in his home that he could expect that his family would care for him just as they could expect that he would care for them. No one need ask anything of one another. But asking still seemed appropriate, still brought welcome response, and still brought welcome appreciation. Asking meant communication, recognition, and closeness. Things worked similarly at the workplace, church, and elsewhere. Everywhere he asked, he found that he would not only receive but that those whom he asked appreciated his request. These interactions were good reminders for him to ask the Father. He prayed even for the habit of asking. Give me breath, Father, give me energy, Father, give me all those things that I might reasonably expect from you, but give me most of all the will and reminder to ask them of you, for all things are yours, and I should receive nothing of yours without attributing it all to you.

Ask, seek, and knock.   Luke 11:9.

Jesus more than once urges us to make requests in prayer of the Father. Ask, ask much, and ask often, for the Father loves to give to those who ask of him. Beyond asking, though, indeed as an extension of asking, Jesus also urges us to seek the Father's gifts, to look for them with the commitment and expectation of finding them. Evidently, from the way in which Jesus described it, prayer sometimes requires searching for the gift and its Giver, pursuing it and him in addition to simply asking for it. Haven't you ever had a family member or friend hide a gift for you? You might have put a gift on your wish list, hinted about it, and hoped for it, but the family member or friend wished to surprise you with it, to give hints of where you might find it if you really believed that you would be so fortunate as to receive it. And there they were too, your gracious giver, when you found the gift. Jesus invites us to pursue the Father's gifts even as we ask him for them and pursue him. Jesus urges us to go to where we would find the Father, even to ask to enter the Father's presence where we would find those gifts. Ask the Father, seek the Father, knock on the Father's door, and he will open the door to himself and the gifts his presence brings you.

Jesus prayed often around his disciples. On one of those occasions, when Jesus had finished praying, one of his disciples asked him to teach them to pray. On that occasion, he gave his disciples a prayer very much like the prayer that he gave in the great Sermon on the Mount, having the same words and structure. He then told his disciples a story to illustrate the attitude of prayer. Think, he said, of going to a friend's house at midnight to ask for loaves of bread. You would receive them not because the friend wanted to get up at midnight, which he surely didn't, but because of the audacity of your midnight request. As if the disciples had not yet appreciated the story's full meaning, Jesus then told his disciples the point of the story, "So I say to you: Ask and it will be given to you; seek and you will find; knock and the door will be opened to you." No one who asks fails to receive. No one who seeks fails to find. No one who knocks fails to have the door open to them.

She found it strange at first but not so strange later. As her prayers grew more frequent, they also grew bolder. In fact, she had begun to feel uneasy about their boldness. Don't prayers require timorous approach and attitude, a sort of quaking and shaking before quick withdrawal to a safer place outside the throne room? She also wondered whether she shouldn't save prayers for the *big* things rather than repeatedly asking for this, that, and the other thing. Maybe she should focus her prayers and only ask for a little every once in a while. Yet she instead continued to pursue God in prayers. Something kept pushing her forward almost as if she were running after him and nagging him. And oddly, even as she did so, she felt closer to him, felt his joy and humor rather than any annoyance or irritation. She concluded that she could not possibly annoy him with prayer as long as her prayers were genuine rather than rote or pro forma. She even felt a little bit like he was drawing her closer to him by placing his gifts just around the figurative corner. So she decided firmly to continue to peek around that corner, to look for him, to knock on his door at any hour in prayer. He would decide what was possible and appropriate, not her.

Ask in Jesus's name. John 14:13.

We have a proper habit of ending prayers by invoking Jesus's name, although when it comes to prayer nothing having to do with habits is fully proper. We do not out of *habit* tell our closest family members that we love them. We instead tell them so genuinely, out of fresh devotion and love. The same must be true of prayer that although we habitually invoke Jesus's name in our prayers, as Jesus told us to do, we do not treat the invocation as if it were an incantation. One does not use any name, not the name of a famous friend, or of a supervisor, or of a pastor, or even of a parent or other loved one, purely for the power that the name may hold. Rather, we invoke any name as a way to confirm our relationship to that person. When we tell a co-worker that the boss said to do so and so, we do not presume that the boss's name in itself holds peculiar power. We mean instead that the boss will soon appear to set everyone straight if we have not done as the boss directed. Invoking Jesus's name in prayer has similar purpose, not for its magical effect but instead to state or imply that we stand under his direction in praying our request. We ask as if Jesus asked.

On the eve of his crucifixion, Jesus had just explained to the disciples that *he* was the way to the Father. He had explained that if they knew him, then they knew the Father. Yet one of the disciples in response had asked Jesus if they could just see the Father, as if to finally satisfy them. Jesus answered that anyone who had seen him had seen the Father because he is in the Father and the Father in him.

He went on to explain that anyone who believed what he had just said would do the works that Jesus had done and even greater things. Jesus continued, "I will do whatever you ask in my name, so that the Father may be glorified in the Son. You may ask me for anything in my name, and I will do it." Jesus wants us to ask in his name, to pray to him and the Father so that he may answer the prayer to glorify the Father in the Son.

She had heard Jesus's name invoked so often at the blessing of every meal and end of every other prayer in her faith tradition. The invocation sometimes sounded more like tradition, but most often it sounded like something quite different from tradition. Most often, it sounded to her as if the speaker spoke with at least some knowledge of who Jesus was, like they were speaking of a brother or friend, not a mechanical sound but a sound almost of intimacy. In invoking Jesus's name, those who prayed sounded like they were praying to someone, the Father, to whom Jesus's name meant a lot, indeed meant everything. She found the same that she could not quite invoke Jesus's name at the end of her prayers without the hair on the back of her neck standing up just a little, like he was present and praying with her. Her heart would soften as she said his name. Her head would bow a little deeper. Even as she said his name, she would sometimes realize that the prayer itself was not the important part. The important part of the prayer was his name. Prayer, she thought, might just be an excuse to speak intimately of Jesus to the Father, hardly a request at all, and instead more like a sonnet or song, an ode to the Father of the glory of the Son of Man. She would pray in Jesus's name, knowing that the name, or more accurately the person whom the name represented, meant more to her than the prayer.

Believe Jesus is able. Matthew 9:28.

No one really wants to waste their time on actions that produce no result. If we are to pray, then we must believe that prayer is effective, that Jesus is able to do as he says. Prayer without belief is no better than wishing for results. Why would God respond to the unbelieving prayer? Try approaching a parent or employer with any request while at the same time saying that you don't even believe that they have the power to grant it. Why would they grant the request of a distrusting and disrespectful petitioner? No judge would grant the request of one who denies that the judge has the authority to do so, especially if the one making the request denied that the judge even exists. Belief is essential to effective prayer because only belief will move the Father to whom we pray. Yet prayer can also take time for God to bring about the result. Indeed, if prayer were instantaneous, producing instant results, then people would pray all of the time because they would have instant gratification in prompt result. We may as well recognize that a challenging thing about prayer is that God answers it on his own timetable, not on ours. But timing is one thing, while belief is another. Just because prayers don't always produce instant results does not mean that prayer is ineffective.

The synagogue leader had asked Jesus to come put his hand on his dead daughter, saying simply and believingly that Jesus's doing so would bring her back to life. Yet the noisy mourners had laughed derisively at Jesus when he had entered the synagogue leader's home, telling the mourners to leave because he was about to bring the dead daughter back to life. Relying instead on the leader's believing prayer, Jesus went in anyway, took the girl by the hand, and brought her back to life. Leaving there, he met two blind men who hailed him as the long-anticipated Son of David, hoping that Jesus would restore their sight. "Do you believe that I am able to do this?" Jesus asked them. They did believe, and so he touched their eyes, saying, "According to your faith let it be done to you," and restored their sight. Believe that Jesus is able. He hears believing prayers, not false or formal prayers made in unbelief.

He believed when he prayed. He had no reason not to believe, knowing that God had long ago blessed him far beyond his paltry belief. It had not always been so. For a long time, he had wondered about if not openly questioned the efficacy of prayer. He would pray then, waiting to see if prayer produced results. Not seeing anything demonstrable, few miracles right before his doubting eyes, he had deepened his inquiry about prayer. Gradually, from study and instruction, he came to realize that he had several misunderstandings about prayer. First, he had not yet prayed in belief. He had prayed instead in *test*, in *challenge* to belief, which he knew now was not the prayer of a believer. Second, he had mistakenly connected miraculous response, something totally out of the ordinary, with answered prayer, when to the contrary answered prayer may look quite ordinary when the results happen. God does not have to make a show to prove prayer effective. Third, he had looked for instant results when the results might instead happen long after he had forgotten his prayer, like next week, next month, or next year. Over time, as his faith grew and God began answering more of his faith-paltry prayers, he realized these and other errors, and so began to pray more, pray in greater belief, and pray with clearer response. Perhaps the instant miraculous prayers come later, he thought, when they would not be proof or surprising but rather the evidence of deep belief and trust. Jesus, he knew, is able.

1.3 Learning

Let no one deceive you. Matthew 24:4. *Do not claim that you can see.* John 9:41. *Clear your eyes.* Luke 6:42. *Hear with your ears.* Matthew 13:16. *Understand with your heart.* John 12:40. *Understand the word.* Matthew 13:23. *Interpret the times.* Luke 12:56. *Let go of traditions.* Mark 7:8. *Gain knowledge.* Luke 11:52. *Consider carefully what you hear.* Mark 4:24. *Be careful of your heart.* Luke 21:34. *Watch for teachers who bear no fruit.* Matthew 7:15. *Guard against men.* Matthew 10:17. *Guard against false teaching.* Matthew 16:12. *Beware of those who teach rules for show.* Luke 20:46. *Do not look for the living among the dead.* Luke 24:5. *Leave blind guides.* Matthew 15:14. *Retain the word.* Matthew 13:23.

It would surprise no one that Jesus spoke often about belief and about prayer. It would on the other hand surprise many that Jesus spoke often about learning. Many associate spirituality with simple belief, with unthinking acceptance of doctrine, statements, assertions, principles, and belief without thought, study, challenge, or examination. Of course, study itself, reason itself, we base primarily on faith, accepting so much of what others have told us without any direct observation, second-hand summary, or basic understanding of their evidence. Knowledge of all kinds proceeds from a substantial base of tradition, presumption, assumption, and theory. Reason would be largely dead, circular, and pointless, without faith, without our nearly unthinking confidence in the orderly, cause-and-effect, vitalizing, forward-moving nature of the universe. God made us to learn about this universe, to search him out in what we study and observe. Among the many things that he said to do and that he did, Jesus gave us many principles for learning. Consider how Jesus said that we ought to learn. Grow in knowledge and wisdom by learning as Jesus would have you learn.

Let no one deceive you. Matthew 24:4.

We often desire the security of knowing what's coming. Cognitive psychologists even have names for the multiple ways in which we happily and gullibly let persons and events delude us. Our powerful minds see patterns in so many things, indeed in everything, even when the patterns are not really present. We flip heads thrice and begin to believe that the next flip will more likely be heads again, or more likely its opposite tails, when the probability remains what it always was, 50/50. We listen to, value, and rely on the predictions of political commentators, economists, financial advisors, and weather forecasters, when their records would often show that their predictions are little better than an almanac. Yet we especially let others deceive us when their counsel comes to matters of fundamental significance, like the meaning and course of life. We adopt as gospel the refrain of a pop song and accept as wisdom the couch chatter of a sit-com television star. We let popular politicians, preachers, and other public personas deceive us again and again, even when we know that their words are deceptive. We are so willing to be deceived that Jesus says simply to stop allowing others to deceive you.

Jesus left the temple again after teaching and prophesying about the destruction of Jerusalem that was soon to come and of his departure and return. As he and the disciples pushed their way through the temple's crowds, his disciples oddly pointed out to Jesus the temple's great buildings. His reply was that every stone of those buildings would topple, leaving nothing to admire. They walked on, probably now in silence, to the Mount of Olives, alone away from the temple's crowds. There, as Jesus sat off by himself, the disciples approached him again, asking him when they would see the temple fall and when Jesus, his departure imminent, would return. Jesus replied, "Watch out that no one deceives you." He then told much more of the great distress that was to come. Finally, he repeated to watch out for those who make false predictions of things to come, even when great signs and wonders accompany them. Only the Father knows the moment of Jesus's return.

The more that he studied the Bible and especially the words of Jesus, the more that he realized that he had previously had no understanding of anything. The things that he thought he understood were simply things that others had told him and that he had accepted. He had not really examined anything, judged the truth of any profound thought. When he looked closely at the words of those whom the public seemed to judge wise, or at least those to whom the public seemed to listen the most, their thoughts were actually not wise at all. They were instead mostly platitudes, not much more than the sorts of things one would read on the side of an expensive cup of coffee. For much of his life, he had let others deceive him without himself pursuing, investigating, and judging truth. In all candor, he had almost wanted others to deceive, welcomed their deception, especially when they packaged it in an attractive manner, perhaps around a particularly successful-looking life, even though he had seen how quickly those successful-looking lives could change their look. So he resolved again to listen to Jesus's counsel to let no one deceive him. From now on, he would judge what was true, and he would do so against Jesus's word as standard.

Do not claim that you can see. John 9:41.

One of the biggest parts of our problem with learning anything is that we think that we already know. Learning begins with the willingness to change one's thought. The definition of learning is to change one's thought in a durable manner. We can study and study and study, but if in the end we are not thinking anew, then we have learned nothing. The closed mind learns nothing. When we think that we know, we have far too little interest in evaluating and changing our thought. Learning begins by connecting new thought to old. We learn first by extending what we know into matters that we previously did not know. We build on what we once thought. To build, we must imagine that we have something to construct. The learner's mind is eager to discover new thought. When we think that we have no new thought to discover, we lose that eagerness, losing with it the will and ability to learn. To learn, we must instead assume that we have not imagined all of the truth, which is of course the only sound assumption. Who knows all other than Christ himself? We must avoid believing that we see everything one has to see. To believe that we see is to be blind. To know that we see only in small part and have much more to discover is to begin to uncover our blindness.

Jesus met a man who had been blind from birth. His disciples asked him whose sin had caused the man's blindness, his own or his parents' sin. Jesus explained that the blindness was not the result of sin but that God might display his works. Jesus then gave the blind man sight. The man's astonished neighbors took him to the religious leaders before whom the man attested to Jesus's having given him sight. The leaders, jealous of Jesus and fearful of his influence, called the man a sinner and threw the man out. Jesus, hearing of their insults, found and consoled the man, saying that the blind would see and those who saw would be blind. Some of the religious leaders heard what Jesus said and asked him directly whether he meant that they were blind, too. Jesus answered, "If you were blind, you would not be guilty of sin; but now that you claim you can see, your guilt remains." Do not reject Jesus while claiming that you can see.

She used to feel superior to many people, confident in what she knew, even though she was still young and in her relative youth suspected that she did not actually know much. Her innocence and naiveté just didn't bother her all that much. She figured that she knew what she needed to know and when she needed to know more would promptly discover it. Right?! Yet as she matured, particularly in her spiritual understanding, she began to realize just how little she knew and how little others around her knew. She suspected too that when she needed to learn something, doing so would be more of a challenge than she had once thought. Her growing knowledge of Jesus was what had turned her from over-confident ignorance, an ignorance that had seemed too much like bliss, to her first real knowledge of truth, knowledge that she nonetheless held very gently and humbly lest it dissipate at any moment. She knew that she was blind and that Jesus had shown her only small glimmers of what she

56

would someday know through him. She also saw that those others around her who were still so confident and even arrogant about knowing what they needed to know were in fact quite ignorant of the truth. She was just fine with not expecting to see enough to claim that she knew. She trusted instead that Jesus would show her what she needed to know as she needed to know it, believing too that she was blind other than through what he enabled her to see.

Clear your eyes. Luke 6:42.

Could it be that we think with our eyes? In the common way of saying it, in the vernacular, to see something clearly means to understand it. When someone fails to understand something, we say that they just don't see it. When they finally get it straight, we say that they finally see clearly. Understanding is the simple ability to describe a concept, principle, situation, or truth correctly in one's own words. Understanding can require literal sight, such as reading the words of a text properly, or assessing a situation properly based on observations of observable conditions. To have something wrong with one's vision, such as to have something in one's eye causing blurred vision, reduces one's ability to observe and can distort one's understanding. That natural connection between clear eyesight and understanding is why we also take seeing clearly to mean understanding things that do not necessarily require sight. Curiously, we call *insight* those other understandings of things that we reason or intuit rather than observe with our eyes, as if we are using an interior or inward-looking eyesight. Importantly, even the insight must be clear, just as the *eye*sight must be clear, if we are to understand things correctly. Insight is just as susceptible to distortion, to blurring, as eyesight is, and perhaps even more so.

Jesus had much to say to the crowd, even as he healed the sick they brought to him. He told story after story that day, one of them about the blind leading the blind until they both fall into a pit. Students can learn no more than their teachers, he cautioned, and the student who finishes training will simply be like the student's teacher. Jesus knew too that we are always trying to teach others before learning ourselves. Speaking to a common crowd whose members were likely familiar with trades like carpentry, he told of a worker trying to remove a speck from his brother's eye while paying no attention to the plank in his own eye. We are so ready to somehow set straight the understanding of others, which is difficult or impossible to do when our own understanding is so distorted. Jesus warned, "You hypocrite, first take the plank out of your eye, and then you will see clearly to remove the speck from your brother's eye." We must first clear our own eyes and straighten our own vision before even thinking that we can help straighten the vision of another.

Her insight had often been keen, oddly in a way that she readily connected with her eyesight, meaning her power to observe. She had always been a close observer of things. She would stand off to the side and just watch until she understood the situation, the motivations of people involved, and probable outcomes. Only then would she act and participate. Her teachers had thought that she was shy, but her standing apart wasn't shyness. She just wanted to observe first so that she could understand the situation. It wasn't that she necessarily trusted her power of observation. She knew that she was often wrong about situations, wrong about the motivation of the people whom she observed. Her own emotions, experiences, and beliefs would distort her observations. Yet those errors just made her more determined than ever to observe, to look before leaping. Then gradually, as she learned more about Jesus and learned to rely more closely on his words, she felt that her power of observation was taking on an interior dimension, as if she could see inside of situations, could read situations at a deeper level. She almost felt as if he was telling her about those situations, helping her divest her own distorting views in favor of his clear view. His insight was one of the things about him that most fascinated and attracted her.

Hear with your ears. Matthew 13:16.

It is funny how we hear but don't hear, just as we see but don't see. Hearing means more than sound waves striking the ear drum. To hear, in the deeper sense of that action, is to recognize and accept the meaning behind the sounds that strike the ear. So many times, we hear what another says but don't register the meaning, no less than accept that meaning. Words pass without recognition. God speaks to us through the Bible, Jesus speaks to us through the gospels, the Holy Spirit communicates with us day to day, and yet we hardly even register the meaning, no less embrace and pursue it. Our hearing is fine so far as it goes. We have the physiological capability of making out the words and cognitive capability of assembling the meaning but simply fail to do so. We hear without hearing, just as we see without seeing. We have the ability without the will. We lack the hunger or desire. The problem is not with our ears or eyes. The problem is with our callous heart and hard spirit. Listen! Jesus says that we must learn to hear with our ears.

Jesus so often used parables when speaking to the crowds that his disciples asked him once why he did so. He answered that he had given his disciples, not them, the knowledge of his kingdom. Those who know his kingdom receive more, while those who do not know lose the little that they have. Jesus explained that he spoke to the crowds in parables because they neither saw nor heard, and so did not understand. He equated them to the callous people about whom Isaiah had prophesied long ago who, hardly hearing with their ears, did not understand enough to turn to God for healing. Jesus concluded, "Blessed are your eyes because they see, and your ears because they hear. For truly I tell you, many prophets and righteous people longed to see what you see but did not see it, and to hear what you hear but did not hear it." Hear the words of Jesus.

She had heard a hundred sermons and probably many more. Had she really heard them, though? She began to listen more closely to what the preachers and pastors were saying. They were saying something extraordinary. Maybe the unusual nature of their message was why she hadn't seemed to hear it. They were speaking of another realm to which she had access right now through Jesus and his Holy Spirit. They were saying that she could live differently and live forever if she only accepted Jesus's forgiving message. She looked around her to see if others were listening. It seemed from what others said and how they acted that some were listening while others were not. As she heard more of the message, really heard it deep down in a way that she had not previously heard it, she began to feel more and more strongly that she wanted to be one of those people who were really listening, who were really hearing. She knew that she had nothing wrong with her ears. She laughed at the thought. What she needed was a turn of her heart toward Jesus. Then she would truly hear, and he would change her. That message is what she was now hearing and pursuing.

Understand with your heart. John 12:40.

The anatomical term *heart* obviously refers to that most important organ that circulates the blood through the body. In spiritual understanding, though, the heart refers to something quite different. We speak of heartache or a heavy heart when we are sad and a broken heart when an important relationship ends unexpectedly. We speak of a glad heart or light heart when happy. The heart is not simply what the mind thinks, nor is it simply what the emotions feel, or what the will intends. The heart in spiritual terms combines the mind, will, and emotions into something nearer the seat or locus of a person, perhaps the person's character or identity. The heart encompasses everything for which we hope, everything we desire, everything that we intend. In that rich sense, the heart had better be willing to accept understanding, just as the eyes must be open to seeing, the ears open to hearing, and the mind open to understanding. We might have the mind but not the will or emotion, or the will but not the mind or emotion, or even the emotion but not the mind or will. We need all together, represented by the heart, to want understanding. The heart must turn, the heart must believe, the heart must desire the Son of Man, or we have no prospect of his blessing.

Jesus spoke frequently of hearing and of seeing, not in the ordinary way of the senses but in the deeper way of the spirit. The Gospels of Matthew and John both quote the ancient prophet Isaiah about the people's hard hearts not hearing or seeing. In Matthew, Jesus himself quotes that passage from Isaiah to explain why he spoke to the crowds in parables because they would not accept his message. John quotes that same passage from Isaiah to explain why the people would not believe in Jesus even after he had performed so many miracles in their presence. The disciples believed, and some others believed, but most people did not believe despite the evidence right in front of them. The passage from Isaiah that Jesus quoted in Matthew and that John's Gospel also quoted held that the people needed to "understand with their hearts" if they were to turn for Jesus to heal them. Understand with your heart, Jesus says. Make it a heart thing.

He knew that his mind was often wrong, just not thinking the way that he knew he should think. His emotions were also unreliable, up one day, down the next. He also had the will some days but not others, when he just didn't feel up to it. On the whole, he felt a little bit of a wreck much of the time, only one-third or two-thirds whole. Yet the one thing that seemed for the past few years to remain right was his heart. Somehow, with the constant help of the Holy Spirit, his whole was lately greater than the sum of his parts. He absolutely knew what it was. He loved, believed, respected, accepted, admired, feared, and pursued Jesus. He *needed* Jesus. The one thing that had not changed over these recent years was that his heart was open to Jesus. He decided to keep it that way as far as he was able with the constant help of the Holy Spirit. That commitment became his personal prayer that the Spirit would abide richly in him so that his heart would see, hear, and understand Jesus, turning to him for healing and blessing.

Understand the word. Matthew 13:23.

While we must have the heart to understand, we also must know *what it is* that we should understand. Our hearts might be ready, but what should our hearts pursue and accept? Jesus makes clear in the following parable and other accounts that his words hold the keys to

61

understanding, to learning, indeed to entering into life in God's kingdom. People open their hearts to many things, sometimes too many things. Some people have a great capacity to learn except that they have little insight into *what* to learn. Indeed, learning occurs constantly, whether we wish to learn or not. We soak up stimuli of all kinds around us, turning stimuli into meaning, whether we wish to do so, commit to doing so, pursue doing so, or not. Advertising is an example. No matter how one resists it, other than to somehow remain out of reach of it, we still pick up its message. Jesus wants us to be selective about the message, indeed to select the Message. If we must learn constantly, as we must and as we should welcome and appreciate that we do, then we must choose *what* to learn just as constantly, be just as consistent in hewing to Jesus's word as we are to accepting and processing the stimuli of learning. Pursue, discover, grasp, and understand Jesus's word.

Jesus had just told the parable of the sower to the large crowds. The crowds were so large that the people stood on the shore while Jesus sat in a boat near shore from which to teach. The sower had scattered seed on different soils, Jesus had said, with different results in the crops that the soils had produced. Of course, only the good soil had produced a good crop, many times the little seed that the sower had sown. The disciples, though, later wanted to know from Jesus just why he taught in parables and also what he meant by the parable of the sower. Jesus first explained that the parables helped the people choose whether to hear and understand. Those who had the heart for Jesus's teaching would learn and understand, while those who did not would treat the parables as having no particular meaning, at least none that they wanted to learn. Jesus then explained to the disciples the meaning of the parable of the sower. The seed was Jesus's word, while the hearers' hearts were the soil. "The seed falling on good soil refers to someone who hears the word and understands it. This is the one who produces a crop, yielding a hundred, sixty, or thirty times what was sown." The ears must want to hear, the eyes must want to open, and the heart must desire to understand and follow.

She liked reading, although she had not always done so. She was glad that she had learned to like reading. Reading opened worlds to her that she would not otherwise have been able to explore. She wasn't quite a fully literate, superstar sort of reader, not one of those persons who had read everything including every classic and every latest book. Yet she was generally well read, increasingly so as her appetite for understanding, knowledge, and meaning grew. Now, though, she liked reading God's word especially. She wasn't sure of the moment that her appetite for God's word had taken hold of her. It might not have been a precise moment at all. Instead, over the past several years she had found increasing exposure to it, and with increasing exposure, she had drawn increasing meaning from it. She had soon discovered that the words of Jesus seemed to discern and judge things for her that she would not otherwise have discerned and judged. Her mind had always judged what she was reading, whether she believed it or not, trusted it or not, and liked it or not. Reading God's word was different. God's word seemed to judge both her and everything else that she read. She eventually felt that while many purported to comment on God's word, God's word was instead commentary on many, indeed on all persons and things. These realizations kindled a fire for God's word within her.

Interpret the times. Luke 12:56.

Culture influences us so readily, as of course must be the case. We are social creatures, learning not only from others but from the accumulated habits, traditions, and practices, and popular influences, of the communities in which we live. We would be lost without culture, helpless in the face of so many ordinary and extraordinary situations. We instead follow the ways of the times, doing as our neighbors and celebrities and leaders do. Yet following the ways of the times can be hazardous. Times change. Times can mislead, indeed routinely do mislead one far from the life and message of Christ. Christ is not of the world, while culture is of the world. As truth and life, Christ judges all things, without having anything judge him. Nothing in the world has the basis to judge God's Son because God created the world, and the created cannot judge the Creator. Christ's life and message give us the basis to judge things of the world, to interpret the times. Jesus wants us to know the times, to see the day's distortion, and to live apart from that distortion so that we can live fully with and in him.

Jesus spoke to crowds of thousands who gathered to hear his authoritative, entertaining, and profound teaching. His teaching was authoritative because he spoke in perfect consonance with the ancient prophets and without ever facing any effective challenge, exactly like one who knew. His teaching entertained because it ridiculed the religious leaders whom the people distrusted and even resented. And his teaching was profound because it revealed the conditions of the times, always striking at the heart of the matter. On this occasion, he had already taught the crowd of thousands for some time, until it seemed like he needed to bring the point of his teaching home, to conclude his gospel message in a manner that would produce the greatest effect on the greatest number. Maybe rain or storm clouds had begun to gather in the distance, making the crowd restless. Jesus told the crowd that they were skilled at predicting the weather from its signs but concluded, "Hypocrites! You know how to interpret the appearance of the earth and the sky. How is it that you don't know how to interpret this present time?" Know the times, particularly where Jesus stands as to them.

He needed in his work to stay abreast of trends in the broader world. Those with whom he met expected him to know not only his own field but how changing conditions were affecting it. He needed some ability to see things before they arrived or at least to know things when they arrived. He could not effectively serve those who expected his help without seeing things, without interpreting things for them. They needed his counsel to connect things that were happening to them and around them with changing conditions in the world. They needed his help to lend meaning to changes in their own lives. He felt at times like he was carrying around a compass for them, showing them which way they were headed and sometimes also why. He seldom revealed Jesus directly as his compass, although some suspected that Jesus was his guide star, and a few knew. He did not hide his close relationship to Jesus and study of his teaching. Jesus's presence as the source of his counsel, the way that he interpreted the signs of the times, would have been obvious to anyone who wished to know. He made sure of that obviousness. Yet he simply knew that fewer would have accepted his counsel had he begun with its source. The heart must lead. He would help them interpret the times, but he would also point them subtly toward the One who revealed the times.

Let go of traditions. Mark 7:8.

How many things do you do because others have done them before you? We tend to think ourselves original, when to the contrary we think, say, and do much as our parents and grandparents did before us, with their having done as others did before them. When we enter a town, trade, or profession, we adopt the local customs, doing as others do whether or not what they do is honest, decent, law-abiding, or consistent. We make a show of our customs as if they were what mattered rather than what we might learn and apply from God's wisdom. We could apply Solomon's wisdom from Proverbs, the very words of Christ from the gospels, or Paul's instruction from his letters, but instead we bind even our religious practices in customs. Traditions bind, constrain, and enslave us, even when Christ's realm beckons. We could live in constantly fresh encounters by leaning on his grand glory, but instead we exchange his invitation for what we did yesterday and others did the day before then. We can rightly treasure traditions particularly when they reflect his love and glory, but we must not let traditions interfere with what he says for us to do, his word being his glory.

Religious leaders and law teachers from Jerusalem gathered around Jesus, questioning him as to why his disciples did not follow the religious traditions as they did. They made a ceremonial washing of their hands, cups, pots, and pans, before eating, while the disciples did not. Their unwashed hands defiled the disciples, the leaders and teachers considered. Why did Jesus put up with these unschooled men? Why did he entrust them with his teaching instead of admonishing them to follow the traditions of the religious leaders and law teachers? Jesus had no patience for their impertinent questions, quoting Isaiah to them that they were honoring God only with their lips while their hearts were far from him. They were teaching human rules while pretending to worship the law-giving God. Jesus admonished, "You have let go of the commands of God and are holding on to human traditions." They were nullifying God's words with these ceremonial rules and other handed-down traditions.

Her family was odd, she had often felt. They had such few traditions. She heard of other families doing the same things year after year to celebrate the annual holidays, things from which they seemed to draw great comfort, although those things also seemed too often to carry great burdens. Her family instead seemed to float through the years without any great fanfare over holiday traditions. Her family had little lore, most of it around the silly things that had happened or that one or another of them had done. Some of their family stories involved pets, while others involved trips or vehicles. Incidents, mysteries, and happenstance were all part of her family's lore much more so than the absent traditions. For a long time she regretted not having those family traditions until she realized how much her family had changed over the years, and changed not just outwardly but in important ways in their life commitments. While they had few or no traditions, they had a capacity to move in and out of communities and circumstances, perhaps adopting briefly their local customs but never really attaching much meaning to the customs, only trying to engage the best of those communities. She finally decided that she could do without the traditions. She still missed them a little now and then, but God was giving her a deeper security and meaning than habit or custom.

Gain knowledge. Luke 11:52.

Oh, to gain knowledge. How many of us do mothers deliver with a thirst for understanding and hunger for knowledge? Most of us begin life as outstanding learners, mastering language as toddlers and writing, math, history, geography, government, citizenship, science, and much more in our school years. At some point, though, the knowledge weighs most of us down. Something begins to douse our fire to learn, or perhaps rather than some*thing* it is some*one* who removes the fuel and oxygen of learning. The rare teacher seems to have the capacity to stoke the fire. The common teacher seems less capable of making any sense of the quantity, organization, pattern, and priority of knowledge. Knowledge does have pattern. It does have priority. The master teacher conveys both priority and pattern. Without the architecture, without the structure and priority, vast knowledge can only be a vast burden. Everything has its place. Everything has its cause. Everything and everyone has a master. The key to knowledge is to know the Master. Knowledge of the Master is the key to the realm. Knowledge fills the realm, none of it burdening the learner whose burden the Master carries.

Jesus reserved his stronger criticism for the religious leaders who professed to be experts in the religious laws. He saw that the teachers among them were just weighing down with impossible burdens those who wanted to learn about God. They were not really helping, not really teaching at all. God had sent their ancestors prophets and wise men whom their ancestors had instead persecuted or even killed. Now these leaders were acting just like those ancestors in opposing Jesus. He was the key to knowledge, his words the key to life. They had only to enter his realm. Instead, they challenged, questioned, and tried to catch and contradict Jesus at every turn. Jesus told them, "You experts in the law have taken away the key to knowledge. You yourselves have not entered, and you have hindered those who were entering." Yet his criticism only caused the leaders to do more than ever to oppose and undermine Jesus. They were not interested in acquiring or sharing knowledge nor in allowing Jesus to teach.

Among her accomplishments that most satisfied her was her vast increase in knowledge. She had learned so much in the past few years. In a clear sense, Jesus had been the author of that knowledge. She felt as if he had unlocked her capacity to learn, to acquire knowledge not particularly of the ways of the world but of the things that govern the world, that move the world, that guide the world. She had learned of the intentions and pretensions of people, how people organize and compete, share and provide, defraud and destroy. She had learned of rights and wrongs, of right ways and wrong ways, of causes and consequences. She suspected that had it not been for the courage and confidence that she drew from Jesus, she would not have attempted what she had, would not have trusted that she could organize, retain, and employ the knowledge that she was amassing. That knowledge would only have been a burden to her, would have weighed her down, and would have distressed and disorganized her. Instead, Jesus and his words seemed to hold it all together, giving her knowledge both cause and application. She only wondered what great thing he would do with her next.

Consider carefully what you hear. Mark 4:24.

Learning has its basis in thought. We must be thinking to learn. Learning involves cognition, meaning to mull, consider, examine, and turn over in thought, in order to make new connections and patterns that will guide future thought and action. Learning is much like building in that it requires constructing foundation and structure, fastening things to things until they take expressive and functional shape. When we let words and ideas pass before us or through us without engaging them, rather simply occupying our mind and senses with them, we are not learning but allowing the words and ideas to entertain us. In case you hadn't noticed, we have more entertainment in our lives today than in prior generations, whether more or less learning. We choose it not for its substance, not for how it will improve and guide our lives, but instead for its ability to occupy and please the senses. When we do turn to things that purport to have substance, we have forgone the capacity for deep and careful thought. Things then pass for truths that don't have truth's quality. We should instead be examining these things carefully.

Jesus was coaching his disciples again, giving them the deeper understanding of things that he conveyed only in parables when in public. He explained that the truth he was sharing is like a lamp that you bring out to shine light on subjects. That light reveals the hidden to anyone who is willing to look and listen carefully. The truth brings out into the light for examination what words, conditions, and circumstances tend to conceal as if they were in the dark. "If anyone has ears to hear, let them hear. Consider carefully what you hear," Jesus instructed, "With the measure you use, you will receive—and even more. Whoever has will be given more, while whoever does not have, even what they have they will lose." The care and clarity with which we examine things determines how much understanding we draw. When we have Jesus's words as the measure, their use gives us more and more. Those who do not have his words, lose even the little that they have, gradually going senseless in their thinking for lack of the authoritative source.

She was still learning how to examine assertions, how to test them for truth. She had come a long way in doing so but knew that she had a way yet to go to develop fully her critical capacity. She could see more of the groundless assertions more quickly, picking them out liking removing the bad berries from the good. She knew how to question the assertion's source, to look for controlling authority. She knew how to compare, contrast, analogize, and distinguish. She found herself doing these things more often because she saw how powerful the practice was to making sound decisions and constructing a sound life. Her ability to examine things carefully was making a difference in her life, and she could see that she was extending that ability to make a difference in the lives of others. Most of all, she knew what to accept as controlling authority for any proposition, beginning in every case with the Source. She had gradually moved from questioning the Source, a fruitlessly rebellious activity, to questioning propositions that the Source showed were inconsistent.

Be careful of your heart. Luke 21:34.

To learn the truth of the words of Jesus, grow in confidence and belief, and mature and remain steadfast in faith, requires an attitude and approach to each day fittingly described as *guarding your heart.*

To guard one's heart is to hold a little something back, to keep just a little something in reserve rather than give it up to nerves, fear, or the over-pursuit of duties and temptations. Frankly, learning and spiritual growth take a special kind of secure resolve, not the kind of attitude that comes easily. Probably, most people fail to learn, grow, and mature in faith because they fail to prepare and guard their hearts for learning. Things instead dissipate them. Events and circumstances, whether their own or those about which they hear in news reports and rumor, worry and weaken them. Often anxious and needful, they submit to temptations in an effort to regain confidence, satisfaction, and control, pursuit of those temptations then further consuming them. For others, the worry is over duties and the effort to fulfill them to everyone's satisfaction. If dissipation doesn't get one, then obsession and compulsion do, as too few hold anything back. Learning, reform, growth, and change? Who has the time, focus, or energy for those things when just getting through each day seems to take everything you've got? And before we know it, time for growth is gone, lost to frantic pace.

Jesus had been through so much with the disciples in the three swift years of his public ministry. He had shown them so much, taught them so much, and been in so many tense and dramatic situations with them. They had walked so far, been to so many places, and fed, ate, learned, taught, healed, wept, and slept under so many different conditions. They had seen Jesus celebrate, grieve, and even party with others. And Jesus had announced the end times of terror on earth and his second coming. Yet in the enormous commotion surrounding his advent, ministry, and prophecy constituting the hinge to history, Jesus still showed concern that the disciples would protect the condition of their hearts to remain steadfast waiting for their salvation to escape all that was to happen. "Be careful of your hearts," Jesus told them, "or your hearts will be weighed down with carousing, drunkenness, and the anxieties of life, and that day will close on you suddenly like a trap." Nothing is too big or terrible to lose your heart to anxiety or dissipation. Guard your heart in order that you can stand with Jesus.

He knew his dissipations, temptations, anxieties, and compulsions. That knowledge made them only a little easier with which to deal. What he needed more than knowing his weaknesses was having a reason not to submit to them. Give anyone a big and clear enough reason to stop the unhealthy chase, and they will generally do so, only too gladly. The most-consumed addict can defeat the habit when the heart gives the addict a compelling reason. The heart is what it takes, he concluded, indeed was what he learned from years of wrestling with his weaknesses. He had heard of guarding one's heart. Now he finally understood enough of what the saying meant to put it into practice. He just learned to keep a little in reserve outside of his compulsions, which made them a lot less like compulsions and more like manageable tendencies. The big thing that he had, though, was the compelling reason to guard his heart, which was to save it for Jesus. He didn't want to be dissipated, weak, over-wrought, and out of touch when Jesus came calling. He wanted to be ready, fit, and able to respond. And the more that he maintained that steady stance in the King's anticipation, the stronger his faith became to withstand greater stresses and temptations. Jesus's Spirit resided in that guarded part of his heart, giving him all the strength that he ever needed.

Watch for teachers who bear no fruit. Matthew 7:15.

While we learn from teachers, choosing the right teacher can be a challenging proposition. How is one who needs instruction in order to learn the subject to know who has the knowledge and skill to instruct? The problem is a bit like the egg having to choose the chicken or the cart having to pick up the horse. By definition, the student does not know what the student is to learn, so how can the student discern who does know what the student is to learn and whether that teacher has the skill to impart it? Here as elsewhere on the subject of learning, Jesus gives sound counsel. Good teachers produce good fruit, meaning that teachers who know what the student needs to know in order to succeed will have succeeded themselves. The fruit analogy makes sense. We know a tree by the fruit that it produces, whether pear, apple, peach, or orange. An apple tree does not a pear produce. A teacher who claims to know what the student needs to learn in order to be able to produce good works should be producing his or her own good works. Seek teachers who live as you would hope to live by learning from them.

Jesus spoke frequently about those from whom we should learn. He not only exhibited the character, evidence, and qualities of the Master teacher but also taught about how we should recognize others from whom we must not or may learn. Nearing the end of his Sermon on the Mount, Jesus told the crowd, "Watch out for false prophets who come in sheep's clothing but are as ferocious as wolves," adding, "By their fruit you will know them." He then reminded his listeners how thistles and thorn bushes do not produce edible fruit. Only good trees bear good fruit, while trees bearing no fruit end up cut down for firewood. "By their fruit you will recognize them," Jesus repeated. Choose teachers who do as they teach and in doing so produce the good works that you would hope to produce.

Somehow, without quite planning it, she had managed to surround herself with people whom she felt that she could be happy, successful, and fulfilled by emulating. These people had knowledge, skills, confidence, generosity, good sense, service to give, and most of all faith. She almost hadn't realized how important choosing sound teachers and mentors is until she started spending time with these people, drawing and learning from these people. They were not all in one place, not all in one organization, not even all in one community. In a way, they seemed to have just shown up in her life. Yet they had not just shown up. Instead, she and others who cared about her had sought them out, not all at once, but little by little, some formally while others informally, some as teachers, others as guides, still others as counselors, and a few as friends. The common denominator with each was not in the way that they talked, thought, or taught. What each had in common instead was personal proof of their soundness and faith. They had walked their talk. She needed no more proof of their qualifications as teachers than that.

Guard against men. Matthew 10:17.

Sad that guarding one's heart and choosing teachers carefully so as to be able to learn and grow spiritually should mean having to guard against others. Circumstances and events certainly challenge us, but should we also have to watch out for others? Conditions do seem to work against us at times, but must we also plan and prepare to guard against *human* agency? So much of our instruction is to love and serve others, and to have compassion for others and take an interest in others. What does Jesus mean then to guard against others? Our unfortunate state is to be as much or more a challenge to others as we are supporters of them. We are social beings, but our society so often frustrates and burdens one another that we must actually take care whom we approach and with whom we relate. We each have only a few who have the character, attitude, personality, stance, and disposition to be open supporters of us. The rest we must studiously avoid, step quietly around, and firmly leave behind. For a few, we must watch out, particularly those who have authority to affect adversely our circumstances. Human agency holds as many hazards for us as conditions and circumstances.

Jesus warned often that others would challenge and undermine the disciples. He explained that in traveling among the people to speak of his Way, the disciples would be like sheep among wolves, defenseless against their ravages. They must therefore be as shrewd in their judgments and relationships as snakes, even while maintaining their innocence like doves. When he sent them out among the Jews, particularly those lost within the religious order, to heal and teach about his Way, he warned them that they many would not welcome them. Just the opposite: officials would arrest and persecute them, although through their arrest and witness they would share the gospel. Jesus said, "Be on your guard; you will be handed over to the local councils and be flogged in the synagogue." They would have to search each town and test each home to locate even one person willing to hear and worthy of hearing their gospel message. They would have to leave many homes and towns for not finding even one willing person.

She wrestled with the question more than nearly any other question: why did she seem to have to avoid certain persons? Why couldn't she get along with everyone, relate to everyone, and please everyone? Some days, too many days, were more like a minefield

73

than a garden, where she seemed to stumble from one tense encounter to another and where few or none seemed to appreciate her, listen to her, and need or want her company. She loved to serve others, encourage others, and please others, but in fact, she seemed able to serve, encourage, and please only a few, and even those few she couldn't manage to please all of the time. Of course, she found defects in others with which she could easily have explained their intolerance for her, things like their haste, insensitivity, coldness toward Christ, and inability to understand and appreciate her good actions and intentions, just as she found defects in herself like her impatience and impulsiveness. Yet that these people didn't care for her company and would not accept her generous service just made no sense to her. Some of her interactions hurt her so badly that she had to learn to guard herself against others. Shrewd she was not, but shrewder she needed to become.

Guard against false teaching. Matthew 16:12.

In addition to guarding against persons who undermine our mission and message, who work against us in our development rather than with us and for us, we must also guard specifically against certain teaching. If we are to learn effectively, then we must not only guard our hearts, identify and pursue masterful teachers, and avoid those who would discourage and defeat us, but we must also examine the teaching itself in order to choose that which informs rather than confuses. Learning involves confirming that the source of information is authoritative, reliable, trustworthy, before we accept it and incorporate it into our learning. We too easily accept information as if others have verified it when to the contrary the information has an unreliable source and would not contribute to our learning. Moreover, some sources are not just unreliable but set directly against authoritative doctrine, intending to disrupt and defeat reliable teaching. Many follow Jesus. Others are indifferent. Still others actively work against him to undermine his message, which is the truth. We must guard against the teaching of those who oppose truth. Discern the source and thus the quality of the teaching.

Judge carefully between sound and unsound teaching. Lots of teaching is out there, some good, much bad. We are whom we follow. We become like those from whom we learn. Do not follow those who teach burdensome rules, like those against whom Jesus warned. Listen to and learn from those who teach the gospel message that gives life rather than rules.

Jesus taught from the most ordinary of circumstances. The religious leaders, both Pharisees and Sadducees, had once again challenged Jesus, this time to show them a sign from heaven. Yet he knew that showing them signs was useless because they did not have the character or disposition to accept his teaching. They were too corrupt even to acknowledge signs from heaven, of which they had already had plenty. So Jesus left them, traveling across the lake with his disciples. When they reached the other shore, the disciples realized that they had forgotten to take bread with them for the meal. "Be on your guard against the yeast of the Pharisees and Sadducees," Jesus remarked in response, referring back to the incident on the other side of the lake. The disciples assumed instead that Jesus was referring to their having forgotten the bread. Overhearing their misunderstanding, Jesus interjected, "How is it you don't understand that I was not talking to you about bread? But be on your guard against the yeast of the Pharisees and Sadducees." Only then did the disciples understand that Jesus had been talking about guarding against their false teaching. They must judge carefully teaching's source and message.

He sensed and hoped that from his extensive studies, which were all informal but nonetheless constant and decades long, he had developed a fine ear for true and false teaching, for how consistent or inconsistent the teaching was with Jesus's message. One can hardly read the Bible cover to cover a couple of dozen times, read and in some cases reread dozens of classic and contemporary commentaries on the Bible, and hear hundreds if not thousands of live, radio, and recorded messages, without developing a strong sense of the core message. Every speaker and author errs to some degree or if not outright errs then at least subtly colors and binds the message by time, place, and era. Some color the message more than others, to the point of distortion and even beyond that to the point of false teaching. He knew that he and others needed little or no discernment to distinguish and avoid those speakers and authors who made no pretense over disputing and denying the message. On the other hand, he knew that he needed every ounce of discernment to be on his guard against the subtly false teachers. Small errors can grow large in their application. He wanted and needed the pure message.

Beware of those who teach rules for show. Luke 20:46.

A teacher's motivation can be as important as the teacher's message. Wrong motive can subtly twist the message, giving it a hue that it does not in its true sense bear. The teacher may have the right message. The teacher may also be a significant member of a close fellowship. The teacher may even frequently produce valuable fruit in a rich ministry. Yet when the teacher's motivation turns from propagating the gospel message to promoting the teacher's program of rules, the teaching has lost its value and meaning. Avoid those teachers. Learn from those who teach with the right motive to point the way to the Master. Jesus did not teach a system of rules. While his instruction includes many things to do and not to do, all of those things point the student toward him in his Father. The point is not the rules, nor especially is it the teacher of rules. Self-improvement literature has lots of programs, rules, and mantras, many of them helpful guides to better living. Their purveyors are often engaging and entertaining even if unabashedly self-promoting. Yet none of them hold forth the prospect for prosperity in spirit that Jesus holds. None of them can save the soul and change the outlook like Jesus. Ultimately, they teach unsatisfactory and even burdensome rules for show. They may have good intentions, but they have wrong motives. We should distinguish carefully between sound teachers who point toward Jesus and those who teach rules for show.

In another one of his debates with the religious leaders who were constantly challenging him, Jesus answered them with story after story until the leaders finally stopped questioning him. He then turned to his disciples to warn them against those religious leaders, with the people still listening to him, "Beware of the teachers of the

76

law. They like to walk around in flowing robes and love to be greeted with respect in the marketplaces and have the most important seats in the synagogues and the places of honor at banquets." Jesus added that the religious leaders and law teachers demonstrated their greed by consuming defenseless widows' homes and inheritances. They also made lengthy shows out of simple prayers, with the purpose of impressing and controlling their listeners. Their teaching promoted themselves rather than the message and Messiah, all to elevate them rather than to inform and equip their hearers with the gospel message of salvation. "These men will be punished most severely," Jesus ended.

She had a keen eye for pride in speakers, probably because she had a keen eye and high concern for pride in herself. Some speakers of the message she respected deeply for their humility. Even as they revealed, interpreted, and exhorted the message with skill and inspiration far beyond any she would ever presume to possess, they simultaneously seemed to point away from rather than toward themselves. They did not teach for show, although they exhibited plenty enough skill in their teaching to attract attention. They also did not teach rules, although the Messiah's message that they taught certainly had clear instructions for things to do or avoid. They instead revealed and exhorted a relationship with the One whose splendor paled in contrast any modest gift of the speaker or listener. Yet then she would see the many who instead taught for show, their pride most evident to her. While others could listen to and admire those speakers, she could not do so. Her spirit fought them, struggled with them, and rejected them not because of the powerful words that they spoke but because of their self-motivation apparent to her if not always to others. She could not hear them even while hearing them, could not learn from them even while they taught. She sought instead the words of the humble few. She wanted a relationship with Jesus, and she knew that exalting one's self is not the way to that relationship. Imitating the showy teachers would do her no good. She instead found merit in the words and humble Christ-like spirit of the few.

Do not look for the living among the dead. Luke 24:5.

So many of the things that we learn are from long-departed teachers and philosophers. We call their ancient writings *classics* and make them the foundation of traditional schooling. We learn, as it were, from the dead, calling into question the extent to which their teaching can convey life to the living. Was everything that they taught for naught? After all, look where they ended up. Their followers, still alive but teaching lifeless rules that only kill the spirit, are themselves like whitewashed tombs, Jesus said, looking good on the outside but filled with dead bones on the inside. We should instead learn from the living, from Jesus and those who follow Jesus into his realm of eternal life. A guide to learning is to look for living teaching, the kind of teaching that generates and sustains life. Reject teaching that weighs you down, tires and discourages you, and burdens you with lifeless rules and dead traditions. Pursue learning that gives energy, vitality, and life, that raises your soul and spirit from their burdens and slumber, and that points to eternal life.

The women who had followed and attended to Jesus in his life went to the tomb on the third day after his crucifixion to attend to his body with more burial spices. When they arrived, to their surprise, someone had already rolled away the large stone at the entrance to the tomb. As they peered into the tomb, to their shock, they saw that Jesus's body had disappeared, leaving no sign other than the grave clothes. As they wondered what had happened, two men suddenly appeared in clothing that looked like lightning. "Why do you look for the living among the dead?" they asked the women, adding, "He is not here. He has risen! Remember how he told you? The Son of Man must be crucified but will rise again on the third day." The women then remembered that Jesus had said exactly that. They were not to look for the living among the dead. They need not treat his many profound words as simply another dead message from a departed philosopher. Let the dead tend to the dead. Jesus was alive! His words carried life among the living. They would go find the living Jesus and tell everyone about him.

She could feel the dead chill surround her, knowing that she had to shrug it off. Knowing that doing so was important to her daily and long-term wellbeing, she found identifying lifeless thinking and teaching easier and easier. It discouraged her, made her down and depressed. She knew that she had to think and learn about life, not death. Death was all around her, like a gloomy companion, especially when she was not paying attention. She had to sort of shoo death away, deliberately turn her thinking, reading, and investigation toward life-giving thoughts. Those life-giving thoughts were also all around her. Pursuing them was almost as easy as choosing to do so, as waking up each day with the deliberate purpose and intent of pursuing life. Neither life nor death had a grip on her, she had learned. She had free will, even if death often tried to tell her that she was destined otherwise. She knew the truth in Jesus. She had long ago chosen his life. Now, she had gained the will to live, to search and find him in every circumstance, to live and learn not among the dead but among the living. The good things are sometimes that easy. She had chosen life. Jesus lived!

Leave blind guides. Matthew 15:14.

Have you ever followed a guide who didn't know where they were going? The proposition is scary, especially when safety or even life is at stake. The moment one realizes that the guide has no clue which direction to take after having led the group afar is a desperate moment, filled with fear and regret. Why did we ever entrust our safety to this blind guide? Look what our trust has cost us! Learning involves following teacher guides. The consequences to learning can be as great as the consequences of other adventures. Learning the wrong thing at the wrong time can create safety, health, and spiritual risks, in the worst cases including mental and emotional depression and even physical injury or death. You don't need blind guides when your long-term future is at stake. The key though is to recognize quickly that they do not know the way so that you do not submit to their instruction, so that their instruction does not mislead you along the way. You may take a first few steps with someone who appears sound of doctrine and trustworthy of soul before realizing that they are neither. Be on the watch. Do not hesitate to leave a teacher, mentor, counselor, or guide whom you discover does not know the word and way of Jesus.

Jesus had once again chastised the religious leaders publicly, once again calling them hypocrites for nullifying the word of God in favor of their many traditions including those having to do with eating food only after a ceremonial washing of hands. The disciples questioned Jesus with what must have been obvious to anyone, which was whether he knew that he was offending the religious leaders. Jesus challenged the disciples with a parable that plants that his heavenly Father had not planted he would pull up from the roots. "Leave them," Jesus said bluntly, "they are blind guides. If the blind lead the blind, both will fall into a pit." The disciples still did not understand, and so Peter asked Jesus plainly what he meant by the parable. After expressing his incredulity that the disciples still did not understand, Jesus explained that the traditions of the religious leaders not to eat food without ceremonial washing had nothing to do with their purity. As teachers of the law, their purity depended on what they spoke, what they said about God and his Son, not what they ate. They were blind guides who would lead to destruction anyone who would follow them.

He was familiar with blind guides. He had read widely when younger, searching for reliable guides. From time to time, he had felt as if he had found one, but before long their insight and inspiration had worn thin. None seemed able to convey life. All taught as if they knew something profound that would make a difference in life, but none seemed really to show that difference in their own life, from what little he could learn about them. More significantly, none seemed able to make a difference in his own life. He kept ending up in dead ends where he found nothing other than their lifeless words. Each time, he would soon leave behind his latest blind guide until gradually he could see the blind guides coming before even engaging and following them. His path was easier, surer, not following those blind guides. Then, he met Jesus. Every step that he followed Jesus was a step in the right direction, leading him as surely and steadily forward, up, and beyond into life as his blind guides had previously led him in the opposite wrong direction. Blind guides no longer.

Retain the word. Matthew 13:23.

The mind is a fascinating and in most cases frightening thing. We each have unique disposition. No mind forms alike. The same words spoken to two or more produce different results. We each hear, understand, interpret, construe, and apply counsel in different ways. The words of Jesus have the capacity to supply each of us with the most extraordinary possible life, to deconstruct and reconstruct each of us for our one unique most fulfilling, meaningful, courageous, and rewarding life. Yet we nonetheless construe Jesus's words in markedly different ways. A few treasure and pursue his words with passion, fierceness, clarity of mind, singleness of purpose, and constant vigor. Many more hear his words with some appreciation but simply do not understand them. They may take a quick and ready interest in his words, but they do not foster his words within them, do not make a seat and home for them, do not dwell and meditate on them in ways that amplify them into their minds, days, and souls. Some hear his words but just as quickly reject them, giving them up to contrary beliefs and principles, dismissing them out of hand, and never giving them a chance to produce anything of merit within the hearer. Although we each respond differently to Jesus's words according to our experiences, personality, character, commitments, and intentions, we each still have the same opportunity and responsibility to understand them. Those who do understand and retain Jesus's words, putting them to use in a committed faith and life, prove their inestimable worth.

The parable of the sower is among Jesus's most-developed parables. Farmers in those days scattered seed by hand in a way that some would land on the paths where birds would quickly eat it up. Other seeds fell on rocky places, Jesus told the large crowd, whose members would have known the result that the plants could not take root. Other seeds fell among thorns that choked the plants. Yet seed falling on good soil would produce a crop of a hundredfold. The parable puzzled the disciples, even as it must have both engaged but puzzled the crowd. Jesus later explained to the disciples that the seed represents the words of his life-giving message. The bird eating the seed on the path invokes the evil one snatching the word from a hearer's heart. The seed on rocky ground invokes a hearer who believes quickly but only until the first trouble comes. The seed among thorns invokes the hearer who allows life worries and wealth's deceit to choke out the word. "But the seed falling on good soil refers to someone who hears the word and understands it," Jesus concluded. Only this hearer produces a crop of righteousness a hundred times as great as the word sown. Know the kind of soil that you must represent for the words of Jesus to dwell richly in you. Understand and abide in the words of Jesus. Do not let evil, shallowness, worries, or wealth interfere with your growth through his words.

She had come to understand Jesus's words at a level that she had only previously barely imagined. She had witnessed how others seemed to let his words take root in them. Those few individuals, whether rich or poor, educated or uneducated, articulate or inarticulate, generally exhibited a sort of power, purpose, and generous production that she much admired, even if she attributed those attributes more to their character than to the character of the words that they had incorporated. She had nonetheless not expected that she would find Jesus's words dwelling in her nearly so richly. She did not even know how those words had taken root in her soul. Perhaps she had after all created a secret place for them and then tended them as if in a garden. The depth of her appreciation for those words and the life that she was now drawing from them made it seem just that way, that they had grown roots in her heart and were producing unexpected but beautiful flowers and fruits for her enjoyment and enjoyment by others. Of course, as she realized how rich, deep, and fruitful the words were, she tended her heart's soil more often and carefully, with new attention, discipline, joy, and vigor. She only wondered what wonderful fruit they would next produce out of her secret garden. She now wanted to understand, retain, and dwell in Jesus's words so often, richly, and deeply.

1.4 Teaching

Tell how much God has done for you. Luke 8:39. *Proclaim God's kingdom.* Luke 9:60. *Be fishers of people.* Mark 1:17. *Acknowledge Jesus before others.* Matthew 10:32. *Teach others to obey Jesus.* Matthew 28:20. *Teach others to keep the commandments.* Matthew 5:19. *Preach the gospel to all.* Mark 16:15. *Tell others of Jesus's resurrection.* Luke 24:9. *Talk with others about Jesus.* Luke 24:15. *Explain the scriptures.* Luke 24:27. *Speak the word with authority.* Luke 7:7.

Just as Jesus said much about how to learn and retain his words, so too did he have much to say about how to teach others about his words. His words about teaching are not only for those very few theologians with advanced degrees, nor even solely for the senior pastors serving congregations. He also expects each of us to both learn and teach his words. What he said about teaching applies to each of us, not just to the theologian or pastor. His disciples were unschooled rather than learned men who nonetheless succeeded in spreading his words to the globe's four corners, fulfilling Jesus's Great Commission, which was not just for them but for all of us. Some of the more effective teachers are those who are still learning, whose knowledge of his words is not so advanced that they are unable, as are some theologians and academics unable, to convey simple truths plainly spoken to open minds in need of them. Too many of us have ears itching for the latest profound insight, when too many of those insights are not insights at all but the proud and self-promoting imagination of the speaker or author. Teachers need to take great care in what, how, and why they teach, but most of all, about whom they teach, the Lord Jesus. Read what he said about teaching and how he taught.

83

Tell how much God has done for you. Luke 8:39.

The simplest and most direct and effective way of teaching God's word is to tell how much God has done for you. The Bible says much about how life works, how to behave for best result, how to please God and seek his favor, and related important subjects, which is all well and good to convey to others. What makes the Bible's instruction come alive, though, is for others to see evidence of its results in the teacher's own life. The saying is "show me, don't tell me." We prefer to see the truth of things over hearing the truth of things. As the Bible says, we must first believe that God exists and that he rewards those who seek him. If a teacher cannot say what God has done for the teacher, then why should the student follow? The teacher should above all know and be able to convey what God has done to make a difference in the teacher's life. If you are a teacher — and remember that *all* of us in the faith are teachers — then be ready, willing, and able to say what God has done for you. Your elevator speech, calling card, or other introductory remarks and parting comments should include at least brief statement of God's good work in your life. That statement may be all that others really need to hear from you.

Jesus encountered a mad man, one so violent and possessed that officials kept him chained and under guard outside of town. The demons possessing the man knew Jesus's power to heal and so begged that Jesus let them escape from the man into a herd of pigs, which they did with Jesus's permission and to the destruction of the pigs. When the townsfolk saw that Jesus had healed their long-violent tormentor who now sat quietly and in his right mind at Jesus's feet, they feared Jesus's power so much that they asked him to leave, which Jesus did. The healed man begged to go with Jesus who said instead, "Return home and tell how much God has done for you," which the man promptly and gladly did. The man had wanted to follow and learn from Jesus so that he could teach others about the great One who had healed him, but Jesus instead knew that the man's testimony of God's healing would alone instruct the people. Tell how much God has done for you.

He realized one day in reading about how best to learn and instruct others in God's word that he seldom if ever simply told people how much God had done for him. He had so many things that he could tell. He remembered swift and long-term healing of a documented serious medical condition just days before the scheduled major surgery. He remembered other bad results of medical tests turning slowly but surely to good results avoiding other serious illness and invasive treatment. He remembered a new job and saving an old job. Then he remembered the big things like parents coming to faith, the birth and faith of a beautiful daughter, and the saving grace of a persevering wife. He remembered most of all the proximity, life, comfort, and mysterious but clear communication of a living God who seemed beyond all sense to want to know and relate to him, care for him, guide him, and strengthen him. And he knew too that God had given him something to anticipate that every person requires for living a good life, a secure and hopeful life, which is sufficient knowledge of the outcome of this life at and beyond death. He knew that God wanted him to trust the truth that he would without any shadow of a doubt one day join Him in celebration. He had plenty to say about what God had done for him, and finally he was ready to do so. Let the doctrinal instruction be the harder part. Telling about God's blessings was going to be easy.

Proclaim God's kingdom. Luke 9:60.

Some find difficult the concept of a kingdom given the scarcity of kingdom's today. Few of us have lived in a kingdom, and so we have lost the sense of what living in a kingdom, or more specifically living in *God's kingdom*, means. A kingdom implies a king, and in the case of God's kingdom, the King of all kings. What makes a realm or country a kingdom is that its subjects both obey and have the protection of the king. The realm extends only so far as the king's authority extends. What happens in the kingdom occurs only with the approval of the king. The kingdom thus takes on the character of its king. The greater the king, the greater is the kingdom. We should each far prefer living in a kingdom with a great king than a minor, weak, corrupt, or vacuous king. Yet in any case, subjects of the kingdom have one primary obligation toward the king, which is to proclaim the king's rule within the kingdom including specifically one's obedience to that rule. The same is true with proclaiming God's kingdom that by doing so, one enters God's realm and satisfies one's primary obligation within it, while simultaneously inviting others to do so as well, which is the point at which the proclamation begins to sound like teaching. Proclaim God's kingdom, and in doing so, teach.

Some whom Jesus encountered sought God's kingdom, while others did not. Wherever he went, Jesus encountered ambivalence over the pursuit of the kingdom. Jesus had set out for Jerusalem knowing that the time was near for his crucifixion, resurrection, and ascension to heaven. Hearing of his destination, the people of one town in which Jesus had planned to stop along the way refused him entry, while another town welcomed him. A man along the way promised to follow Jesus wherever he went, to which Jesus replied that he could not even find a welcome place to lay his head. Jesus asked another man to follow him, but the man wanted first to finish the funeral of his father. Another man wanted to follow Jesus but only after returning to his family to say goodbye. To the man intending first to bury his father, Jesus replied, "Let the dead bury their own dead, but you go and proclaim the kingdom of God." Those who dwell in the kingdom of God do not die but live, while those who do not dwell in the kingdom are already dead. God is Master of the living. God's kingdom does not include the dead.

She was slowly gaining a sense of what it meant to live in the presence of God, to live in his kingdom or realm. The concept was so foreign at first and remained foreign for quite a while before gradually taking hold. She did, though, sense two realms, one without God and one with God, even though the two realms were not always evident or distinct to her. She knew that the two realms, one with God and one without, could not in any direct sense overlap. God was either Master of the realm with its subjects willingly under his authority, or he was not Master of the realm where instead the subjects were free to do as they wished without his presence and protection, God help them. She also knew that she wanted to live only in God's realm. Living without his protection and outside of his authority frightened her. She wanted no part of that realm. This last thought was what led her most to seek God's realm, to look for it, and beyond looking for it, to talk about it especially to herself but also a little to others. She finally even began proclaiming God's realm every time she thought of it, acknowledging in silent and public prayer that she and those who agreed with her gladly submitted to God's beneficent authority. As she did so, she soon began to feel emotionally and recognize logically that indeed she had a new allegiance with all of its glorious rights and responsibilities. What a difference a realm makes. She had more than a country. She had a kingdom and, with the kingdom, the King's allegiance.

Be fishers of people. Mark 1:17.

The way of faith is not a lonely way. Yes, faith is individual. We live and die and rise again, obtain blessing or suffer curse, by our individual beliefs and commitments, one by one. No one else other than Christ himself can gain your salvation for you. You alone need acknowledge it, receive it, accept it, and commit to it. Others may join you, or they may not, and still you alone will receive the forgiveness and gain the blessing. Yet faith nonetheless has a huge communal element to it. Faith inevitably involves a community because only through fellowship in the word does one receive the knowledge and understanding to accept and commit to faith. The communal or collaborative nature of faith is as simple as the statement that *they cannot believe if no one tells them.* Others who do not know the Lord depend on us because we are the only ones who will tell them of the Lord in ways that will show them the truth, reliability, mercy, and grace of faith. The spread of faith in Christ depends not on conquering new lands or old peoples. Faith in Christ instead depends on the loving communication of who he really is and what he really says and does. We must be intentional about reaching others who do not yet know the One who is Love. To know and follow Christ means to attract others along the way. One can hardly love Christ without obeying his command to care enough for others to have them join us in Christ. We must within our faith think about the faith of others and in some strong sense intentionally promote that faith through proclamation, witness, and instruction.

The time had come shortly after Jesus's baptism, his testing in the wilderness, and his first proclamation of the good news of his coming, to designate the disciples who would help him spread the word. The good news must at first travel by word of mouth, meaning that it must have knowledgeable, skilled, and committed men and women, especially believing men and women, to carry and proclaim it. Jesus walked the roads of Galilee telling people that the time had come, God's kingdom was present, and that they should turn and accept this good news for what it was. As he walked, Jesus saw his first two disciple candidates Simon Peter and his brother Andrew casting their fishing net into the beautiful inland sea. "Come, follow me," Jesus told them, "and I will send you out to fish for people." Something about Jesus made both Simon Peter and Andrew drop their nets to join Jesus immediately. They had spent life fishing for fish. The Son of Man had now invited them to fish instead for men and women. How could they sensibly resist?

He seldom considered himself an effective witness for Christ. Doing so seemed in itself presumptuous as if to think that he was anyone as skilled, capable, or interesting as to attract others to Christ. He found little or nothing within himself that would make him a fisher of men and women. Yet he experienced such clarity, power, and purpose pursuing the way of Christ that he definitely wanted others to join him. He did not feel that he should have such blessing only for himself, especially knowing that the blessing was inexhaustible. Faith wasn't at all like something that others would use up, leaving too little for him. The opposite seemed true that the more persons of faith shared with one another, the greater the faith grew. He would simply love to be an effective witness for Christ even if he knew himself incapable. He kept thinking though of the disciples whom Jesus himself recruited. The gospels did not represent them as particularly capable. They instead often came off as unschooled bumblers even to the point of seeming to frustrate Christ. And then they abandoned him. Still, Christ called them back and forgave them, particularly Peter. In short order, they became powerful witnesses for Christ. Maybe he could witness to some effect after all, too. He knew one thing, which is that he would try, suspecting that even in his own bumbling way, God would use him.

Acknowledge Jesus before others. Matthew 10:32.

You may wonder how one gets started teaching about Jesus. The entrée, invitation, or prelude to teaching is simply to acknowledge Jesus before others. To acknowledge Jesus before others is, more than anything, to speak positively of him, mention him, credit him, or in some other way honor him when in the presence of others. We speak well of others all of the time whether they are pastors or preachers, presidents or other politicians, sports or film stars, or simply neighbors and friends. We say things like, "Oh, she's wonderful," "You'll love listening to him," or "Did you hear about the generous thing that they did?" Praising people rolls off of our tongues with little difficulty, as indeed it should. Praise is far better than gossip. It attracts us to others, engages us with others, and builds our trust in others. Yet how seldom do we similarly acknowledge Jesus before others? You may feel it awkward to do so, which may be exactly the obstacle to overcome. The opportunities are abundant and natural. We often see a sports figure make the sign of the cross or point heavenward after every on-field success. Wouldn't our saying "thank the Lord" be just as natural in any other setting? No matter how we would feel about doing so, awkward or not, the acknowledgment would accomplish its purpose of pointing the hearer toward Jesus. Teaching may follow, whether by you or another.

Jesus was sending the disciples out to heal and instruct in the course of his public ministry. As he did so, he warned them repeatedly that they would meet challenges in telling others about him. He gave specific advice about how to deal with those hostile others who would hate them because of Jesus. When the message brought them hostility in one place, they were to take the message someplace else. Even their own families would reject those who embraced and shared the message of Jesus. Yet the strongest advice that Jesus gave was to stand firm to speak his gospel message despite the hostility. Jesus said, "Whoever acknowledges me before others, I will also acknowledge before my Father in heaven." Jesus explained to his disciples that if they did so, then God would save them. The Father would protect them from harm, especially guarding their souls. If to the contrary they disowned Jesus before others, then so would he disown them before his Father in heaven. Acknowledge Jesus before others. Do not let fear or a false sense of propriety keep you from lauding Jesus as you would so readily laud others. Let others know that you think and care about Jesus. Then watch what opportunities arise to tell more about what he has done for you.

For a long time, he seldom spoke directly in acknowledgment of his Lord. Oh, he certainly prayed openly at every meal and on special occasions where others expected it. Yet in polite conversation at work and around town, he just didn't find the opportunity to acknowledge the Lord and would in any case have felt it out of place. That uneasy feeling though nagged at him. He knew well Jesus's frightening statement that those who refuse to acknowledge him before others, he will refuse to acknowledge before his Father in heaven. He finally felt that the Holy Spirit was guiding him to address that uneasy feeling. So he began with a little mention here and there, testing simple little natural expressions of thanks, grace, and appreciation. Sometimes it was "thank God," other times "God bless you" or "you have my prayers to the Lord," and still other times "there but for the grace of God" or "Jesus only knows." He soon learned which expressions felt and sounded most natural and authentic, as he also learned to avoid expressions when they sounded platitudinous or trite. Before long, he had surprised himself on more than one occasion with an authentic acknowledgment that he would not have made if he had thought it out in advance. He had finally learned to acknowledge Jesus freely before others. Although he only rarely had anyone object, he cared more about Jesus and the souls of those who heard of him than he cared about the objections of those few. He also noticed that others outside of his faith community now frequently associated him with his Lord, giving him new opportunities to answer questions and share words of encouragement in faith. Indeed, he realized, he should long ago have been acknowledging Jesus before others.

Teach others to obey Jesus. <small>Matthew 28:20.</small>

The fundamental point of teaching about matters of faith must be to teach others to obey Jesus. Too often, those who have not read the Bible with any care think of Jesus as a man of love, care, great sentiment, occasional wisdom, and frequent miracles. They may even know of the historical events of the faith, whether Jesus's virgin birth, baptism, transfiguration, triumphal entry, crucifixion, resurrection, appearance, and ascension, and the descending of the Holy Spirit at Pentecost. We would do well to teach of such things. Would though we do even better to teach what Jesus taught? Jesus did more than miracles. He told us that to love God is to obey. He then told us what to obey, not just a few things here and there but in abundant detail. Jesus told us so many things to do and so many other things not to do, and with great specificity. Remarkably, his instructions were not culture bound. They did not have to do with long or short hair, covering or not covering the head, or wearing skirts or pants. They did not have to do with washing pots or hands, or eating certain bread or avoiding eating certain meats. His instructions were instead clear things, timeless things, and by and large things that one could readily do or not do just as the instruction required. They were achievable and sustainable things, sound things, consistent things, and lots of things, without being arcane or peculiar in the way that would prove burdensome. Jesus taught with the intent that we obey. Teach others to obey Jesus even as you teach what Jesus taught.

After his crucifixion and before his ascension, Jesus in his resurrected body had at times walked, talked, and eaten with the disciples, appearing and leaving them only to appear again. It was finally time for his ascension. The disciples had gone to the mountain at Galilee where Jesus had told them to meet him for the last time. They worshiped him there, as he prepared to give them their great commission. The Father had given Jesus all authority. They were to go to all nations, baptizing believers in the name of the Father, Son, and Holy Spirit. Yet they were to do more than baptize believers. "Teach them to obey everything I have commanded you," Jesus concluded, adding, "And surely I am with you always, to the very end of the age." The disciples were not only to teach *about* Jesus but also to teach others to *obey* Jesus. Jesus expects obedience. He wants and expects us to obey. And he wants the teachers among us, which at some point includes each of us and all of us, to teach others to obey him. His instruction was not for interest, exposition, or principle. His instruction was for obedience. We show our love for Jesus through obedience to his instruction. Obey Jesus, and teach others to obey Jesus.

She loved the kids in Sunday school. They had such energy, they were so entertaining, they were so endearing, and they were so *funny*. Even on the cold and wet days, and the dark days of winter, she never really minded getting up and getting to church for the first service, and then teaching Sunday school during the second service, knowing that the kids would lift her spirits. She also cared about the kids, wanting to see them do well. She made sure that she was prepared for the lesson each week, and she took special care to watch for the child who needed something special, some encouragement, some guidance, or some attention. Yet beyond her natural care and concern for her energetic little charges, she also wanted them to realize that they had someone to obey, and not particularly to obey her, although that would help now and then, but to obey Jesus. She wanted these children to know that Jesus said to do certain things and not to do other things. She wanted them to know that these things were not recommendations but instructions. She wanted them to know that obedience was alright even for proudly individualistic, emotionally secure, upwardly mobile, and firmly independent Americans, when the question was obeying Jesus. They didn't have to follow her every instruction, although that would help. They didn't have to stay in line when singing or dancing, although that would look more orderly. They didn't even have to stay in their seats if they were particularly fidgety, as some of them were routinely. They just needed to obey Jesus. Children, parents, everyone, she thought: obey Jesus.

Teach others to keep the commandments. Matthew 5:19.

We miss something important, though, if we stop at considering Jesus's teaching as merely instructions that he wants us to obey for our best welfare. Obedience also has to do with our ability to enter his presence and the presence of his Father. God is holy. One does not bring disobedience into his presence. We cannot enter the kingdom of heaven with our half-hearted obedience and frequent transgressions following us. Jesus wants us to teach others to obey God's law as God's commandments. Notice the difference between a command and a request or instruction. One does not ordinarily disobey commands, without suffering special consequences, because of the offense to the one giving the command. Disobey an instruction, shame on you, but disobey a command, shame on God. God cannot let disobedience to commands go unaddressed, or they are no longer commands but only recommendations. By telling us to teach others to obey the commandments *as commandments*, Jesus reminded us of the divine and holy quality of God and God's law. Commands one obeys at all costs. Instructions one generally follows at some probable inconvenience if not. This obedience thing is serious business because it involves our relationship with and access to God. These are not self-help programs but matters of the divine.

In his great Sermon on the Mount, Jesus taught more about the deep nature of obedience. Some thought that Jesus might be giving them new commandments to take the place of the Ten Commandments that Moses had given the Jews so much earlier. Some thought that they no longer needed to obey the old law. Jesus corrected those errors, saying that he came not to abolish the commandments but to fulfill them. The old law was not disappearing. Instead, Jesus would shed his blood to cleanse us of every transgression and give us the Holy Spirit so that our hearts pursued the intentions behind the great commandments. Far from casting aside the old commandments, Jesus explained, "Whoever practices and teaches these commands will be called great in the kingdom of heaven." Indeed, the only way to enter the kingdom of heaven was to have more righteousness than the religious leaders and law teachers had, which hardly seemed possible without Jesus.

Jesus explained that the old law was not simply about avoiding actual murder but also about avoiding the anger that precedes murder. The old law shows us so much of what we should be doing, while Jesus absolves us of not having done so and gives us the Spirit to guide our intentions that we may obey better.

He thought long and hard about the Ten Commandments to the point of memorizing them, repeating them frequently, and meditating on them. On their surface they seemed straightforward enough to understand and also to obey. He was not to make an idol of anything, but when after all had he carved any graven image? He was not to murder, but when after all had he ever aimed a gun at anyone with the intent to kill? Adultery and theft, these too were pretty easy things to recognize and avoid. Yet as he thought of what Jesus had said, extending the commandments into their roots in anger, greed, desire, and other states of mind and dispositions that were all too familiar to him as to anyone, he realized how offensive he must seem to God much of the time. The commandments were frustratingly difficult to satisfy, even impossible to do so if he were honest with himself and took the commandments in the deep and thorough way that Jesus taught and intended. His reflections on the depth and holiness of the commandments turned him steadily back to Jesus whose sacrifice gave him the only hope of entering God's kingdom and whose gift of the Holy Spirit gave him the heart to continue to pursue that entry. He developed a new appreciation for God's law and through whom one must approach it, giving him the confidence to share that appreciation through teaching.

Preach the gospel to all. Mark 16:15.

Jesus makes it perfectly clear how central his good news must be to any sound teaching. The good news is of course that we have his sacrifice on which to rely for entry into God's kingdom. God cannot embrace the unholy, and so he instead embraces us as the consenting image of his entirely holy Son. We also have Jesus's glorious resurrection following his sacrifice, as evidence and guarantee of our own eternal transformation. He has done it, proven it, made it manifest, and in doing so he plainly says that the same is ours for the asking. The gospel has an aspect of formula to it, which may be why he encourages us to *preach* the gospel. The gospel is not complex. One hardly even *teaches* the gospel because it takes only oration or assertion. We need only *state* it, not explain it. Yet we must emphatically state it. No one who does not hear it will somehow through reason divine it. Although it takes no particular deep exposition, as teachers we must still make the gospel evident. And ultimately, the gospel is not a formula but relationships with the forgiving Father, sacrificing Son, and Holy Spirit who must dwell in us for our hearts to desire the gospel and accept it. Preach the gospel to everyone. You may be their first, best, or last chance to hear it.

Jesus's appearances to the disciples after his resurrection were not simply to prove to them that he had indeed risen, although his appearances certainly had that effect. Some of them had continued to doubt even after hearing about the empty tomb and the remarkable reports of the women who had seen the tomb and also seen him. His appearances to the disciples removed that doubt. In the process, his appearances also changed them from fearful men hiding behind locked doors to preachers of the gospel to everyone who would listen, including the religious leaders whom the disciples had most feared. Yet again, Jesus did not appear in order solely to convince the disciples of his resurrection. He also shared more instruction, even giving them marching orders in the form of a commission. While he taught them several related things, ultimately Jesus said to them, "Go into all the world and preach the gospel to all creation." Those of us who believe, and whom he washes of sin, he saves, but those of us who do not believe and do not accept his cleansing, the Father must condemn. The disciples were now to carry to the four corners of the earth the good news of his personal sacrifice for our sin, our ready access through him to the Father's kingdom, and his resurrection in which we have the guarantee of eternal life in that glorious kingdom.

She in no sense considered herself a preacher. Public speaking of almost any kind would make her knees and stomach weak, and keep her up nights. Preaching was for others. Yet Jesus said to preach the gospel to everyone, and she took his words on this subject just as seriously as any other subject. She just didn't know how or to whom she was to preach when she had none of the characteristics of a preacher and didn't seem to have an audience for the message in any case. After all, her friends were believers, and much of her activity she spent around the church. So she decided to pray about it. As she prayed, she began to discern that she had plenty of acquaintances with whom she had not yet spoken of Christ. Those acquaintances included all kinds of goods and service providers with whom she dealt in her many household and ministry transactions. They also included people whom she saw frequently around town going about their daily tasks just as she did. Jesus said to preach the gospel to everyone. For her, *everyone* must mean these people. She began to listen for the Holy Spirit to give her the words to preach. Her preaching wouldn't be from a pulpit but with the Spirit's guide. In the context of her good works and kind spirit, it just might have the effect that Jesus intended.

Tell others of Jesus's resurrection. Luke 24:9.

Among our conceptual teaching, instruction, and preaching, one solid detail, one historic artifact that we must convey is that Jesus lived again after his death on the cross. We fail to convey the gospel message if we leave out the resurrection. *Resurrection* is not simply a theological concept, not alone an important doctrine. Jesus's resurrection was a historic event, a moment in time, place, and history when a dead man, albeit an extraordinary one-of-a-kind Son of Man, lived again after his death. If Jesus did not rise again, then our belief is false and our faith vain. We must believe that he rose from the dead just as Jesus foretold that he would rise, just as he spoke about again after he did rise, and just as the gospels and book of Acts record from multiple witnesses. We can share all of the valuable wisdom and insight that we wish to share from Jesus's teachings, but in the course of doing so we must not hesitate to tell of Jesus's resurrection. Wisdom is good, but resurrection is better. Tell of Jesus's resurrection just as Jesus told, the women told, and someone told you, leading to your believing. The resurrection is an indispensable part of the gospel message.

The two women had just encountered at Jesus's empty tomb the two gleaming men who had told them that Jesus had risen. The men had also said not to look for the living among the dead. For the women, their encounter and the thought of the risen Christ must both have been momentous. Gleaming men dazzling like lightning do not just appear and tell of wondrous things. And dead men do not just rise. The women had seen Jesus die and seen him placed in the tomb three days earlier. They *knew* that Jesus was dead, and yet now they were hearing from these extraordinary messengers that he was instead living. They must at that momentous moment have needed some reckoning, some explanation, something to resolve the mind-splitting contradiction. Then the women remembered that Jesus had told them, "The Son of Man must be delivered over to the hands of sinners, be crucified, and on the third day be raised again." So the women returned to the disciples to tell them everything, reminding them of Jesus's words about his resurrection. They told of Jesus's resurrection, just as Jesus told of his resurrection and we must tell of Jesus's resurrection.

She didn't feel that she had a particularly critical mind. If the gospels said that Jesus rose from the dead, which the gospels surely did say, recording many witnesses who observed it, then she was more than willing to believe it. She wanted to believe it and did. She had no reason to question it and every contrary reason to accept, endorse, and apply it. The Old Testament had foreshadowed it, Christ had foretold it, and the gospels recorded it. Plenty of other unusual things had happened in the course of history, much more unusual than a dead man rising. Unusual things had happened to her. The things that she read that scientists were endorsing without much or any direct observation, whether big bangs, black holes, bent space, slowed or sped-up time, and other cockamamie phenomena, were plenty strange enough for her to accept Christ rising. What she had a harder time doing was telling others about it, particularly those whom she expected to be hostile to it. She didn't want to argue, didn't want to have to explain or justify. How could she do so? She wasn't trained in apologetics, debate, logic, or argument. No one would believe her, anyway. So she just stuck to it, stuck with the truth that so many others had believed to their eternal advantage. She wouldn't debate, prove, or argue. Jesus's rising was Jesus's rising. She finally resolved in her mind that uncritical confidence in his resurrection would be her stance before anyone who wished to either agree or disagree with it. Jesus said to tell it, and so tell it she would. Let others take their own responsibility for whether they would believe that he had in fact risen. She knew it in every fiber of her being, which was enough for her. As much as she might care about them, care about their salvation, whether the truth of Jesus's resurrection was enough for anyone else was ultimately their problem. She could believe herself and tell them but not believe *for* them.

Talk with others about Jesus. Luke 24:15.

Teaching can include simple talking. Jesus is an unendingly fascinating person and his life an unendingly fascinating subject. Teaching need not be formal instruction, like a lesson. Teaching about Jesus need not be preaching, like a formal message. Good teaching is often more like conversation or discussion. Simply talking with others about Jesus can lead to greater interest, awareness, curiosity, and discovery than offering formal instruction. Think of your own experience. Haven't you learned about Jesus from quiet conversation with friends? Isn't your heart more ready to receive instruction when instruction is not the purpose? Many of us have the habit of evaluating, assessing, questioning, and critiquing instruction, which can be fine particularly when we have reasons to question the instruction's soundness and source. Yet a critical attitude can keep us from discerning important truths about any subject including particularly Jesus. Conversation can be the antidote to a critical spirit. Those who will not listen to a sermon or lesson may listen to the conversation of a friend. Plain talk in plain circumstances can reach an open heart that would be closed in the classroom or chapel. Talk with others who share an interest in Jesus. See what you and they would learn from your conversation. Jesus may just join you in Spirit.

The two on the road to the village of Emmaus near Jerusalem just could not stop talking about Jesus. They kept going over with one another everything that had happened in the last several days including his triumphal entry, rumor of a last supper, then his arrest late that night, and an unprecedented middle-of-the-night trial. Soldiers, at the behest of the religious leaders, had hauled Jesus before Herod that same night, kept him in a pit overnight, and then taken him before Pontius Pilate who had tried to release him until the crowd, paid by the religious leaders, had forced Pilate to condemn Jesus, releasing the insurrectionist Barabbas instead. Then the soldiers had flogged Jesus and crucified him next to common criminals. And yet the sun had mysteriously disappeared when Jesus died on the cross. Spirits had come from the graves, and the temple's curtain had torn in two. Two of the religious leaders had buried Jesus in a tomb with a great stone rolled to close it, but then the stone had rolled back, and his body had disappeared along with reports of gleaming angels. The two on the road just could not stop talking about Jesus, as if they were on fire with the knowledge of these wonders. Then Jesus himself appeared to them, although in disguise, asking them, "What are you discussing as you walk along?" They were surprised that their unknown companion had not heard of all the events surrounding Jesus's crucifixion, and so Jesus listened to them tell excitedly about those events.

She candidly believed that she had learned more about Jesus from her friends than anyone else including some very learned and wise instructors. Oh, she had learned lots and lots from pastors and preachers, radio and television speakers, organized and planned Bible studies, and old and new authors. She was as up on the latest and greatest instructors as anyone in her fellowship circle. She had nearly the same appetite and interest for formal instruction as anyone. She had done year-long studies, half-year studies, month-long studies, group studies, individual studies, and other studies. She drew and shared much from all of these activities. Yet what she remembered most from them was how her family members and friends had reacted to them, interpreted them, incorporated and recalled them. The conversations in the car on the way home, around the dinner table, and in bed at night, meant as much or more to her as the instruction itself. She learned as much in talking *with* friends and family about Jesus as she learned from the pastors and preachers talking *to her* about Jesus. She had heard of aural and oral learners, people who learn by listening and talking with others. She felt that she must be one of those who teach themselves and teach others by listening and talking. She also felt that Jesus was nearer, that the Holy Spirit was in her, more so when she was talking about Jesus than when she was listening to others talk about Jesus or simply reading about Jesus. She began to think that *walk and talk* was her favorite Jesus time, when she and her best friend would walk their dogs and talk about Jesus. Talk, teach, and learn.

Explain the scriptures. Luke 24:27.

The Bible is a couple of thousand pages long depending on its format. Its many authors wrote over a period much longer than a millennium, possibly closer to two millennia. During that entire time, they wrote repeatedly in ways that predicted and foretold of Jesus's coming in the particular time, place, and manner that he did actually come. The ancient scriptures told of his character, demeanor, life, purpose, actions, death, resurrection, and ascension. Jesus's coming was no historical accident, not even surprising when it finally occurred. Angels gathered shepherds to witness his birth, which the scriptures so clearly predicted and was so long anticipated and specifically heralded that wise men came a great distance to the precise place and moment of Jesus's birth, bearing the precise gifts recognizing his status and purpose. Hearing the same prediction from his own religious scholars, the local ruler then slaughtered all of the area's children in an attempt to kill and defeat Jesus. Prophets at the temple where his parents presented him for circumcision had long awaited him and instantly recognized and honored him. Mother, father, uncle, aunt, and cousin all knew who he was and what his coming fulfilled and represented. We are simply to know and share the scriptures that tell these historical facts that frame his advent so extraordinarily and perfectly. We are to share what we know of these extraordinary scriptures.

The two walking on the road to Emmaus had finished telling their unknown companion, whom they could not recognize as Jesus, all about the events of the prior week surrounding Jesus's crucifixion. Jesus might have appreciated their interest and excitement but not their ignorance of what the ancient scriptures and he himself had foretold about those events. Jesus said to them, "How foolish you are, and how slow to believe all that the prophets have spoken!" He then explained to them everything that the scriptures from Moses through all the prophets said about him, the dozens of prophecies and frequent foreshadowing of exactly what had just occurred during Holy Week in Jerusalem. His explanations took some time, indeed all the way to Emmaus, where they finally recognized him as he broke bread over a meal with them and disappeared. These things that Jesus had just explained to them, they excitedly shared with the disciples as quickly as they could return to the disciples in Jerusalem. Know the scriptures that foretold of Jesus so that he need not chastise you in your ignorance. Explain those scriptures to others just as Jesus did to the two on the road to Emmaus, and those two did to the disciples in Jerusalem. The scriptures reveal God's long-standing plan fulfilled in Jesus.

He had wondered what would happen as he read and reread the scriptures cover to cover, over and over, across the months, years, and decades. Would they finally grow so familiar to him that they would lose their unique fascination for him, like a great film or sporting event, every turn and the final outcome of which become so familiar that it loses all interest for him? He need not have worried. The scriptures were simply magisterial, unparalleled, and utterly profound, whether judged as history, literature, poetry, prophecy, moral or spiritual writing, or a combination of all forms. They were inexplicable as anything other than a fully divine work, no, *the* fully divine work because one could find no equivalent, parallel, or superseding other. The scriptures continued to hold such fascination for him that he found that more and more parts of it left him in quiet trembling, reverential awe, or similar transformed state or condition. He seemed to have few real opportunities to explain the scriptures to anyone because no one recognized him as that kind of teacher. Yet when he did have the opportunity, words wanted to pour forth like fire, so much so that he nearly had to bite his tongue not to let his excited manner put off his hearer whom, he felt, probably needed to take his passion in smaller doses.

Speak the word with authority. Luke 7:7.

Teaching can take on different hues. Some teaching is hesitant or propositional, inviting the student to conjecture, hypothesize, evaluate, and consider. Other teaching is negative and critical, encouraging the student to challenge, doubt, and reject. Although teaching by definition intends learning and so must have some degree of content, teaching nonetheless often takes the stance that the student is the authority, that the student must judge what is right or true *for the student*. Whatever content the student chooses to believe from the teaching, the teaching's hidden message is that nothing is authoritative and instead everything is subjective, for each of us to construct or choose. Jesus is not a post-modernist. He represents and communicates objective and thus authoritative truth. He instructs that we teach accordingly in an authoritative rather than propositional manner. Because his words, the words of God, carry authority, we must not present them as alternative or optional truths for listener's to consider and accept or reject. If we speak God's words in a manner other than authoritatively, then we misrepresent the fundamental aspect of those words as truth embodied, truth represented, truth conveyed. To teach God's words with authority does not mean to throw them at people like stones. The teaching may and often should be gentle and inviting. Yet the teaching should always be authoritative, even if quietly authoritative.

A soldier whose servant was so sick as about to die heard that Jesus was nearby, and so the soldier sent elders to ask Jesus to come heal the servant. The elders pleaded with Jesus to do so because of the soldier's love for their nation. Jesus was on his way to the soldier's house when the soldier thought better of his request and so sent friends to Jesus to tell him, "Just say the word, and my servant will be healed." The friends explained to Jesus that the soldier had said that he did not deserve to trouble Jesus but that he too, like

Jesus, was under authority that gave him authority. The soldier believed that Jesus's word alone, conveying the authority of his Father, would be enough to heal the soldier's servant. The soldier's faith in the authority of God's word amazed Jesus who had not found such faith anywhere else in the nation and whose word therefore promptly healed the soldier's servant. Jesus's words carry authority. We should speak and teach those words in confidence, trust, and faith, recognizing and conveying their authority. We too should amaze and please Jesus in treating his words as authoritative so that he may promptly hear our prayers, answer them, and in doing so instruct those whom we teach. Even as we examine scripture carefully to convey its meaning, we have only one way to treat Jesus's words, which is with authority.

She knew quite well how easy it was to misunderstand Jesus's words, even to twist them to justify and achieve whatever one wished to do. She had heard pastors get it wrong occasionally, or at least it seemed wrong to her, and like everyone else had heard of pastors using God's word for their own ends, sometimes even for obviously corrupt ends. She had also witnessed lay individuals using those words to dupe and prey upon others. God's word carries authority, and people will misuse authority, even God's authority. Yet she also knew quite well that people misusing God's word does not make God's word any less authoritative. Even though she questioned how people—including herself—used and applied God's word, she trusted what Jesus said to do and not to do more than she trusted anything else. As his parable said, his words really did have the character of rock rather than sand. The words never really changed. They instead simply stood. They stood out and stood up in every situation. They were faithful, reliable, constant, and consistent. They had a character that nothing else had, a character she well knew was authority. Human authority seemed to vacillate constantly, whether political, governmental, social, or even scientific authority. Yet profound authority was in the world in at least one place in God's word. In her conversations with friends, in whatever opportunities she had for teaching, she always treated God's word as authority.

1.5 Speaking

Speak what Jesus tells you. Matthew 10:27. *Speak just what you are taught.* John 8:28. *Do not speak on your own.* John 7:16. *Speak no careless words.* Matthew 12:36. *Stop wailing.* Luke 8:52. *Speak faith over problems.* Matthew 17:20. *Do not swear an oath.* Matthew 5:34. *Do not justify yourself to men.* Luke 16:14.

Believing and praying, and learning and teaching, were all big subjects for Jesus. Jesus was also concerned with how we spoke, not just when praying or teaching but in the ordinary course of life, simply when communicating with others with ordinary intentions. The quality of our communication expresses or fails to express faith. Simply by communicating, we show others where we stand with respect to fundamental matters of faith. People of faith are often able to identify others of faith without either one saying a word explicitly about faith. That discernment is possible because the ordinary words themselves convey faith or absence of faith. People who know and trust God's word recognize dozens of subtle markers by which they pick up faith in the ordinary speech of others. If people of faith can perceive faith in others simply through their communication, then people who lack faith, although they may not be able to judge the presence or absence of faith overtly, must also be influenced by the faithful or faithless communication. That influence may be why Jesus taught about how to speak. He wants our ordinary words to represent him as effectively as do words that we speak in prayer and teaching. We are to some degree always in prayer, always communicating with God, and always communicating faith or lack of faith to others, whenever speaking.

Speak what Jesus tells you. Matthew 10:27.

Speech reveals us. You can hardly say a word without beginning to disclose who you are, what you value, what you think about how the world operates, and what you accept as truth. We choose what we say. No one forces words from our mouths. The speech that comes out of us tells others of our allegiances, whom we follow. For humankind, speech is as inevitable as it is self-defining. We each daily speak thousands of words, even tens of thousands of words. Among those words is every clue as to what we believe to be authoritative, whom we believe to constitute authority, whom we obey, whom we reject, and whom we trust and value. Thus with speech inevitable and self-defining, we should speak what Jesus tells us. To leave Jesus's words out of our common speech is to define ourselves as apart from Jesus. We love or reject Jesus, obey or disobey Jesus, and honor or dishonor Jesus largely by the words we use in everyday discourse. Jesus gave us many words to share with others, all of them organized around a soul-piercing and soul-uplifting message. We should speak those words frequently, constantly, and consistently if we are to take on the Christ-like image for which God made us and help others to do likewise.

Jesus gave several instructions when sending out his disciples for the first time, including instruction specifically on speaking. Jesus had spoken to the disciples for some time by then, had given them many words. They knew by then how he spoke, what were his frequent subjects, what was his central message. They could either speak their own words, or they could speak like Jesus spoke, repeat words that he had chosen telling stories that he told and sharing meanings that he shared. Jesus made it clear that the disciples were to speak his words, never mind the consequences. "What I tell you in the dark, speak in the daylight," Jesus said, adding, "What is whispered in your ear, proclaim from the roofs." In doing so, Jesus gave as reason that the disciples may as well disclose the concealed and reveal the hidden because people were going to learn the concealed and hidden anyway. The disciples had no reason to hide that they spoke about and for Jesus. People would learn anyway. You cannot hide faith, and therefore you should not hide faith. Faith is evident from speech alone and should be evident from speech alone. People will object to Jesus's words, but God will protect those people.

He was incredibly conscious of his own speech and always had been. He had always sensed that his words defined him, which scared him. He knew that he was what his words represented but seldom felt that his words represented whom he hoped to be. His words revealed and represented his inadequacy, which just made him all the more self-conscious in speaking. Some called him shy, but his reluctance to speak wasn't due really to fear or lack of confidence when among others. His reluctance was much more the instant incompleteness that he felt the moment that he uttered a word. His hollow words would echo back to him for hours or sometimes even days or down through the years. Yet as he discovered more of Jesus, he grew progressively less fearful of how his speech defined him. In sharing the words of Jesus, he found a reassuring definition. He was then fine with how he thought of himself and how others thought of him as he spoke the words of faith in Jesus, even when those others thought less rather than more of him. He realized that his mistrust of communication had more to do with mistrusting the world without Christ than anything to do with embarrassment in speaking. He was fine with embarrassment before others and even rejection by them as long as he had the identity and confidence of Christ. He knew that the only way to have that identity and confidence was to speak Christ's words, quietly, faithfully, and consistently.

Speak just what you are taught. John 8:28.

Jesus spoke precisely the words that his Father gave him. Jesus knew that he pleased the Father by sharing the Father's thoughts and expressing those thoughts in words that his hearers could understand and follow in their own love for the Father and pursuit of him in obedience. Jesus spoke both to please the Father and to teach us how to do so. We also please God when we speak what he has taught us. We may possibly please God speaking unique and original things in his honor, and yet we know that we please him speaking his own words, words that he specifically gave us as trustworthy. God knows how to move hearts and minds in his direction. The living and dynamic words that he gave us have special power to do so. People appreciate the spontaneous nature of speech, but they can often appreciate even more the referential nature of speech, how a single word here or there, or a few words strung together, can point the hearer to a complete and well-developed body of thought, particularly God's thoughts, which are always higher than our own thoughts. Jesus gave us so many profound things to say. We have no great and frequent need of substituting our own words for Jesus's words in communicating the grace, mercy, blessing, and divinity of the Trinity. We might instead do very well to read carefully what Jesus teaches us to say and then to say those words, just those words that he taught.

Jesus sometimes taught in the temple courts near where visitors placed their offerings. His doing so was dangerous because it invited the religious leaders' inspection and investigation, that which would soon lead to Jesus's crucifixion. Indeed, well before the dramatic Holy Week events that led to the crucifixion, the religious leaders who heard Jesus teach in the temple courts challenged the authoritative way that Jesus spoke, arguing that his testimony about himself was invalid without supporting authority and witnesses. Jesus assured them that he held unique authority, but even so, that he stood with the Father who had sent him, thus satisfying the religious leaders' demands for both authority and witness. Jesus explained that he had come as the Father's trustworthy representative, adding, "What I have heard from him I tell the world." They still did not understand, so Jesus told them, "I do nothing on my own but speak just what the Father has taught me." Jesus explained that the Father was with him because Jesus always does what pleases the Father. And as Jesus spoke, many who heard him believed in him.

She found that she was developing quite an ear for God's words. She had never felt particularly literate or articulate, although she read often. She did not even highly value the articulate. Leave fancy words to others, she often thought. She preferred plain speaking in herself and others. Yet she had developed a pure passion for God's words, for his precise meanings to the extent that the English words translated from Hebrew, Greek, or Aramaic were able to convey those meanings. She just sensed that they held a power beyond any other words. They were in a sense the source of her kingdom life, as they were the source for others sharing her kingdom life. That passion for God's words led her to begin to memorize them, which surprised her. She had once memorized a poem in grade school only through great effort. She hadn't memorized anything substantial since then. She did not regard herself as a strong learner or as one quick to recall, especially to memorize. And yet she did it, memorized a verse, then a passage, then a whole Bible book. In doing so, she found that she was sharing much more often just what those words taught. She didn't particularly want to be a person who quoted scripture for everything, although she also felt that nothing would be wrong with that. She just wanted the power of God's words and to be able to share that power in her ordinary speech. She had learned to speak just what God taught.

Do not speak on your own. John 7:16.

We are so powerfully bound within our own interests and experiences that we inevitably speak out of those interests and experiences. Our desires to some degree drive us, forming not only our actions but also our speech, just as our experiences also color our speech through perspective. We speak on our own, like little authorities. This tendency to speak on our own we must strongly resist. Whether highly educated and experienced or not, we still have little basis to claim authority and even less basis to claim attention. Jesus said quite clearly not to speak on our own but instead to speak in ways that we learned from him and that turn the listener's attention to the Father, just as Jesus consistently spoke. We should want our speech to attract hearers to Jesus and his Father, not to us. When we formulate our own premises, draw our own conclusions, and propagate our own thought, we inevitably introduce errors of experience, errors of the peculiar. Listen to any expert who professes unique experience, and you will hear subtle error because truth does not arise out of unique personal experience. Truth is a God commodity, one that we share widely as believers. Avoid speaking on your own, and you will far less often look and sound foolish. Speak the words that you hear from Jesus and the thoughts that you share with the Father, calling attention to the Father.

Jesus sometimes taught at religious festivals where crowds would gather. On one such occasion, the crowds who heard Jesus disagreed about his intentions, whether they were good or evil, although they kept their thoughts to themselves for fear of criticism from the religious leaders who made those decisions for everyone. Yet before long, Jesus moved right up to the temple courts to speak and teach. His words amazed the devout persons whom he found there. They didn't recognize Jesus as one of those whom the religious leaders had schooled for teaching, and so they wondered where he had learned his deeply authoritative message. Jesus told them, "My teaching is not my own. It comes from the one who sent me." He added, "Whoever speaks on their own does so to gain personal glory, but he who seeks the glory of the one who sent him is a man of truth." Jesus did not speak as if he was his own. He instead spoke the words of the Father who sent him. Those who speak on their own inevitably call attention to themselves rather than turning their listeners' attention to the Father. In doing so, the speakers prove themselves prideful and false, when speaking instead in ways that turn the listener's attention to God would prove the speaker humble and true.

She had a strong aversion for people who seemed full of themselves, who were always sharing their own opinions and thoughts. On the other hand, people who had fewer of their own opinions and were more willing to share others' thoughts attracted her. She felt the same way about her own personality and communication that she was better for herself and others when she was less full of herself and more interested in sharing the thoughts of others. Yet in faith in Christ, she felt a special bond with others. She had experienced the truth of how Christ bridges all people across all ages, cultures, and other gaps. Speaking the words of Christ and exhibiting faith in Christ connected with other believers in fellowship, even when other affinities were obviously lacking. Especially when she was among unfamiliar faces, she tried not to speak out of her own personal experiences, preferences, and references but tried instead to speak the words and act the ways of

Christ, at least until her new acquaintances were familiar with her. She had no special pride about herself such as what she had earned, experienced, or accomplished. She held no strong personal views except the view and perspective of Christ. And oddly enough, in speaking his words rather than her own, she felt firmly as if she was assuming her most attractive, secure, and sound identity created uniquely as her own. She had learned that sometimes you have to give up what you think is or should be your identity, give it up specifically to Christ, in order to discover the identity that is truly your own.

Speak no careless words. Matthew 12:36.

Empty words carry away the speaker's spirit. We are what we speak. What we say shapes not only what others think of us but also how we think of ourselves. We form speech from thought while we simultaneously form thought from speech. What we say also shapes how God thinks of us, which is the more-important perspective than what we think of ourselves. When we speak empty words or, worse, words that offend the Father, deny Christ, and reject the Holy Spirit, we take on the character of disobedient rebels. God requires that we account for our words. When one thinks of how much we speak and how many careless words pass our lips in a lifetime, the thought of accountability for our words should drive each of us straight for the cover of Christ. That need for shelter from and forgiveness for what we speak may be another reason why our words should never offend the Holy Spirit. Careless in our speech we may often be, but special care we should take to maintain the relationship and means by which we would gain God's forgiveness. We should not test God by speaking carelessly, and we should especially close our mouths and guard our hearts in ways that preserve God's willingness and way to show us mercy.

Jesus criticized the religious leaders often but once went so far as to call them a *brood of vipers,* not exactly a term likely to improve their reputation or Jesus's relationship with them. The crowd must have either cringed or howled in delight at his criticism, or both. For sensitive observers, though, the occasion may have especially seemed to warrant Jesus's criticism. Jesus had astonished the crowds by healing a man who was both blind and mute, instantly making the man so that he could both speak and see. The crowds must have sensed that they were witnessing the advent of God's great representative, one whom their murmurs indicated they were prepared to give the honorific *Son of David*. The religious leaders would have none of it. They claimed instead that Jesus healed using the devil's powers. Imagine attributing the work of God to none other than the *devil*. Jesus easily refuted the charge. How after all could the devil do good works? Clearly, Jesus worked through the Spirit of God when healing as only God, not the devil, would do. Jesus wasn't so concerned when the religious leaders criticized him back but said instead that they were committing a great offense when speaking against the Spirit. Be careful what you say, Jesus was saying. Jesus concluded, "I tell you that everyone will have to give account on the day of judgment for every empty word that they have spoken."

He had no more-frequent regret than the careless words he had spoken. Time and again, others had shown him mercy and grace despite his harsh, insensitive, and thoughtless words. The mouth was indeed a spark, setting the soul afire, he knew. Yet his mouth continued to offend God, himself, and others. He recognized many offenses and surely, he knew, missed recognizing many other of his offenses. Occasionally others took the task upon themselves to caution or correct him. He appreciated each correction, whether his careless mouth showed it sufficiently or not. What he wanted most, though, was that the Spirit would dwell more richly in him so that his mouth had a reliable guide and inspiration. He knew that others close to him would properly regard him as kind and gentle, a regard that he sought and desired as evidence of the good that he hoped to bring to them, only to the degree that his mouth had the Spirit's steady influence. He shuddered at the thought of his rudderless mouth, indeed of life in any respect, without the Spirit. Let his mouth never offend the Spirit, he thought, without whom all life-giving communication was hopeless.

Stop wailing. Luke 8:52.

One gets the distinct impression from the following account that Jesus did not appreciate griping, complaining, or wailing, even over something so significant as the loss of a loved one, at least when Jesus was present to answers prayers relating to the cause for the grievance or grief. To *wail* is to protest loudly, including howling, whining, or moaning. Life gives us plenty of cause to moan, plenty of cause short of the death of a loved one and then more cause when loved ones do indeed die. Every day brings its share of small or large grief. The more one counts one's challenges and curses, the easier wailing becomes. Nearly anyone can find cause to gripe and moan, and most of us do, giving frequent expression to things that we regard as undesirable, out of order, oppressive, and undue. For many of us, those challenges, as frequent and as great as they are, we bear with any grace only because of the power, presence, and purpose of Jesus. The singularly unbearable work of Jesus on the cross turns our sorrow into joy, our pain into gain, because it defeats death itself. Jesus does not reject mourning. He knows our grief and reckons it just. What he graciously invites and reasonably expects though is that we turn our grief over to him who can turn it into God's glory. We need not wail, indeed should not wail, in the presence of the one who brings back the dead and grants eternal life.

Jesus would surely raise the synagogue leader's daughter back to life shortly after she had died in her father's house due to illness. The events on his way to that miracle though tell us something additional about our communication, about how we naturally respond to and communicate about events and how we should alter that response. When someone told the synagogue leader not to bother Jesus anymore because the leader's ill daughter had now died, Jesus, overhearing the news, told the leader not to worry but to have faith and believe. The leader must have listened and believed because Jesus did as he said in bringing the leader's daughter back to life. Yet when they first arrived at the leader's house where the daughter laid dead, Jesus encountered all the people there wailing in their grief.

Those wailing at the leader's home may have been close family and friends, professional grievers, or both. One gets the impression from the brief account that Jesus did not appreciate their wailing in his presence. "Stop wailing," Jesus told them simply and directly. Stop the chorus of faithless grief. Jesus was on hand, and when the Lord is present, one has no reason to wail or moan.

She hurt over plenty of things, just as others also hurt. She seemed to suffer frequent small and large sleights, wounds, and oppressions, at least her fair share of them as others suffer in their own lives. She had cause to complain, and she occasionally acted on it. Yet something usually checked her grief, stopped her whining. When the really big losses occurred including the death of loved ones, she felt the intense loss that she expected to feel but somehow managed better than she expected. No bitterness took root. She knew that she must turn to Jesus, take her grief and sorrow to him. She expected him to turn that sorrow to joy, prayed for that transformation, and gave her grief over to him. She knew that he was a man of sorrow who yet changed grief to dancing. She knew it because he had shown her that her grief was temporary while her joy would be eternal. She knew it because she had asked him to confirm her faith in him that he gave life to the dead. She asked him not to test him but instead saying that her faith told her that he would honor her request. He had given her the evidence that her faith told her he would provide. She had no cause for wailing. He had turned her pain to confidence that her joy would soon be complete. Her pain was now more like anticipation than grief.

Speak faith over problems. Matthew 17:20.

Problems, issues, challenges, and questions confront us frequently, even daily or multiple times each day. Major problems may come along only once in a while, but few years or seasons go by without one. We can look back at nearly any year and agree that it was a hard year for the big unexpected and unwelcome things that we faced. Moderate challenges we face more frequently, perhaps monthly or weekly, while small issues we face daily. The moderate monthly or weekly challenges test us and our resolve, character, and commitment. The small daily issues nag us, drag on us, tire and depress us, never quite seeming to go away. The problems may be physical, psychological, emotional, relational, financial, legal, circumstantial, or situational. They vary widely, but they come with unrelenting regularity. Yet with God's help, we face them and by and large defeat or at least get around and eventually overcome them, or survive enough of them to maintain our sanity and spirit. In retrospect, we find it easier to see that we should have faced each challenge with greater faith. We should have spoken and acted with greater confidence and faith in the midst of each challenge before it resolved or first turned in the direction of resolution. If we had done so, if we had spoken words of faith in the midst of challenge, then we would have fared better just as others would have fared better around us. God could then have acted more swiftly and received more glory from drawing us past and out of the problem. We could have accomplished more for ourselves and for others while giving God greater credit for his ability and willingness to act on our faith. We ought to more often speak in faith when encountering problems.

Jesus had just returned from the mountain where God had acknowledged and transfigured him before Peter, James, and John. As at other times, a crowd met Jesus bringing the sick for Jesus to heal. One man reported to Jesus that the disciples had been unable to heal his son of seizures from which his son suffered greatly. Jesus first chastised the perverse unbelievers around him with whom he would not long stay or put up. He then had the man bring his son whom Jesus promptly healed of the seizures with a rebuke to the demons possessing the boy. The chagrined disciples approached Jesus afterward asking why they had been unable to heal the boy when Jesus had done so promptly. Jesus answered, "Because you have so little faith. Truly, I tell you, if you have faith as small as a mustard seed, nothing will be impossible for you," even moving mountains. Jesus tells us to speak out of faith when addressing problems. Speaking without faith is pointless in the face of problems.

He had little clear concept of how much faith he really had. He simply didn't know whether it was as small as a mustard seed or as large as an orange. If the disciples barely had a mustard seed's worth of faith before Christ's resurrection, then he doubted that he had any more, except that he did know the resurrection. Maybe the fact that we live in a post-resurrection world makes all the difference in the strength of our faith, he realized. Indeed, he had prayed over large and small issues, even huge issues. He and his family had faced and overcome most of those issues in a manner much better than he could reasonably have expected, which was not to say that life had been easy but that things had worked out much less wrong than right. In retrospect, he could see how in a few particular instances, the steady faith that he and others most close to him showed might have moved God to act more quickly and beneficially. Not to take credit in any respect for God's wholly merciful work, he could still hardly explain how God had blessed him and his family through those times, events, and circumstances without believing that God had answered his prayers and the prayers of others for him, just as he solidly believed that God had answered prayers he made for others in their own difficult circumstances. Judging the quality of his own faith would always be difficult, he concluded, and so he didn't want to make too much of it. But he would continue to speak in faith whenever confronted with the world's many problems. God just might appreciate and honor it.

Do not swear an oath. Matthew 5:34.

To not swear an oath seems pretty easy with which to comply, among Jesus's many admonitions. After all, how seldom do we actually testify in a judicial proceeding? And even in court, officials typically administer oaths by asking if the witness will swear *or affirm* that the witness is about to tell the truth, the affirmance option intended to enable Christians to comply with Jesus's edict. When you hear a witness answer, "I do so affirm," you can be pretty sure that the witness is making that effort to respect what Jesus told us to do in not swearing an oath. Yet court proceedings are not the only place one hears oaths. One hears frequent assertions that the speaker speaks truth in ordinary conversation, with speakers relying on all manner of oaths from "I swear" to "honestly," "no kidding," or

"Scout's honor." As Jesus's admonition reveals, the concept of an oath turns the reliability of communication inside out or on its head: nothing is necessarily true unless the speaker specially marks it out as such. Discourse filled with oaths must then be discourse filled with lying between the oaths. Those who rely on oaths to convince their listeners of their honesty are thus inherently untrustworthy in all communication. A wise judge once said that despite the oath, people lie in court more than anywhere else because in court they speak out of self-interest. Another wise person once said that an oath is a prelude to fraud. We have an inherent bent toward self-serving speech. The oath simply highlights that bent. We should instead speak honestly all of the time.

Jesus spoke against oaths, or more accurately against lying, in his great Sermon on the Mount. Every day has its habitual oaths, things that people repeat almost automatically to endorse their own speech. From the examples that Jesus used in his sermon, habitual oaths of Jesus's day must have included swearing to fulfill vows to the Lord, swearing on heaven, or perhaps swearing on the altar. The idea must have seemed sound to those who endorsed the practice. Lying about things related to God would add offense to God and the one listening. Yet when he said, "Do not swear an oath at all. Say simply 'Yes' or 'No,'" Jesus must have meant to indicate that lying about anything offends God. Could we please God by cheating our neighbor to fulfill our pledge to God? Could we please God by keeping an oath to God while otherwise defrauding our customers? Jesus explained that any lie and all lies come from the evil one. When we speak with the evil one's tongue, we offend God, no matter the subject. We offend God in stealing, lying, cheating, and defrauding at all, not merely when the offense relates to the temple, altar, oath, or vow. God is not venal, concerned only with himself and subject to bribe. God is instead holy, concerned with our own holiness in any relationship to him. We gain nothing by oaths in general or by restricting our oaths to things of God. We should simply let our yes be yes.

Moved by Jesus's admonition, he listened carefully for a time to the truth-telling quality of his speech. He began immediately to notice small exaggerations that he had not noticed before. His exaggerations in one sense seemed harmless. They usually involved estimates or predictions anyway, so who could object? Yet they continued to disturb him. He must have a reason for the exaggerations, and indeed he did, which was to make whatever premise that they supported more acceptable than it would otherwise have been. He realized that even as small as they were, they nonetheless subtly undermined his communication, the trust that others should show for his words and propositions. So he began to correct those estimates and predictions, to pull them back to where they belonged in all candor, without the shadings and colorings that made them look stronger and more reliable than they actually were. As he corrected his speech to make it more accurate, honest, and reliable, he noticed that the corrections gave him less a sense of always striving and selling, and more a sense of balance and equanimity. It was now alright if people didn't accept his premise, on whatever subject that he would previously have felt so ready to argue for using his small exaggerations. His yes was yes and his no was no, although he would keep listening to and watching carefully for the honesty of his speech.

Do not justify yourself to men. Luke 16:14.

We all justify. We all rationalize. Explanation is a big part of modern discourse. We each feel that if people simply listened to us, simply understood us, they must agree with us and approve of our actions. So we constantly speak in justification of those actions. We urge and guide to, and advocate for, the conclusions that we want others to draw particularly when those conclusions are about us. We thirst for approval while hardly even realizing it. How different we would be if we cared less for what people thought and more for what God thought, truly thought about and valued God's judgment rather than others' judgment. And how different we might be if we let people think, judge, and speak as they wish, particularly about our own actions. Instead of *just listen to me*, we might say *what do you think*? We might then learn something from others, adjust our actions to suit others better, and improve our relationships. We would also relieve ourselves of the nearly constant effort of justification.

118

Justifying fatigues a person and strains relationships. Justifying requires so much energy, so much thought. Rationalizing can involve the wrong kind of thought endorsing what we have already decided or done rather than considering consequences and better alternatives. We should just stop justifying. Let our actions be what they are, whether good or bad. Let our heart reveal itself in the quality of those actions. And don't let our mouths try to change others' impressions. Let others draw their own impressions, and think about God's judgment instead.

Jesus had instructed his disciples about how to handle money, not for the love of money but in trustworthy fashion and to gain friends. He used an extended parable showing how to use money. The religious leaders who loved money overheard and objected to his teaching. They made disrespectful faces toward Jesus, chiding his teaching in front of the disciples. Jesus told them, "You are the ones who justify yourselves in the eyes of others, but God knows your heart." The religious leaders tried to make themselves look a certain way outwardly to people, a self-serving practice that people oddly valued and respected. Appearances were important to the religious leaders because people valued appearances, and the religious leaders wanted the people to regard them highly through their appearance, no matter how their hearts were inwardly. So the religious leaders made a show of things, whether the show was in their fancy dress, flowing robes, pristine grooming, prominent seats, or long prayers. They also justified their actions to others, always explaining why they were right in doing as they did. No one could challenge them because they always had the rationale for why they were right and others wrong. Yet Jesus explained that people value things that God rejects. He then went on teaching in parable after parable.

She didn't feel much compulsion to justify herself, even while she recognized that others did. She listened carefully to the speech of others, both those close to her and those not so close. In that speech, she often heard the effort to explain and rationalize why others spoke, acted, and related as they did. Some people constantly justified themselves. Others did so only occasionally. Yet pretty much everyone rationalized to some degree. And she found that those who did so most often seemed least likely to be pursuing a sound course. The funny thing was that they also seemed to know it.

The more they justified, they less that they seemed to believe that they were doing the right thing. The justification was like a warning to themselves, which they seemed to recognize, even though the justification at the same time meant that they were going to go ahead down that path, natural and probable consequences notwithstanding. She found their habit at once sad *and* funny, funny because their justification was not even convincing themselves but also sad because they knew better. Her amusement didn't last long, only until she started to recognize her own voice of justification, less often expressed than others but still present. She too needed not to justify. Let her words and actions be as they are, and let her change them to please God rather than explain them away with that poisonous voice of justification.

1.6 Serving

Do justice. Luke 11:42. *Lay down your life for your friend.* John 15:13. *Be a servant.* Matthew 20:26. *Be ready to serve.* Luke 12:35. *Serve all.* Mark 9:35. *Wash one another's feet.* John 13:14. *Feed the hungry.* Matthew 25:35. *Invite in the stranger.* Matthew 25:35. *Invite the poor, crippled, and blind.* Luke 14:13. *Clothe the naked.* Matthew 25:35. *Look after the sick.* Matthew 25:36. *Heal the sick.* Luke 10:9. *Visit the prisoner.* Matthew 25:36. *Do as Jesus does for you.* John 13:15.

Anyone who knows the story, words, and actions of Jesus recognizes that he embodied and advocated service to others. His life was a life of service, indeed the ultimate life of service in which he gave his life for others. He washed, fed, healed, advocated, and protected, all in service to others. He also spoke frequently about service, explaining how and why we should serve, and whom we should serve with what actions. Not to listen to Jesus about service is to lose huge opportunities for meaningful work and life. God blesses us with such energy, so many resources, and so many causes, that we must see and seize the opportunity to serve. God plans our good works in advance of when we first see the opportunity to do them. We often overlook that others serve us richly. Others are constantly providing for us, some whom we see and others whom we don't see. We should serve others likewise. Listen to what Jesus said about service and watch how he served. Then go and do likewise.

Do justice. Luke 11:42.

In choosing and instructing actions, Jesus concerned himself most deeply with justice. Justice is to do for others what they deserve, particularly to provide the means for others to succeed in their reasonable endeavors. Justice is a particular concern among the poor and powerless who far too often cannot meet basic needs without the help of others. We all depend on others, and in fact we are all at some time poor and powerless, whether in infancy, youth, disability, or old age. The poor and powerless depend on others more acutely. They can often provide for themselves only with an assist from others that gives them access to the resources and means by which others having more wealth provide for themselves. While justice is a peculiar concern for the poor and powerless, justice is essential to society at all levels. Societies do not produce wealth without justice. Societies do not flourish in their freedoms, arts, culture, and economies without justice. Justice is not a resource solely or even primarily of government or the rich or famous. We do not receive justice from the elite, not only from lawyers and judges. Rather, justice is a property of the place and age, a cultural commodity that expands or contracts with the hearts and dispositions of the majority of ordinary citizens. Jesus made it so when urging us to do justice. Many doing justice within a community makes for a just community. Justice fails when pursued by only the few.

A religious leader had invited Jesus to eat with him after Jesus had instructed growing crowds. Jesus accepted the invitation and reclined at the meal with his host and other religious leaders, although without the ceremonial washing of hands. Noticing his host's surprise at Jesus's transgression of the religious tradition, Jesus told him that the religious leaders should concern themselves not with outward appearances but with generosity to the poor reflecting a clean inward disposition. Jesus added, "Woe to you religious leaders who tithe a tenth of the smallest things but who neglect justice and the love of God. You should have practiced the latter without leaving the former undone." Tithing even down to the smallest thing is fine, but do justice and love God. Jesus told them other woes, each illustrating the religious leaders' outward show but inward corrupt condition. He knew that he was insulting the leaders because one of them told him so. Yet he kept on with his instruction and then left. From then on, the leaders fought him at every turn, plotting to catch him saying something for which they could condemn him.

She had a growing passion for justice in large part because she had learned how important justice was to her savior Jesus. For a time, she had concerned herself little with how others fared, being more concerned instead with how she was faring. Gradually, though, her heart grew to see injustices consuming others. She had long suspected that some of the world's pain was unfair, the result of skewed rights and unfilled responsibilities. As her heart to advocate against injustice and for justice grew under the benign and passionate influence of the Holy Spirit, she began to encounter people experiencing specific instances of injustice. God was simultaneously giving her the skill to help address those instances. Those instances did not always seem so clear cut and simple. To the contrary, they were routinely muddied and complex, hard to tell the precise line between justice and injustice. Yet she still found a calling to engage against injustice, to struggle and advocate particularly for the powerless and poor. She knew that her Savior wanted her to do justice, and so she was ready to try.

Lay down your life for your friend. John 15:13.

To lay down one's life implies sacrifice. Service has an inevitably sacrificial sense to it. When we serve others, we give of ourselves. Service takes time, meaning that when we serve others, we give up time that we could have spent on ourselves when we may need or want that time for real personal benefit. Service takes effort, sometimes blood, sweat, and tears. When we give effort on behalf of others, we sacrifice that effort from things we could have pursued for ourselves including things that might have made a significant difference to us. Service takes talent, meaning exercising skill and capacities that others, particularly the ones whom we serve, do not have. When we use our talents for others, we give up the opportunity to use them for ourselves, sometimes for considerable personal benefit. Each such act of service is laying down one's own life for the life of another. Some of those acts are more obviously sacrificial, such as giving blood or even a kidney or bone-marrow transplant. Others of those acts, like helping a challenged child learn to read, are less obviously sacrificial but carry some personal impact nonetheless. When Jesus tells us to lay down our life for others, he meets the obstacle to service head on. We doubt the wisdom and value of giving something of ourselves, until he says instead that doing so is exactly wise and valuable in his own incomparable image.

Jesus had finally reached the ultimate point in his long discourse following the profound Last Supper. His disciples were above all to love and to love one another. They would be Jesus's friends, no longer just his servants, if they simply loved one another. Love was the one essential, the one greatest command. Yet Jesus had a particular kind of love in mind, not the sentimental love or the emotional love of the world but instead the sacrificial love that Jesus himself represented and demonstrated. Jesus summarized, "My command is this: Love each other as I have loved you. Greater love has no one than this: to lay down one's life for one's friends." The disciples must lay down their lives for the lives of others. They must give up things that they think are most important for themselves in order to share those things with others. They were to break their personal bounds to participate in, support, and celebrate the lives of others. Sacrifice is not a popular word, but by urging the disciples to lay down their lives, Jesus could hardly have been clearer in his intentions for service.

She felt better with each little sacrifice, which she did not initially expect but which later stood to reason. Her service was ordinary, usually through programs that others created and administered. She liked it that way, leaving it largely to others to judge the value of the activity, although she still had to decide whether to join in it herself. She regularly did join, whether for one-time events or across seasons or school terms or years. Regular simple service seemed to be her niche, her defining activity. Initially, she had expected that it would severely impact what she could accomplish for herself. She later guessed that her service did have some impact, although on the other hand in retrospect she seemed to have accomplished just as much or more for herself as she would have if she had not engaged so regularly in the service activity. Yet she was also fine with it now either way. Maybe she would have done a lot better for herself at school or in work, health, comforts, recreations, or relationships, if she had forgone the service. She didn't care. She was doing things His way. She was no hero at service, she knew perfectly well. Others whom she knew were making obvious sacrifices to serve, even profound sacrifices. She had not heard the call to do so as yet, even though she someday might. For now, she felt that He was pleased with her regular service and enjoying every one of her small sacrifices, which helped her enjoy them, too.

Be a servant. Matthew 20:26.

Who wants to be a servant? You don't get many volunteers. Service, though, has the nature of being a servant under a master, a worker under a supervisor, an employee under an employer. We should admit that others are in charge to some degree when we serve. Serving is hard to accomplish without taking on the role of submitting to the will and interest of another. Our actions are not necessarily service if we insist that we know what others require and then go about providing it, providing what we want to provide, rather than fulfilling the request and need of another. Many of us have the natural inclination to offer only what we want to offer rather than to provide what we could provide responding to an actual need. The soup kitchen needs meats and vegetables, but we supply rice and noodles. Sunday school needs a kindergarten teacher, but we volunteer for the choir instead. The neighbor needs a ride to dialysis, but we mow their yard instead. One of the harder things to do is to discern and provide the need as a servant would do. Servants have the heart of looking out for their master, of supplying quickly and without complaint what the master wants and needs. If we could just see our neighbor in need as if he or she were the Master, then perhaps we would jump more quickly to fulfill the request rather than provide our lesser alternative. The heart of a servant aims to please the other, not to find satisfaction in the fact of having served.

Do everything as if for God, and you will have found the heart of the one true Servant.

The mother of James and John had asked Jesus to let her two sons sit at his right and left hands as places of special honor in his kingdom. The other disciples who heard this extraordinary request grumbled at it, even though Jesus had answered that the Father would make that judgment, not him. To address the division that the request had created among the disciples, Jesus called them together to explain the kingdom's different nature. Among non-believers, those who do not know and pursue the kingdom, those who are in charge indeed do take the places of honor in order to lord it over everyone. Yet things work in the opposite way in God's kingdom. "Instead, whoever wants to become great among you must be your servant," Jesus explained, "just as the Son of Man did not come to be served, but to serve, and to give his life as a ransom for many." If we seek recognition and elevation, then our ambition should be to serve, not to promote ourselves to higher position. Let others promote us if at all then through our service. Most people know that those who serve best lead best. If you want promotion, then take the sacrificial assignment.

Oddly, he loved the servant aspect of service. He felt uncomfortable when others were serving him, although he received and appreciated services often, whether at restaurants or the doctor, dentist, optometrist, dry cleaner, or other service provider. In his own home others served him frequently, so often that he recognized almost daily that he did not know the number and nature of those generous acts of service. Everything that he needed seemed to just show up, although it did so only because of the constant service others provided him. He tried though to reciprocate, and trying pleased and satisfied him. He knew his Master's heart, and although he had no pretension of the ability to imitate it effectively, he could at least try in small and sometimes larger acts of service performed as much as he could fathom in the manner of a servant. Doing so at work was easier, where most everyone expected his prompt service, not to suggest that others failed to appreciate it. Most recipients seemed to appreciate his service even while recognizing that his role, as he too interpreted it, was to serve. He tried to do his work service though in a way that truly met the needs of those whom he served, that kept their needs ahead of his ability to earn a living. Everything just seemed more right in approaching service in that fashion. He was the beneficiary of such frequent and effective service, particularly from his one great Master, that he wanted to return the favor to everyone.

Be ready to serve. Luke 12:35.

An unusual thing about service is that the opportunity for it can arise at the most-unexpected time, in the least-expected place, and through the least-expected manner. Many who intend to serve believe that they will do so on their own timetable. They may expect a polite call and fair notice for convenient service. They may expect to choose the time, place, and manner of their service. Indeed, they may feel that they should get to choose their service, given their belief that service is voluntary, optional, additional, and provided out of surplus. Service tends not to work that way. Sometimes it does, but then just as often it does not. Our resources and skills, which after all are God's resources and skills for his use and application, are effective under other circumstances than those we might choose out of convenience. The needs we are capable of serving arise at times outside of our preferred schedule. Wednesday evenings or Saturday mornings may be most convenient, but the opportunity and responsibility to serve may instead arise on a Sunday afternoon, Monday morning, or Friday evening. We may think that our service should be in one community or neighborhood when God instead requires it in another. We may think that our service should be administrative and managerial when God expects it instead to involve daycare or physical labor. If service is by nature sacrificial, then part of the sacrifice is that we do not control it so closely. Let service take on its own life rather than fitting it to your life. Be ready to serve at all hours, in all places, and in all manners. Be ready.

Jesus coached the disciples repeatedly on how they should serve. In the middle of one of those lengthy teachings on how the disciples should guide and serve others, Jesus introduced a service principle

127

within a service analogy, in the manner that he so often taught mixing principle with analogy. "Be dressed ready for service and keep your lamps burning, like servants waiting for their master to return from a wedding banquet," was the way that Jesus put it. He then explained that the wise servant is ready whenever the master comes because the master is likely to come unexpectedly, maybe even in the middle of the night or in the very early morning at daybreak. The disciples questioned whether Jesus really meant that they and not others should be so ready to serve, perhaps as if they expected instead to have places of honor along with the Lord their master. Jesus answered with another parable suggesting that the disciples should be like wise managers whom the master entrusts with his household and who therefore had better have fed and supervised the household's residents, no matter when the master returns. When the master gives much, he reasonably expects much. When the master gives less, he expects less. Jesus expected a lot from the disciples to whom Jesus had given so much knowledge of the kingdom of heaven.

He wondered about both his ability to serve and his effectiveness at service. Both were difficult to judge, each holding their own doubt and hazard. If he agreed to serve in places where he did not have the time and resources, then he might do more harm than good. Likewise, if he agreed to serve and then actually did attempt service where he lacked the skill to be effective, then he might again do more harm than good. He saw no point to being willing to do a job poorly. He wanted only to do the few things at which he knew that he was good, things that he did often and effectively, where he had the confidence, skills, resources, and connections to ensure favorable outcomes. Those limitations were how he conducted himself generally, whether in his home, trade, or profession, and so he figured initially that he should limit his voluntary service to others accordingly. Yet so much time passed without much service opportunity that he began to question his self-constraint. Jesus might have meant something else when he said to be ready and that he expected much from those to whom he gave much. So here and there he began saying *yes* rather than *no* even when he felt like the service request was a little outside of his area. Evidently, others felt him qualified. Maybe they were right that he had broader skill than he had surmised. And indeed, as he served more and more often, he found both that his current skills were reasonably effective *and* that he was developing new skills and capacities for service. He began to feel a little more like the wise manager always at the ready and a little less like one whose caution meant denying services to the poor.

Serve all. Mark 9:35.

We may like to choose whom we serve, but Jesus's message is to serve all. Choosing whom we serve gives us an opportunity to make friends, pursue causes, influence people, and gain reputation. Choosing whom we serve reduces the challenges, messiness, and dissonance of service because we tend to choose those with whom we have relationships and affinities. We choose maybe by language, culture, and community, or if not then by time, manner, and place. We also naturally feel that some merit our service more so than others. We do anyone a favor by serving, and so we should get to pick and choose whom we should favor with our service. Jesus though says otherwise. In Jesus's kingdom, those who can serve should serve all. Those who have the capacity to serve have the responsibility to do so for anyone who would benefit, whether or not the benefit is to any degree reciprocal for the one who serves. You mean serve those nearest me, those dearest to me, right? No, Jesus means to serve all, including those who seem farthest from and least attractive to us.

Jesus at times took the disciples aside secretly for instruction. During one of those most critical times when he needed to tell the disciples again what would happen to him, he took the disciples through Galilee telling them that men would soon kill him but that he would rise again in three days in resurrection. They had heard him say the same thing before but still did not understand it. The disciples were also too afraid to ask for an explanation. So instead they argued among themselves as to who would be the greatest. When they reached a house in Capernaum, Jesus asked them why they had argued on the road. Although they did not answer, he knew. So he sat down and called the disciples to him for another lesson in service. He explained, "Anyone who wants to be first must be the very last, and the servant of all." Not just the last but the *very* last, and the servant not of one or some but of *all*, and so *last in line* and *servant of all*. Jesus had no room or patience for self-promotion, for leading by place of honor and show. His disciples must instead lead by serving and by serving *all*. Jesus was dead serious about service. He had come to reach and serve all and expected his disciples to do likewise.

She knew whom she liked to favor and whom she didn't. She loved to serve friends and neighbors. She also loved to serve the nearby and friendly poor, the cheerful folks in cheerfully charitable places who just needed a little help and who were much appreciative of it. She liked to serve independently more so than in groups and like anyone preferred that her service not carry threats or risks. She wanted to be wise rather than foolish in service. Also, patience had not been her greatest quality, more like her least. Like anyone, she didn't appreciate those who wasted her time or insulted her character or intelligence. She also had ideas of not wanting to foster dependence, not being an enabler, and not wanting to have someone take advantage of her generous but still-limited resources. She was thus for a long time fairly selective about whom she served, a little like turning a spigot on and off. Yet as she served, her heart for service and for whom she served grew. She gradually cared less for her previous fine distinctions. She found opportunities to help others well outside of her own community with whom she had no particular affinity. She cared less for any particular criteria and trusted less her ability to discern. In the end, she just wanted to serve all and let Jesus make the judgments about to whom to send her.

Wash one another's feet. John 13:14.

Washing one another's feet has both literal and figurative applications. Jesus literally washed the disciples' feet. His act was one of direct service. Sandaled feet exposed to dirt and dust on an all-day hike need a good washing, particularly when coming indoors for the evening. Jesus was definitely doing the disciples a favor. Yet washing guest feet was for servants, not the role of a leader or honored guest. Washing another's feet is not as easy as it may sound. You must get very low to the ground, hands extended awkwardly forward, fumbling with water and towel to scrub ground dirt off the foot's peculiar surfaces, while the owner of the feet towers over you. Washing another's feet makes about as clear as one can the relative standing, servant to master or guest, of the involved parties. Masters had good reasons, both practical and political, why they did not wash the feet of servants and why they had servants wash their own feet. To reduce or eliminate political, social, spiritual, and other hierarchical distinctions were presumably why Jesus chose foot washing to illustrate his service lesson. Government, religious, corporate, communal, and family leaders were to serve. Leadership was a responsibility rather than a license for privilege. Leadership meant works, not perks. Leadership meant hard and awkward work, work that others might consider demeaning, like foot washing. In any service situation, try discerning what others most avoid because of its difficulty or inconvenience, and then do it. You may see instantly how effectively your act serves, the swift relief and accommodation it brings to everyone within reach of your service. You will also have changed however slightly the attitude of the group, organization, or initiative of which you are a member, toward the service that it is to perform.

With the Last Supper in progress, Jesus suddenly rose, removed his clothes, and wrapped a towel around his waist. Drawing water from a basin, Jesus proceeded around the low table at which the disciples reclined, washing each disciple's feet and drying feet with the towel around his waist. When Jesus reached Peter, Peter objected because he could not see Jesus as his servant. Jesus insisted, Peter relented, and Jesus finished washing the disciples' feet. He then explained that although the disciples properly thought of him as their Lord and teacher, he intended to show them how a Lord and teacher properly acted by serving. Jesus urged, "Now that I, your Lord and Teacher, have washed your feet, you also should wash one another's feet." He added that he had meant specifically to set an example. The disciples should in the future do as he had just done, and God

131

would bless them if they did so. The moment must have shocked the disciples. It certainly discomfited them, as Peter's response showed. Jesus had done more than just take the lowest position among them. He had given himself the lowest position among the household servants, who were already below the disciples who had worked as fishermen, tax collectors, or perhaps tradesmen like Jesus rather than as household servants. Even servants have rank. The disciples had all probably seen household servants take on every other task ahead of washing feet, leaving foot washing to the lowest-ranked and least-fortunate servant. Jesus had made himself as low as he could under the circumstances in order to serve, just as they should thereafter do.

Her favorite sacrament at church was actually foot washing. While she loved the other sacraments, too, especially communion but baptism, too, the foot-washing ceremony, performed only once a year in her church was such a perfect demonstration of her servant Lord's heart. She loved service, but she also loved the leveling aspect of foot washing, having little patience for people who thought more of themselves than they should. As she watched the senior pastor in his entire regalia stoop low to wash a parishioner's feet, she thought of how washing feet leaves no room for pride of place or status. She tried to think of what was the modern equivalent to foot washing so that she could pursue that service, but no one thing came to mind. Instead, she started to think of several small things that everyone knew had to be done but that everyone also seemed to avoid. She was not particularly surprised to find those things everywhere, whether organizing chaotic storage rooms at church, cleaning up the staff kitchen at work, or the many small things that it took to keep an orderly and efficient home. As she kept at those low tasks, she so often found the Lord's presence there more so than she did in the high places. She realized that he was indeed the reason for her service. She would gladly go wherever he went.

Feed the hungry. Matthew 25:35.

The soup kitchen is the classic place of service. We can conceive of no more-representative places of frequent, common, and ordinary service than the food banks, pantries, soup kitchens, gleaners, co-ops, and similar places that feed hungry persons unable to provide regularly for themselves. These places are the first ones that one usually recalls when thinking of charitable service. Hunger, we understand. Hungry, we have all been. The thought of going without food is a concern with which we are all familiar not because we have all experienced poverty but because we have all been hungry. We all know how quickly and deeply lack of nutritious food affects us, how little we can accomplish and how badly we suffer without it. We know that people starve to death quickly, while we also know that people who get only irregular nutrition suffer bad health and all of its related effects. One cannot think clearly, concentrate, learn, act, work, or provide for one's self or others for very long without decent food. One also finds it much more difficult to worship and love the Lord. Just as an army marches on its stomach, faith requires physical sustenance in order to devote energy and attention to prayer and worship. Although voluntary fasting can promote devotional states, believers generally find it harder to pray on unwillingly empty stomachs. Jesus gives us readily understandable instruction when he says to feed the hungry as our act of service. Know and support the soup kitchen in your community.

Jesus taught for a long time one of those last days on the Mount of Olives outside Jerusalem, telling several long parables while also speaking of what was to come for all his listeners. One parable in particular, of the sheep and goats, had much to say about service. He spoke about his glorious return with the angels, when he would sit on his throne to judge the nations. Then, he would "separate the people one from another as a shepherd separates the sheep from the goats." The criteria that the King would apply would be their service. The righteous, the sheep, would have served their needful fellows, but the unrighteous, the goats, would have failed and refused to serve. About the righteous sheep, he would say first, "For I was hungry and you gave me something to eat." About the unrighteous goats, he would say first, "For I was hungry and you gave me nothing to eat." The sheep he would place on his favored right side while the goats would go to his left. He would then bless the sheep with eternal life but call the goats cursed for eternal punishment. Jesus expects us to feed the hungry, equating himself with those in that need. He will reward those who do but punish those who do not.

The two of them, father and young daughter, made a small habit of it, shopping Saturday morning once a month or so in order to bag up groceries to take to the church's food pantry. Although the food that they bought was imperishable, they would date the bags to be sure that none remained in the pantry longer than was safe for the canned and boxed items. They need not have worried though because often the pantry was empty of bags by the time that they planned and executed their next visit. They would check now and then with the person at church who directed needful families to the pantry, to be sure that they were purchasing helpful items. They tried to buy only things that they themselves would consume rather than cheaper goods, but they also tried to be wise about purchasing proteins and other nutritious things that would sustain the body. They also tried to buy combinations of goods that would make sense to a hungry family. Of course, they watched for sales and clipped coupons, but they also usually did that for themselves. They both felt that the simple service made a bad or good week better. The task was usually over before they knew it. They also recognized that they were sharing time with one another that they would not otherwise have shared. They received blessing just as they gave blessing, which they knew was part and parcel of service.

Invite in the stranger. Matthew 25:35.

Jesus also wants us to invite in the stranger. Invitations are special. The dentist does not *invite* someone to a root canal, just as the doctor does not *invite* someone to a major surgery. An invitation implies that something welcome, beneficial, enjoyable, and generally good lies on the other side of the invitation. We invite family and friends to a holiday meal. We invite our closest friends on fun day trips, special vacations, or to the movies on a rainy day. We invite new neighbors over for coffee and new co-workers out to a group lunch. Wherever we see and want to solidify and celebrate ties, we make invitations. That purpose of course is the jarring part of Jesus's admonition to invite in strangers. So much of Jesus's instruction involves turning the world's ways on their head, setting them aright with the kingdom of God, which has better ways. In the worldly way, we invite family and friends. In the kingdom, we invite strangers. Remember that Jesus did not come to save the righteous but the sinner. The kingdom has plenty of righteous celebrants glorifying God. The kingdom has plenty of room for more celebrants covered by the saving blood of Christ. Among the strangers whom we encounter, many will not know, trust, or otherwise have a relationship with Christ. Our invitation to the stranger is an invitation to Christ. Prisons have re-entry programs to help newly released prisoners establish new lives in their most-critical first few days and weeks of released time. Think of the stranger who does not know Christ as a recently released prisoner facing that critical time.

As Jesus told the story of the sheep and goats, he listed several acts of service that, beyond simply feeding the hungry as a first act of service, would help him distinguish one from the other, the blessed from the cursed. After feeding or not feeding the hungry, he listed giving or not giving the thirsty something to drink. Feed the hungry, and give the thirsty something to drink. The parable's context did not make clear whether Jesus meant these acts literally or figuratively, although one is often safe to assume that he meant both. Feed the hungry literally, but also give the spiritually hungry the substance of Jesus's words as the bread of life. Give the thirsty something literal to drink, but also give those who dwell in a spiritual desert Jesus as the spiritual water of life. When Jesus then added to his list of acts of service that "I was a stranger and you invited me in," he may again have intended both literal and figurative meanings. We probably ought to invite strangers into our lives and even our homes, but we also probably ought to share our faith in Jesus with those whom Jesus does not know. People will get to know Jesus because we know Jesus. When Jesus reserved punishment for those where "I was a stranger and you did not invite me in," he may not so much have meant that he will punish us if we do not invite in literal strangers as much as he meant that he punishes those who remain strangers to him. Makes sense, doesn't it? Help others make acquaintance with Jesus. Do not let others be strangers who failed to invite him in.

This one is going to be hard, she thought, as she read Jesus's admonition to invite in the stranger. Some people seemed to have the knack for open hospitality. Their homes were always filled with different people. That knack was not her knack. While she felt more than usually hospitable, she also felt that her home was a bit of a haven from the world's craziness. She also doubted her capacity and her family's capacity to tolerate much of that craziness at least if it came within their home. The home was a place of solitude and rest, to regain and restore normalcy, not to further disrupt it. Strangers we call *strangers* for a reason, which is that they are strange to us. When we don't know a person, how can we trust that we can put up with them and that they can put up with us? Yet she did know people who while not complete strangers on the one hand, and not close friends on the other hand, were just well-enough known to her that she believed that she could invite them in to get to know them better. Maybe those near-knowns was who Jesus meant when he said to invite in the stranger, or at least what he meant to her. While hoping that he understood and forgave her lack of courage in not inviting in complete strangers, she planned the occasional dinner party or holiday meal at which she mixed friends and near-strangers. And years later, those times were the ones that she remembered best as a celebration of human kinship and spiritual fellowship. Her stranger guests, or better put as *guest strangers*, enlarged her circle and enlightened her view, just as she hoped that her hospitality had warmed and encouraged them.

Invite the poor, crippled, and blind. Luke 14:13.

We do tend to favor those who favor us, particularly when planning our invitations. Whom did you invite to your last gathering? No one who invites friends, families, and neighbors is unusual. When we want to share a good time, we generally choose those who know how to have a good time, with whom we might share a good time at their place in the future. Reciprocity is the coin of invitation. We tend not to invite those who we believe would be unable or unwilling to reciprocate. In doing so, we probably most of the time feel as if we are just doing what is right, making everyone happy, and keeping everyone comfortable. Jesus has different instructions. He says to invite those who *cannot* repay us. He refers specifically to those who are too poor to do for us as we would do for them if they joined us for a meal, party, or holiday celebration. He also refers to inviting the crippled, whom we might understand to mean those whose appearances don't fit with everyone's expectations, whose physical condition or mental state might make others uncomfortable and who probably get few or no invitations because of it. Jesus also refers to inviting the blind, whom we might understand to mean both the literally sightless but also the figuratively undiscerning, again ones who probably get few or no invitations. Jesus wants us to please God, to do things that enable *God* rather than others to reward and repay us. Jesus gives us a distinct lens on service as working for a Lord whose payment will be far greater than any ordinary payment.

A prominent religious leader invited Jesus to a meal one Sabbath. Knowing that others closely watched him as he ate, Jesus called their attention to a sick and swollen man whom Jesus promptly healed after asking his suspicious watchers if healing was lawful on the Sabbath. He then quizzed his watchers whether they would pull a child or ox out of a well into which they had fallen on the Sabbath, to which they could not answer without looking foolish, and so they did not answer. As the meal went on, Jesus kept observing and teaching. Jesus soon turned to his host saying that next time he held a banquet not to invite his friends, relatives, or rich neighbors, each of whom would promptly pay back the host. Instead, Jesus explained, "When you give a banquet, invite the poor, the crippled, the lame, the blind," who cannot repay you, so that God will repay you at the resurrection of the righteous. Jesus continued to give uncomfortable lessons and tell challenging parables as the banquet continued.

She and her friend had sort of come up with the idea together. They each wanted to give the other credit, even though neither cared

137

for credit. They just thought that it was the neatest thing. They wanted to have a community dinner to which the church invited anyone but especially those having the hardest time with fewest resources. They wanted, either literally or figuratively or both, the poor, crippled, and blind to bless them with their presence. And so she just got the banquet planned, funded, advertised, and started with great help from everyone at the church, staff and membership included. Invitations went out to the second-hand stores, social services, and ride services where the poor, crippled, and blind mixed. Other churches, she knew, fed the poor and hungry monthly, weekly, or even daily. She had worked in those regular services before, and she valued and respected them just as everyone else did. Yet this meal she wanted to be more like Christ's banquet story, not a desultory regular meal but a real banquet. The church raised the funds for fine cuts of meat. A staff member with a chef's skills planned and cooked the entrée while a volunteer with a catering business made exquisite dessert. A florist donated flowers from which volunteers made beautiful centerpieces. The budget afforded white linen tablecloths. Band members serenaded with song. Rich served poor, and all had a good time. Invite the poor, blind, and crippled to your banquets. Throw parties for the poor and let God reward your banquet service.

Clothe the naked. Matthew 25:35.

As in so many other lessons, when Jesus said to clothe the naked, he presumably intended both practical and conceptual applications. If your business is making or selling clothing, then his instruction probably means something practical to you. Use your skill to provide clothing. That clothing may be warm enough to withstand a cold winter, safe and comfortable for work, or just winsome enough to get a person a job in an interview. Clothing, the saying goes, makes the man, which although an exaggeration nonetheless carries an element of truth that persons depend in nearly all situations on appropriate clothing. Those who lack clothing lack something quite important. Watch the homeless mission send its poor onto the streets on an early winter morning. Look at the families standing in line for food distribution. Your close inspection will reveal to you need for appropriate clothing. You need not even have special access to clothing resources. Your own clothing, or your own finances to buy another person clothing, can do just as well. Yet do not overlook Jesus's figurative meaning. Each of us has had the need for mental, emotional, or spiritual cover, perhaps in the form of understanding, forgiveness, respect, trust, confidence, or privacy. We may have had the need because of our own sin or the sin of another making us their victim, which may hardly matter when it comes to the need for figurative clothing. God, the Bible says, shelters us under his wing. Indeed, God made clothing to cover both Adam and Eve in their nakedly sinful shame. Clothe the naked. You would be doing no less than the loving Father did and the loving Son directs.

To clothe the naked was another one of the service acts that Jesus listed at the Last Supper as criteria for sorting sheep from goats. Those who clothed the naked, Jesus would sort, treat, and bless as sheep, while those who failed or refused to clothe the naked, Jesus would sort, treat, and punish as goats. The disciples would have understood the difference between sheep and goats even if the modern reader might not. Sheep were mostly docile, gentle, and harmless but also quite productive, providing both wool and meat. Sheep were also generally obedient followers especially when recognizing the image and call of their shepherd master. On the other hand, goats were stubborn, mischievous, and frequently destructive, while barely having their productive uses. Communities treasured, guarded, and relied on their sheep but barely tolerated goats, even having a tradition of periodically turning one loose into the wild carrying the community's sin as a *scapegoat*. Jesus judged the blessed sheep, "I needed clothes and you clothed me," but judged the punished goats, "I needed clothes and you did not clothe me." Give clothes to those who need clothes. Then also cover the embarrassment, offenses, and shame of those who need that cover.

His particular work had revealed to him the shame of many, just as the work of others reveals shame. Schoolteachers see the physical evidence and crayon depictions of suspected child abuse, he knew. Social workers learn the shame of the deranged and addicted, he had witnessed. Doctors see the results of domestic violence, knowing or suspecting the perpetrators. Letter carriers learn of illicit interests. Lawyers learn of the promise breakers, cheaters, and swindlers. Judges learn of the drunk drivers and deadbeat parents. Prosecutors see the shame of the child pornographers and tax evaders, while police officers see the shame of just about everyone. Even trash collectors learn a thing or two about the neighborhood revelries. Many of us see much shame, he knew. The question was how we would each treat it in any one instance. Disclosure to the right persons at the right time in the right manner, he knew, was critically important. Yet so too was to maintain confidences under the right circumstances, to help others recover from their inevitable shame, no matter who or what inflicted it. Over time, he saw how some persons, professionals, and communities learn how to punish, correct, monitor, and prevent wrongs, even the most-serious wrongs, without unnecessarily destroying, and instead while respectfully clothing, involved persons. He was glad of the verses that he had learned, by which he practiced, and in which he abided, having to do with appropriate cover, not ignorance or complicity but humane cover, for the shame of others. He was especially appreciative when he saw others extending that cover. Clothe the naked, he kept thinking, as his work and the work of others continued to reveal the shame of a community.

Look after the sick. Matthew 25:36.

Looking after the sick is certainly an act of service. Sickness by definition debilitates. Hunger, thirst, homelessness, and poor clothing may be one's norm, things that a person can get used to for a time or season at least. Sickness is the opposite of normalcy. In its acute nature, it attacks, injures, destroys, and disrupts. Whatever we were doing before sickness, we must stop doing during sickness until a return to good health. In severe sickness, we cannot even care for ourselves. Sickness with care may mean a swift return to full health. Sickness without care may mean death or permanent disability. The smallest act of health care, like getting a person the right diagnosis and vitamin or medicine, may fully restore a person's good health. In other cases, sickness requires exhausting care, constant and close care over long periods. Care for the sick can be especially sacrificial, often more so than feeding the hungry or slaking thirst, not only because of the constancy and concentration that care can require but also because of exposure risk to some care providers. To treat contagious disease is to risk succumbing to disease one's self. Yet Jesus admonishes to care for the sick as he so often attended to and healed the sick. In doing so, we bring Jesus to those for whom we care, just as Jesus brings us to them. As we minister to the sick body, we minister to the oppressed spirit. Look after the sick, and you will be doing the work and will of Jesus. You may also be helping Jesus cure a much greater spiritual sickness attending any absence of Jesus.

Yet another act of service that Jesus listed at the Last Supper, as criteria for separating blessed sheep from cursed goats, was to look after the sick. "I was sick and you looked after me," Jesus told the disciples of his sheep, just as he instructed as to the goats, "I was sick and you did not look after me." After his sheep judgments, and then again after his goat judgments, Jesus included in his parable the response of first the righteous sheep and then the unrighteous goats, "When did we see you sick?" His answer to each was consistent, to the sheep that "whatever you did for the least of these brothers and sisters of mine, you did for me," and to the goats that "whatever you did not do for one of the least of these, you did not do for me." When we care for the sick, especially the *very* sick, indeed the *least* of the sick, Jesus said that we care for him. Can you imagine Jesus as the person who lies in the bed before you needing your loving care? Could we have any greater incentive to loving care? By using his own care, the care we would show for *him*, as the yardstick, Jesus meant to give us the greatest possible inducement to care for the sick and to do each of the other acts of service he listed at the Last Supper. Jesus was serious about service and wanted us to be so. Great rewards await those who serve including those who care for the sick.

They had both witnessed much loving care for their sick parents in their parents' last years. They had made good acquaintances, even friendships, with the skilled and committed staff members in their increasingly frequent visits to hospital intensive-care units and emergency rooms, assisted-living centers, nursing homes, and hospice units. Rarely, a staff member would have a bad day, leading to confusion, offense, or disagreements. Routinely, care providers instead displayed great patience, cheerful endurance, acute sensitivity, generous thought, much forgiveness, and tender care. Their observations of these care providers heartened and lifted them through the difficult times of their parents' steady decline and ultimate demise. They relied heavily on those care providers, indeed most of the time entirely on those care providers, even drawing their own comfort, solace, and energy from them even as they cared for their elderly parents in demise. They tried to be thoughtful, bringing a card, gift, or remembrance now and then, and offering to share whatever bounty that they brought their parents. Nearly all offers, the care providers politely but firmly refused, whether out of personal propriety or the requirements of their employers. They regretted that they could not do more, although in a sense, that they could not pay back these care providers for their unstinting care of their parents they suspected was alright. Care providers truly win their reward in heaven.

Heal the sick. Luke 10:9.

As kind and thoughtful as it is, we are not simply to care for the sick while they lay succumbing, if by *care* we mean only sentimental concern and comfort. Rather, Jesus says that we are to *heal* the sick, which means that we are to care for them in ways that directly promote their recovery. We should care for the sick using the effective means that God provides and with the intent and confident expectation of their recovery. You can and should make a difference in the healing of those for whom you care. Watch an effective care provider, and you will see that the care provider is acting to make things not just tolerable but better. Care can and often should be active, creative, thinking, planning, and assessing. God provides so many means for healing, all of them through the power and purpose that he invested in Jesus. Jesus gives us the will, commitment, and ability to heal, not simply to care. God then provides expertise for evaluation, discernment for diagnosis, medication for cure, and therapy for strengthening, each of them in their own way requiring and depending on miracles of healing. God also and primarily gives us access to his powers through our prayers for the sick, and again not just prayers given for solace but prayers for miracle healing. We also pray for healing not just of the body but of the spirit, for those for whom we care, that they see, accept, depend on, and love Jesus. Heal the sick even while caring for them and as an object of caring for them.

Jesus appointed more than just the disciples to serve the communities that he entered. He wanted more workers doing what he and the disciples had been doing. So soon after Jesus had sent out the 12 disciples, he appointed 72 others to go ahead of him in twos to serve in advance the places that he was going. He wanted his message and good works to precede him. With God's kingdom so near, with Jesus present and so willing, the people had so much good work to do, and yet so few were doing it. After appointing the 72 others, Jesus gave them specific instructions, much as he had instructed the 12 disciples before them. He told the 72 to stay in whatever home welcomed them, letting their service in the town be the consideration for whatever food and drink the home's keeper gave them. "Heal the sick who are there," Jesus instructed the 72, "while telling them, 'The kingdom of God has come near to you.'" Some towns would not welcome them, Jesus cautioned, in which case they must warn those towns that things would not go well for those towns later. So the 72 went out, returning with glad reports that even demons they encountered had obeyed them, just as demons had obeyed Jesus. The 72 had healed the sick, as Jesus had instructed.

He often sought to console and exhibit care but less often sought to heal. He knew it was true. He heard stories of miracle healing and had even seen and experienced some himself, but those experiences had merely planted seeds of faith that had not yet taken root. He certainly did not doubt that healing was possible. Of course much healing occurred, whether sudden or slow and progressive. People by and large expected healing from most diseases, and healing in fact occurred from most, even if new diseases constantly seemed on the rise. Yet overall, he had a growing sense that all healing, again

143

whether sudden or slow and progressive, was God's work. Why should anatomy, physiology, biology repair itself? What particular will to organize, defend, and repair did any unthinking cell, group of cells, or biological system really possess? None, of course. Although medical and scientific statements are rife with suggestions of such will to survive and replicate, no physician or scientist expressly attributes intent to organic processes that have no capacity to form it. Healing instead occurs through an invariably inexplicable life-giving presence and purpose having no conceptual paradigm other than God. While physicians diagnose and medicate to influence organic processes, God gives the processes their positive power and human purpose. God intends, and so cells respond. God desires it, and so systems organize and repair, sometimes with medical help but often without it. He would now pray more often and with greater understanding and faith, for God's swift and sure healing. The seeds of experience had taken root.

Visit the prisoner. Matthew 25:36.

One of the first things that one realizes in a prison ministry is that the people on the inside are an awful lot like the people on the outside with the exception of the conviction and its consequent constraint. If you have never been to a prison or communicated with a prisoner, then you may have an artificial or exaggerated sense of the prisoner population. In that population, though, one finds men and women, old and young, rich and poor, educated and uneducated, and members of every affinity, ethnicity, and national origin. One finds in the prisoner's mind every justification and rationalization that one finds in the free, and many of the same temptations and corruptions. In the prison community, one finds social hierarchies, good and bad reputations, and good and bad relationships. One also finds skill, knowledge, and insight, and no surprise here, faith, what many would call *jailhouse* faith but that which seems earnest and authentic nonetheless. When Jesus instructed to visit the prisoner, he doubtless intended that those who did so engage and support the prisoner's faith, to listen, agree, encourage, counsel, and advise in ways that bring prisoners closer to Christ. Christ's forgiveness and redemption can easily mean more to the prisoner, whose surroundings speak redemptive need, than those who perceive themselves free. Jesus may also have meant that we find practical things to do to help prisoners reenter communities with greater prospects for success. Yet Jesus may also have meant that we look after the figurative prisoners who bind themselves to ideologies that condemn and constrain. We should look after one another mindful that anyone can be a prisoner, anywhere.

The last of the acts of service about which Jesus spoke at the Last Supper was to visit the prisoner. "I was in prison and you came to visit me," Jesus said to the righteous sheep, and "I was in prison and you did not look after me," he said to the unrighteous goats. Among the six acts of service that Jesus specifically mentioned including feeding the hungry, giving drink to the thirsty, inviting in the stranger, clothing the naked, and caring for the sick, visiting the prisoner seems the oddest, maybe the hardest, and the most out of sync with current sensibilities as to what should constitute charitable service. Soup kitchens and clothing ministries we understand, but not everyone is cut out to visit a prison. While we occasionally run across the hungry, thirsty, threadbare, sick, and strangers, prisoners are truly the gone and forgotten, which may be why Jesus made them the last and ultimate of his six service populations. If you truly want to see the lost, hopeless, and lonely, then visit a prisoner. The prisons of Jesus's day must have been worse than modern prisons, especially American prisons where prisoners have constitutional rights, but prison remains prison. They are grossly inhospitable places holding against their will the desperately lost. Looking after the lost sounds like something that Jesus would do. We have no better place to find the lost than among prisoners including those recently released from prison.

They had never done anything quite like it but in retrospect were always glad that they had and sometimes were pulled to return to it. They had been a part of a prison ministry only for a little while, a year or two of jail visits one night a week. They had taken a weekend and a few evenings for training and then had committed to the weekly visits, she visiting on the women's side of the jail and he on the men's side, each with other men and women with whom they met and prayed for a little bit before starting. Those other men and women included veterans who had participated in jail ministry for decades, newbies who would end up giving it a try for only a short time before giving up, and others in between who found a season in which to do it but then found that the season had ended in favor of a new season for other service work. Their experiences varied week to week. Some weeks included inspirational moments involving expression of deep faith, sometimes by the incarcerated but also sometimes by a visitor or jail administrator or guard. Other weeks seemed ordinary, like chatting with a new acquaintance on the street. Other weeks were frustrating and disappointing for lack of interest or open rejection by inmate, administrator, or guard, or lack of insight by the serving visitor. They often felt wholly inadequate to the role despite their abiding faith, sound Bible knowledge, good training, and helpful resources. Yet they knew that Jesus instructed it, desired it, and even commanded it. And they knew that he was wholly adequate, even out of their most depressing visits.

Do as Jesus does for you. John 13:15.

The ultimate act of service would of course be to do for others as Jesus does for you. In any pursuit, we benefit not just from instruction but from models. Teachers, instructors, mentors, coaches, counselors, and guides are good. Sometimes, a model to imitate is better. We do not know how accomplishing something looks until we see it done, whether that act is to roller skate, ice skate, ski, dance, drive a car, pilot an airplane, or captain a boat. Then the light bulb goes on and we think, *oh, that's how it looks*, and we find it easily done. The same is true of service. We might think service difficult, when Jesus serves with ease. We might think servants deadly serious, when Jesus serves with humor and levity. We might think service to take extensive plotting and planning, when Jesus serves spontaneously. We might think service draining, when service renews and invigorates. We might think service distracting from the mission, when service in Jesus's name is the mission. Jesus's model of service is a constant corrective for misimpressions that we might

146

draw even from the lessons that Jesus shares about service. We must hear how *and* see how to get the true sense of how service works. We must also ground and localize service in the fact that Jesus served us. No one provides service as completely and effectively as the one who appreciates the degree and quality of service received. If the Golden Rule is to do unto others as we would have them do to us, then its service equivalent is to do for others as Jesus does for us.

As he washed the disciples' feet at the Last Supper and told them to do likewise, Jesus also said, "I have set you an example that you should do as I have done for you." Jesus not only spoke and instructed about service, exhorted and guided about service, but he also served. Each of the six services that he urged in his discourse at the Last Supper he performed at times and in ways, along with many other services. He fed thousands of hungry with fish and bread while also feeding the soul with the words of life. Jesus gave inexhaustible drink to the woman at the well and many others. He invited odd outcasts and players at society's margins out of tax-collector booths, chains, and fishing boats, and in Zacchaeus's case out of a tree. He cared for and healed the sick, and made sure that John the Baptist in prison felt his fellowship and heard his word. He then gave his perfect life in the ultimate act of service, laying it most painfully and shamefully down in the dust to die that we should live. So when Jesus told the disciples that night that they should do as he had done, they had the complete and perfect role model, the meaning and embodiment of service, which is to do as Jesus did. His admonition to follow him, imitate and mimic him in service, was no weak or empty instruction but the best of all possible guides. Rest assured that none have served as completely and effectively as he served, and none will ever do so.

Her old church gospel choir used to sing, in what many regarded a little humorously and even scandalously, that *nobody do me like Jesus*. The song's valid point seemed to be that no one has made or can make the sacrifice for us that Jesus made. Oh, yes, one hears stories from time to time of someone giving up their life for another, perhaps a first responder rushing into a burning building to save a resident while losing the responder's own life, or a parent jumping in front of an oncoming car to knock their child safely aside while losing the parent's life. These acts, she thought, were supremely noble and

147

sacrificial nearly in the sense that Jesus sacrificed his own life. Yet she recognized that certain things distinguished Jesus's sacrifice from that of the parent or first responder. Jesus's suffering was intense beyond belief, not a moment's horrible realization or few seconds or minutes of pain but the worst form of death then and maybe ever known to humankind. Jesus's murderers also intended his demise to be shameful rather than noble. Likely, few or none at the time thought that Jesus was doing anything particularly noble or even worthwhile. Jesus accepted not merely physical agony but also government condemnation and bitter religious judgment in the course of his ignominious death. Yet some might still say that he gave his life needlessly, unlike the noble first responder or parent, the very point which may be Jesus's greatest sacrifice. He knew the ultimate truth, the present and attainable kingdom, and so badly desired it for us that he gave himself for that purpose while knowing that many, perhaps even most, would misunderstand, deny, and reject it. He served to the point of death, hoping that we might live as we have not yet lived and could never otherwise live without him. He served to the point of death for something far greater than our sin-condemned lives, which was his offer and the Father's offer of eternal life. He both sacrificed more and achieved more than anyone who will ever deign to serve. Now, go and do as Jesus did.

1.8 Working

Do not serve money. Luke 16:13. *Do not store up for yourself.* Luke 12:21. *Store up treasure in heaven.* Matthew 6:20. *Put money to work.* Luke 19:13. *Be trustworthy with a little.* Luke 16:10. *Pay your taxes.* Luke 20:25. *Guard against greed.* Luke 12:15. *Lend without expecting it back.* Luke 6:35. *Tithe.* Matthew 23:23. *Bring out good things.* Luke 6:45. *Bear fruit or else.* Luke 13:9. *Work for food that endures.* John 6:27. *Do God's work.* John 9:4.

While we recognize plenty of service occupations, in the spiritual sense serving carries with it the connotation of volunteer, uncompensated activity devoted to the good of another. Yet Jesus also had much to say about working, about things that we might consider more in the nature of *compensated* activity, or least activity for which we expect some reward. Jesus taught about what kind of rewards for which to work, how and why to work for rewards, and what to do with rewards. That Christ spoke much about working for and earning rewards may seem surprising to those who first see in Christ the sacrificial servant and draw from it a volunteer service ethic. Yet his teaching about compensated work, rewards for work, made sense to his hearers then and should make sense to us now. Who does not expect reward for work well done? Who does not justly expect causes to have predictable effects, for a certain order and fairness to govern our strivings? God's kingdom would indeed be an unusual place if perseverance in righteous faith had no outcome, no consequence, no recognition, and no reward. Christ made sure that his hearers understood how justly the kingdom operates, far more just than does the world in which we find so much unfairness in factions, oppressions in institutions, and grievance against governments. And yet the kingdom's justice is God's justice, not human justice, and the kingdom's reward God's reward, not human reward. For all that he taught about working, Jesus must have believed that our understanding of the subject was important. Listen to Jesus instruct on working for eternal rewards.

Do not serve money. Luke 16:13.

The thought that money is a master demanding service may at first seem odd. Money is inanimate, unthinking. How could we possibly serve it? Yet that inconsistency may be precisely the point that Jesus was most making when he said not to serve money. Indeed, we cannot serve money in the way of a true master because money is only a thing and not in any authentic sense a master. It cannot guide, counsel, instruct, or command us. We nonetheless *do* serve money as if money was our master, even though money has no such capability to be a master. What we do when we treat money as a master is listen to our own greed while pretending that our greed is apart from us. We project our greed onto the inanimate to placate our conscience. We do so by attributing money with the characteristics of a master, and with our own greedy characteristics, to say for instance that money is insatiable, that money never has enough, that money will fly away unless one jealously guards it, that money should keep us constantly thinking about how to satisfy it when instead we are only pursuing our own greed. One cannot pursue money as a false master while pretending to obey God, particularly because God's attributes are utterly unlike a greedy money master. God is instead generous beyond imagination with those who love him. One either serves the true God or the false master money.

Jesus certainly told parables and gave straight instruction about money, whether in his great Sermon on the Mount or at other times. In one of those other times, he told the disciples the parable about the shrewd manager whose rich employer suspected of waste and from whom the employer demanded an account. Knowing that he was about to lose his job, the manager struck good deals with his employer's debtors so that the debtors would support him after his firing. The rich employer ended up commending the manager for his shrewdness. Jesus gave the parable's lesson as to use worldly wealth to make friends so that heaven welcomes when the wealth is gone. We must handle wealth in ways that God regards as trustworthy in the kingdom, not in the greedy, accumulative, and acquisitive ways that the world expects us to handle wealth, which only serve the wealth and not God. "No one can serve two masters. Either you will hate the one and love the other, or you will be devoted to the one and despise the other. You cannot serve both God and money," Jesus concluded. The pursuit of money was just as much an issue in Jesus's day and just as much an issue for the religious leaders of his day, as it is an issue for us and our leaders.

He kept thinking how easy it was to articulate financial goals and how hard it was to articulate spiritual goals. A program of which he was a part required that he set short-term, intermediate, and long-term goals well into the future. The financial goals came to him easily, he knew *too* easily, as he ticked them off one by one. He wanted to increase earnings to a certain level, decrease expenses, pay off debt, accumulate a certain amount of savings, build retirement accounts, and save for children's education. All well and good. Then he turned to spiritual goals. What did he want to happen long term in his relationship with Christ? What short-term and intermediate objectives might he set to reach those long-term spiritual goals? The answers came much more slowly, which concerned him. He knew that he wanted Christ as master, not money as master, yet it seemed pretty clear from his familiarity with money's goals and demands that money was indeed his greater master. So he set to work over the next little while setting clear spiritual goals for the short and long term. He wanted to read the Bible at least annually and better yet all the way through at least twice a year for enough years to be intimately familiar with it. He wanted to develop and memorize a list of key verses until he found them guiding him in daily decisions. He wanted to pray, meditate, and be silent until he heard Christ's voice daily, and to journal his experience until he had evidence that his devotion had enabled Christ to approach and guide him more closely and often. His list of spiritual goals went on and on until he was satisfied that God, not money, was his one true master.

Do not store up for yourself. Luke 12:21.

We sow, we reap, and we sow and reap again. The virtuous cycle keeps our hands busy and our stomachs full, while enabling us to be generous to others with any excess in our earned provision. We do sometimes reap excess just as we sometimes reap but still lack because of the short crop. Jesus gives us a lesson in what to do with the excess. We are not to hoard excess so that we can indulge. Rather, we are to be generous with excess, sharing it with others. We are to be generous with excess because God was generous with us in providing the crop from which we drew for our need and accumulated any excess. God owns the full crop. We are stewards for God because God holds our lives in his control. We live and work on his terms and timetable. He decides how large the crop will grow and how long we will live to sow and harvest it. When we store up wealth, as in times of special plenty we occasionally must, we are to share that wealth generously rather than live in luxury on that excess. Storing up wealth may at times be necessary. Who can blame one for bringing in a larger-than-needed crop? Jesus's admonition is not to store up *for one's own self.* Sow often, water and tend the crop as it grows, and bring in the plenteous crop, storing it appropriately. But then share the excess.

When the crowd of thousands had gathered and Jesus started to teach them, he began with the parable of the rich fool storing up surplus grain in ever-bigger barns to live a life of ease, until God suddenly took it all from him, indeed took his life, and gave all his hoarded grain to others. Jesus concluded, "This is how it will be with whoever stores up things for themselves but is not rich toward God." Jesus made a priority teaching the crowd how to treat the abundance that God supplies. Surely, farmers, carpenters, traders, fishermen, shepherds, money changers, and others in the crowd had experienced abundance. Even if they had not, then they still would have hoped and perhaps expected to do so. Jesus's lesson in how to treat those earnings, how to treat an abundance of earnings over what their sustenance strictly required, was that day the most important of lessons because it was Jesus's first lesson. They were to be rich toward God, which in the case of handling God's abundance, meant not to hoard it. Hoarding God's abundance displays attitudes that God rejects, dislikes, and even abhors. Those attitudes include distrust of God's provision, which is also disrespect to God, and a lack of generosity and concern for his people for whom he has the greatest concern.

She might be thought miserly for the limits that she kept on her personal consumption. Although she could afford any clothing that she wished, she shopped for casual wear and even for business attire at the thrift store. She packed lunches rather than ate out, and cooked often, making an excess for leftovers to eat for the rest of the week. She wore out clothing rather than threw out clothing. She clipped and used coupons, shopped at the warehouse stores, and bought groceries and any other necessary items on sale. She hardly ever treated herself with a spontaneous luxury purchase. Yet for all her thrift, she hoped that she was sufficiently rich toward God and others. For as little as she spent on purchases, she was not in heart miserly. She just had little interest in acquiring, holding, or consuming goods. She found no particular security in her property and was not particularly interested in a life of any ease. She wanted to work, engage, and be productive, and felt that her sound savings were just being responsible for her own care and that of her family. To be sure that she was generous to God and others, she committed to regular giving at her church, listened carefully for special needs to satisfy, and was particularly generous with friends and neighbors. She hoped and prayed not to have a hoarder's heart but to be a most generous giver. She even looked forward to the day that her giving might be greater, if God should provide her with a greater excess.

Store up treasure in heaven. Matthew 6:20.

We produce goods with different qualities. Some of those goods, like the woven cloth, milled wood, and cut stone of the workers who heard Jesus's messages on the hillsides around the Sea of Galilee, or our smartphones and computers of today, are physical commodities that one can see, seize, handle, buy, sell, and store. The quality of those goods is tangible, measurable, and real but also surprisingly impermanent. What will the woven cloth or cut stone of Jesus's earthly days bring you today? Indeed, what will yesterday's flip-phone bring you today with the latest smartphone beckoning the masses? Commodities fluctuate greatly in value in many instances entirely unrelated to the effort that they take to produce them. They also do not necessarily represent any social value. They may one day bring great security, healing, relief, or enjoyment but the next day none. The hot products of today are the junkyards of tomorrow, eyesores and useless. An entirely different class of goods exists in God's kingdom. These goods directly represent social value or perhaps more accurately that odd word *righteousness* representing spiritual value. These goods do not decline over time in value or rust away, and no one can ever take them from us. If anything, their value grows rather than diminishes over time as we approach our full entry into the kingdom where they await us as reward. These goods are the goods that we should pursue presently to store in heaven.

Jesus was more explicit in the great Sermon on the Mount about what to do with God's abundance than simply to be sure to not store it for one's self. Jesus first reminded the large crowd listening on the hillside how hard things make it to store up wealth in the first place. Moths, rats, or other vermin destroy the cloth, grain, and other kinds of goods that members of the crowd were used to storing. Thieves break in and steal other kinds of wealth, such as if the owner is rich enough to procure and hoard gold, precious stones, and coins. Jesus admonished instead, "Store up for yourselves treasures in heaven, where moths and vermin do not destroy, and where thieves do not break in and steal." Where you store treasure is where your heart will be, Jesus added. Jesus wanted people's hearts to be with God and their neighbors, not bound to their material acquisitions. People matter, not wealth. The living God, not your inanimate things, deserves your heart. Be rich toward God, not your material possessions. Place your security in God, not in hoarded things. These were Jesus's admonitions.

He delighted in the thought and pursuit of God's own economy. He had a strong sense of economic responsibility, about acting appropriately within the world's workplace and household economy. He wanted to do what the Bible itself said to do, which was to provide for himself and his family rather than leave doing so to others. Given God's daily grace, he had the current capability not only to provide for today but to save for tomorrow to ensure no burden on the next generation, taxpayers, or others. Yet that whole earthly economy of savings accounts, retirement accounts, stock markets, and financial managers just didn't seem entirely secure, meaningful, or fulfilling. While it seemed *responsible*, it didn't seem *holy*. While it seemed forward looking, it didn't seem *eternal*. While it felt prudential, it didn't feel *guaranteed* or *certain*. He knew that nothing in the world was guaranteed, but he sensed and from his studies understood that everything in God's kingdom was certain because God promised it. He wanted God's promise more than he wanted an economist's forecasts. He wanted the certainty of God's love more than he wanted the probability of diversified stock portfolios. And the good thing, the really sure and predictable thing, was that through his Lord Jesus Christ, he had entrance to God's kingdom. He would be operating in God's economy, storing up treasures in heaven.

Put money to work. Luke 19:13.

When we do have an excess of earnings, as God's abundance may allow, then Jesus tells us what to do with it, which is to put it to work. Resources beget resources. Capital aids labor. Savings employed do more than savings hoarded. To simply hold money is to deny its benefit to others. In the wonders of a vital and just economy, one can instead deploy, invest, control, and multiply money, meaning make additional earnings from it, without losing it. To do so, one must make a fundamental shift in one's perspective on money. We learn to see money as the product of our labors. We learn to treat money earned from our labor as the item of exchange for goods and services necessary for our survival. The labor-earned and necessities-expended concept of money is the only one that many of us have for money. That concept alone would naturally lead us to hoard an excess of earnings to hold against a rainy day, for what other use has money than to provide for necessities? Yet Jesus gave us another perspective on money, which is to see it as accumulating capital to invest in promoting greater welfare. One can reasonably extend Jesus's perspective beyond money to any gifts that God grants, whether gifts of property, tools, equipment, time, proximity, or talents. God's bounty begets ever greater bounty. Those who have and use will gain more, while those who have not or have but fail to use will lose what they have.

Crowds lined the streets to see him as Jesus passed through Jericho on the way to Jerusalem. The crowd was so thick that a short man, a wealthy tax collector, climbed a tree to be able to see Jesus over the crowd. Seeing him in the tree, Jesus called him down and then blessed his household when the man promised to share his wealth with the poor. Jesus then told the crowd that had gathered to see Jesus's exchange with the wealthy tax collector a parable about putting money to work. The story, known as the parable of the ten minas, had a man of noble birth calling together his servants and giving them money, ten minas, while he left the country for a period. "'Put this money to work until I come back,'" Jesus quoted the man of noble birth as saying. When the man returned, two of the servants had indeed put his money to work earning more money, for which the man rewarded them handsomely. But a third servant had laid away the single mina that the servant had received from the man of noble birth whom he believed to be a hard master. The man of noble birth punished that servant and the others who had not trusted him enough to employ his assets. Jesus wanted the people to engage the talents and gifts that the Father gave them so that they could show the Father the many good things that those talents and gifts produced for him.

She had learned many good ways of putting money to work and was learning new ones all of the time. Of course, she wanted enough money to provide for herself and her family, but rather than jealously guard what she received each year, she instead trusted God to continue to provide as he had done for so long and so generously. She had been a good steward of those funds, which properly deployed had earned additional funds. Her growing bounty enabled her to give away and put to other good use ever larger amounts and percentages of her family's income. She had long hoped that she and her family would be able to do so, to be more and more generous, even if she had not made specific plans or arduous efforts. Instead, she had continued to trust God, draw ever nearer to Jesus, and pray for more of the Holy Spirit to give her the confidence and guidance to manage God's abundant blessings. Gradually, she was able to be more generous, not only in charitable giving and support of ministries but in just helping out with individual needs and community initiatives, whether the help required time, talents, or money. The more she gave, the more she received, not even yet counting any other rewards that God held for her in heaven.

Be trustworthy with a little. Luke 16:10.

Money requires trust. Money in itself is valueless, not worth the paper on which the government prints it. Start a fire with it, maybe? One might as well, if the money has no exchange value. Yet the kind of money to which Jesus referred when telling us to be trustworthy with a little is money that has exchange value, real money, credible money, money that in the right hands can accomplish things like purchase needed goods or services, or finance a new business venture, or employ a productive worker. Money gets things done, which is why one must be trustworthy with it. Money represents the ability to accomplish things, when God wants us accomplishing things using whatever abundance he gives us including material abundance, and including cash money. To misplace the money, forget that one has it, let a thief steal it, or allow it to sit idly by when it could accomplish something if put to use, those actions are being untrustworthy with money. To waste it on frivolous consumption, such as to gamble it away, or to give it to someone else who is untrustworthy and will waste it, is to be untrustworthy with money. Trust with money means prudential treatment and productive use. Money management reveals character, when God concerns himself deeply with character.

After Jesus told the disciples the parable of the shrewd manager who cut the bills of his master's debtors so that he would have friends on whom to depend, Jesus extended his teaching into a related instruction. After telling the disciples to use wealth to gain friends so that when wealth disappears God will welcome you into heaven, Jesus spoke about being trustworthy with any wealth, whether great or small. "Whoever can be trusted with very little can be trusted with much," Jesus told the disciples, "and whoever is dishonest with very little will also be dishonest with much." The amount in one's care matters little. The care is what matters, whether the amount is large or small. Dishonesty depends less on degrees of damage than it does on the quality of the action. Stealing is stealing even when stealing a little. Greed is greed even when being greedy with a little. A lack of diligence toward money is being careless even when the matter involves only a little. People with more to give one will notice whether one takes care of what little one has. So too will God notice and give or withhold depending on the diligence of the care. Jesus then further explained what he meant, saying that the one who is dishonest with worldly wealth God cannot trust with God's true riches. The one who is dishonest with others' money God will not trust with that one's own riches.

From when very young, she had been cautious about how she handled money. She learned early how to keep an account, a tiny savings account, and then a checking account with its confusing but important account statements and register. She also learned early lessons in investing, seeing value come or go with the degree of risk, care, and diversification in investments. Her only interest in managing finances had to be with being responsible. She otherwise had no particular attraction for money. She just didn't want to lose it unnecessarily and wanted instead to make it work as it should, understanding that money indeed had working value. She could certainly see in the families around her how money either worked or didn't work for them depending on how they regarded it. She saw that money revealed the godly character of some individuals and families in their appropriate level of care and concern for themselves and others, while trusting in God, or the godless character of others in too great a concern for money or for themselves, and too little concern for others. She just didn't want her money, the money with which God had blessed her, to reveal her as anything other than responsible, thoughtful, caring, generous, and productive. She knew that money was judging her, in a sense, revealing the degree to which she obeyed and trusted in God.

Pay your taxes. Luke 20:25.

No one likes to pay taxes. Everyone should do so. Some may find surprising that Jesus said to pay taxes. And indeed, the religious leaders' effort to trick Jesus with unanswerable questions may have been the primary reason why Jesus said to pay taxes, in the context in which he said it. God may not concern himself much or at all with whether citizens pay government taxes. Taxes may not be a divine edict, and paying taxes may not be a biblical principle. Yet behind the instruction to pay taxes lies an important lesson. We will owe obligations in this world different from the responsibility that we owe God. And we can often fill those worldly obligations without offending God, and should fill those worldly obligations so as not to offend others who might then think less of God. If Jesus had allowed the religious leaders' trick question to cause him to make a statement that would oppose God against government taxes, then we would have a major problem. Christians would stand against secular authority in a way that would undermine secular authority, Christian participation in society, and how others regard Christians under God's authority. Reconciling public duties with responsibilities to God can be difficult. But doing so is possible, and when possible, it is also wise. You may not like taxes, but pay your fair share so that you will have respected public authority while helping public authority respect you and Jesus. The government money with which you pay taxes has far less value than your heavenly coin.

The religious leaders had enough of Jesus teaching the people in the temple courts, undermining their authority while giving God authority. They thought of one trick question after another with which to try to catch Jesus in a way that would diminish his popularity, turn the people against him, and enable them to condemn and punish him. One of their questions had to do with paying taxes, whether everyone should pay taxes to Caesar. They figured that if

159

Jesus said yes, pay Caesar, then the people would turn against him because of the heavy tax burden. If Jesus said no, then he would have committed a serious crime that Caesar would punish. Jesus though saw their trick. Asking for a coin, he asked the religious leaders whose image was on it. Caesar's image, they answered. Jesus replied, "Then give back to Caesar what is Caesar's, and to God what is God's." Jesus had answered in a way that respected God's authority while also respecting Caesar's authority, and without angering the crowd. Jesus was far too smart for the religious leaders to catch with trick questions. Paying taxes with Roman coins is only giving back to Caesar what Caesar had minted. But the people including the religious leaders must give to God what is God's.

Jesus's instruction to pay taxes, or to give government what belongs to government, while reserving for God what is God's, helped him understand how to distinguish earthly and divine kingdoms and how to proceed responsibly in each of them. He found the distinction increasingly important. Life requires one to deal in the world, whether that means paying taxes or managing other legal rights and responsibilities associated with home mortgages, licensure for driving or employment, and other things of trade, property, and citizenship. He saw that the two kingdoms, earth and heaven, related to one another even though the latter, God's kingdom, was nonetheless wholly distinct because holy in constitution. He could not behave dishonestly in worldly dealings while aspiring to God's kingdom. Nor could he ignore God's kingdom while aspiring to succeed in the world. He needed above all to seek God's kingdom even while ensuring that his actions in the world pleased God. He wasn't going to shortchange the government on taxes, that much was sure. Doing so wouldn't work well in either kingdom. Yet he could also let imperfect and even unjust governments do as they would, advocating responsibly for just government while preserving his true devotion for God. Obey authority, but first save the soul. He loved Jesus's instruction.

Guard against greed. Luke 12:15.

160

For many of us, for much of our lives, we have the capacity to earn, whether in large or small amounts, but to earn. While God certainly wants us to employ the capacities that he gives us including the capacity to earn a living, that capacity can turn itself from a blessing to an idol if we indulge, pursue, and value it beyond valuing things of God. Earning is satisfying. Who doesn't like a paycheck? Yet when we look for satisfaction in how much or how consistently we earn, we will find nothing but temptation to greed, for God did not design us to find satisfaction in earning. Appetite for any wrong thing is insatiable. The more we feed it, the more it hungers. The same is true for unearned income, whether from investments, inheritances, gifts, or winnings. Who doesn't appreciate a windfall? Yet when we look for satisfaction in how much or how often we receive unearned income, we will find nothing but temptation to greed, for God did not design us for satisfaction in winnings. We will always want one dollar more. When God is present and available to us, which by the way is all of the time that we are present and available to him, we must not turn our face away toward money or any other material thing. We should continue to keep our mind and devotion on God, even while accepting and valuing his blessings.

In the same setting in which Jesus taught not to store up for oneself but instead to be generous with others, he also instructed to guard against greed. The crowd of many thousands that had gathered around Jesus included that one man who had asked Jesus to command his brother to divide an inheritance with him. Jesus's rebuke had been sharp, certainly much sharper than the man had at all anticipated. After all, the man had only asked for what he perceived to be justice. Here was a King whose concern should be justice, the man might have thought, and yet that King replied, "Man, who appointed me a judge or an arbiter between you?" Jesus's next statement might have struck home with the man even harder than Jesus's initial rebuke. Jesus continued, "Watch out! Be on your guard against all kinds of greed." He then continued to teach with the parable of the rich fool building bigger barns to store his wealth for a life of ease. The man asking for help obtaining an inheritance might have been wondering how he had shown greed. We don't know the details of the man's claim, which in fact may have been groundless and thus unjustly greedy. Yet no matter the merits of the man's claim, here was the King who at the moment that the man had demanded money had been teaching how the King would acknowledge the faithful before God in heaven. To desire money more than Jesus's recognition in heaven is most certainly greed, no matter the merits of the claim to the money. Watch out for all kinds of greed, even that claim that appears based on merit.

He knew that he had to set clear bounds on his pursuit of things, all things, even and especially the things that were generally good to pursue. His recognition came in part because of a compulsive or obsessive nature that he felt he had inherited as a family blessing or curse, he was never quite sure which one. Whether his drive to do things, sensible things mostly, but just to do things constantly, was a blessing or curse, he had learned that he must limit and control it, or better yet let the Holy Spirit help him control it. He had learned that pursuit of anything, even a good thing, can quickly turn to greed when one over-pursues it. That temptation was certainly true about working, earning a living, accumulating money. Yet it was also true about being generally productive, keeping busy, keeping clean, building a career, building a service record, or building a reputation. He had learned that one could be greedy about anything, meaning that one could turn one's face slightly away from God to pursue other things more than God asked. The one thing that he was learning that he could safely pursue without limit was not a thing at all but a relationship to a person, God in Christ. He must value the Giver more than the gift, keeping his face turned toward God.

Lend without expecting it back. Luke 6:35.

One way that we put our earnings, gifts, or accumulations to work is to make loans. One could make a loan to a family member, neighbor, or friend, or in an investment account buy government or corporate bonds, which are loans of their own sort. In doing so, we would ordinarily expect repayment. We define a loan in that manner, funds given now in exchange for funds repaid in the future, disregarding here whether the loans bear interest. A loan implies at a minimum repayment of principal. Jesus, oddly, says to make loans without expecting repayment, and indeed, to make those loans to enemies because God will pay us back. The instruction seems odd because loans involve repayment, we hope to be good stewards of funds, and why would we loan to enemies? Yet in the case of some loans, the borrower is not the one who pays the loan back. Parents sometimes guarantee their children's loans and, for better or worse, voluntarily or involuntarily, pay the loans back. So do spouses, business partners, insurers, and others. Borrowers do not repay every loan. So think again of what Jesus said. God repays the lender who loans generously to enemies. God is the guarantor of peace-making, generous, forgiving debt. He is also the One who rewards our generosity. Try it. Lend without expecting it back.

Jesus had already spoken several clear lessons to the large crowd filled with people from Jerusalem all the way to the coastline. He had summarized for them just whom God would bless and when God would bless them, and who would instead face God's woe. He had gone so far as to urge the crowd to love, pray for, and serve not just friends but also enemies. Then he went farther, urging the crowd to lend not just to those from whom they could expect repayment but to lend to enemies whom they knew would not repay them. What was this strange instruction to make loans that were not loans but gifts without repayment? What kind of economy did Jesus conceive? He explained that the credit that the crowd should seek was credit in heaven, not repayment on earth, credit in God's kingdom, not worldly return. Jesus instructed clearly and firmly, "Lend to them without expecting to get anything back." The reason, Jesus said, was that then your reward, greater than just getting your ordinary money back here, would be rewards in heaven and not just as an ordinary lender but as children of God. So God operates, Jesus explained, being kind to those who don't merit or appreciate it. God loves even the ungrateful sinner so much that God gives without expecting back.

They were ready to forgive the loan the moment that they made it. Indeed, although their borrower had insisted on repayment, they had not even structured the transaction in their own records as a loan. They had accounted for it in their own finances instead as a

163

gift. They knew that their irresponsible borrower would not repay it. They also believed that their borrower did not deserve or warrant the loan, that others would have been not only more-creditworthy borrowers but also more-deserving borrowers. The only reason that they could think of for having made the loan was that this irresponsible borrower had asked, and God said to lend to enemies without expecting repayment. While they did not regard the borrower as an enemy, indeed they could think of no enemies that they had, they certainly regarded the borrower as one with whom they had no desire to curry any particular favor. The absence of any interest that they could gain by making the loan was a big part of why they made it. They probably wouldn't be frequent lenders to irresponsible borrowers who didn't deserve the funds, probably wouldn't put them to particularly good use, and wouldn't do anything in return for their favor. But they were listening to God on this one, and God said that he had a reward for them greater than the reward of this irresponsible borrower's repayment.

Tithe. Matthew 23:23.

The tithe is certainly an ancient practice, one involving giving a tenth of one's income to God. In practice, to tithe means turning those funds over to the ministers of God who will devote the funds to the support of the religious institution, temple and synagogue then, church or synagogue today. Different churches place different emphases on tithing, some strongly or not so strongly encouraging adherence to it, others deemphasizing or disregarding it entirely in favor of the personal offering of whatever amount or percentage the giver discerns. Churches that encourage or even require tithing may differ on whether the percentage is on gross income or net income after taxes, and on whether a tithe is due from retirement or investment income or instead only on earned income. Along these spectrums, churches also differ on their interpretation of what the Bible and Jesus instruct regarding the tithe. Without purporting to resolve these differences, we can nonetheless do well to listen to Jesus instructing others that they should not neglect tithing, even while they do more-important things of God.

As seemed so usual for this Son of Man whose fame spread throughout the region, Jesus in this instance had crowds attending to his every word. Religious leaders must have been among the crowds on this day because after Jesus had spoken to the crowds about the religious leaders, he began to call out the religious leaders directly with woe after woe. In the midst of his condemnations of their practices, Jesus described how the religious leaders followed the practice of tithing to God a tenth of their income right down to the tiny spices but in doing so neglected other more-important concerns of God. Those concerns that the leaders neglected included justice, mercy, and faithfulness. Jesus explained, "You should have practiced the latter, without neglecting the former." Jesus told the religious leaders not to neglect tithing, which was all well and good, even as he told them to attend to the more-important matters of justice, mercy, and faithfulness. Tithing remains an opportunity and responsibility, even if other things mean more to God. God concerns himself more with righteous actions but when it comes to money also concerns himself with regular giving to God.

Years later, they were both relieved that they had been members of a church that encouraged tithing and that they had committed then to doing so. Of course at their first serious thought of it, the practice had alarmed or at least disconcerted them. They had not in their minds or household budget made that much room for God. They were also not really sure that their giving was going to God. Yet they continued to read and study the Bible, listen to pastors and other message-givers, listen to the Holy Spirit, and pray. Before long, they had recognized some power, purpose, and effect in the practice of tithing that they could begin to see and feel in their not-quite-tithing giving. Gradually, their commitment to the practice grew. At first, they were less regular than tithing formally required, despite their commitment. They were probably, if they had thought clearly about it, short-changing God. But gradually, their spirit changed, they grew more confident and generous, and they heard Jesus's words and other words of the Bible more clearly through their prayers and the Holy Spirit. They were tithing, and the sky had not fallen. They were tithing, and God was blessing.

Bring out good things. Luke 6:45.

How often do you think of the quality of what you produce, not whether it has literal errors or defects but rather the merit that it would stand in God's kingdom? What good does your activity produce? Jesus urges us to ask and answer these questions. One can go through life producing a lot of anything. For most of us, time is actually on our side. A life's work involves a *lot* of labor. Activity, busy-ness, is the human condition. We flit about like busy bees, doing whatever we do, in a hive of activity. Stop though to think of the quality of that activity. Does all that activity do much good? Sure, we can earn and earn, accumulate and accumulate, and indeed we generally should do so, keeping busy using whatever time, talents, and resources God gives us. Yet Jesus urges us to think now and then about the quality of that activity. Sometimes we need not think too deeply because whatever the activity is produces other benefits, like a paycheck, health insurance, and the necessities that both will provide. But other times require that we assess the connection between what we produce and the value that God gives it. In God's kingdom, activities and what they produce have different value than the value that an employer and its paycheck give them. We must also ask what our communications with others produce, whether peace and encouragement on the one hand or strife and division on the other, what our recreations produce, whether good health and spirit on the one hand or bad health and spirit on the other, and what our studies produce, whether wisdom and a good heart on the one hand or corruption and an evil heart on the other. Bring good things out of a good heart.

Jesus had taught the large, diverse crowd from all over the area for a while by the time he got to the lesson about the good tree and its good fruit. The crowd had heard of blessings and woes, love for enemies, and not judging others, and soon would hear of wise and foolish builders. Yet here deep in his message, Jesus spoke about the

166

significance of the *quality* of what we produce, not simply that we should use gifts and resources productively but that the quality of what we produce should be in itself good. Jesus introduced the concept by saying that good trees bear good fruit, giving the example of figs from fig trees, and good plants good fruit, the example grapes from grape vines. Thorn bushes don't bear figs, and briers don't produce grapes. Jesus urged that to have others consider you good, you must bring good out of the good that your heart stores. Hearts can store both good and evil. We choose what fills, or who fills, our heart. We then draw good from the good heart or evil from the evil. Fill the heart with good, Jesus was saying. Then draw out that good, for the mouth will speak that which fills the heart. We cannot fill the heart with evil and yet produce good. Jesus urged his listeners to be the good person who produces good from a good heart.

That she could often see so clearly the difference between a good person producing good and an evil heart producing evil amused her. Her amusement had to do with why the people producing evil did not see it as clearly as others did and, well, *stop* producing it. Some people were simply wrecks causing others wreckage, when everyone but the wrecker seemed to be able to see the wrecks coming. Yet as she reflected on the obviousness of the evil that some others were producing, she also began to look more closely at her own life. Every heart, she knew, has the capacity for both good and evil. Every mind, she knew further, has the capacity for deluding itself about the distinction between the two. She certainly didn't want to do evil, although she suspected that sometimes she did so out of things that she had not yet fully discovered and rid from her heart. More than simply avoiding evil, though, she wanted to do *good* things, sound things, sensible things, and things that people valued, actually things that *God* valued because people seemed to value all kinds of crazy things. So that assessment became her commitment that she would think often of what God thought of what she was producing. She knew, too, that she would need to fill her heart with the good Spirit of Christ if she had any hope of avoiding self-delusion and producing the good things that God desired. No wrecks, for sure, but also good things, really good things, out of the abundance of her activity.

167

Bear fruit or else. Luke 13:9.

Many mistake Christianity to be merely a faith of do-gooders who expect to earn their way into heaven. When they see little or no difference between the good that Christians and non-Christians do, a judgment by the way that is impossible for anyone to make reliably from personal observation or public account of individual behaviors, they assume that they can gain whatever heaven or other reward Christians gain simply by continuing to do whatever large or small good that they are then doing. Those who think this way are right in one sense but wrong in another. Jesus did make doing good both a survival imperative and point for reward. We must bear fruit or else. Yet he simultaneously indicated that relative judgments of the quantity of right- or wrongdoing are not the measures of who gets into heaven. We are all sinners, none of us doing sufficient good to earn our way into heaven. Comparing oneself to a Christian who does too little good is no way to rationalize yourself into heaven. We must instead turn away from evil and accept Jesus's payment for the evil we have already done and will inevitably do, while embracing Jesus's heart for good. We must bear fruit to get into heaven because the fruit will have evidenced our repentance and embrace of Jesus. No one repents and embraces Jesus without producing good. Bear fruit by embracing Jesus.

Jesus made clear in another parable the life-threatening implications for a person who does not turn from evil to produce the good fruit of a clean heart. Jesus had been speaking to a crowd in the Galilee region when some of its members told him that the region's governmental leader had ordered killed some of the local citizenry. Their implication was that those citizens must have been serious wrongdoers. Jesus corrected them, saying that they had been no worse in their wrongdoing than any other local citizens, or indeed than the citizens of Jerusalem, all of whom needed to change their ways to stop the evil that they were doing, or they too would perish. He then told a parable in which the owner of a vineyard ordered cut down a fig tree that had produced no fruit for three years. The vineyard manager pleaded with the owner to spare the tree for one more year while the manager fertilized it, after which he would cut it down if it still bore no fruit. Bear the fruit of a good heart, Jesus was saying, or perish in the evil drawn from an evil heart that refuses to turn from sinning. Jesus thus gave the way and warning to turn, and the imperative to turn in failure's mortal consequences.

He hardly considered himself a do-gooder. He had no delusion that he did any greater quantity of good, or that the good that he did do had any greater quality, than that good that many others did. In fact, he felt or knew that he did less good than many others, and he had plenty of evidence in their good works to support his conclusion. He also did not sense within his own mind any peculiar commitment to do good, or any passionate drive to do good, that others did not readily appear to exceed in their words and actions. He neither felt peculiarly good nor peculiarly effective at doing good. Instead, he almost felt as if any good that he accomplished was in spite of himself more so than because of himself. Whenever a small fruit of good appeared that he could not definitively attribute to another and had thus to attribute to himself, that fruit almost surprised him. Oh, he didn't regret doing good in any way. To the contrary, he wished that he could and would do much more of it. He would have loved to have been copious in producing good and in bearing much more fruit than the small fruits that appeared that he could not dismiss easily as the obvious work of others. He just knew that he, personally, did not have it in him. On the other hand, he also knew that one very good-loving and good-producing God inhabited him in at least some small measure and that he increasingly clung to that God for everything including his turning from evil. He only hoped that as time went on and his passion for the Father and Son grew in the way that he prayed that passion would, they would begin to produce more of their big fruit through and around him. He had seen big fruit before and wanted more of it nearer him. He had no will to perish.

169

Work for food that endures. John 6:27.

Isn't Jesus's assertion true that we so often and diligently work for mere food, the kind of food that only temporarily fills our stomachs, when we could be working for things that endure eternally. Given that natural hunger is insatiable and thus inevitable, we seem to face the choice constantly whether to move ourselves to satisfy our hunger or instead to think and pursue things of God. One suspects that fasting is a spiritual discipline precisely because of that constant choice in which we routinely pursue food over God's sustenance. If only periodically, if only for a meal, morning, or day, or at most a couple of days, we should consider not pursuing satisfaction of our hunger, simply to remind ourselves to pursue God in those moments. That both Moses and Jesus fasted for forty days is no mere happenstance or coincidence. The pursuit and presence of God are worth sacrificing the food that only temporarily relieves a continual hunger state. Although fasting is a spiritually healthy discipline, we nonetheless can of course both eat and pursue God through belief in Jesus Christ. Indeed, one suspects that the spiritual discipline of prayer before meals is, like fasting, precisely to remind us of pursuing Jesus even as we eat often and eat much. Eating as often as we do, we have few better ways to remember Jesus than to speak of him every time we eat. In any question over eating, fasting, praying, or pursuing God, though, we should remember that we are better off to pursue God than to eat. To work for food that spoils has a second, less-literal connotation that we should also know and value. Work apart from God, outside the will of the Father, the words of the Son, and the approval of the Holy Spirit, is work that spoils. Work with God lasts for an eternity.

Jesus had miraculously fed the crowd of five thousand from but a few small loaves of bread and a couple of fish. He had then moved quietly away up the mountain so that the crowd could not install him as a ruler by force. The disciples left across the lake by boat, where Jesus joined them in the night by walking across the water. When the crowd realized that Jesus and the disciples had gone, they also got in boats to find Jesus, finally locating him on the other side of the lake while wondering how had gotten there when the disciples had left alone in the boat. Jesus corrected them that they were not really searching for him because of the miracles he had performed but because he had filled their stomachs with free food. Jesus must have known that they were after him for the free food and filled stomachs, not for the miracle life of God. Jesus cautioned them, "Do not work for food that spoils but for food that endures to eternal life, which the Son of Man will give you." The crowd then asked Jesus what they must do to do the works of God, to which Jesus answered that they must believe in the one whom God has sent. The crowd needed to see Jesus for who he was, the Son of God, and in doing so they would have done the work that God expected of them. Jesus must have seen their doubting hearts.

Her life seemed centered largely around two things, the continual feeding of hungry stomachs and the happy pursuit of the things of God. Anyone would understand the stomachs part, particularly a homemaker with spouse, child, animals, neighbors, and friends. No one near her was in any danger of starving. Yet everyone with whom she spent her days was continually getting hungry. It was true. No sooner had one meal or snack ended than she needed to be thinking about the source, preparation, and timing of the next meal. Of course, she did better than wait for one meal to end before thinking of the next one. As in so many other households, she planned, shopped, cooked, and served on weekly, half-week, two-day, meal-to-meal, and snack-to-meal schedules. The point was that she was *always* thinking about meals, and not just because she was pretty much always hungry but because everyone was pretty much always hungry. Only occasionally did she resist, regret, or resent the whole food thing. Most of the time, she valued the opportunity to feed her family including its animals and to extend generous meals to neighbors and friends. Indeed, these works of love were precisely what endured. As God filled her heart with the love of Christ, Christ filled her days with loving service, works that she suspected endured not just until the next meal but eternally. As long as she had enough of Christ in heart and work, she suspected that he was counting her cooking and serving as *food ministry*.

171

Do God's work. John 9:4.

Jesus made it even clearer in another incident that we are to work together with Jesus to do God's work. Yes, to work for food that endures is to do God's work, that is, to do work that God recognizes and rewards. God's work may not, though, be just any good work. Good work that we do for our own credit, or good work that we do for a handsome monetary reward, or good work that we do by coercion such as under sentence or force, is probably not doing God's work, even though God would naturally prefer good work over bad. God's work has aspects of both being good but also being done for God rather than for other cause or credit. Good work would seem most to be *God's* good work when the work was both good and for the credit, account, and honor of God. Compensation for the work would not necessarily cancel the credit, account, or honor for God. That the work benefitted the one performing the work would also not necessarily make the work something other than God's work as long as God continued to get the credit, account, or honor for the work. Workers are worth their wages. Yet the worker must likely do the work *for* God, to God's credit, on God's account, with honor to God, for the work to be true God's work. Do the good work on account of God, with God getting the credit. Consider Jesus's example in the following account.

Jesus and the disciples were walking along together when Jesus noticed a man who had been blind since his birth, a man who had never had sight. The disciples made a study of his condition, asking Jesus whether the man had sinned or the man's parents had sinned to cause him to be blind from birth. Jesus corrected them that the man was not blind because of sin. The man was blind, Jesus explained, so that God's work might be on display in him. Jesus, it seemed, was about to act, about to do the work of God in the man. Jesus continued, "As long as it is day, we must do the works of him who sent me." Notice that he said that *we*, presumably referring to the disciples who accompanied him, must do God's work. Jesus added that night was coming, when no one could work. Jesus also said that *he* was the world's light as long as he was in the world. Jesus then made mud from having spit on the ground, put the mud in the man's eyes, and told him to go wash in a certain pool, after which the man was suddenly able to see. The man told the astonished people who recognized the now-sighted previously blind man that Jesus had given him sight. Jesus had done God's work.

This question of who should get credit for work bothered him more than most any other subject having to do with work. He was fine with work generally. He almost never minded work and instead candidly enjoyed many aspects of it including the people, energy, challenge, and monetary reward. What puzzled him, confused him, and distracted him from work was when people gave him credit for working or for work performed. He did not feel creditworthy. Those people giving him credit probably felt that they were simply encouraging him, recognizing him, and showing him appropriate appreciation. And when someone did give him some recognition or credit, he did feel an instant's relief, sometimes just enough to thank the person for the brief recognition. Yet his real sense was that he deserved no particular credit. He wanted to deflect the credit, and quickly, lest the recognition change the nature or quality of the work. After more reflection, he decided that he wasn't doing the work for his own credit. Indeed, he had an overriding sense that the more credit that he got, the less value the work had to him and probably to others. He was just doing his job. If the job had worked out in some creditworthy respect, then God deserved the credit. If anyone saw anything especially good happening, then he wanted them to see God in the work. He wanted to work for the account of God.

1.8 Persevering

Lift your head in troubles. Luke 21:28. *Do not worry about tomorrow.* Matthew 6:34. *Do not worry about your life.* Luke 12:22. *Do not worry how to defend yourself.* Luke 21:14. *Do not let your heart be troubled.* John 14:27. *Do not be afraid.* Mark 5:16. *Do not fear persons.* Matthew 10:28. *Take courage.* Matthew 14:27. *Stand firm.* Luke 21:19. *Stand firm to the end.* Matthew 24:13. *Persevere producing a crop.* Luke 8:15.

Work does not always appear to succeed, to accomplish our objective, at least not at first try. Jesus's instruction on persevering comes to us at just the right moment, when few or none of us would justly feel that we could ever do anything quite like Jesus did. Our natural response might be why bother even trying? Maybe we should give up before we even start. Beyond the conceptual challenge that Jesus seems to present us in urging us to do as he did, he who was the strongest, wisest, surest, and most vital human who ever lived, we face the challenge of adversity. In a perfect world, we might believe, pray, learn, teach, and serve, and even approach on our best days doing so as Jesus did, nearly accomplishing what he sets before us. Yet we do not live in a perfect world. Adversity rears its ugly head at the first step we take in belief or prayer, learning or teaching, or service. Of course, we are part of a spiritual struggle. We do not often comprehend that struggle's participants. Apparently, as God has revealed to some, angels fight demons all around us, the forces and effects of which we constantly face and sometimes even sense. Thinking about angels or demons, or even spiritual struggle, presents a special dilemma for the modern mind, one to which this book offers no solution. No matter its conception,

175

the point of Jesus's instruction that this section addresses is that he expects us to persevere. Listen to Jesus on perseverance.

Lift your head in troubles. Luke 21:28.

We might well draw two things when Jesus says to lift your head in troubles: first that troubles will come; and second that those who persevere, Jesus will serve well. Jesus would not have told us to lift our heads in troubles if he did not expect us to suffer troubles. No one really needs convincing that troubles do come, although a reminder now and then that Jesus predicted them can help us maintain the faith. We are not uniquely cursed or even cursed at all when we suffer trouble. Troubles come to all, even the righteous like Job whom Satan caused to suffer greatly until God restored twice his fortune. That trouble will come makes helpful Jesus's admonition to lift our head in trouble. To lift one's head has special meaning, when you think closely about it. Studies show that physical posture affects mental disposition. Holding your head up high and confidently can improve your outlook, which in turn can help you persevere through challenges. Thus to lift your head is both a colloquialism for persevering while also a remedy or aid to perseverance. Jesus likely intended from his instruction that we recall, value, and pursue perseverance. He may also have meant literally that we lift our head up in trouble to help us great through the trouble. Get through trouble, but also do the things that help yourself get through trouble. Sometimes you need a little boost, and your posture itself can be that boost.

Jesus did not always paint a rosy future, not even for believers. He instead had a clear apocalyptic vision, one that involved enormous stresses and challenges. Jesus predicted that people of faith would especially face great challenges, even while having his promise of the kingdom of heaven. "They will seize you and persecute you," Jesus told the disciples after having taught for a last time in the temple courts. Times would be hard for everyone as nation rose against nation. Jesus explained that the land would suffer great distress in earthquakes, famine, and pestilence. Jerusalem would suffer destruction, as the people fled to the hills. Even the righteous would face great wrath, with people fainting from fear over what was happening. Everyone would hate the righteous because of their love for Jesus, even their brothers and sisters. Yet Jesus admonished, "When these things begin to take place, stand up and lift up your heads, because your redemption is drawing near." Standing firm in the faith would bring them life because God's kingdom would be near. As these awful things happened, Jesus would be coming with power and glory.

As he trooped around his usual route on his daily walk, he lifted his head now and then to view the trees, hills, and sky. He realized then how deep in thought he had been, how dark his world seemed, and how hard he had been struggling to comprehend it to improve his situation in it. He didn't feel like he had much that he could do. Lifting his head alone seemed to take more effort than it was worth. He trooped further along, thinking for a moment how his desultory posture must look to anyone who happened to observe him. He didn't really care what others thought, but he did want to get out of this awful rut. It felt a lot like a spiritual challenge more than anything else. As he assessed his situation over and over, he confirmed that he had no foundational reason to hang his head, to pity himself, to be down in the mouth. God was just as good now to him as always. Christ was still at his side and in his heart. To get through the myriad small things that seemed to be nagging at him so effectively, maybe all that he needed to do was to persevere. Maybe all that he needed to do was to lift his head. He tried it for a few steps again, feeling a little lift as he did so, and then laughed to himself, even letting a smile appear on his forlorn face. Tests make us, shape us, refine us, he knew. Tests and challenges would come, he knew. He only needed to persevere in faith. He kept his head up the rest of the way around his daily loop.

Do not worry about tomorrow. Matthew 6:34.

We do worry about tomorrow, don't we? Too many of us spend way too much energy wondering and worrying what will become of us tomorrow. As today goes on, bringing us all that we need and also a lot of what we don't particularly need but may well desire, instead of enjoying God's blessing today, we worry about whether God will bless us tomorrow. Indeed beyond worrying about tomorrow, we burden ourselves with striving for tomorrow's provision before even having exhausted today's. Think about how much energy you have spent at times trying to plan and ensure that things will go well for you tomorrow while missing opportunities to love, care, and serve today. Today brings challenges, and so likely will tomorrow. We live day to day. We have no capacity to live in the future, only in the present. Time is funny that way in that it takes us in linear fashion from today toward tomorrow without tomorrow ever arriving. We will do tomorrow what we must, although it will then be today. Yesterday we did as we must have done, while waiting for today's doing. It is always today, never tomorrow, never yesterday. These are not word games but truths about living in the only moment that one can live, applying one's mental energies to affecting only what one can affect. If as is often the case we need to prepare for tomorrow, then we can still only do what today permits. We should worry less, and when we worry, we should promptly translate that worry into what we can do about it today. Rather than worry about tomorrow, act today.

Jesus spoke at length about worry in his great Sermon on the Mount. He had already taught much in the Sermon when he reached the subject of worry. He said not to worry about eating, drinking, or clothing, things that probably consumed the crowd to whom he spoke as much as they consume us today. He encouraged the crowd to consider how God cares for the birds that were probably right then flitting freely about the hillside, and how God clothes the beautiful flowers that probably right then covered the same hillside. Jesus pointed out that non-believers run after eat, drink, and clothes, while the Father knows already that we all need these things. He urged the crowd instead to God's kingdom and righteousness so that God could give eat, drink, clothing, and other blessings to them. Jesus summarized, "Do not worry about tomorrow, for tomorrow will worry about itself. Each day has enough trouble of its own." He then continued his great Sermon on other subjects, having addressed so thoroughly avoiding worry. Do not worry whether God will provide. Instead do as God directs, and let God provide generously without burdening yourself with worry.

Every time that she read it, she always felt that Jesus's statement that *each day has enough of its own trouble* was sad and true but also funny. That each day brings trouble was sad, she knew, because days should fill with joy rather than difficulty and sorrow. From her perspective, which she felt that she probably shared with a lot of others, the world had plenty of trouble and far too little joy, even if God's kingdom also brought incredible daily blessings. Jesus was certainly describing days accurately when he said that they bring trouble, all kinds of trouble. She took *trouble* especially to mean things that challenged her faith, kept her on her spiritual toes, on the lookout for things that might undermine all that she knew and sought in God's kingdom. Hardly a day went by when she didn't have to catch herself, remind herself, pull herself together, and persevere in her faith, some days much more than others. Yikes, she often thought, couldn't days bring a little less trouble? At the same time, she had learned that God was giving her just enough of his own Spirit for her to survive each day and, somehow, to prosper in her own spirit. She was tough in a way, although tough of a spiritual kind, more like *disciplined* to think only about today's faith challenge. She expected God to allow her to experience just enough challenge tomorrow, too, to increase her perseverance just as much as she was able, to grow in her faith just as much God knew she could grow. She came to the point of appreciating trouble not for the sorrow that it carried but for the choice that it gave her to occupy the kingdom rather than the world. The world she knew to be a troublesome place, while the kingdom was utter refuge even from trouble.

Do not worry about your life. Luke 12:22.

While we worry about having enough for tomorrow, we also worry about our life. We worry not only that tomorrow will bring shortage, want, hunger, and need, but also that today will bring the end of our life, or if not our literal death, then the end of life as we know it and wish it to continue. We invest ourselves in what we think that our life should be. Our investment sets our expectations and guides our actions. We do what we think will produce the life that we see for ourselves. We then worry when things do not seem to be going as we planned for our life, when events, obligations, and opportunities intervene. This approach to life that so many of us take so much of the time, projecting expectations and then worrying when circumstances look like they will frustrate them, is not the approach that Jesus instructs. Jesus says not to worry about our life. His instruction suggests a sort of casting away of expectations because expectations are the foundation for worry, which is to show concern that the future might not meet those expectations. We worry that we may suffer something that we would rather not suffer, face something that we would rather not face, or fail to achieve something that we want and expect to achieve. Worry has to do with anticipating the negative, foreseeing what we don't want to foresee and then regretting it before it even occurs. Jesus's admonition not to worry is not an instruction to stick one's head in the sand, to ignore probable consequences of things that we control and choose today. We should still act responsibly, thinking of natural and probable consequences. Rather, Jesus's admonition has to do with diminishing our expectations of what *will* occur. Do right, but let God determine the consequences, and know that God has acted for your benefit no matter how those consequences contrast with your expectations.

Jesus had spoken first to the disciples, and then to a great crowd that had gathered, before turning again to the disciples. The disciples he had warned against the hypocritical religious leaders who were following Jesus and the disciples closely to catch them in punishable blasphemy. When someone in the crowd called out to Jesus to make a brother divide an inheritance fairly, Jesus told the crowd to watch out for greed because life is not about abundant possessions. Jesus then gave a parable of a rich fool who, amassing plenty, decided to build bigger storehouses so that he could live a life of merry ease, only to have God take his foolish and greedy life that night. Jesus then turned again to the disciples, telling them, "Do not worry about your life." Jesus saw how others kept pursuing things rather than God and in doing so offending God while losing out on the bounty that God would provide them in the kingdom of heaven so near. Do not worry about your life. Worry about pleasing God who creates and sustains life, and rewards those who earnestly seek him in his kingdom.

He had long ago found meaning in the Apostle Paul's insight that *godliness with contentment is great gain*. He wanted both godliness and contentment, just as he hoped for concomitant gain. Yet Jesus's instruction not to worry about one's life, and his revelation that those who give up their lives will save them while those who cling to their lives will lose them, gave him additional clues about reaching that contentment. He had always had expectations for his life, as he thought that most everyone else had expectations. He began to realize, though, that those expectations were often not met, which produced a kind of confusion, anxiety, disappointment, or worry, a sense that something must be wrong either with him or the world or both. So he tried to moderate those expectations and before long to largely give them up. Oh, he still maintained what he felt was an appropriate ambition to do better for himself, his family, and others. He had every interest in improving his knowledge, wisdom, insight, and skills. He just no longer depended on what happened next to maintain that ambition. God would do as God would do. God might present him with an opportunity and task that he had never imagined. Why should he worry if God supplied something different from what he expected? He was learning not to worry but to believe, pray, learn, teach, serve, and trust.

Do not worry how to defend yourself. Luke 21:14.

We probably spend far more time and energy than necessary preparing to defend ourselves against things generally and around our faith specifically. Jesus says not to do so, that is, not to worry about defending yourself when the time comes to answer for your faith. In so saying, Jesus may have been referring to what many have discovered and shared since from a different perspective, which is that one of the worst ways to convince someone is to argue with them. Argument begets argument. Obsessing over elaborate justifications for one's faith in advance of any time when called on to give that defense may simply be preparing one's self to undermine one's own faith. Simple, confident, Spirit-led statements of faith may have far more powerful effect than arguments crafted from insecure faith, as the powerfully effective witnesses of the Apostles Peter and Paul quite well demonstrate. Live secure in your faith, which is not to say that words are completely unnecessary. Jesus also makes clear in his instruction that we will have words to speak, only that he through the Holy Spirit will be the one who gives us those words. Another insight Jesus may be asking us to draw from his instruction is that our words, which would be the words that we plan in advance out of our anxiety over defending our faith, have no power like the words that he supplies through the Holy Spirit. We must particularly rely on and dwell in the Spirit when answering for our faith. One might even profitably extend Jesus's instruction beyond defending one's faith to defending one's self generally. The more that we attempt to justify out of our own anxious words whatever we have done, the less we accomplish, while the more that we speak the Spirit's words over and around our beliefs and actions, the more we accomplish. Let Jesus's Spirit lead your defense, and you might be surprised what you accomplish, or more accurately, the Spirit accomplishes.

Jesus did not sugar-coat the future that the disciples would face for having followed him. He several times told them of their contrary great challenges including arrest, trial, and imprisonment. Even as he told of their perilous and difficult future, Jesus simultaneously reassured them nonetheless, "Make up your mind not to worry beforehand how to defend yourselves." Don't worry how you will defend yourself when the time comes to do so, Jesus was saying. One might assume that planning in advance for making a vigorous self-defense would simply be prudent, in preparing the rationale and justification for why one had supported Jesus. Yet instead, Jesus said that *he* would in effect prepare their defense. *He* would give his disciples words and wisdom that no one, not their worst adversaries, would be able to contradict or even to resist. The key was simply to stand firm in what they knew of Jesus. They had no cause for preparing elaborate defenses and certainly no cause to worry about how to defend. Although nearly everyone, even family members, would hate and betray them, none would harm so little as a hair on their heads if they simply stood firm in their faith. They would speak the words that Jesus gave them, and those words would do their powerful work of witness including the disciples' defense.

He had always been naturally quick to his own defense. He could guess why from family and psychological circumstances, which may have been exactly the point. He should not be relying on his personality, psychological makeup, and family dynamics to shape the quality and character of his communication. The more that he acted out of that makeup, the less he seemed to accomplish. He almost had to take a deep breath sometimes and to simply step back rather than jumping with his own words to his own defense. That little voice seemed to just prime his verbal pump with justifications in his own defense, when those justifications he could hear and realize himself were doing little more than undermining his own beliefs, character, and actions. Slow down, he would tell himself when speaking anything about why he did or was going to do something, and slow down the inner voice, he would tell himself when planning to speak in his own defense. Leave room for the Spirit to influence and speak. Things, after all, would be alright as long as he continued to think and act in pursuit of the things that Jesus represented and instructed. Live in the Spirit and speak in the Spirit, leaving out the worried defense.

Do not let your heart be troubled. John 14:27.

The world must be a troubling place, given Jesus's admonition not to let things trouble our hearts and not to be afraid. Of course, the world does bring much trouble and many things to fear, understanding that the *world* means conditions and experiences apart and distinct from God's kingdom. The world includes only natural life that ends with natural death, not God's eternal life. Death is a scary thing without God's eternal life. The world includes disease without God's healing, pain without God's comfort, want without God's provision, and confusion without God's purpose and plans.

183

Trouble is everywhere and peace very hard to find. The little peace that the world offers without God is only an ignorance-is-bliss peace, one that ignores current and future hazards if only for the little time that they allow such ignorance. Soon enough, those worldly troubles will once again be upon us, whether financial, legal, social, medical, psychological, or spiritual. The world does not offer the deep and lasting answers, the confident and reasoned peace, that faith provides. The world offers only a troubled heart, while God's kingdom offers eternal peace. To not let your heart be troubled is to recognize Jesus and follow him into the kingdom. We have no sound and reasoned alternative to God's kingdom that equally enables us to engage the world fully as kingdom work in complete peace. Do not let your heart be troubled. Pursue Jesus into God's kingdom to have the kingdom's peace.

Among the many profound revelations and critical instructions that Jesus shared at the Last Supper were his words about how we find peace in a troubled world. Although Jesus had so many things to say, he also said that his words that evening as at other times were not *his* words but the *Father's* words. One wonders at the detail of the record of his words that evening, wonders that the disciples were able later to recall and share so many of Jesus's words, but the disciples had the Holy Spirit's help in doing so. Jesus told the disciples that evening that the Father would send the Advocate, the Holy Spirit, to remind and teach the disciples about these many things that he said while Jesus returned to the Father. Jesus would not leave the disciples orphaned but would come to the disciples and live with them, the disciples in Jesus and Jesus in the disciples. Jesus then said, "Peace I leave with you; my peace I give you. I do not give to you as the world gives. Do not let your hearts be troubled and do not be afraid." Whenever Jesus said to do or not do something, he was giving the disciples such clear instruction. They were not to let their hearts be troubled and not to let themselves grow afraid. They had a choice to make, which was either to receive the peace that Jesus was giving them and leaving with them or instead to let their hearts be troubled and their minds afraid. Peace is a choice, just as troubled hearts and fear are choices. They may be bold choices, but they are choices, or Jesus would not have given the disciples this instruction.

184

She sure knew a troubled heart and fear. One could easily say that anyone does, although some are more calm and peaceful than others. Her natural disposition, proven to her a few times too often when she was young, as hearts prove themselves to anyone young, was probably more to the end of the troubled-heart scale than the peaceful end. That natural disposition made her deep peace of late all the more surprising. While hardly realizing it, she had sought that deep peace all of her life, finding instead only brief periodic peaceful interludes from her generally troubled heart. The fear itself for a long time concealed her nearly subconscious search for peace. Yet her glimpses of peace grew stronger as she matured and learned more deeply about the faith that she had nurtured since she was a child. Coming to Jesus was not her fundamental question because she had so long ago done so. Hearing, understanding, and obeying Jesus was what her maturity, coached by the Holy Spirit, achieved for her. With that obedience came peace. She had peace because she heard Jesus say that she had the choice of it. He had given her the gift of peace if she only obeyed him to accept it. To some, his words might sound too much like a formula for peace, just to choose it, but those who believed so would have misunderstood him. Jesus possessed the peace as his own. He was Peace in all its love, assurance, and contentment. This gift of his own is what he had given her, and she had finally come to the peace of fully appreciating and accepting it. Now, rare fear and a briefly troubled heart were all that reminded her of his kingdom gift of peace, now available to her as often and fully as she chose it.

Do not be afraid. Mark 5:36.

The source of perseverance presents a mystery. Why do some persons persevere while others do not, and why do each of us perceive sometimes but other times not? Jesus gives us a clear clue in his admonition not to be afraid. Jesus links the will to proceed with persevering to the decision not to fear. We persevere until fear overtakes us. When we submit to fear, the effect is to discourage and

185

soon prevent our persevering. Jesus wants us to persevere in trials and challenges, to hold fast to faith that overcomes the challenges. To do so, he says that we must not be afraid. His instruction both reveals and answers an odd conceptual challenge having to do with the nature and cause of fear. Many likely believe that fear is something that comes upon us. Well, I was *afraid*, we say in explanation of why we succumbed to our condition and ceased to persevere, as if we have little or no control over fear. We treat fear like an ungovernable emotion, when to the contrary, given Jesus's instruction, fear simply must have some element of our control. Jesus would not tell us to avoid something that we cannot avoid. He would not instruct us to attempt an impossibility. If he says not to fear, then we must have the ability to fulfill his instruction. We must be able to choose no-fear over fear, or he will have asked of us the impossible. Fear is no explanation or justification for failure. Fear is instead the choice not to trust the persevering action's outcome. Fear is thus unbelief in disguise. When we refuse to persevere in faith, we do so not because we fear a negative outcome, although that excuse will be our rationalization, but instead because we have lost faith in the positive outcome. *Do not be afraid* is not a gentle mother's reassurance, not in the way that Jesus says it. It is instead a King's command to trust him because he is trustworthy. Fear is failure, not emotion.

On his way to the synagogue leader's house to heal his daughter, Jesus overheard some people tell the leader that their effort was too late because the leader's daughter was dead. Jesus turned immediately to the synagogue leader with an instruction. His instruction had to do with the leader's persevering in the faith that the leader had already exhibited in calling for Jesus to heal his daughter. Jesus wanted the synagogue leader to persevere even when confronted with this apparently insurmountable new challenge that the leader's daughter was no longer merely sick but now was dead. Daughters simply do not rise from the dead. No one could have blamed the leader if he had thanked Jesus for being willing to heal his sick daughter but called off any further effort because the daughter was now dead. The leader had every sound reason to give up, to refuse to continue rather than to persevere. Jesus, though, did not tell the leader precisely to persevere but instead not to *fear*. Fear, apparently, confronts and overtakes perseverance. You cannot have one with the other. Either you fear and quit, or you refuse fear and continue. Jesus told him, "Do not be afraid," even as he told the synagogue leader to believe him. They then resumed their trip to the leader's house, although Jesus would only let the three most-prominent disciples Peter, James, and John accompany them. Might it have been because he wanted no company other than those who did not fear?

She had not thought of herself as particularly fearful, although she was still discovering things that she likely had once feared. She had accepted various challenges, healthy and positive rather than foolish and daredevil challenges, despite that many of her peers including some of her friends had foregone those challenges. She had risked, persevered, and invested, where the outcome was not assured but possible and, if achieved, more than worthwhile. She had not even had much confidence in herself that she was more than potentially capable, and only with a lot of help and God's providence and protection. What was most interesting to her was that she now saw that her growing faith had been the source of her growing courage. The tiny fears that her faith had revealed, her faith had also banished. She thus felt that she had not accomplished these things as much as her faith had accomplished them, which was to say that the Spirit of Jesus had accomplished them through her because she knew that her faith was the faith of Jesus. She had operated largely without fear because she had operated on the faith of Jesus who knows no fear. She had not ignored or somehow willed her own courage. She had instead relied more and more heavily on the powerful Spirit of Jesus, feeling like the Spirit had carried her along on this wonderful journey that she could not have achieved, indeed would not have foolishly dared, if she had acted on her own inclinations. Do not be afraid, she thought, because Jesus is not afraid.

Do not fear persons. Matthew 10:28.

Sad to say, but one of our common fears has to do with people. Yes, disease might be a fear, along with natural disasters like lightning, earthquakes, and tornados, and then animals like reptiles, sharks, and spiders. We might also fear motor-vehicle accident, home fire, air crash, or other mechanical and artificial disasters. We might even fear financial meltdowns, legal liabilities, or losing home, farm, or other property rights. None of these fears, though, has to do with one other great fear, an overriding fear of many, which is the deliberately competitive, destructive, or otherwise interfering intent of persons. We may find in the world more reason to fear the intent of a person than circumstances or events. People purposefully harm people, particularly when they cannot otherwise have their way with those people. Efforts to stand apart, to do as God says rather than as people demand and generally do, may well increase the risk of harm by those other people whose demands we do not fulfill. Jesus said as much when instructing the disciples not to fear others who had the capacity and interest to harm them, and indeed would in some cases harm them. His instruction not to fear intentional physical harm by others that would actually occur bears special notice in that he explicitly coupled it with God's saving the soul. The person who forgoes the body to save the soul need not fear the body's destruction because God will resurrect the body of the saved soul. We should instead fear God that we not lose our soul, having hell then destroy both body and soul. Do not fear that others will kill you, where fearing would have you deny Christ and in doing so cost you your soul. Save your soul in Christ, and God will save your body.

In instructing the disciples how they should persevere on their first trip into the mission fields, Jesus told them not to fear those whom they would encounter, who would actively oppose them. Jesus said, "Do not be afraid of those who kill the body but cannot kill the soul." The disciples must not fear those who might even go so far as to kill the disciples' bodies. Fearing what people said or did in response to the disciples' gospel message, even fearing that they might kill the disciples in body, could cost the disciples their souls. If they denied Christ, then they would have lost their souls in a futile attempt to save their bodies. Jesus continued to say that the disciples should instead fear the one who can destroy both body and soul in hell. Denying Christ would leave them in hell. While the natural body would die in either case, whether killed by the disciple who stood for Christ or lost to the inevitable natural death, the losing one's soul to hell by denying Christ would destroy all prospect of a resurrected body. The choice Jesus instructed was simple, to save the soul, because the body is lost to natural death either way. The disciples must instead always think first and last of saving the soul. Jesus's instruction was to stand for him always, even when threatened with death.

He found it awfully hard to admit that he probably feared people more than anything else, maybe even more than death. He could not explain his fear of people, although he had a vague sense of its worldly psychological and emotional source. He didn't so much fear violent people, like a sudden and unexpected attack from a hidden adversary. No, he feared *all* people, without reason or distinction. His fear wasn't even quite a fear of physical harm but more a fear of existential denial. He feared not that people would hurt him but that people would deny him, and not that they would deny him what he wanted because he didn't want that much, but that they would deny his immanence, in some way denying that he *was*. He hardly realized it for most of his life, but he depended on people in order to validate him, not just to validate his merit or worth but to validate *him*, his very existence. The most frightening thing was that he also feared himself, the dark power within him to deny his own immanence, meaning that sliver of divinity that gives each of us intrinsic, unjustified, pre-existent life. He learned though from a close and meditative reading of Christ's own words that these fears none other than Christ could banish. He *could not* lose his soul if Christ were to dwell in him and if he were to live in Christ. His choice to accept and obey Christ, and to live in God's kingdom, was his only choice. He was nothing outside of that kingdom, only a figment of the dark power's imagination.

Take courage. Matthew 14:27.

Not to fear is one thing, while to take courage is another. Banishing a negative state like fear is certainly possible. We can in a figurative sense wipe the emotional slate clean. We can once again assume a neutral stance or state, neither negatively fearing nor positively anticipating the next moment or event. We can make ourselves non-committal either to hope or despair, faith or fear. Yet on our journey away from fear, we should prefer to take the next step beyond the blank-slate uncommitted neutral to the positive hope expressed in faith. Jesus instructs exactly that. Beyond banishing fear, we are to demonstrate resolve. We are to act with courage, be courageous, show some substance, and develop some finer mettle. We have lives to live, each of us a life that he has planned for us, a life certainly not of fear but also not of a safe or inoffensive kind of languor, sluggishness, or listlessness. His life for us is one of forward-moving and confident action, of resolute commitment to a course. As we take courage, he takes action through us, creating opportunities and outcomes that we could not have seen no less obtained for ourselves. We must only take courage and have faith. Banishing fear makes a good start, but then grasp and exhibit courage.

Jesus had more to say about persevering than simply prohibiting fear. He also gave the disciples the flip-side positive instruction to be courageous. The specter of Jesus walking out across the lake's water to them in the boat unnerved the disciples just as it would anyone, especially because the disciples did not at first recognize that the specter was Jesus. An unknown water-walking apparition would bedevil any of us, just as it did the disciples that night. Jesus had a prompt response to the disciples' terror, though. The passage says that Jesus *immediately* called out to them. Jesus's presence, his revealing his identity to the disciples by saying *it is I*, was instant even if still only partial reassurance to them. Peter wanted verification, and he got it in the form of Jesus's invitation to walk to Jesus on the water. Yet in the midst of this back-and-forth ghostly communication, Jesus gave the disciples that positive instruction, "Take courage!" Do not merely banish fear but also grasp the character of confidence. The words and presence of Jesus should have given the disciples mettle and resolve that they required straining to make out an unprecedented apparition. The disciples had no reason to fear any apparition but instead to fear, in the sense of *obeying*, only the commands of Christ.

She had grown up thinking that her immediate family, her own household, entirely lacked any degree of courage. She saw in other families what she construed at the time to be great acts of courage, while her own family looked to her like a bunch of what people her age called *wimps*. They never did anything bold or daring. Stultifying caution seemed instead to be their approach to all things. Yet as she aged from early and middle childhood into late childhood and then early adulthood, her family's approach looked less like timidity than plain old common sense. Simultaneously, as the sense of her family's actions took shape to her, she also began to notice things that looked to her like real courage, authentic courage, not the things that she saw in other families that were now beginning to look to her like foolhardiness and even obviously destructive behavior. As she matured further, she saw more evidence of her family's courage in just the place that she was learning to place it herself, which was in faith. As it turned out, her family was about as bold and courageous in its faith as any other family she knew, and maybe a little bit more so, in just the ways that she was learning herself. Oh, they were not daring missionaries, when maybe they should have been. She had recently found plenty of quiet models and heroes of that particularly courageous type, to which she suspected her family would never come close to measuring up. But she also suspected that courage has its own types and measures for each, including for her, and that she should pay closest attention to taking of courage what she could. And she knew precisely where to find it, in Christ.

Stand firm. Luke 21:19.

Perseverance has more than one expression, connotation, or illustration. Yes, to take courage is to persevere, courage impelling us to hold fast to our faith and act on our faith while setting aside and leaving behind fear. Yet to persevere could also be to *stand firm*, as Jesus also admonishes. Sometimes, faith requires taking courage and moving with that courage. Other times, faith requires standing firm and not moving. As with so many of Jesus's other instructions, to stand firm has both literal and figurative meanings, each of which to some degree Jesus likely intended. Maintaining one's faith in the face of imminent desolation, whether destruction of property or injury to person, sometimes means literally not running, not moving, and instead standing in the same place. Flight often follows fright. Rather than flee in fear, we find times when faith demands that we simply sit tight, hold our ground, maintain the battlements, and stand in the breach. The figurative meaning of standing firm would be not to give up spiritual ground, not to deny Jesus, not to adopt a secular, godless stance when challenged in our faith. Once we learn the truth, recognize the historicity, authenticity, and rationality of faith in Christ, we should not unlearn that truth when persons or circumstances challenge it. Standing firm on conceptual ground is like standing firm on physical ground in that it takes a sound and sure commitment. Stand firm in the face of fear, and stand firm on faith in faith challenges.

As Jesus described to the disciples the temple's soon-coming destruction and the desolation that would accompany it, he had a consistent message for the disciples that they were not to crumble along with the temple. The temple would not stand. Fine buildings, no matter how sound and spectacular, do not survive wars and marauders. Buildings fall, bodies of course fall often long before buildings, but godly souls, meaning souls finding their righteousness solely in Jesus, survive. With the survival of souls, God resurrects the fallen body into eternal life. So about the coming destruction that he foretold, Jesus also told the disciples, "Stand firm, and you will win life." The kingdom into which Jesus invited the disciples and invites us is an eternal kingdom where the Temple who is Jesus reigns forever, and we reign with Jesus. Even as he foretold destruction including crumbling buildings, national demise, and bodily death that the disciples might most fear and regret, Jesus simultaneously said in short to ignore it, not at least to worry about it, and instead to stand firm in the face and occurrence of it. What the disciples had to fear was fear itself, the solution to which was simply to stand firm.

His work had taught him much about standing firm. It had first taught him that he should choose with care the ground on which he decided to stand. No point in standing firm when the ground itself will soon give way. Discernment in choosing positions and sides to take enables one to stand firm. Making foolish and unsound commitments in the first place soon undermined one's willingness and ability to stand firm. So he had to get first things first, to build the solid foundation on which to stand. He had also learned that once you choose the ground, you must stand to defend it even when in the face of attacks it begins to look or feel like the wrong ground. That undermining of confidence is what challenges do. If he took the ground on good cause in the first place, then he must stand firm to defend it even in times that it looked, well, indefensible, as long as his stance still stood for first principles. He learned that he could live with losing a good fight, again as long as the fight was from first principles. None of these lessons was easy. They were all hard lessons to learn but necessary lessons. They had shaped him, he was sure, and he was just as sure that the lessons would keep coming. The last thing that he had learned, though, was to welcome the lessons. Better to be in the good fight standing firm than to flee the fight or watch from the sidelines.

Stand firm to the end. Matthew 24:13.

The admonition to *stand firm* is great as far as it goes but leaves the question open as to how long one should stand. History gives us multiple accounts of military officers, politicians, scientists, philosophers, missionaries, and others who stood firm until their end or the conclusion of their cause. These individuals find their place in history because of their having remained so steadfast. History also gives us multiple accounts of individuals who left their position early, leaving it to others to defend to the end. We learn of those individuals in history only because of their fecklessness. Yet history also gives us accounts of individuals who stood firm in adversity's face for a good long time but who abandoned their position just before the end. History preserves for us the names and record of these individuals because of their tragic near miss at glory, their sometimes enormous and heroic effort lost at the last moment, with the loss going all of their reward in glory. These individuals include the explorer whose bones and note pads lie just short of the goal of discovery, the military officer who lost the war for having finally given up the critical winnable battle, and the scientist who recorded but never published the ground-breaking formula. Standing firm means nothing if one does not stand firm to the end.

When the gospels give us multiple accounts of Jesus's teaching on the same subject, even when describing the same moment, they sometimes give us small differences in the account of what Jesus said or how he said it. Those differences do not mean that one account is correct and the other incorrect. Jesus may have said both things precisely as recorded, in parallel repetition as speakers, particularly teachers, often do to ensure their audience's understanding. Alternatively, both accounts may have been fair interpretations of something slightly different that Jesus had said. And when reading the gospels, we are after all reading translations of writings reproduced and handed down from what were initially oral accounts. Whatever the explanation for these slight variations, the words and their meanings remain important. In a different gospel account of the temple's coming destruction, Jesus told the disciples not merely to stand firm but to stand firm *to the end* in that "the one who stands firm to the end will be saved." Jesus concerned himself and concerned the disciples with finishing, with ending in the right place, as we should concern ourselves accordingly.

He was nothing if not a finisher. He was so driven to complete things that he strongly suspected that it was a character defect, an obsession and compulsion, and one that he must watch carefully lest it be his demise rather than his salvation. Whatever he started, or others started within his responsibility, he *had* to finish, whether that meant right at the moment or through thick and thin in utter diligence. Some things he could finish instantly, while other things were going to take a few hours or maybe a few days or even weeks. Other things he knew would take years, even decades. One way or the other, though, he was going to see them through. And every one of them he treated as a matter of life and death, or more accurately, he treated as if he might die before he finished them if he did not act promptly, diligently, and surely. Gradually, though, he began to connect his compulsion to finish with his faith. Maybe finishing jobs, tasks, projects, initiatives, and commitments was only an expression of remaining steadfast in faith. Maybe finishing *things* mattered not at all, when finishing *faith* was instead the critical ingredient. He began to think that as his ability to complete things waned and projects paled in significance that he must be sure that his faith did the opposite, growing in strength that he would stand firm to the end.

Persevere producing a crop. Luke 8:15.

Why persevere? What precisely is the point? Salvation, we learn, is through Christ. Christ persevered to the point of completing his glorious mission, of which we are eternal beneficiaries. So what difference then does *our* perseverance make? Jesus clearly taught that our perseverance does make a difference. When we persevere, we produce things of value. Certainly, perseverance in pursuit of worldly things often produces worldly rewards. If you want to earn a larger paycheck, acquire more material goods, or gain greater fame, then persevere in the kind of worldly activities that produce those worldly rewards. Work longer hours with greater discipline overcoming more obstacles to achieve those goals, and you will very probably come closer than you would have if you had given up at the first challenge. Perseverance has its secular expression. We know perseverance often works in the world. Yet the crop that Jesus wants us to produce is not the world's crop. He probably cares not at all for the size of our worldly paycheck, home, fame, or reputation. Rather, persevering in his kingdom produces the kind of kingdom crop that he values and rewards. When we persevere in faith, we produce a crop of kingdom righteousness bearing eternal reward.

Jesus's parable of the soil, told to a large crowd, holds such meaning for us in large part because of Jesus's explaining it afterward to the disciples. The farmer had spread his seed on the path, rocky soil, thorn-choked soil, and good soil. Only the seed on good soil took root, grew, and produced a crop one-hundred times what the farmer sowed. Later, Jesus explained to the disciples what the seed, path, rocky soil, thorns, and good soil represented, giving wondrous insight not only into the parable but also into the manner by which Jesus taught. Jesus finished his explanation to the disciples by saying about the good soil, "Those who hear the word, retain it, and persevere produce a crop." Jesus was urging nothing in particular about literal seed planting. The large crowd may well have included many farmers, but Jesus was not teaching farming. He was teaching about his hearers' hearts, how his hearers should act in ways that fairly represented and demonstrated his good Spirit within their hearts. The members of the crowd and disciples must persevere if they expect in any way to produce good things, righteous acts and faithful character that God values and rewards in his kingdom. One enters the kingdom through Christ, but one earns a kingdom reward through perseverance with Christ.

She had not been a particularly persevering person when young, and she knew it. Yet she was undoubtedly remarkably persevering now. She felt a tiger-like passion for perseverance lurking within her, even when she felt physically and emotionally drained, which was more often than she wished. She could be as tired and discouraged as she might, and still she felt that she could and should forge ahead with whatever initiative God had given her, of which she had many. That passion she indeed attributed to faith, to God in Christ, Christ in God, and Christ in her. She knew of no other source for that vitalizing drive in life than the one great Source, knew of no other reason to rise in the morning when her body and soul did not really want to rise, knew of no other reason to persist when her hands and spirit did not want to persist. She also found in faith that she believed that her rising and persisting was making a difference, not necessarily in the results that she saw, for too often the results looked meager or even appeared negative, but in the results that she *anticipated*. Somehow, the Spirit had helped her accept, adopt, and *incorporate* that belief that good results were accruing from her persistence in Christ's righteousness, and even beyond good results, good *rewards* were accumulating in the kingdom. And so onward she went, whether lame or blind, weak or discouraged, from glory to glory in his kingdom.

1.9 Succeeding

Do not seek praise from people. John 5:44. *Do not love praise from people.* John 12:43. *Do not love the important seats.* Luke 11:43. *Take the lowest place.* Luke 14:10. *Do not exalt yourself.* Luke 18:14. *Humble yourself.* Matthew 23:12. *Be humble when only doing your duty.* Luke 17:10. *Guard against hypocrisy.* Luke 12:1. *Hunger for righteousness.* Matthew 5:6. *Let your light shine.* Matthew 5:16.

People may reasonably believe odd that Jesus should have to admonish us about success. Of all of the things with which we should be able to deal, success might seem to have been the one. If we cannot deal properly with success, then what chance do we have of dealing properly with challenge, loss, hardship, or failure? Success should be easy, which may be the problem. Success holds the allure and expectation of ease, and indeed some opportunity for ease. Success builds confidence, and not just confidence in God and his wonderful bounty, but also *self*-confidence, the larger the success, the greater the self-confidence. Indeed, with much success, we might just feel as if we do not need God, do not need to listen to and follow Jesus's instruction. We could claim the success as our own, due to our own skill, insight, and capacities. What, after all, did God have to do with it? We also might begin to value success, to love and cherish success, more than we value, love, and cherish God. Who needs God when one has success? Thus a little thought quickly demonstrates our need for clear and strong advice on dealing with success. We may need more and stronger advice on success than we need for failure. Failure is a great teacher, while success is a poor teacher but one with great allure. Listen carefully to Jesus on his instruction about success. Follow Jesus rather than love and pursue success without him.

197

Do not seek praise from people. John 5:44.

So many of us live for the approval of others. Wanting to do well by others is not a bad thing but a good thing. We should be good sons, good daughters, good employees, and good neighbors. When we act fitting for the circumstances, whatever those circumstances might be, we may justly accept and appreciate the recognition of those before whom we act. The problem begins when we act not because doing so is fitting, proper, and approved of and commanded by God, but instead in order to achieve those strokes of approval. *People pleaser* is one term for those of us who emphasize gaining the approval of others over the obligation, responsibility, satisfaction, and righteousness of doing proper acts. When people pleasers do not focus on God and his commands, admonitions, and desires, and they focus instead on pleasing people, their distortion soon undermines their service or work. Work becomes a show rather than a service. Anything done for show is only halfway done because the work concludes when the honor dissipates. Moreover, you cannot please people enough to fill a personal need for approval. No one can fill for long your tank when empty of approval. The people pleaser ultimately disrespects the people and the work, just as the people disrespect the people pleaser. And if working solely or primarily for the approval of others does no good for us, then doing so does no good for those from whom we seek approval, either. We call them *flatterers, sycophants,* and *brownnosers,* those who heap false praise on those who seek and need approval of others.

Jesus had healed a man who had been an invalid for decades, telling the man to pick up the mat on which he had lain so long, and walk. The man had miraculously done so. The religious leaders saw the man carrying his mat on the Sabbath, which violated their rules. They told him not to do so, but he replied that the unknown man who had healed him had told him to pick up his mat and walk with it. When the man later met Jesus at the temple and realized who he was, the man told the religious leaders, who began to challenge Jesus over it. In reply, Jesus told them that he is always at work because his Father is always at work. He then explained much more about his relationship with the Father including that Jesus was the One about whom their scriptures testified. He then said that he was not seeking the religious leaders' approval because unlike the religious leaders, he does not accept human glory. He added that they sought the approval and regard of other humans rather than seeking God's approval. Because they were concerned only with human affairs rather than God's affairs, they did not even recognize and believe in Jesus. Jesus asked, "How can you believe since you accept glory from one another but do not seek the glory that comes from the only God?" They should have sought God's approval rather than the honor of men.

He knew that he was far too much a people pleaser. He knew precisely what being a people pleaser did to him, how it did nothing more than twist him into unhappy knots, first in making too much effort and then, when not gaining all the approval that he wanted and felt that he deserved and needed, making too little effort or even abandoning the work. He knew that being a people pleaser made him proud at times and despondent at others, far too often high or low, and always acting for a show. He even knew why he was such a people pleaser, including his family history, psychological makeup, situational challenges, and obsessive disposition. The sad thing had been that for years, his knowledge of his broken condition was alone not enough to help him stop seeking the praise of people. What he needed was a *do* more so than another *do not*. He suspected that he could not stop pleasing people until he found something or someone else to please. And then he discovered whom to please, a God who both accepted glory and gave glory in its full measure and weight. Pleasing, he discovered, was definitely not a bad thing. He had just to decide whom he would please, which by that point was an easy decision.

Do not love praise from people. John 12:43.

Some things that we seek, we nonetheless hate. Other things that we seek, we come too much to love. Those of us who are people pleasers, seeking the praises of others over simply doing good works, may or may not love the few praises that we obtain. Loving those praises that we do obtain causes new problems beyond seeking them. Attributes like vanity, pride, narcissism, and arrogance come easily to mind when thinking of the person who loves the praise of others. These are not attractive attributes. They are instead deadly attributes, comprising character that leads quickly to condemnation and ultimately to death. When you sense in yourself that love of the praise of others, call it what it is, and flee from it. You cannot love praise on the one hand and God on the other. To say that God is jealous of praise is no knock. If he were anything else, then we would have no hope for us because self-love of that kind leads directly to destruction. To love praise from others is indeed self-love, a turning inward to value highly regard for oneself as measured in the praise of others. God did not create us for turning inward on ourselves but for turning first to God and then in his Son's image to others. We have divine origin and destiny, not solely human origin and destiny. Self-love measured in the praise of others cuts off divinity. God does not relinquish his praise to others. Let God praise you, and love no other.

Jesus had spent three years of public ministry performing miracles, healing, and teaching. The religious leaders' opposition to him had grown from the time that they first learned of Jesus, who continued to teach drawing ever larger crowds despite the leaders' opposition. He had then made his triumphal entry into Jerusalem during the great festival. The end of his public ministry, and his crucifixion and resurrection, drew near. Over the prior three years, many in the crowds and even some among the religious leaders had come to believe in him. While the crowds thronged and cheered his triumphal entry, though, the religious leaders did not, not even those who had come to believe in Jesus. The Gospel of John gives as the reason that the believing leaders would not openly acknowledge their belief in Jesus as their fear of the other leaders putting them out of the synagogue and that "they loved human praise more than praise from God." Jesus continued to tell them, "I have come into the world as a light, so that no one who believes in me should stay in darkness." The leaders who believed Jesus but feared the other leaders and loved human praise needed to come into the light.

He saw only subtle differences between loving God's praise and the praises of others. Those differences he was still exploring. Part of his problem distinguishing was that some people did love godly actions and would say so. Was he then pursuing those people's praises for the godly action or pursuing the praises of God for the same godly action? He decided to keep his focus on God's pleasure as much as he could rather than listening very much to people's praises. If people wanted to praise something, then let them do so, but just don't pay it much attention. Listen instead to God. Maybe the difference was subtle, but it also seemed important. Yet he also saw only subtle differences between showing humility before others particularly in not seeking and loving their praises for being godly, but then beginning to make a show of false humility. He would rather accept a compliment straight up than show false humility in order to gain further compliment for his godly showing of humility. So again, he decided to keep his focus on God's pleasure as much as he could rather than rejecting people's praises in order to appear humble. He knew that these distinctions were particularly important for him because he knew that he could far too easily decide to love such a powerful intoxicant as the praises of people. Reflecting on Jesus's admonition made him commit to doing more good work that people could not see without necessarily doing less that they could see. Better not to let praises tempt him. Better to store up things that only God could praise.

Do not love the important seats. Luke 11:43.

Nearly everywhere one goes, hierarchy is evident. In formal settings like graduation ceremonies, weddings, funerals, and even regular church services, prominent people take the prominent seats. Organizers often mark and save those seats for the prominent parties, but even when they don't, the prominent people end up in those seats. The same is true in business meetings, commission meetings, courtrooms, and other institutional settings, where the important people take the power seats. The practice even extends to informal settings including parties and other social and recreational gatherings. Even in prisons, the leading inmates take the important seats. Watch people closely, both the high and mighty people and ordinary people, and they all share a fine sense of who ranks and who doesn't rank. To some degree, rank is inevitable. What is not inevitable is to love the high ranking. You may in fact be quite important to a certain proceeding, whether formal or informal. You may be prominent in the community in which it takes place. Be careful, though, not to love your prominence. One practical way to discourage love of prominence is not to take prominent seats in gatherings. The practice of taking the back-row seat, while artificial, can serve as a check on pride of place. Better yet, no matter where you literally sit, maintain an attitude and approach that gives others, particularly the ordinary and low, more prominence in the proceeding. Give Jesus's admonition not to love your prominence both literal and figurative expression. Keep your sense of prominence firmly in check.

Jesus had begun to criticize the religious leaders heavily, on the occasion that a religious leader had invited Jesus into his home to eat along with other religious leaders and teachers of the law. Jesus was so hard on the leaders that one of the teachers of the law cautioned him that he was also insulting the law experts. Jesus instead turned his criticism to those very law experts. One of Jesus's criticisms that sparked this exchange was that Jesus had said that the religious leaders would suffer because "you love the most important seats in the synagogues and respectful greetings in the marketplace." Jesus must have seen the scene repeat itself in so many synagogues and marketplaces, the religious leaders basking in the honor of their most-special synagogue seats and soaking up the praises of the shoppers in the marketplaces. Because of their love for the honor and approval of others, Jesus said that the religious leaders were like dead men, like unmarked graves in that while they were indeed dead, others did not recognize them as dead. The teacher of the law actually did not correct Jesus, only indicating that what Jesus said was insulting. Jesus's criticism hurt because of its accuracy, not its errancy. The teacher of the law may have known just as well of its accuracy. Both he and Jesus knew the religious leaders' hearts and self-aggrandizing practices.

She really had no interest in prominence and was amused at others who did. She could see so clearly those who sought out the important seats because they valued their own importance. She never wanted to be like them and for a long time believed that she wasn't like them. Yet now and then, she found evidence of her own natural will to prominence. As disappointing as it was, she slowly discovered one area after another where she actually did have pride of place. Those areas may not have been in large or formal gatherings. She had no problem taking the low seats there because she had no interest in that kind of prominence. Her problem areas were in other smaller and more-routine settings. She found in those ordinary settings that she actually drew substantial encouragement from her physical place and the small privileges that it afforded. She then recognized that she felt entitled to those places and their privileges. If someone had displaced her from her seat, even though just an ordinary seat in an ordinary setting, for a lower seat, then she would have quickly drawn insult, as she found that she occasionally did. So she committed to banishing even these commitments to entitlement. She wanted to draw *all* of her standing from Jesus, not from where she literally sat, which in retrospect seemed such a foolish and worthless thing.

Take the lowest place. Luke 14:10.

So, if we are not to seek and love the seats of honor, then where do we sit? Jesus instructs specifically to take the lowest seat, and he gives good practical reasons why, as shown in the next paragraph's account. Of course, though, the instruction to take the lowest seat has much less to do with simply where you sit than it does with your broader approach to people and places. Jesus did not intend that Christians get hung up on where they sit in a rules-bent formal practice. The deeper lesson is far more important. We naturally tend to look to the interests and influence of powerful and prominent people, probably because we seek to draw on that power and prominence. We likewise naturally tend to seek, preserve, and promote our own power and prominence again because of the way in which we believe doing so prefers, secures, and suits us. When Jesus says to take the lowest seat, he may simultaneously be saying something like to seek the perspective and serve the needs of the low and ordinary, those people whom you discover in the low places. The curious thing about that low-seeking practice is that you may just find the honor there that you would without the instruction have sought in high places. Try it sometime. Pick the lowest places in your community, go there, and meet and serve the people. Chances are good that you will end up on the newspaper's front page for your unusually inspired insight and service. God exalts those who seek the low and lost.

Jesus had another occasion on which to remark and instruct on the right way to approach honor among others. Once again, he joined a meal at a prominent religious leader's house, this one being the time that he healed another person attending the same meal and the religious leaders were prepared to criticize him for healing on the Sabbath. After healing the man and explaining to the religious leaders why he did so, Jesus watched other arriving guests as they picked the places of honor around the table. He then instructed those at the meal that when invited to a wedding feast not to take the place of honor lest someone of greater importance arrive, requiring the embarrassment of moving to a lower place. Indeed by then, with all of the decent seats taken, the guest who must move will end up in the worst seat at the banquet, feeling humiliated. Jesus said instead, "When you are invited, take the lowest place, so that when your host comes, he will say to you, 'Friend, move up to a better place.'" This practice brings honor without seeking honor. Jesus then made the point of his example even clearer, explaining that those who exalt themselves end up humbled, while those who humble themselves end up exalted.

He had no intention of promoting himself when he began his weekly social service at the soup kitchen nearest his workplace. He had done this service at other places before, and here, he figured, was a new opportunity. Although the place was gritty, possibly a little unsafe at times, and many of the people badly broken in various respects, he nonetheless came quickly to like the place after getting over his initial unfamiliarity and its accompanying discomfort. The same process had occurred at his other, prior service places. Seeking the low places had been scary at first, but he had adjusted quickly to the point that he felt comfortable, confident, and adjusted, even at times inspired. Indeed, he found such perseverance among the people in those places. He may not find much skill there, but he found plenty of heart, a lot more than he found in some other, higher places. He may not find much education in the soup kitchens and other low places he had served, but he found plenty of wisdom and some of it just as good as or better than what he found in the high places that his vocation required him to frequent. No matter, though. He was in the low places doing as Jesus had said and liking it. Then one day a newspaper stringer came into the soup kitchen's social service area having heard through one of the soup-kitchen patrons of his service. Although a news story, award, and recognition followed that he appreciated, he felt in retrospect that he would have preferred simply to continue quietly the service in low places.

Do not exalt yourself. Luke 18:14.

Somehow, someway, we do find small and large ways to exalt ourselves. Some of those ways are only internal as we speak to ourselves about who we are and what we do or don't do relative to who others are and what *they* do or don't do. Our personal nature, poured as we are into these corporeal vessels, too easily leads us to those us-them, me-you comparisons. Comparisons of any kind then too easily lead to contrasts. First our thinking and then our words reflect that *I* do *this*, while *you* do *that*. As we begin to ascribe attributes and characteristics to ourselves and to others, our subjective and self-interested view of all things naturally helps us ascribe the better things to ourselves and the worse things to others. These thoughts and, when we express them, words soon lead to behaviors in which we promote ourselves while denigrating others. The practice of self-exaltation, though natural, is at the same time unfortunate and curious because self-exaltation almost inevitably ends up reflecting poorly on the self-exalter. Self-exaltation, self-promoting, and self-aggrandizing behavior does not work. Popular history and culture are replete with sad and sordid examples of the fall from grace of the exaggerators and self-promoters. Self-promotion may look like it works for some at least some of the time, but in truth and depth it works for none, never. Jesus instructs to let others exalt you.

Not surprisingly, Jesus found among the crowds people who felt so confident of their own righteousness that they looked down on the others around them. He, like others, could probably have picked these people out from a mile away. One day, Jesus gave a lesson specifically to and for them. His parable of the religious leader and tax collector had the religious leader going right up to the front of the temple to pray in thanks to God that he was not a sinner like these other people, particularly this tax collector who had entered the temple area beside him. The tax collector instead hung back in fear and respect of God, beating his breast, looking down, and asking God to have mercy on him as the sinner that he was. The crowd, although not its prouder members, must have known whom Jesus was going to praise, the humble tax collector. Jesus concluded the parable, "I tell you that this man, rather than the other, went home justified before God. For all those who exalt themselves will be humbled, and those who humble themselves will be exalted." Jesus wanted them to let God exalt them in their humility, which God will do. Look indeed at how Jesus exalted the breast-beating, downward-looking, sin-confessing tax collector, while Jesus parodied and humiliated the proud religious leader.

He knew self-promotion like the back of his hand, even though he hated it, at least officially. That tension was precisely his problem. He knew that he should avoid self-promotion at all costs. Yet he also knew how good recognition by others, high position for oneself, and privilege of place could feel. What he had to keep reminding himself was that those good feelings of recognition were only fleeting good feelings that could never satisfy him, as they were never able to satisfy any other. He knew their unreliability. Sense of importance passes very quickly, sense of self-importance even more quickly. The world structures itself to give ample room for self-exaltation, he knew. Its means and inducements for self-promotion were immediately at hand, whether social, virtual, occupational, political, or other. The world seemed to him all about self-promotion, its implicit and explicit message being that no one else will do your promotion for you. But he had also learned that the world was wrong when positioning each of us as left to our own mechanisms to survive and just possibly prosper. God, he knew, will promote you. He wanted place in God's kingdom much more than he wanted pride of place in the world.

Humble yourself. Matthew 23:12.

Just as Jesus provides instruction and lessons in *not exalting* oneself, he also addresses the flip side of that instruction in urging us to *humble* ourselves. One supposes that we can with some care and attention avoid exalting ourselves, at least in its most obvious ways. We can sit in less-prominent places, let others speak as often as we speak, and choose to serve those in need more so than those who have power and influence. We can speak less often and less positively about our own merits and accomplishments while more often recognizing the accomplishments and merits of others. Avoiding self-promotion, we have seen, is a good thing. Yet Jesus takes the instruction a step further in urging that we humble ourselves, which is to take an additional step of lowering ourselves, removing ourselves, and diminishing ourselves. To be *self-effacing*, which serves as a synonym for *humility*, has the connotation of removing one's face from whatever good character, behavior, or action one has undertaken or accomplished. Let your good character, behavior, and actions take the face of others, perhaps of those who participated with you in whatever activity gained you the good remarks or reputation, but particularly of God in Christ. Give God the credit because God is due the credit. You didn't form yourself or even wake yourself up in the morning; God did. You didn't prepare the circumstances of your life for the good work that you attempted; God did. You didn't complete the good work that gained you the remark or reputation; God did. Lower yourself, deliberately putting the face of others, particularly God's face, on the good that others see in you or through you. Do so not in false humility but in true humility. God is author even of your striving.

Jesus had yet another lesson for the crowds regarding how to treat success, this one another reminder to remain humble, but one in which Jesus used different examples. Jesus had yet again spoken against the practices of the religious leaders and teachers of the law, who did everything so that others could see and appreciate them. Beyond their sitting in places of honor and walking proudly through the marketplaces, they even made their clothing to attract the attention, respect, and praise of others. The members of the crowd must have noticed how the flowing robes got bigger and their tassels longer as the religious leaders and teachers of the law claimed more and more honor. Prominent seats, frequent compliments, and flashy clothing were not even enough, though. They also loved to be called *rabbi, father,* and *teacher,* for the honor that these titles brought them and the way in which these titles lifted them above others. Yet Jesus told the crowds that no one should call others by these titles or seek to have others call them so. Instead, everyone is to acknowledge and accept that they have only one Teacher, Father, and Messiah, in heaven, leaving these titles of honor to Him. The way to honor was through humble service, not self-promotion. Jesus said again, "The greatest among you will be your servant. For those who exalt themselves will be humbled, and those who humble themselves will be exalted."

She found her home in humility. She had for a long time been searching for her spiritual residence on earth, which didn't seem a particularly hospitable place for her spirit. Few things in the world captured her spirit, gave her spirit a sense of coziness and comfort. Indeed, the world consistently did the opposite, jarring her spirit, telling her that she had no place in the world other than what mean and low place the world gave her or what slightly higher place to which she could exalt herself. Survival of the fittest, the world seemed to say to her every time she sought solace, comfort, or place in the world. Only then did the thought strike her: humility *was* her place in the world. She felt perfectly at home when she felt humble. She began to remove her face from things, not so much literally, although she could do that, too, in her virtual world, but more so from a spiritual and internal standpoint. The world was not hers to consume, control, or destroy. What she did in the world was not to her credit or debit. She was instead a pure child of God, completely dependent on Him not only for breath and sustenance but also for place and merit. If God wanted her to have a higher place than her deep humility, then let God exalt her.

Be humble when only doing your duty. Luke 17:10.

One special time to remain humble is when only doing your duty. Those who expect profuse thanks, long breaks, and special rewards for only doing what they should do are not the kind of workers whom God or anyone else would wish to hire. We joke today about how everyone needs so many strokes for ordinary performance, whether in school, the workplace, the home, or other institutions needing and reasonably expecting performance. Everyone gets a blue ribbon. Everyone gets a cookie. Everyone gets an atta-boy or atta-girl even when only doing the most ordinary task expected of anyone. The expectation is a joke because we know that it undermines the very performance that we are seeking. Giving generous kudos for routine tasks appears to the person completing the tasks to make their performance optional or contingent on continuing recognition, when performance is neither optional nor contingent. What builds performance is solid expectation of performance without recognition, when no one is looking, and generous appreciation for going beyond the call of that duty. For society and institutions to function, we all want and need duties filled when no one other than God will know that the doer has filled them. More significantly, God wants that same kind of stable, consistent, and devoted performance.

On one of those many occasions when Jesus was teaching the disciples, an occasion on which Jesus had much to say, he reached the point of speaking to them about sin, faith, and duty. Sin would come, he told the disciples, but just hope that sin does not come through you. Jesus told them about faith that if they had even a tiny speck, then God would work through them. Yet Jesus also spoke about their need to recognize that they owed duties to God for which they should expect no special appreciation. To illustrate, Jesus asked the disciples if they would expect to thank and excuse a servant who was only doing the servant's job of plowing soil or tending sheep. No, they would expect the servant to do that job and any others expected from them within their role. One does not thank another for ordinary duties that the other fulfills, or at least one does not excuse them from further duties. Pride drawn from doing what one should do is false pride that serves no one. Jesus concluded this part of his long lesson, "So you also, when you have done everything you were told to do, should say, 'We are unworthy servants; we have only done our duty.'"

The days, weeks, months, and years passed by, and then the decades. The expectations that others had for him over that entire period, and the duties, obligations, and responsibilities that he was to fulfill, were so consistent that the routines that he had to follow to perform them gradually ossified. While no day was exactly the same as another, and new matters were constant challenges, the small beginning-of-day and end-of-day routines, and many of the routines in between, never really changed. He had repeated every little thing so often, literally thousands of times. He had also gradually improved the efficiency of each of those little routines until they eventually each seemed to command that he do them exactly as the day before. For a while he thought that he had become an obsessive compulsive but finally decided that he had just grown so familiar with every routine that any little deviation amused more so than annoyed him. Now and then, he would hear others complain that no one seemed to appreciate what they did and had to do each day. He seldom if ever felt that way. Somehow, some strange way, he felt as if God was nearest him not when he was taking on a new challenge, figuratively climbing a new mountain, but instead in those tiny daily routines. He just felt as if God loved those who took pleasure in fulfilling small duties day after day without complaint or recognition. His amusement and satisfaction grew thinking that he performed each tiny routine, fulfilled each modest duty, at the pleasure of God. He prayed that it was so.

Guard against hypocrisy. Luke 12:1.

Jesus gives us another great warning relating to success when saying to guard against hypocrisy. Hypocrisy is to attempt to appear more successful than one is, to appear one way while acting another way when the appearance is better than the action. Hypocrisy involves pretense, pretending, and deception. To be a hypocrite, one must attempt to deceive others into believing that one is better than one actually is, but then one only deceive oneself. A hypocrite becomes a hypocrite when others see the attempt at deception but the hypocrite does not see or care that others see the hypocrite's attempts. Hypocrites only fool themselves. By instructing us to guard against hypocrisy, Jesus highlights that we are all susceptible to hypocrisy. Putting a better face on one's actions and intentions than they deserve is so inviting and easy, and so readily satisfies one's need for acknowledgment, status, and endorsement. Those who do not perceive God as valuing them, and also do not see others as doing so, fill themselves and attempt to fool others with illusions of their worth. The allure and power of that self-deception and deception of others makes the hypocrite not so much one to condemn as one to pity. Set your guard against deceiving others over your success when you are likely only to deceive yourself.

Thousands had gathered again to see and hear Jesus, trampling one another, probably hoping to witness yet another miracle. Jesus prepared to begin another extensive teaching. First, though, Jesus addressed his disciples, saying, "Be on your guard against the yeast of the Pharisees, which is hypocrisy." Jesus had on other occasion referred to sin as yeast but here referred to the specific sin of hypocrisy, of trying to hide one's intentions and actions in a veneer of respectability. Jesus explained that no one could really hide things in the way that the religious leaders tried. He said instead that everything hidden in darkness would appear as in daylight, and everything whispered as if shouted from the rooftops. The people could tell that the religious leaders were hypocrites, and God certainly knew. Jesus didn't want the crowd to aspire to be like the religious leaders in their hypocrisy. They must instead be on their

211

guard. Don't worry about what the religious leaders might do to them, Jesus said, but worry instead about what God wants them to do.

He hoped that he had a fine sense for hypocrisy in himself but knew at the same time that he couldn't be sure. While he felt reasonably effective at constructive introspection, he also knew the power of self-deception. Now and then, he would get a glimmer, just a little peek, at how he deceived himself in trying to appear certain ways to others. He knew that everyone, particularly adults if not so much with children, in small and large ways constructed how they wished to appear to others. He knew that he chose his own words, shaped his own actions, to make appearances and keep up appearances. Although he hoped that in doing so he was only acting graciously and responsibly instead of for show and reputation, he also knew that inevitably he would fool himself, disguise his hypocrisy, as he now and then glimpsed. While those glimmers of insight into his own hypocrisy disturbed him, he learned to welcome and embrace them rather than shut them out. He wanted to be on his guard against all things false and pretentious. He figured that the only way that he could do so, and then change his exaggerated practices, was to listen to the Holy Spirit showing him his many sad conceits.

Hunger for righteousness. Matthew 5:6.

So what does success really look like? When, or how, is one truly fulfilled? Jesus describes success differently from the way that the world would describe it. Success in God's kingdom, true success, eternal success, is not the accumulation of worldly wealth marked by big bank and retirement accounts, homes, and cars. Success is not finally reaching the top of whatever educational, workplace, professional, governmental, social, athletic, service, or other hierarchy of which you are a part. Success is not the perfect family, figure, or face. It is not even good marriage, good health, good reputation, or good character, although any of those things could be enjoyable blessings. The one ultimate success is filling by God,

212

nearness to God, the presence of God, satisfaction in God. To conceive of filling by God as ecstasy would at once both suggest and yet still misrepresent and fall short of what that ultimate kind of success means. Success in some sense means a pinnacle reached through and in experience, implying both a process and condition or state. The condition or state of filling by God should address, fulfill, and complete every possible positive sense, sensibility, ambition, or yearning, and yet beyond such perfect state, do far more, perhaps by leaving one still fully responsible and able to worship God. Now, let's hope *that* success sounds better than arrogance, self-aggrandizement, and pride.

Right at the beginning of his great Sermon on the Mount, Jesus taught what we know as the *Beatitudes*. Crowds had followed Jesus up a mountainside until he sat down, his disciples gathered around him, and he began to teach. Blessed are these, Jesus taught, and blessed are those, he taught again. Each of his several serial statements described those who had access to the blessings of the kingdom of heaven. God would bless the poor in spirit, the meek, and the mourner. He would bless the merciful, pure in heart, and peacemaker. Those whom God would usher into his blessed kingdom were not the ones who generally made their own way into positions of favor in the world. The world favors the rich in spirit, not the poor, and the mighty rather than the meek, the judgmental rather than the merciful, the manipulator rather than the pure, and the violent rather than the peacemaker. Each whom Jesus said had kingdom access would nonetheless receive from God their special blessing fitting to their station and need, comfort for instance for those who mourn. In the middle of these blessings, Jesus described those whom God would *fill*, those who in the kingdom would find the only kind of success that satisfies and lasts. This special reward of God's filling God would reserve, Jesus said, for "those who hunger and thirst for righteousness." God's filling, the only full satisfaction, would be the reward of those whose ambition it most is to please God, the mark of *righteousness.*

He loved the thought of hungering to please God, thirsting to do as God intended. The thought was so pure, positive, and unassailable by any contradiction. The effort to please God, the

213

commitment to please God, also seemed to be the one thing that had no bounds or limits, the one thing that he and anyone else could not overdo. On the other hand, he had what he consistently felt was too little insight, information, or wisdom on what it meant to hunger for righteousness, to please God. His studies nonetheless showed him that hungering for righteousness, loving God, and pleasing God, largely meant to do as God commanded, to *obey* God. He didn't want to fall into formalism, to make a system or performance out of pleasing God. He knew that pleasing God must involve relationship, true love, authentic dedication, passionate devotion. Yet obedience would still mark or evidence each of those things. From there, he realized more fully that to obey God, he must learn what he could of what God commanded, especially through the words and actions of the Son of God, Jesus. Jesus's statement that God fills those who hunger after righteousness then became another marker for him. He began to understand, believe, and expect that if indeed he was approaching the subject of pleasing God correctly in studying and following the words and actions of Jesus in passionate devotion, then God would fill him as Jesus said. This, he thought, was going to be special. And special it was and is, he began to discover.

Let your light shine. Matthew 5:16.

Jesus's admonition to *let your light shine* evokes in the minds of many the joyful children's song to let it shine, let it shine, let it shine. The song has the children sing of their *little* light, which may be because they are little children who sing it or may instead be just what any of us feel about the small visibility of the small and few truly good works that we do. The song, like Jesus's teaching, is about how to deal with doing or having done good works. Humility might have us hide our good works, which is good as far as humility goes. Yet how are others to learn of God's goodness, the pure servant hearts his love produces, if they never see its evidence in the lovingly dutiful works of others? Although the song is for children, its message, like Jesus's instruction, holds profound meaning. The song and instruction are not simply to let one's light shine from the good works you have done or are doing. They are to let one's light shine so that others will see and glorify God. The song and instruction create an appropriate tension between the humility we must maintain over good works that they are far less our accomplishments than the work of the pure heart, devoted hands, purposeful plans, and abundant resources with which God blesses us. He is the source of all goodness. One strongly suspects that Jesus has in mind a particular kind of humble shining of a particular kind of godly light, just the sort that the children's song so poignantly captures, rather than the glaring spotlight of self-promotion.

The mountainside crowd had settled in to listen to Jesus teach the disciples. Most likely, they were quickly in rapt attention as he spoke the blessings of the Beatitudes over them. He then compared them to the salt of the earth, good seasoning unless they lost their saltiness, and then only good to be cast out the door for trampling underfoot to keep the dust down. Or, he said, they were the light of the world, like a great town built high on a hill for everyone to see or a lamp placed on a stand to light the whole house. No one would light a lamp and then promptly place it under a bowl, hiding its light. It should instead light up everything in the house from its prominent lampstand. Jesus then summarized the lesson, "In the same way, let your light shine before others, that they may see your good deeds and glorify your Father in heaven." They were to let others recognize the light, salt, and Spirit of God working through them as they did the good deeds that the Father had planned for them and for which he had equipped them. They were not to hide God's light from others but instead to let it shine so brightly as to illuminate their households, towns, and cities.

They gave her the verse as her verse, the verse that described her, marked her, guided and in some sense completed her. How the program leaders had known that this light-shining verse should be her verse, was in a sense already her verse and had likely always been her verse, she would never know. Some people have a life verse, while others seem not to have one. She now had one from the moment that they gave it to her while giving other youth their own different verses. She could tell that some of the other youth were indifferent to their verses and some excited. She didn't show any emotion over hers. Doing so would not have been like her. She never wanted to be the center of attention or make a big fuss, which she suspected the program leaders had recognized and may have had something to do with their verse choice. She just loved God, loved good works, and loved right doing, and maybe also wanted others to do so, which again gave her a clue why the program leaders had given her that verse. She wondered how long she would really remember that they had given her this verse and how long she would feel that indeed it was *her* verse. At least for this one day, she hoped that it would be a lifetime.

1.10 Giving

Give. Luke 6:38. *Do not steal.* Luke 18:20. *Use wealth to gain friends.* Luke 16:9. *Give out of your poverty.* Mark 12:44. *Give in secret.* Matthew 6:4. *Give freely.* Matthew 10:8. *Give to the believer.* Matthew 10:42. *Sell what you have to give to the poor.* Luke 18:22. *Be generous in giving to the poor.* Luke 11:41. *Give to the poor.* Luke 18:22. *Give to the one who asks.* Matthew 5:42. *Give to everyone who asks.* Luke 6:30. *Use gifts.* Matthew 25:21.

The prior three sections on serving, earning, and succeeding all imply vocation, calling, aptitude, and capability, the kind of motivation, initiative, and activity through which God produces abundance. We know from what Jesus said about these activities that we are to share generously with others the abundance that God produces through us. Yet how does one do that? How are we to give, share, and be generous? The answer, simply to give, might seem easy. But giving in God's way must be at least somewhat harder than simply giving appears, because Jesus took it upon himself, took so much time and trouble, to teach so much about giving. We would not need Jesus's instruction if giving were as easy as it looks. People then must have been making errors in their giving, just as people today would make similar errors. Giving in God's way must have a particular purpose and design different from purposes and designs that we commonly assume. We should not only want to give and give frequently and generously, but we should also want to give as God would have us give. To do so, we need Jesus's model and instruction. Consider what Jesus says and what he did about giving.

Give. Luke 6:38.

We do first have Jesus's direct and simple command to give. To give is to relinquish something of value, to take something that one has and from which one gains at least some benefit, and to let go of it voluntarily with the intent that others receive and benefit from it. To give is not to lose something or have something stolen, nor to discard something that has lost its value to the giver and perhaps to others. We have not given when losing a watch or having a wallet with $100 stolen, and we are not giving when filling the trash barrel to put out at the curb. To give implies at least some value deliberately forgone for the benefit of others. Giving is God's work, godly work. God himself is a giver, just as Jesus showed the incomparable depth of his own generosity in giving his own perfect life in sacrifice. Jesus gave all that anyone could give and then much more. Others might also give their life, but Jesus gave his perfect life. Jesus gave a life that no other could give. None of us have a perfect life to give. When Jesus submitted to public scourging and crucifixion, he also gave up a position of equivalence with God that no other possesses. We would lower ourselves at least somewhat to submit voluntarily to physical punishment and execution, as Jesus did. But deep truths be told, we each have much in us to condemn. None of us sits at God's right hand, so our lowering to submit to punishment would not be so much, not even nearly like what Jesus gave up in lost position. The point is that Jesus sanctioned giving first by instruction and then by example. When Jesus says to give, he meant to *give*.

On the occasion that Jesus taught such a large crowd from all over the area, when he gave both blessings and woes, and taught about loving enemies, not judging others, and several other big subjects, he also interjected a few words about giving. Jesus placed his few words this time about giving in the midst of his teaching about not condemning others and instead forgiving them while examining one's own self for sin and errors. Apparently, from the way that Jesus connected the subjects, to avoid judging others too harshly and instead to forgive them connects well with the willingness to give generally. Jesus might have been saying that to judge is to take away, while to forgive is give. In any case, the few words that Jesus added about giving are one of the best-known of his passages, one often repeated in some churches where poverty, and thus giving, is a bigger challenge and issue. Jesus said, "Give, and it

218

will be given to you. A good measure, pressed down, shaken together and running over, will be poured into your lap. For with the measure you use, it will be measured to you." In candor, maybe we like the passage so much because Jesus connected *giving* so closely with *getting*. We may like to give, but we sure like to receive. Jesus certainly made that connection that the generous giver will generously receive, just as the parsimonious giver will receive only little. One suspects that the crowd liked at least this part of his powerful message.

She loved giving. For a time, she had thought that she had no particular spiritual gift, not for preaching, prayer, tongues, interpretation, discipleship, or administration. Then she realized that giving was her ministry. Although she followed a few giving guidelines and hewed to her own giving practice and conventions, to whom she gave hardly mattered to her. Often her giving was to a church ministry but sometimes a national or global ministry, an orphan, or disaster relief. Often her giving was to a neighbor or friend. Other times her giving was to a needful stranger. Sometimes she gave to the rich and sometimes to the poor, although of course much more often the latter. Her giving to the rich constituted only kindnesses to those whom she knew. She loved giving to pastors and their spouses but also gave to butchers, bakers, and candlestick makers, or so her generous giving seemed. She gave to hairdressers, letter carriers, checkout cashiers, and coffee baristas. Sometimes her giving was a small extra, more than a tip certainly but nothing extravagant. At other times, her giving approached extravagance to the point that her family would gently counsel her. Yet as richly and often as she gave, she never felt tired of it or burdened by it. She instead felt only more and more richly blessed herself. Giving, she knew, was the best possible ministry, indeed the very way in which Jesus had ministered most to her.

Do not steal. Luke 18:20.

Many probably think, *well this command is an easy one,* because they believe that they have not stolen. The command might not be quite as easy as that. Giving and stealing have a subtle relationship. The admonition to give has a helpful corollary in the command not to steal. If giving is relinquishing voluntarily to another something of value, then stealing is to *take involuntarily* from another something of value. Although our understanding of stealing is straightforward and common in the manner of outright theft, we nonetheless give different connotations to stealing than that obvious form of theft. Stealing, while usually involving taking property from another against their will, could also involve refusing to give to another something of value that was their due. Technically, the law might call *embezzlement, fraud,* or *conversion* the concealing and retaining of something of value, beyond any time permitted, when that something belongs to another. We still properly think of that wrongful act as a form of stealing. Stealing fundamentally involves depriving another of something of value. Stealing thus indeed bears a more-subtle relationship to giving than one might first think. God says to give. If just the right opportunity for giving presents itself, and a corresponding obligation to give arises as in a direct command from God to give, then have we stolen by not doing so, by instead retaining that which God has commanded as gift? We might on close reflection see little difference between outright stealing of the usual kind on the one hand and refusal to give what God has commanded as gift. Either way, one ends up with something one should not have retained. Yes, be sure not to steal, but also look carefully at what God calls you to give, recognizing that everything is his and that retaining something of his that he has commanded given could be stealing from God and a theft-like offense toward the one to whom he expected the gift.

Jesus fulfilled the law. He did not overturn or replace it. On one occasion, a certain ruler, calling Jesus *good teacher,* asked him what he must do to inherit eternal life. Jesus first asked the ruler why the ruler had called Jesus good when no one is good other than God alone. The ruler's statement, Jesus seemed to be saying, was the same as identifying Jesus as God, in which Jesus did not chastise or correct the ruler, just that the ruler should know what the ruler was saying by calling Jesus the Good Teacher. The account does not record a reply from the ruler. Jesus simply continued answering. "You know the commandments," Jesus said, beginning, "'You shall not commit adultery, you shall not murder, you shall not steal, you shall not give false testimony, honor your father and mother.'" Jesus listed several of the Ten Commandments. The ruler told Jesus in response that he had kept the commandments since he was a boy. Their colloquy continued from there, as another account below summarizes, but in the exchange to this point Jesus had clearly pointed the ruler to keeping the commandments, one of which was not to steal.

The more that he reflected on what Jesus said about giving, including what Jesus said about not stealing in the context in which he said it, the less confidence that he had that he was following not just the letter but the spirit of the commands. Everything began to look to him like a close call. In every transaction, he realized that he needed to take more care to give full measure and to give it timely no moment later than giving it was due. He began to see more-frequent small, silent cheating, stealing, or theft in the current and prevalent practices of others and sadly in his own former practices, and less honest dealing and proper giving of the kind that God could abide. He had never thought of handling property, finances, and obligations, as so fraught with the hazards of greed, self-interest, and dishonesty, until he gained this fuller appreciation for the hazards from the words and Spirit of Christ. He was sure that he must now give much closer attention to giving whatever is due whenever due, guided by the Holy Spirit. He no longer had any delusion that he was free from the temptation and influence of stealing as rank sin.

Use wealth to gain friends. Luke 16:9.

Jesus's instruction to use wealth to gain friends has both an attractive and also somewhat odd sound to it. We might first take from his instruction that we would be better to gain friends from wealth than, for instance, to increase and amass wealth, hoard wealth, deny others any benefit from wealth, or trust in wealth for our security. We should see and appreciate the generosity of making friends with wealth over any of those other ways in which people commonly do treat wealth, increasing, amassing, hoarding, and trusting in it. Other than the regret we might feel for spending wealth, any of us could with ease probably follow that instruction to use wealth to gain friends. An adventure here, a banquet there? We might enjoy making friends using wealth, just as those new friends would also enjoy it. Yet the instruction also has a bit of an odd sound to it. Doesn't wealth have some higher purpose than to *make friends* with it? Shouldn't we start a charitable foundation, build a hospital, staff an orphanage, or pay for a poor child's college education with wealth instead? Making friends with wealth sounds a little cavalier if indeed doing so is to be our aim and end. The answer to this tension probably lies in the fact that Jesus did not stop at saying to use wealth *merely* to gain friends, as if gaining friends should be our aim and end. He actually said a little more than that, which changes our understanding of the instruction in the following account's manner.

In the midst of his parable of the shrewd manager, told to his disciples, Jesus made a fascinating statement about the nature and result of giving, and our motivation to give. After telling of the manager's impending firing and how he cut the debts of those who owed his employer so that they would welcome him after his firing, Jesus said, "I tell you, use worldly wealth to gain friends for yourselves, so that when it is gone, you will be welcomed into eternal dwellings." Set aside for a moment the questions raised by the manager's shrewd action in cutting apparently just debts simply to win favor. In giving the instruction to use wealth to gain friends for welcome into eternal dwellings, Jesus first confirms what we should have known that giving makes friends. Those who receive appreciate those who give. The nature of giving is to bless the recipient, which is a powerful and apparently godly process. Also, the result of giving is to make a friend of the recipient, which is a powerful and apparently godly effect. The motivation for giving, Jesus's instruction next confirms, should lie in our desiring to please God. Jesus says to make friends here, not to have the blessing back of those friends here through their favor and gifts in return, but instead *so that* God welcomes us into his eternal dwellings. We should give to gain God's approving welcome, to gain access to his place where he welcomes us. Jesus instructs that we should desire to please God through our giving so that we may dwell in God's welcome. Nothing gets better than that.

222

He had long ago noticed how spending wealth made friends, not that he had then had much wealth of his own to spend. He was still far too poor to appreciate directly wealth's friend-making effect. He instead saw others spending wealth, not always but occasionally, in ways that quickly made many friends. Oh, he saw the wealthy amass, hoard, and hold tight to wealth, too. He probably saw much more of that holding than of the spending. But he had seen wealth spent generously and quickly, too, rather than hoarded, and in those instances he had seen fast friends, indeed notoriously fast friends who didn't look at all like they would have been friends without the spending of much wealth. That wealth the fast friends had squandered so quickly on riotous partying that when the wealth was gone, so were they. The friend-making effect of wealth was too obvious in those instances, which in no sense looked like they included godly behaviors. He thought again of Jesus's words that while we should use wealth to make friends, the purpose of using wealth to make friends is actually to gain God's welcome into his kingdom. Although he didn't know directly and might be over-reading Jesus's parable, he nonetheless suspected that God might consider the kind of spending and kind of friends when determining whether to extend the welcome. After all, the shrewd manager had reduced debts of those doing trade with his employer, whom he suspected represented God in the parable form of Jesus's teaching. Maybe, he thought, the idea was to reduce the debts of others who owe those debts to God, that is, like Jesus to cover and forgive their sins so that God can welcome both the forgiver and the forgiven.

Give out of your poverty. Mark 12:44.

We surely understand that God values sacrificial giving done out of poverty more than God values giving surplus out of wealth. We can see just as Jesus saw that giving everything one has means giving more than giving a little of one's lot, in godly measure. Jesus's parable to that effect is nonetheless an important lesson with multiple valuable corollaries. On the surface, one might reasonably assume that giving $100 means more than giving $20, no matter the wealth or poverty of the giver. In a world of limited resources, $100 has five times the value of $20 to the worldly recipient, whether that recipient is a charity, agency, or other institution, no matter who is the giver. Foundations name buildings and funds after wealthy donors who give a lot, not poor donors who give all of their little. Yet we still understand intuitively the giving-out-of-poverty parable. God does not live in a world of limited resources. He is without limit, his resources are without end, and everything is his. The parable confirms implicitly these valuable corollaries. Because everything is God's, including both the money that we give and the money that we hold, the kingdom register in which he records our transactions does not measure the total of his treasury but instead only measures the extent of our generosity toward him. In a strictly logical sense, the only satisfactory gift at the temple is to always give everything, which is what the widow in that instance did. Try giving out of your poverty. God appreciates how you handle his money out of your heart toward him.

Jesus had taught in the temple courts, the large crowd listening to him with delight. He taught so clearly, with such authority, and making such imminent sense of the ancient scriptures. He had taught of the coming of David's Lord and Messiah, which was Jesus himself. He had also warned against the teaching of the religious leaders, making a show over their own importance. When he had finished, he sat where he could watch the people putting their money into the temple treasury as offerings. He saw rich people throwing in large amounts, their coins likely announcing their generous offerings to anyone who could hear the coins' noisy clatter. But then he saw a poor widow put in two very small copper coins worth barely anything. Jesus called over the disciples, saying, "Truly I tell you, this poor widow has put more into the treasury than all the others. They all gave out of their wealth. But she, out of her poverty, put in everything—all she had to live on." God measures giving in his own way, in the poor widow's instance out of the sacrifice she had made for him and trust she had shown in him, so like the sacrifice and trust of Jesus. The rich giving out of wealth means less to God than the poor giving out of poverty.

She hungered for the righteousness of giving out of poverty, even as she hesitated to trust and believe that much. She was not poor, so giving out of poverty was not necessarily an everyday opportunity. Yet she knew fully what giving out of poverty meant and what it would require of her if she did. She could see many more ways to give than she was currently giving, and she could see giving much more than she currently gave. She had multiple concerns and justifications for not giving sacrificially including that the money she gave was not hers alone but her family's money, too. She also knew that she needed to provide for her family out of the money to which she had access and also believed that God called her to be a good steward of his blessings. Still, though, she knew that she could give sacrificially if she simply chose to do so. The next withdrawal she made or check she wrote could be larger, large enough to leave her short of paying for perceived needs. As she reflected over the years on this important question of giving sacrificially, her giving grew. Small opportunities arose for her to give at a moment when doing so seemed sacrificial and probably was so in small respect. She and her family had to cut back here and there to do so, for instance, or she had to do without or trust for a windfall of income to replace the gift with which she had parted. She hadn't yet spent her last as the poor widow had, but almost like courtship, God seemed to be giving her gentle opportunities to show her trust and love through small sacrifices of sometimes-large giving. She hoped and prayed that his Holy Spirit would continue to shape and inform her heart over this powerful question of sacrificial giving.

Give in secret. Matthew 6:4.

Giving raises an important question that most and probably all givers face. What should others know of the gift? The recipient may of necessity learn the identity of the donor, although not in every case when the gift goes through an intermediary such as a church or charitable organization. Even then, though, staff or other members of the church or charitable organization may know or learn of the gift. Givers often have some control and in some cases complete control over who learns of their gift. So again, givers face an inevitable question of gift notoriety. Jesus of course recognized that issue just as he would know all things. The important point is that by addressing the issue so squarely, Jesus teaches us that gift notoriety is consequential. Giving is not as simple as just giving. How the giver treats the method or process of giving makes a big difference in the quality of the giving act. Jesus's instruction is, in short, to give secretly. Don't call attention to your giving. Others should learn of the gift only if they need to know. Calling attention to the gift implies pride in giving, the desire that others note the generous or righteous character of the giver. Pride in giving destroys the character of the giver and gift. It places the reputation of the giver over the generosity of the giver. The giver may in fact be generous, but when the giver calls others' attention to the gift, doing so undermines the generosity. Calling attention to the gift makes it evident that the giver has reputation among others as at least one motive and possibly the prime or only motive for the gift. Obeying God in giving is a good thing, just as is having the compassionate and generous heart to give. Giving so that others believe one has an obedient and compassionate heart has a negative rather than positive quality. Pride corrupts.

In the middle of his Sermon on the Mount, Jesus spoke about giving to the needy. In that part of his sermon, he did not directly urge to give to the needy. Instead, he assumed that those who were listening to him were doing so already without his urging. He assumed that his hearers were already practicing righteousness, but he warned not to do so in front of others for the purpose of their seeing. He assumed that his hearers were already giving to the needy, saying, "So when you give to the needy," but he warned not to announce that giving with trumpets as hypocrites were doing in the synagogues and on the streets. Can you picture trumpets calling attention to the wealthy person who was making a gift either in the synagogue or right out on the streets? What a grand but hypocritical show it must have made, with the hypocrisy in the prideful honor that the trumpets gave to the giver when the honor should have gone to the righteousness of the gift. The crowd listening to Jesus on the mountainside must have seen that prideful show repeated frequently, a show that may well have irritated and even angered them. Note here, though, that Jesus was not in this part of his sermon exhorting to give but rather instructing *how to* give. Giving has proper and improper methods. An improper method of giving would be to announce it to others for public credit. Jesus then continued with the proper method of giving, "But when you give to the needy, do not let your left hand know what your right hand is doing, so that your giving may be in secret. Then your Father, who sees what is done in secret, will reward you."

He once had ambivalent feelings about the notoriety of his giving. On the one hand, he had no particular interest in others knowing when he gave or didn't give, or how much he gave when he did. Each to his own, he thought. Although he didn't mind being well thought of in his community rather than believed to be some sort of scoundrel, he didn't particularly depend on high esteem among others for his own self-worth. He had no interest in taking a prominent place in philanthropic circles, for instance, even though he deeply respected the giving of those who did. On the other hand, he saw the efforts that faith, charitable, and other organizations of which he was a part made to publicize the identity of givers, and he understood a part of their purpose and message in making that publication, which they said was to by example induce others to give. Yet he also felt pride's pull. He realized that recognition tempted him, just as, he supposed, it tempts anyone. At that point, though, he felt that he had identified the enemy sufficiently to vanquish or at least resist it. He would do as Jesus instructed, to give without seeking recognition for it. While some would necessarily learn about some giving, and others would note giving for whatever positive institutional purpose they could accomplish with the disclosure, he decided firmly that the more circumspectly that he could give, the better to resist the temptation for recognition. He might not always be able to give in secret, but God would give him plenty of opportunity to do so.

Give freely. Matthew 10:8.

The quantity or degree of giving is another question that most or all givers face. When do you begin, and when do you stop? How often and how much does one give? We probably ask that question of ourselves believing that resources are limited. We only earn so much in a paycheck, have so much in a checking or savings account, and have so little in a wallet or purse. We only have so many hours in a day and so much energy in our limbs to use for service. And we also rightly think of the importance of being good stewards of whatever financial resources we earn or receive, and whatever productive time and capability we manage. We should be paying the rent or mortgage, buying our own food, and otherwise acting in a financially responsible manner, just as we should be showing up for the job and putting in the hours notwithstanding alternative opportunities for charitable service. That said, Jesus still says to give freely. From God's perspective, resources are unlimited, not limited. God can increase what we earn or receive, and he can replace what we give, just as he can take away from us what we do not share freely. God knows and likely respects that we have needs and responsibilities of our own. To give freely may mean to stretch just beyond what we think that we can afford to give or manage to do charitably, just as God stretched in giving his Son whose teaching, example, life, blood, sacrifice, and redemption we receive so freely. When we give freely, stretching what we perceive to be our limited means and capabilities, we learn how generously God gives and replaces. When relying on and trusting in God, we are usually capable of far more than we estimate or perceive. Jesus invites us to increase that trust and to watch our giving increase with it, even as we learn to appreciate more fully just how generously God gives for us to receive.

When Jesus sent out the twelve disciples with his authority and power to heal, he gave them specific instructions to be generous in their giving. He also told the disciples why they should be so generous. Jesus first told them where to go, which was to the lost within the nation of Israel. He did not explain whom he meant by the *lost*, although his instruction as to what to do for the lost, which was to resurrect and heal, probably gives us the definition we need. Jesus instructed them to heal the sick including those with leprosy, drive out demons, and even raise the dead. Thus the disciples were probably to go not among the healthy and wealthy prominent people but among the diseased, sick, and dead who knew that they needed new life and healing and would therefore accept it from the disciples.

Yet after giving these instructions about whom to serve and how to serve them, Jesus also instructed as to the generous character their service should possess, and with that instruction also told the disciples *why* their service should be so generous. Jesus put both points succinctly, saying, "Freely you have received; freely give." The disciples must give freely, which we can reasonably take to mean without expectation for return. Give without hesitation, qualification, or condition. Give freely. And do so because God gave to the disciples so freely. Indeed, Jesus prefaced his instructions here with the command to tell those to whom the disciples gave freely that the kingdom of heaven has come near. The disciples were to herald the near presence of the kingdom, to point to God's present kingdom those to whom they gave so freely because God had given so freely to them. The disciples walked the kingdom with the King, where giving is most generous.

Years later, indeed more than two decades later, she could still recall with regret one clear time when in retrospect she felt that she had not given freely. Oh, she could recall plenty of times when she had declined to give, chosen not to give, not volunteered to give, or in some other way just not given. Solicitations to give wash over us in telephone, television, newsprint, social-media, email, and other communication waves. No one other than God himself could give to all who ask if one counts mass inquiries. Yet that distinction was precisely her problem with this one instance that she recalled with such regret. That request was not a mass inquiry. Someone, whom she knew not well but with whom she was nonetheless acquainted, made a specific request of her for funds for a specific purpose. She had wrestled a little with the request and then quietly declined it even though she would have been able to honor the request without denying herself or others. She recalled much later that she had rationalized at the time why she should not give as requested, which was in part that she could think of better uses for the giving, even though the person who asked felt the activity well worth pursuing and thus the request well worth asking. She was much later not even sure that she would make a different decision if the same person made the same request of her then. Still, her refusal bothered her. She felt in retrospect that she had not done as Jesus had instructed.

229

She decided that she had not listened closely enough to his guiding Spirit.

Give to the believer. <small>Matthew 10:42.</small>

While we should go to the sick, dead, and lost with our giving, Jesus also counsels that a gift to the believer, one who follows Jesus, brings the giver a sure reward. Faith finds support in community. Fellowship favors faith. To walk alone presents challenges best addressed by walking with others. We must be solicitous of our communities of faith. We must consider and care for fellow believers. We should be especially concerned to support with generous giving those who carry the faith to others, the followers of Jesus who attract and encourage new followers through their own generous giving, even if the giving is of time and talents rather than treasure. To support the work of a missionary is to give where giving may count most. To support the work of one who nurtures faith in others is to give where giving counts much. We do not restrict our gifts solely to give to the righteous, and not only because we have little prospect for making reliable distinctions between the righteous and unrighteous, believer and non-believer. Our generosity with the lost may be God's way of saving the lost. We must still give special regard for providing for the believers who do that work of God in speaking to, serving, and loving the lost.

Jesus had given long instructions to his disciples as he prepared to send them out with his authority and power. He told them so many profound things that the disciples must have wondered how he would end his long instructions. He did so by referring to the special regard that the disciples should have for the community of believers. In their travels on his behalf, the disciples would have some people welcome them but many reject them. Jesus first said that those who welcomed the disciples were simultaneously welcoming Jesus. Through their generous giving, the disciples carried Jesus with them to those people. He added that those who accepted the disciples thereby also accepting Jesus would then also be accepting the Father who sent Jesus. Jesus carries the Father to those who accept Jesus. Jesus then spoke of the reward that those who welcomed prophets and righteous persons would have, indeed, the same reward that prophets and righteous persons have. Jesus then concluded with a simple statement about those who did more than merely welcome the disciples but actually *gave* back to the disciples. He said, "If anyone gives even a cup of water to one of these little ones who is my disciple, truly I tell you, that person will certainly not lose their reward." Notice Jesus's three points of emphasis that even the *smallest* gift to a disciple of Jesus, he *truly tells us*, brings a *certain* reward.

They occasionally spoke with one another about whether they should or would have made competent missionaries. They had missionary acquaintances and of course heard inspiring accounts of missionary work, which they valued greatly. Yet they agreed that they had no sense of call to that ministry themselves, and more so, possessed no particular personality or skill that would appear to equip them for effectiveness. They could not picture themselves being good in the mission field and suspected that they would instead be ineffective burdens on whatever mission team or organization that might consent to send them. Their reluctance might have been fear or lack of faith or vision, as they were both readily willing to admit, but still nothing seemed to move them from their reluctance. Maybe mission work would come later, God willing, they thought. On the other hand, they did have those acquaintances who involved themselves in such remarkable mission work. And like millions of others who stay at home but pray and send, they knew that they could and should include missionaries and disciple-makers in their giving. Maybe, they laughed, they were living vicariously, but if so, it might be just the kind of vicarious living that God respects and appreciates.

Sell what you have to give to the poor. Luke 18:22.

Jesus gave his well-known instruction to sell all possessions in order to give the poor and follow Jesus, specifically to a certain rich ruler, and not from the account itself necessarily as a general instruction to anyone. Yet generalizing the instruction may well be appropriate to some degree and in some cases, or may be appropriate in full degree in all cases. As with much of Jesus's other profound instruction, each of us will have to discern the instructor's specific intent as to each of us and the instruction's specific application. One general point that anyone could reasonably draw from the account, though, is that possessions can interfere with both the willingness and ability to give. We can certainly give more out of the sale of possessions than we can give clinging to those same possessions. If selling things is a good tactic to pay down debt, which it often is, then selling things would presumably work just as well for increasing giving. Holding onto possessions also interferes with the willingness to give in that it promotes and fosters that false sense of security that we draw from hoarding. The proposition seems counterintuitive, but experience teaches at least some of us that the more we let go and give, the easier letting go and giving becomes. The hardest gift is the first, not the last. Sell something once in order to give, and selling something twice in order to give generally becomes easier. Selling in order to give teaches that our happiness, security, personality, and comfort do not have to be, and indeed should not be, in our possessions.

The rich ruler who wanted the eternal life that Jesus offered had assured Jesus that he had kept the commandments since he was a boy. Jesus told him that he still lacked one thing for eternal life, adding, "Sell everything you have and give to the poor, and you will have treasure in heaven. Then come, follow me." The account then states that the ruler looked very sad because of the great wealth that he would have to relinquish, highlighting that the quantity of wealth can be an influence against generous giving. Indeed, Jesus looked straight at the ruler, telling him outright how hard, indeed seemingly impossible, the rich find not just giving up their wealth but how hard they find entering God's kingdom. Jesus's statement might have surprised the wealthy and the religious leaders who courted them, or if not surprise, then his statement may at least have dismayed them. Some who heard Jesus's statement asked how anyone could then find salvation. Jesus replied that although entering the kingdom might look impossible, God made anything possible. The disciple Peter pointed out to Jesus that the disciples had left everything behind to follow Jesus, who reassured the disciples that anyone leaving home or family behind for the kingdom will receive both the kingdom and a rich reward. Entering the kingdom is more than possible. Jesus assures entry along with that entry's just reward.

She watched her parents closely as she grew up, just as she watched everything else closely, cautious and curious observation being her nature. Some of the more curious observations she made had to do with how her parents treated things, particularly their household property. Things seemed to come and go from her home frequently, especially *go*, much more frequently than in the homes of her friends. She even had to watch out a little or *her* things would disappear in a garage sale or as a donation to the thrift shop. Once in a while, a family heirloom would make its way into their home, under circumstances where she would think that it had a better chance of remaining long term. But, no, the heirloom was soon on the way out the door to the garage sale or thrift shop, too, although sometimes later bound for recovery when the donor relative got wind of the transgression. Her family's constant gifting away, donating, selling, and general winnowing of things for a time concerned her that her family could not afford its possessions, but the suspicion turned out not to be true at all. Gradually, she came to understand instead that her family just did not value things in the way that many other families valued things, whether new, old, or sentimental. She learned, too, that they valued things other than material possessions, like wanting to give generously but above all valuing their relationships with her own Lord and Savior Jesus. In the end, at maturity, she accepted and agreed that she too had no security in her possessions but great security in her relationship with Jesus and security of the same source in her family.

Be generous in giving to the poor. Luke 11:41.

So yes, give in general, give especially to believers who are making disciples of others and also to the poor, and even sell what you have in order to give to the poor. Jesus instructed each of these things in different ways and contexts. In yet another setting, he also instructed to be *generous* in giving to the poor, in case that inference was not apparent in his other instructions. Giving to the poor is one thing. Giving generously to the poor is another. You may have witnessed less-than-generous giving or may even have recognized it in yourself. We do make or find justifications not to give too much to the poor. One hears or reads about not wanting a generous gift to foster dependency, not wanting an unnecessary gift to reduce a poor person's dignity, not wanting generous gifts to fund corrupt behavior, and not wanting generous giving to attract other needy. We make or find plenty of rationales to give cautiously and only in modest amounts. Yet Jesus tells us instead to give to the poor generously. His instruction may well be because the poor need and benefit from generosity, and that generosity reflects the character of Father and Son. Still, in at least one account, Jesus revealed what generous giving to the poor does for the giver. Do not underestimate the power of giving generously to the poor. See in the following account what Jesus says that generous giving to the poor accomplishes even for the greedy and wicked.

The religious leader who invited Jesus into his home to eat and who noticed that Jesus did not wash for ceremony got from Jesus a lesson on the futility of ceremonial washing. Jesus told the leader frankly that while they were busy cleaning the outside, their insides were filled with wickedness and greed. Jesus called those religious leaders foolish, explaining that God had made both their insides and outsides. They had no way to hide from God, their creator, the bad shape of their insides simply by washing their outsides ceremonially. The ceremony did nothing for God, who saw both inside and outside. Yet in the midst of rebuking the religious leader, for Jesus would in a moment have several more rebukes, Jesus told the religious leader how to clean both the inside and outside. Jesus said simply, "But now as for what is inside you, be generous to the poor, and everything will be clean for you." Even though Jesus then resumed with his rebukes, notice the ready solution that he offered the religious leader, simply to give generously to the poor. Giving generously to the poor, Jesus told him, cleans *everything* for you. From the sounds of Jesus's many rebukes, one can easily imagine that the religious leader might have felt that the poor were not worthy of generosity, which may be precisely why Jesus gave that instruction. The Lord's words reach their mark.

She had learned the power of giving generously to the poor. Sure, she knew that generous giving could make big differences in the recipients' lives. One good acquaintance she had known, a person whom others would easily have counted among the poor when she first met and got to know her, had over the span of many years parlayed small and large generosities into two college degrees and a great job and career. That person was now giving generously to others. She had several times seen or been able to reasonably infer the positive effect of generous giving on jobs, vehicles, homes, and even marriages of the low income and poor. A little here and a little more there can simply make a big difference to a household's welfare and survival. These differences were natural, apparent, and of course highly satisfying to the recipient. Yet she had also seen significant effects on the giver. Giving seemed in some cases to have transformed persons whom she knew or at least deeply affected them. It could simply have been her impression of the giver that had changed rather than the giver actually changing, but she instead felt that the transformation was deep and real. Not only that, but she sensed the powerful cleansing effect that generous giving to the poor had in her own soul. Giving's biggest personal benefit seemed to be to take her mind off herself, to direct her spirit to God who made the giving possible and a high priority, and to direct her soul toward the person who received the gift. Those changes of mind, spirit, and soul were alone reward enough.

Give to the one who asks. Matthew 5:42.

One of the most natural and practical things that Jesus taught us about giving was to give to the one who asks. We probably sometimes make too big of an issue over whom to give our gift. When we do so, we may be fooling ourselves into not giving at all or at least temporarily avoiding giving, to satisfy our greed, insecurity, lack of trust, or other flaw. The question to whom to give may be a bit like the law expert who when Jesus said to love one's neighbor asked who was his neighbor, the account tells us, *to justify himself*, which we might safely take to mean to justify having many times not loved neighbors. Jesus responded to the law expert with the parable of the Good Samaritan who helped quite generously the person whom robbers had beaten on the road, when religious leaders had walked right by that same person. Similarly, we ask to whom we should give, just like the law expert asked the identity of his neighbor. Jesus promptly answers us that we should give to the one who asks us to give. Appreciate again the unhealthy power of self-justification. When others ask us to give, we find many reasons not to give, whether those reasons have to do with our present financial condition, the character or circumstances of the one making the request, what we think that the one making the request will actually do with the gift, and so on. Listen to your own rationalizing the next time you hear a request, particularly one directed at you individually. "Who, *me?*" your small inner voice may say and then answer itself, "No, they must be directing the request at someone else," or with similar justification. Yet no getting around it, no justifying. Give to the one who asks.

Jesus was well into his Sermon on the Mount when he reached the subject of giving generously to the one who asks, although he introduced the subject from a different direction. Jesus first spoke of not resisting an evil person, for example, one who slaps you across the cheek. Turn the other cheek to that person, Jesus said, for another slap. If someone sues you, Jesus continued, then give the claimant not just your shirt but also your coat. If someone forces you to walk a mile, Jesus said, then walk two miles with them. Jesus may in these instances of violence, lawsuits, and forced demands, have been encouraging peacemaking, the softening of hard hearts and anger, and the mending of division, through acts of generosity and love. Whatever the interpretation, Jesus then shifted the teaching from others who might force performance, in which case Jesus said in essence to over-perform for the one doing the forcing, to the person who simply *asks* for a gift or loan. Here in the case of simple requests, Jesus used no hyperbole, no doubling of the request on gift or loan, as he had in the instances of forced demands, where doubling the demand might indeed have been necessary generosity. Instead, Jesus said to simply make the gift or loan. Jesus summarized, "Give to the one who asks you, and do not turn away from the one who wants to borrow from you."

In a way, he appreciated how seldom others actually asked him for something directly. Oh, he had plenty of requests, but by far the majority of those requests were very modest and primarily for things that he would have done out of ordinary duty rather than in generous giving. Instead, people were for the most part remarkably restrained and respectful when the time and opportunity came to ask for something bold and generous. His appreciation was not so much that their reticence meant that he had to give less often, although he suspected that flaw of his was indeed a small part of why he appreciated having had so few requests. He worried, too, that he might have signaled to others that he was an unwilling giver, although he did not believe that to be the case, despite his natural insecurity with money that sometimes led to an unfortunate stinginess. On the whole, he actually seemed to give more often and more generously than many others as far as he could tell, although he knew that really knowing where his giving fell in comparison to others was impossible and also probably not healthy. Better that no one know or rely much on the relative giving of others, he concluded. In the end, he discerned that the reluctance of people to ask for something just made him respect the diligence and perseverance of those people all the more. He decided that worrying that someone might ask for something generous was a waste of time and that he should instead worry that someone might *fail to* ask when he would gladly have provided. He then had what he felt was a healthy new outlook on giving, one that should make him feel more generous and act more generously.

Give to everyone who asks. Luke 6:30.

Probably, givers today, especially those who give often and much from family, corporate, or community foundations, make substantial efforts to distinguish among the merits of those seeking the gifts. Anyone who has tried knows the challenge of writing successful grant applications, where the grantor seems to require the crossing of all letters "t" and the dotting of every letter "i." Foundations grant processes aside, many of us as individuals take a similarly cautious and even business-like approach. The requests for support come in bunches, and we carefully or not-so-carefully consider each of them, or many of them, or, well, a few of them before deciding which if any to fund. And again, as we follow our thoughtful or not-so-thoughtful winnowing process, we gradually justify its usually less-than-generous result. We may or may not have actually articulated valid and reliable criteria for our decision whether to give, but whether or not we have, we still find justifications to deny some, many, or all of the gift requests, whether made by family, friends, neighbors, employers, charities, causes, churches and ministries, or strangers. In doing so, though, we miss Jesus's instruction to give to *everyone* who asks. Jesus lived in a different day, one in which we might think that people faced fewer gift requests, but to the contrary the gospel accounts and following letters show plenty of examples of demands and requests, not to mention begging, and need far greater than that of our day. We may be missing something critically important in not hearing Jesus's instruction to give to everyone who asks.

Jesus was well into his instruction to the large crowd on the plain, teaching about loving enemies and to turn the other cheek, much as he had taught in his Sermon on the Mount. Here, though, he departed in small ways from his Sermon on the Mount message. Rather than someone suing for your shirt to whom you should give your coat, Jesus instead gave the example of someone taking your coat to whom you should give your shirt. Jesus or the one recording the account of his teaching on the plain then omitted the Sermon on the Mount's example of walking two miles with the one who forced a one-mile walk. Jesus instead proceeded on to the Sermon on the Mount's instruction to give to the one who asks but in his message on the plain altered his Sermon on the Mount text to include *everyone* who asks you. Jesus said, "Give to everyone who asks you, and if anyone takes what belongs to you, do not demand it back." Note the specificity that Jesus gave this form of his instruction to give to everyone who asks *you*. Note also the generality that he gave the instruction to give to *everyone* who asks you. Giving to everyone who asks broadened Jesus's instruction in the Sermon on the Mount when he said to give to *the one* who asks. Jesus then gave the crowd what

238

we know as his Golden Rule to do to others as you would have them do to you.

She decided to try something different for a change. Instead of putting up her guard against every giving request that she heard, especially in her outreach-mission church where the requests for support were deliberately and justly many, she would try to accept and act on every request, at least to some degree. She would try giving to everyone there who asked. To her surprise, she found the requests were not quite as often as she had believed. The number of times that she actually reached into her purse for money or pulled out her checkbook to write a check was fewer times than she expected. She realized that in putting up her guard against giving, she had likely exaggerated the number of requests, developed a negative attitude greater than the situation warranted. She next realized that she could give something in response to all requests without significantly affecting her finances. That discovery truly surprised her. She had thought that to answer every request would have required taking on at least one and maybe two or three new jobs. Where, she used to think, would she ever get all the money? As it turned out, she already had the money but just needed to open her ears and heart to giving it. Her last and most pleasing discovery was that her heart changed with her giving generosity. Quickly, she was not wincing at requests, trying not to hear them, but instead listening intently for requests and, to a degree that surprised her, actually welcoming them. What a difference an open and generous heart makes, she realized, just as Jesus had said.

Use gifts. Matthew 25:21.

Jesus's many instructions to give, to give generously, and to whom to give, together imply a related important instruction that Jesus spelled out in other lessons and parables. We are to use whatever capacity that we have to give, whatever time, talent, and resources we have to employ on behalf of others. We are not to sit idly on our capacities and resources, lazy, comfortable, and indolent.

239

We are instead to rise, move, and act, deploying whatever resources we own or control. If time is what we have, then we should use that time. If skills are what we possess, then we should use those skills. If money is what we hold and control, then we should share that money with others and invest that money in others. God blessed us with life and blesses us daily with breath, discernment, and sentience. He reasonably expects us to apply our natural and capable activity, motion, energy, and vitality, in service of others, which simultaneously accomplishes our service to him. God has invested himself in each of us and has every right and reason to expect a full return. If we held someone else's money for investment, whether as a financial advisor or fund manager, then we would not just lock those funds in a vault to gather dust until the person requested the money's return. We would use the skill that had caused the person to entrust the money to us. When God blesses us with whatever skill or resource we receive, we have the compelling obligation to use those blessings. If you need any further incentive, then consider that those who earnestly deploy resources for productive good, God blesses with even more.

As he was leaving the temple courts during the festival week just days before his betrayal and arrest, Jesus had lingered one last time to teach the disciples. His instruction was lengthy, including parables, prophecies, cautions, and instructions. One parable involved three men, whose master had given each a different number of bags of gold. The man who received five bags had put them to work to earn his master five more bags of gold. "'Well done, good and faithful servant,'" Jesus quoted the master as saying, adding, "'You have been faithful with a few things; I will put you in charge of many things.'" The man given two bags also put them to work to earn two more, receiving the same lauding from his grateful master. But the man given just one bag had hidden his bag believing his master to be hard, and thus earned none. The master condemned that man for laziness and wickedness, giving his one bag to the man who had ten. Jesus reported the master as saying that whoever has, the master will give more, but whoever does not have, the master will take what little they hoard.

He had such a fire, such passion, to use his time, skill, and resources for productive good, for the benefit of the people whom and institutions that he served, that when no one was looking he would literally run back and forth between workstations. He knew that his passion was at least a little unusual and also knew that it could look scary to others, less like earnest care and more like obsession or compulsion. He had to take care not to let it interfere with others, with his family, or with his own health. He also recognized that greed, pride, and other corruptions could just as easily take hold of his passionate energy to distort if for bad rather than good. The quietly furious pace at which he often operated also exhausted his mind and body, although he had learned to have less concern for the exhaustion. Any worker knows what being tired at the end of a productive day is like. He wanted to be tired if doing so meant that he had put his all into another day in service. His greatest concern about the nearly manic pace at which he operated was that he be sure to direct it in ways that his Master approved. In the end, he figured that he should not ignore, frustrate, or waste his energy because his Master had made him this way. He should just use it as his Master directed and deployed.

1.11 Receiving

Do not set your heart on food and drink. Luke 12:29. *Do not worry about eating and drinking.* Matthew 6:25. *Eat whatever others give you.* Luke 10:8. *Fast without showing it.* Matthew 6:17. *Hunger.* Luke 6:21. *Do not worry about what to wear.* Luke 12:22. *Report what good you see and hear.* Luke 7:22.

The subjects of service and giving make so much sense for Jesus to have addressed because we know that love and care for others are the command and heart of the Father. We do well to attend to Jesus's instructions on generous giving. On the other hand, that Jesus spoke not just about giving but also about *receiving* can be a little surprising. We should nonetheless listen closely to and follow Jesus's words about how, when, and what to receive, and what to say about the good things we see of others. To have the right attitude about serving, giving, loving, caring, and other important acts, we may also need the right attitude about receiving. Giving and receiving have close relationship. We find it hard to get one of them right without the other. Look at those who seem to do well in service, and you will probably find that they do equally well with respect to the issues that receiving raises. You may not have anticipated that receiving should raise any issue, but Jesus's instructions show that it raises several. We all have certain needs to fulfill and certain opportunities to receive that which would fill them. We also each have certain desires to manage if we are to remain healthy of body and sound of mind and spirit. Listen then to Jesus's words and follow his actions around receiving.

Do not set your heart on food and drink. Luke 12:29.

243

Food and drink are two of the things that we hope, expect, and critically need to receive regularly, meaning that we inevitably think often and necessarily about receiving them. To think about the next meal, though, is one thing, while to set one's heart on food and drink is another thing. One common response to Jesus's instruction not to set our hearts on food and drink is probably, well, sure, we should manage our calorie consumption responsibly. After all, obesity is a health and lifestyle issue. If we pursue food and drink too often and too aggressively, then we will have weight and health problems, some of them serious and even life threatening. If the drink is alcoholic, then we will have substance-abuse problems. So sure, let's be wise about food and drink. Yet Jesus's instruction probably has a little less to do with the body and physical health than it does with spiritual matters. Health certainly affects one's spirit. Our bodies are our temples. We should not make such marked distinctions between the mental or spiritual and the physical. Our bodies, made by and after the image of God, are a part of who we are, even if they await resurrection with our spirits. But again, Jesus's instruction not to set the heart on food and drink probably applies just as much to the fit and healthy as it does to the unfit and obese. You can be perfectly fit and healthy, and still think about, occupy yourself with, and pursue food and drink to such great degree that you miss life's point and purpose. While God gives us food and drink to sustain us and even to enjoy, Jesus's instruction is a warning against making food and drink our constant occupation. Be conscious of your thoughts. Listen to how often you find yourself thinking about, planning, and anticipating your next drink or repast. Fast now and then to break the mental occupation with food and drink. Enjoy food and drink, but don't make it your heart and mission.

Speaking to the disciples in the midst of a crowd of many thousands that had gathered around him, Jesus spoke about the common needs of food and clothing. His admonition was not to worry about either. God clothes the grass and flowers, and God feeds the tiny sparrows. How much more then will God feed and clothe us? Yet Jesus then extended his instruction beyond not just worrying about food and drink, trusting instead in God's provision, but also to avoid pursuing food and drink as ends. Worry is one thing to avoid. So, too, is pursuing food and drink a destructive end.

The way that Jesus put it was, "Do not set your heart on what you will eat and drink." His instruction was about the direction or setting of the heart, not to food and drink but to the desires of the Father. Jesus immediately explained that the pagans of the world, those who imagine many gods rather than knowing the Father, run after food and drink. Setting their hearts on food and drink, they pursue food and drink as the most important part of their day. Jesus corrected that view, saying that the Father knows the need for food and drink, and that the disciples should therefore pursue instead the Father's kingdom. Do not set the heart on food and drink.

As he headed to his vehicle for the ride home after another challenging work day, his first thought was of the drink, not alcoholic but a drink nonetheless, that he might get on the way home. Even as he did so, he laughed silently at his misguided focus. He knew well the preoccupation that food and drink, for him especially drink, could hold. Who didn't think now and then of something warm and comforting, or cold and refreshing, to drink, whether in the morning to get going, mid-day to get restarted, or end of the day to slow down? We seem to have a drink for every mood or moment, he thought, as he mulled whether to stop here or there, and whether to get something sweet or sour, warm or cold, large or small. As his mind wandered over the subject of drink, he remembered again how misguided was his focus. God had blessed him richly this day, even if the day had included its usual challenges. God was near, present in this moment, even if the moment was only another long drive home. He began slowly to turn from the thought of the blessing and nearness of God, and how his day had in some respects included kingdom work, to prayer to God. His prayer and communion lasted a short and refreshing while, broken only by the approach of the exit where he usually made a drink stop.

Do not worry about eating and drinking. Matthew 6:25.

Setting your heart on eating and drinking can distract you from healthy reflection on the blessings and desires of God. *Worrying* about eating and drinking presents a different set of concerns. Jesus admonished both to avoid setting your heart on eating and drinking, *and* not to *worry* about what you will eat or drink. To set one's heart on something implies devotion to and desire for it. By contrast, to worry about something implies anxiety or concern over whether that something will take place. Worrying about eating and drinking can take several forms. One concern that people who worry about food and drink might be expressing is that they will not find food to eat or drink to satisfy thirst. Certainly, hunger and thirst are legitimate concerns for many who have inadequate access to food. Worry might still not be the answer for addressing those concerns, but the concern itself we should understand and respect. Jesus may have been speaking instead about those of us who have adequate access to food but nonetheless pretend, act, and worry that we do not. For some of us, it takes only a small delay in the next meal or drink to begin to whine and worry that we will promptly expire without it. We just don't like to be hungry, even though hunger may in our case be only a temporary and small inconvenience, and no cause whatsoever for concern, no less for worry. Jesus might have been saying not to complain and worry when you are hungry, and your next meal is right around the corner. We should show a little perspective, discipline, and maturity, when God has provided so richly, rather than worry over abundant food and drink.

In his Sermon on the Mount, Jesus gave a similar instruction about food and drink to the instructions that he gave the disciples and crowd on the plain, although with some differences that provide further lessons. In the Sermon on the Mount, Jesus gave similar instructions not to worry about what to eat, drink, or wear. The Father feeds the birds and clothes the flowers, and so would feed and clothe the disciples and crowd. He also referred in the Sermon on the Mount, as he had in his message on the plain, to the pagans running after food, drink, and fine clothes, when they should have known that the Father would provide them and that they should thus focus on the Father. In the Sermon on the Mount, though, Jesus was more specific in discouraging what the disciples and members of the crowd might have said and must have heard repeatedly. Jesus said, "So do not worry, saying, 'What shall we eat?' or 'What shall we drink?'" Jesus seemed to be addressing more closely and specifically the fear, anxiety, worry, and lack of trust in God that hunger can generate.

246

Jesus did not say not to hunger. He said instead not to worry about what to eat or drink. The response to hunger and thirst should not be asking yourself or others worrying questions over what to eat or drink.

She suspected that this instruction, not to worry about food and drink, was especially for her. Maybe her high metabolism contributed to her propensity to show concern for her next meal because indeed she was quickly hungry after any prior meal. Or maybe she was just so accustomed to regular meals and had never had circumstances force her to go very hungry. Then again, maybe she was just soft and needed to toughen up. Or maybe some of her concern had to do with the quality or lack thereof in the food because indeed she tried to eat healthy. Whatever was the cause for her concern, she knew that she exhibited worry over her next meal far too quickly, far too vociferously, and far too often. She had never deliberately gone hungry, that is, never deliberately fasted, but maybe the time to do so was now. A small voice was telling her that her worry over food was not metabolism, privilege, or even weakness, but spiritual misunderstanding. She had discovered another obstacle in her path into the kingdom. She was going to worry less over the next meal.

Eat whatever others give you. Luke 10:8.

We get picky about food and drink for a lot of different reasons. One reason is pure taste. We each like certain foods and dislike others, although some of us like more foods and others fewer foods. Some of us are pickier than others of us. Some of us are particularly picky about food ingredients or preparation, sometimes for good reason because of allergies or food-borne illness, others for less reliable reasons. Some of us also avoid certain foods out of ceremony, particularly religious dietary laws. Some of us also have stronger feelings than others about eating the offered food and drinking the drink of a poor host, or of any host, that one should not burden another with one's appetite. Jesus may or may not have meant his instruction, to eat whatever others set before you, to address any or all of these reasons. One implication of his instruction that the setting in which he gave it strongly suggests is not, when carrying his word and fellowship, to refuse food and drink thinking that we are not worthy of it. Sharing God's word with a host merits the host's hospitality including food and drink. Don't hesitate to have your fill of what you have earned. Yet Jesus did say to eat *whatever* others put before you in that setting, at least possibly suggesting that dietary restrictions, particularly of the ceremonial and religious kind, should not impede us, and also possibly suggesting that we should not let our pickiness undermine our host's appreciation for the word of God that we carried.

Jesus had just appointed seventy-two others to follow the disciples into the mission field where, he said, the harvest would be plentiful. He had specific instructions to give these seventy-two others, in most respects like, but in some small respects different from, the instructions that he had given the twelve disciples who went before them. They were to go ahead of him two by two into the towns where Jesus was about to go. In the towns that they entered, they would find or make opportunities to enter some residents' homes. In homes that welcomed them, Jesus explained, residents would likely offer them food and drink. What were they then to do? Should they decline the offer so as not to burden their hosts or to prove their willingness to carry Jesus's word for free? Should they follow strict dietary laws and eat only approved food, declining any other? Or should they leave without eating or drinking? Jesus instead instructed, "Stay there, eating and drinking whatever they give you, for the worker deserves his wages." They were to eat and drink whatever their gracious host offered them. No food and drink restrictions, no polite refusals, just eat and drink, Jesus was saying, adding that they would have earned whatever their host had offered.

He knew that eating it would be hard, but he was just as sure that he was going to do so. In candor, he would have admitted that he was a picky eater. He ate home food and certain restaurant food, particularly the corporate-franchise kind that was so fungible and reliable. He did not eat much else. He particularly avoided party food, banquet food, and potluck food. He just didn't like the looks or taste of it, or even trust it. While if he were hungry enough at a gathering, he might take a couple of crackers with some reliable-looking cheese sliced onto them, he absolutely avoided mixed dips, potato salads, and the like. He would think at each such offering, who knows what's in there? On the other hand, he never would have let any host know of his pickiness and hoped that it was not too evident. He didn't in the least want to offend anyone who was so generous as to offer him food and drink. He knew that pickiness can easily offend. And that was precisely his dilemma at this moment. His host who had entertained him so graciously in the spirit of faith-filled fellowship had just set a dish of his own before him. On that dish was everything that he would ordinarily not eat. If he did not eat it, then his host would notice and might take offense, undermining their fellowship. So, eat he did. Down the hatch, smiling.

Fast without showing it. Matthew 6:17.

Fasting is a long-established spiritual discipline. Moses and Jesus both fasted for extended periods, Moses on the mountain and Jesus for forty days in the wilderness. To voluntarily go without food for a period has its spiritual effects particularly when done as a spiritual discipline. Hunger is so compelling, and food draws, entertains, and satisfies us to such a great extent, that putting both hunger and food deliberately aside to attend to one's relationship with God focuses the body, soul, and spirit. Holding hunger at bay and refusing food entails sacrifice, signals devotion, and creates concentrated time. Done in the right way under the right circumstances, particularly the influence and presence of the Holy Spirit, fasting can contribute to intense spiritual awareness and awakening. Fasting has much to recommend it. On the other hand, fasting probably has few or no effects on our relationship with God when not done as a spiritual discipline and done instead only to lose weight or to have more time for work or play. Jesus, though, makes it quite clear that fasting has no influence on God when done to impress others with one's purported godliness. Listen to Jesus teach about fasting.

Jesus spoke about the practice of deliberately going without food for a time as if people did it as a matter of course. When he spoke about fasting in the Sermon on the Mount, he did not expressly recommend fasting, not at least in so many words. He instead told the crowd gathered to hear him on the mountainside *how* to fast. His giving that instruction about how to fast could have been an endorsement of fasting, or it may instead only have been a corrective to the way in which people were then fasting, without any intent on his part to encourage fasting. His instruction was certainly the latter, a corrective. On its face, Jesus's statement about fasting simply assumed that people would be fasting, again which could be a powerful endorsement of the practice, as if to say that of course people would be fasting, or it may not. Yet consider the corrective for which he certainly intended it. Jesus said, "When you fast, do not look somber as the hypocrites do, for they disfigure their faces to show others they are fasting." Jesus said that by showing others that they fasted, they had already received their reward in full. Jesus wanted them instead to act and look normal, grooming themselves as they would on any other day when they were not fasting. Then, Jesus said, only the Father would know, and the Father would reward them for what they did in secret. Jesus's implication from indicating that the Father would reward secret fasting appears to be that the Father favors fasting. Just fast for the Father, not for show.

For seasons, they had periodically fasted together. They found it hard to fast separately. Eating in households and elsewhere is social. They, at least, tended to eat together when home together. When they were trying to fast separately, one would be eating and expecting the other to eat, when instead the other was fasting. Fasting together eliminated the awkwardness of one of them eating while the other fasted. Fasting together almost made fasting a little easier, although they agreed that fasting was not easy. They laughed together that at the first missed meal, their bodies seemed to yell at them that their bodies were dying. Their bodies seemed to say, Hey, you, we need food, a lot of it and quick! Talking to one another in this way about how they were feeling as they fasted helped them persevere. They picked one another up. When they were both down during a fast, they just tried to keep away from one another so as not to bring the other one further down. Misery loves company, too much. The down times during fasting when they kept apart were when they each turned silently in prayer and meditation to God.

250

They agreed that these were the important times, often the powerful times. They also agreed that not eating and not *thinking* about eating, or at least trying not to think about eating, gave them what seemed like so much more time to dwell so much more richly on God. The other thing that they both agreed about fasting was that they would try not to make a big show of it. They might share between them that they were fasting together, but they wouldn't go advertise it to anyone else.

Hunger. Luke 6:21.

One of the clearest ways in which we measure whether we are receiving what we feel is due us is to ask whether we are hungry. If we are hungry, then we feel deprived, which is perfectly natural, just as it should be, a necessary inducement to seek food. The same would be true for other kinds of hunger, perhaps hunger for care, closeness, comfort, meaning, or relationship, that those appetites lead us forward toward their fulfillment through God. It is fine to hunger from time to time, or for seasons in life, we should think, because hunger is an important inducement in life, not at all to say that deprivation itself is a good thing. Yet somehow, we take hunger a step farther than its biological, social, and spiritual basis alone would warrant. In the world's ways, to hunger is not just a signal to seek food, but beyond that, is also to fail, to be left out and left behind, and a condition that others may blame. Hunger is not just a difficult thing but a bad thing, a judging and condemning thing, making one not just in need of food but a failure in the world, a reject and outcast. Jesus rejects those implications by saying instead that the hungry will be satisfied. The important implication from Jesus's statement about the hungry being satisfied is to not let hunger, again whether for food, care, comfort, relationship, or intimacy, convince you that you do not have the favor and kingdom of God. Our attitude in the face of hunger should not be to give up, lose faith, and reject God thinking that he has rejected us. God does not love only the fat, happy, and fulfilled. God loves the hungry every bit as much as he loves the full and satisfied, especially when that hunger leads us forward in faith

251

to seek fulfillment in him. If you are not receiving everything that is yours, everything that you need for your filling, then don't give up on God because his kingdom is still yours. Who cares about hunger when we have God's kingdom?

In his sermon to the large crowd on the plain, Jesus gave several instances when the members of the crowd would find themselves blessed. The poor and hungry, those who weep, and those whom others hate and exclude, would each find themselves blessed nonetheless. The poverty and hunger that some suffer, and the condemnation that others have for the poor and hungry, are no obstacle to God's kingdom. Blessed are the poor, Jesus said, for *theirs* is God's kingdom. As to hunger, Jesus said specifically, "Blessed are you who hunger now, for you will be satisfied." In saying that blessing would follow the poor, hungry, weeping, hated, and excluded, Jesus did not say whether those would be blessed *because of* their circumstances or instead *despite* their circumstances. Being poor certainly does not feel blessed. We call it *poverty* precisely because the condition is the opposite of what we define as *blessed*. Nor does being hungry, or weeping, or being excluded or hated feel like being blessed. Indeed, weeping is not merely a circumstance but an emotional response to a circumstance. One weeps precisely because one is *not* feeling blessed. Jesus was thus not saying that to weep or hunger is to *be* blessed. Rather, his words were that those who weep or hunger now *will be* blessed, the implication being that the blessing follows the weeping or hunger. Weeping and hunger have no merit in themselves except to the extent that they lead us forward to God's kingdom where none weep or hunger. One does not do better to weep or hunger than to smile and be filled. Jesus was simply saying that those who weep or hunger, or suffer in poverty, will be satisfied and laugh because *theirs is the kingdom of God*. We each have access to the kingdom of God, where we will find no poverty, hunger, or weeping, and where we will instead find fulfillment in God.

He was often hungry, although all of it was voluntary, not at all out of deprivation. A point comes in life when the body just no longer needs the calories that the stomach nonetheless demands. The nature of stomachs is to want to be filled, even when the metabolism has slowed to the point that the body no longer needs a filled stomach. Such is the cycle of life. He felt that he had developed a healthy approach to his hunger, which was to let it keep pushing him forward in faith. He initially saw no connection between hunger, satisfying that hunger, his expanding waistline, and his growing or diminishing faith. What did God have to do with hunger? Gradually, though, he realized how preoccupied he was with food because of the small hunger he tried to allow and endure in order not to gain so much weight as to not fit his clothing. Nearly everyone at some point battles weight. He knew that his battles were very small battles compared to what some others must endure. Yet the greatest help that he received in those small battles came from turning the battles into ones of faith, using hunger and the time that hunger freed from eating to turn to God in meditation, prayer, study, and reflection. He also had work, family, and recreations to occupy him, of course, but devotion became more and more a part of his response to hunger. He knew though that the hunger he experienced was nothing like unwilling deprivation and was especially glad that the deprived had just as much, and maybe even more, access to God. Hunger only for a time, and then live filled with God.

Do not worry about what to wear. Luke 12:22.

When the subject comes to what we wish for ourselves, what we hope to gain or receive as we proceed through life, we probably think as much or more about our bodies, our physical appearance, than just about anything else. We inhabit these glorious temples, but the temples have a way of attracting more of our attention, and more negative attention, than may be healthy or spiritually wise for us. Of course, a large part of our challenge in this respect is culture. Living in a media-driven society that makes one's body image the measure of one's status and worth certainly does not help us keep this need in any perspective. If the high rate, large quantity, and substantial cost of cosmetic surgery is any fair indication, then we have collectively lost that battle. Body shapes, and our negative perception of them no matter how normal and healthy they actually are, have spawned their own eating disorders that have cost the lives of far too many young women in particular. We are obsessed not only with our bodies but with what covers them, with our fashion or dress. Not too long ago, the world scorned and a nation deposed an international figure in part because his wife had indulged the inconceivable luxury of hundreds of pairs of shoes. Today, international celebrities flaunt their hundreds of shoes and showy outfits. We throw out or throw off clothing far more than we wear it out, while always looking for what will make our bodies look just a little bit more like what we think others think that our bodies should look. Jesus says simply not to worry about our bodies or what we wear to cover them. His admonition would resonate with the disfigured and destitute, those who had too little clothing and disabled bodies. Yet his admonition should resonate just as much with those of us today who obsess over our bodies and clothing.

This crowd had been the one that had grown so large into the many thousands that individuals were trampling on one another. Jesus had thus begun by teaching his disciples, only gradually drawing the restless crowd into his lesson. His teaching had drawn the crowd in, causing him to address the crowd with a preliminary parable, the one about the rich man who built bigger barns to live a life of ease off of his bountiful harvests. Jesus had then turned back to his disciples to tell them to instead not worry about their lives, what they would eat, their bodies, or what they would wear. Jesus said specifically, "Do not worry about your body, what you will wear." He then continued by saying that worrying helps nothing, not even the clothing and body. God had made the wild flowers more beautiful than the richest and most resplendent man in the world Solomon could even manage to look. Jesus said to leave looks to God, for "how much more will he clothe you — you of little faith!" Thus Jesus had moved from a parable teaching about what to do when blessed with more than one can consume, which was the parable of the rich fool who built bigger barns, into specific instructions to his disciples about the extra attention that they should not be giving their lives, consumption, bodies, and clothing. His do-not-worry instructions were thus not just to trust God's provision but also to not obsess over our bodies and clothing because nothing we do will be like what God does for us in resurrecting our bodies. Imagine: God will clothe us. Until then, anything we do as to clothing, even if we had all the money and means in the world, is worthless.

She realized that she probably took just a little less care for her clothing than she ought to by the strict and formal measures of at least some members of her family and community. The thrift store was by far her favorite clothing outlet. Even after years of shopping at the same small hand-me-down thrift store, she was amazed at the acceptable, even desirable clothing that she found and bought there. She had sweatshirts and jeans that she had bought there a decade earlier and still wore regularly but still loved going as often as her schedule and conscience permitted her. In her case, the thrift store wasn't really a money thing, although she definitely appreciated the very low, often ridiculously low prices. She could have afforded almost anything she wished at full-price outlets. And rarely, she did shop at those full-price outlets, particularly when she felt that she really should satisfy those family or community members' taste on one or more special occasions, by purchasing and wearing something according to the day's tastes. She didn't want to disrespect others on those occasions. Overall, though, she just wasn't that deeply concerned with what others thought of her appearance, as long as she was reasonably comfortable. She wanted to care for herself but not attract attention to herself or try to meet the expectations of others. God had made her as she was, which she knew in God's eyes was beautiful, and he would someday be clothing her in exactly the fashion that would make her even more beautiful.

Report what good you see and hear. Luke 7:22.

One other way in which we should think about receiving gifts is to recognize and acknowledge what others are doing. We naturally tend to take the most notice when *we* receive something, writing thank-you cards, spreading the word of our blessing, and making other appropriate shows of recognition. We like to receive blessings but also hope to acknowledge appropriately when others bless us, not wanting to be ungracious, show ingratitude, and receive the ugly label of an ingrate. After all, it is all about us, right? Jesus takes a broader view that we should not just recognize and share the good things that we receive, the good things that happen to us, but that we should report the good things that he does for others. The shift that Jesus invites us to make is subtle, but think of its value. In addition to going around counting and reporting our blessings, which to an extent is good but nonetheless self-involved and -focused, we should be looking around us at the wonders that Christ does in the lives of others, and celebrating those things with others. You may be one of those who does so, or you may know someone who does. The outlook has powerful effect on both the one who holds it and those who witness it. Keeping your eyes and ears open for the wonders that God accomplishes through Christ is a revolutionary way to live when contrasted with the general self-focus we ordinarily maintain. Look not for your own blessing, although celebrate and acknowledge it when it comes. Look instead for the blessing of others, and report it especially to those who need its encouragement.

The crowds naturally grew as they followed Jesus from town to town where he taught, challenged, blessed, healed, and even raised the dead. The time was still early in Jesus's public ministry. The local ruler, though, had imprisoned Jesus's cousin John, the well-known herald who had recently baptized Jesus in the Jordan River when the Holy Spirit descended on Jesus. John's disciples had been among those who had followed Jesus from town to town, listening to his teaching and witnessing his miracles, which they reported back to John in prison. Their reports made John want to hear Jesus confirm that he was the Messiah, so John sent his disciples to Jesus as messengers with that request. Jesus replied to the messengers, "Go back and report to John what you have seen and heard: The blind receive sight, the lame walk, those who have leprosy are cleansed, the deaf hear, the dead are raised, and the good news is proclaimed to the poor." After the messengers went on their way back to John, Jesus told the crowd that John was indeed the one whom the scriptures said would herald the Messiah.

He loved being around people who spoke about what Jesus was doing for others. He had been almost completely unfamiliar with that perspective of God's action in the world until joining an actively spiritual congregation where, it seemed, nearly every member had that perspective. In that congregation, he heard nearly constant report of what Jesus was doing here, what Jesus had done there, and what Jesus was going to do somewhere else. He marveled at the consistency and power of the congregation's outlook. The congregation's members were individually not particularly blessed as blessing generally went in the region, although many of them were significantly more blessed than they had been before pursuing Jesus, and the congregation had itself definitely grown in health and welfare over the years according to its pastor and members. Yet once immersed in that perspective of God's action in the world, he could see from small hints how others from outside that congregation also had that kingdom perspective. In each instance, he realized how refreshing the perspective was both for the one who held it and those who heard it. He supposed that the perspective might jar those who did not know Jesus. He even once heard a pastor from another congregation complain about people who were always talking about Jesus. The pastor's comment surprised and disappointed him, even though he suspected that he had misinterpreted it from the fashion in which the pastor intended. No matter. He sensed the power that reporting the work of Jesus had not just on those who already followed him but on those who didn't yet know of the miracle life that he provided.

1.12 Judging

Do not judge others. _{Matthew 7:1.} *Do not judge by human standards.* _{John 8:15.} *Stop judging by appearances.* _{John 7:24.} *Make right judgments.* _{John 7:24.} *Do not condemn.* _{Luke 6:37.} *Show sinners their fault.* _{Matthew 18:15.} *Rebuke those who sin against you.* _{Luke 17:3.}

Believing and praying, learning and teaching, serving and working, persevering and succeeding, giving and receiving. One can see from the above sections that Jesus taught about subjects that relate closely to one another, that when properly understood work with one another rather than against one another. We should believe, while we also pray for God to help us believe. We should learn, but we should also teach. We should serve sacrificially but we may also work expecting reward. We will have to persevere through formidable challenges, but when we do we succeed in receiving just reward. We should give, but we must also attend to how we should receive. The next subject on which Christ taught, when and how to judge or not judge, presents a similar sort of dichotomy. Judging, or discerning right from wrong, and distinguishing the should-do from the must-not-do, is obviously important to a rewarding life in Christ. On the other hand, and to the surprise of many, *not judging* also turns out to be critically important to not having God judge us. Judging has two sides, doing so with discernment on the one hand to ensure that we are not committing our own or ratifying another's sin, but also *not* doing so in a way that unforgivingly condemns others with the result that God condemns us. Listen carefully to Jesus speak about the important subject of judging. Get judging right, just as you get other important actions right.

259

Do not judge others.   Matthew 7:1.

Jesus was crystal clear on his instruction not to judge others, the result of which would be that God would judge you by the same stringent measure. By not judging others, Jesus likely meant not to condemn others unduly for their sin. He could have meant not to judge them worthy, worthwhile, excellent role models and mentors. Rather, though, Jesus clearly meant from the additional context that he gave to his instruction that we should not judge others negatively. One might construe several possible reasons for Jesus's instruction not to condemn others. We might, for instance, not have the full information and perspective we would need to make sound judgments. You may have judged another harshly, maybe even someone close to you, only later to learn that they were without guilt or responsibility in the matter. Another reason not to judge could be that the authority and responsibility to judge may be someone else's than yours to judge. You may be sticking your nose into something that should be none of your business. We might also not have the skill to judge, not knowing God's word well enough and just not having the perspective and wisdom. While all of those reasons not to judge could be sound in any one instance, Jesus gives a different reason not to judge, which is that God may judge us just as we judged others. The prayer that Jesus taught us to pray is that God should forgive us as we forgive others. When we judge others harshly, we give God grounds to judge us harshly, which outside the blood of Jesus would be very easy for God to do. Jesus did not come to judge sinners but to save them. We should act accordingly, not as the judges of others.

Late in his Sermon on the Mount, Jesus shared an instruction that may have relieved the crowd listening to him on the mountainside. Jesus had already said much in the way of things that people should do and not do. Distinguishing right action from wrong action must have been important, his listeners would easily have concluded, because Jesus had so many instructions. So far, so good, because Jesus was clearly telling of things that were important. Yet as to any number of his instructions so far, they may also have felt the judging eye of the person sitting next to them on the mountainside for their having disobeyed that instruction. Some would not have given to the needy, prayed, or fasted as Jesus had already instructed, while others would have stored up abundantly in bigger barns, against his instruction. One can easily imagine the crowd's restlessness growing as tension mounted between seatmates who now held veritable grievances against one another based on their prior violations of Jesus's instructions. Jesus's instruction not to judge another must have quickly resolved that tension. They were all sinners. Jesus said, "Do not judge, or you too will be judged. For in the same way you judge others, you will be judged, and with the measure you use, it will be measured to you." They must think generously and forgivingly of others. As Jesus went on to explain, they should take the lumber out of their own eye before trying to remove the speck of sawdust out of their neighbor's eye. Monitor and correct your own sin rather than judging the sin of another, he was telling them.

Time and circumstances had taught him that in any large enough group of people, he would discover one who somehow did not meet his standard, just as at least one would discover that he did not meet their standard. He had lived, worked, and served by then in enough different communities to know that not everyone can get along with everyone all of the time. Someone somewhere, indeed someone everywhere, was going to annoy him just as he was going to annoy someone. He had also learned over time that when he gradually identified that person whom his own spirit seemed so badly to want to judge that he needed then to be especially patient with and solicitous of that person. He needed to work overtime not to think about that person, not to speak negatively about that person, and to always show that person special kindness precisely because he did not feel like it. Otherwise, if he let his own judging spirit take over, neither that person nor he would have any peace around one another. He hoped and prayed then that those who did not like, respect, trust, or believe *him*, and who felt that they had good grounds to condemn *him*, would instead look the other way and forgive him. In later years, he was so very glad that he had learned that lesson. He certainly did not want God judging and condemning him.

Do not judge by human standards. John 8:15.

Life makes essential some degree of judging of at least certain things. We make judgments all of the time, necessarily. If we were to throw away our judgment, then we would either be fools or robots, senseless things whom no one could tolerate. We have just seen in the prior section, though, that Jesus does not want us judging and condemning others. We might better reserve our judgment for ourselves, first of all, and then next for situations and circumstances involving us in which we need to make and should be making discerning judgments based on God's word. So certain kinds of judging of certain things at certain times is no problem and, just the opposite, properly expected and instructed of us. Yet beyond Jesus's caution not to judge and condemn others, we find another of his instructions not to judge by *human standards*. We do have many human standards, some of them social, others cultural, traditional, normative, professional, scientific, medical, business, regulatory, or legal. These human standards may each be helpful in their own way and for their own subject. On the other hand, when we judge the things of God, particularly the core things like *who is Jesus*, then we must apply the standards of God. God's kingdom does not operate by human standards. Human standards may govern certain human activities reasonably well, although many will dispute even that much. Human standards are always poor judges of the things of God. Human standards often judge God's things and the people of God to be foolish, but we should concern ourselves far more with God's standard of humans, who in judging God prove themselves the fools.

The religious leaders had lost any patience with Jesus and were by now trying in every way to catch him in order to be able to condemn and silence him. Jesus had turned back to the crowd to teach again, this time calling himself the *light of the world* and saying that anyone who follows him would never be in the dark but always have life's light. These words were so close to blasphemy that the religious leaders spoke up again, saying that Jesus didn't have the independent witness to testify to any such thing. The religious leaders were referring to the important question of judging the truth of Jesus's extraordinary assertion. The law required two witnesses, while Jesus was only one. The religious leaders must have known that they had so intimidated the crowd and controlled the people that no one else would stand up for Jesus. They thought that they had Jesus in a corner, trapped by the very law that he claimed to fulfill. Yet on that important question of judging, Jesus answered them, "You judge by human standards; I pass judgment on no one. But if I do judge, my decisions are true, because I am not alone. I stand with the Father who sent me." Jesus went on to explain that he did indeed have the necessary two witnesses to establish the truth. Jesus was one witness and his Father, the One who had sent him, was the second witness.

His days certainly involved working under human standards, indeed unavoidably so from several standpoints. He simply could not ignore all of the laws, rules, regulations, policies, and protocols for doing what he did. He would hardly have lasted a day if he had attempted to do so. Yet he increasingly understood aspects of God's standard. He was beginning to develop a discerning eye from the standpoint of Jesus's instruction, things that made sense in God's kingdom rather than the human institutions within which he operated. He could also begin to see when the standards differed, not to say that they outright conflicted. The human standards seemed to require him to perform in certain ways in certain situations. God's standards seemed to operate at a different level more like a moral or spiritual level, or maybe within a different realm more like a spiritual realm. What fascinated him was the degree to which the Holy Spirit seemed to be weaving God's spiritual realm into his earthly institutions. While human and divine institutions were definitely different, they were not entirely apart. The divine unquestionably influenced the human, even if the human did not appear to alter the divine. He soon realized, too, that he needed to discern, act, and proceed under God's standards as surely and consistently as he had devoted himself to human standards, or indeed more so. His prayer had for a while now been that God would help him do so. In the words and life of Jesus, he was finding more and more answers to those prayers.

Stop judging by appearances. John 7:24.

How often and how easily we misjudge a book by its cover. The saying, indeed Jesus's teaching, is of course *not* to judge by appearances. To some extent and perhaps a great extent, we can and should judge by appearances, if by appearances one means observation and evidence. Scientists, detectives, medical examiners, investigators, and forensics experts all to an extent judge by appearances, by the data that they collect, analyze, and observe through their senses. Yet *appearances* in the saying's usage must mean *superficial* observations that are not valid and reliable evidence for the supposition we are drawing. Appearances fool us in exactly those ways that we let them tell us more than they really mean. We take them to be proof of that which they are not. Our special challenge, though, is not to misjudge the things *of God*, particularly the identity, actions, and instructions of Jesus. When Jesus warned not to judge by appearances, he was responding to confusion over who he was and what he was doing and teaching. While not to judge by appearances may be sound advice for any situation, Jesus's primary or sole concern in giving that instruction clearly appears to have been that we recognize who he is, when he is present, what he is doing, and what he is teaching. We must not judge things of God by the world's invalid and unreliable standards.

Although the scriptures had long predicted him, and the people of Israel saw many signs fulfilled that he had indeed come, the coming of Messiah might confuse any people. Yet one extra challenge that the people faced was that Jesus did not appear in his dress, demeanor, relationships, social status, and other ways in the manner that they thought of Messiah. As one gospel account shows, the crowds that gathered around him whispered about him, disagreeing whether he was a good man or deceiver. Their debates were only whispers because they feared the religious leaders whom they knew would make their own judgment. One occasion when Jesus was teaching in the temple courts at the time of the festival illustrated that tense dynamic. Jesus's authoritative teaching amazed the people on one hand, but the fact that no one had taught Jesus confounded them on the other hand. He didn't have the standing and status of one of the religious leaders' star students, which may have been part of why the religious leaders were already plotting against him. Jesus told them that his teaching came from God who sent him and asked why they were trying to kill him for it. Apparently unaware of the leaders' plotting, the crowd called him *demon possessed* for fearing nothing. Jesus warned them to get things straight. His Sabbath miracle that they had just observed was perfectly consistent with the scriptures. To address the source of their confusion, Jesus then added, "Stop judging by appearances, but instead judge correctly." They were misreading something into Jesus's appearance that was not there. They couldn't recognize the Messiah standing before them and teaching.

Her experiences, and experiences that others had shared with her, had gradually taught her to avoid judging by appearances. For a long time, she had operated in the world as the world had taught her to operate, trusting whom the world told her to trust and listening to whom the world told her to listen. That is, if the event, information, and interpretation had the look, feel, and other trappings of general approval, the limelight, attention, and high production values of worldly things, then she would have accepted them as true and reliable. She would have embraced and followed their message. Over time, though, many of these messages proved unreliable. Their sources proved corrupt, and the consequences of pursuing their messages proved corrupting. Her disillusionment caused her to turn increasingly to the ancient message that, indeed the Ancient One whom, she had once in her youth and young adulthood followed. As she returned with ever more mature devotion to Him who once held her youthful devotion, the trustworthy appearance of the world's messages dissipated. She increasingly saw through and past their *trappings*, a synonym for their *appearance* that in itself should warn anyone, to the corruption which was their essence. She simultaneously saw through the plain garb in which the world had dressed the King, to see more and more of the King's glory.

Make right judgments. John 7:24.

Not to make wrong judgments, especially in judging by appearances, is definitely a good step in the right direction. Yet not making wrong judgments is only half a step in the right direction. We then need to make *right* judgments. Avoiding a wrong judgment is a qualitatively different act than making a right judgment. As the above section suggests, to avoid a wrong judgment, one must recognize and avoid applying invalid criteria, like the education, dress, and social standing of a certain ancient Teacher. Don't judge the book by its cover. Covers are not valid and reliable criteria for the contents inside. One cover may be unattractive, while the next may be attractive. The cover, whether attractive or unattractive, is not a valid or reliable criterion for the contents inside. Yet rejecting invalid and unreliable criteria for judging is again only the first half of what needs to be a full step. Instead, judge the book by other valid and reliable criteria, like the table of contents, introduction, authority, argument, analysis, conclusion, and bibliography. Look inside. Find sound standards by which to judge. Finding and applying sound standards by which to judge requires different insight, resources, and skill than does rejecting unsound standards. Finding Jesus, welcoming the Holy Spirit through whom we discern, and finding God, are wholly different accomplishments than simply learning not to judge by appearances. Grasp, understand, organize, frame, recall, and apply the words of God. The scriptures foretold of Jesus, whom we must accept for entry into God's kingdom. Jesus revealed the will of the Father by which we can judge all things.

As the prior section shows, Jesus taught not just to avoid judging by appearances, in other words not to make wrong judgments especially about the things of God, but also to make right judgments. Jesus's words to the religious leaders were, "Stop judging by appearances, *but instead judge correctly.*" Jesus said so in the midst of explaining the scriptures by which Moses had long prior acted and that Jesus was right then fulfilling. Jesus in other words was applying the standard of God's word even as he was fulfilling and revealing those scriptures. As the same gospel began by saying, in Jesus was the word of God, and Jesus was the Word of God. The Word of God is living and active, judging all things. Nothing passes outside the word and judgment of God. The world holds nothing apart from God. No circumstance is so outside the will of God not to be accountable to God's standard. God's word judges all things, and nothing judges God's word. The One positive standard we have on which to rely is the Word of God. We must do more than reject appearances. We must also accept the Word of God. This gospel account taught these things about Jesus.

As so many had before him, he had finally found the divine standard judging all things, or better stated, the One who judged all things. That the standard would be a Person bearing the identity of the Word, rather than a theory, formula, text, or thing, was both surprising and satisfying. He had investigated many such things, finding none nearly satisfactory to serve as standard. The Word become flesh satisfied all things, addressed and answered all things. The incarnate God made both the natural matter and the supernatural matter more. The Trinity knit together all things, from origin to purpose, plan, and prophecy, and from conception to death and eternity. He embraced the divine standard, letting the King judge all things, ensuring that every theory, ideology, and philosophy would bow with every knee. Although he knew his personal fallibility, he tried to judge nothing by any standard other than this divine standard so that every judgment would be true. If the divine standard had no judgment to make, then he had none to make, too. All that mattered to him was what mattered to his King.

Do not condemn. Luke 6:37.

While we are to make right judgments using his divine standard, Jesus simultaneously tells us not to condemn. To judge is not to condemn, although many, particularly those who reject Jesus and his followers, but even some of his followers too, equate the two. Many believe that those who follow Jesus are judgmental, meaning that Jesus followers unnecessarily condemn others who do not accept and follow Jesus. Some of those who reject Jesus purport to hold that any judging, any holding to a standard, any distinguishing of right from wrong, is unnecessarily judgmental condemnation. Yet we all make judgments of right and wrong, even those who claim that judging right from wrong is itself wrong. Do you see how impossible rejecting judging is because to reject anything is to judge? Any belief, even the rejection of belief, requires a standard, requires judging. So if we all judge, what is the difference between permissible judgment and impermissible condemnation? Judgment implies discerning, drawing right conclusions about things. By contrast, to condemn is to assign guilt to, convict, and denounce, even doom, a person. Judging requires discerning truth and drawing sound conclusions from it. Condemnation requires nothing more than standing over another whether or not one has any basis for it. The lawless dictator condemns, while only those who discern authoritative standards can judge. Jesus permits sound judgment of situations and circumstances under his standard but prohibits condemning others under any standard.

Jesus had many things to teach in his sermon to the large crowd on the plain. One of them was that those who followed him must not condemn. Jesus said, "Do not condemn, and you will not be condemned." Jesus taught not to condemn by speaking this sort of reciprocal couplet, first not to condemn and then that those who condemned *would be* condemned. The couplet form of his statement clearly implied that those among the crowd who heard him were not to condemn *others* or another, particularly God, would condemn them. Indeed, Jesus strung three of these couplets together, first not to judge or another would judge them, then not to condemn or another would condemn them, and finally to forgive so that another would forgive them. From these couplet forms, and from the immediately prior teaching in which Jesus said to love enemies, Jesus made it clear that the problem to avoid was judging and condemning *persons*, not necessarily discerning and judging events, situations, and circumstances. Members of the crowd who heard Jesus were to love and forgive others, even enemies, not condemn them.

She wanted to love, not condemn. Condemnation was easy, she had found, far too easy. She heard others condemn people outside of their hearing so often, speaking so badly about others behind their backs, using words that denied their value, worth, and standing as children of God, like those others had no right to exist. She discouraged most of that talk, although she also found that sometimes, she hoped rarely, she would tolerate the deadly talk, even agree with and promote it. She usually managed to bite her tongue,

268

but even then she would occasionally find herself getting the condemnation conversation started, only to recognize it too late and then regret it deeply afterward. Her mind and heart would trick her repeatedly, offering rationale and justification, fueling her emotion, and then her pride would kick in, and off she would go, condemning another, while she told herself that she was just cautioning others, helping others, or seeking insight and affirmation from others. But no, she was condemning. And then, she stopped, almost like something had finally broken or submitted within her. Jesus said not to condemn, and that those who condemn, God condemns. She thought at first that she would feel shortchanged or burdened by no longer joining others in their frequent condemnations, but instead she felt relief. Let God judge and if necessary condemn others. She was having no part of it, fearing her own condemnation, a fear she wanted to face no more.

Show sinners their fault. Matthew 18:15.

While we are not to condemn another, the admonition does not extend to showing others their fault. We are in a sense our brother's and sister's keeper. We can and should to a degree be their conscience, just as we hope that they will be our conscience. Of course, this responsibility creates a fine line, on the one hand not to condemn and on the other hand to speak to others about their faults. In a society as committed to personal liberties as is our society today, this responsibility also makes the modern person shudder at the thought. Yet we do still draw lines around behaviors where society is willing to do more than just give counsel, even to charge and convict. We also recognize the value of models and mentors, and in some places even the value of wise fathers and mothers, whose roles are not to coddle but to counsel and even to discipline. And in any case, Jesus instructs it, whether or not culture today supports the thought of showing sinners their fault. If you still hesitate at the thought, then notice and address the effect of language. Words like *sin* and *faults* carry deeper and heavier connotations that many persons will resist when they would not resist *counsel, advice,* or *guidance.* Helping the person begin to accept the deeper and heavier meanings of sin and fault, particularly their eternal consequences without the blood of Christ, is precisely the point of counsel, advice, or guidance. We show sinners their faults and hope that they show us ours not to burnish reputations but to obey and follow Christ.

Jesus had a particular way that he instructed the disciples to show others their faults. He had just told them the parable of the wandering sheep in which the owner of the sheep will not leave even one behind and will be happier at finding the lost one than about the other ninety-nine sheep that did not wander off. The *wandering* in the parable may be the equivalent of *sin* and the owner's going and getting the sheep may be the equivalent of *counsel,* although the parable has other deeper interpretations, particularly in the love and sacrifice of Christ, and his rescue. The very next thing that Jesus told his disciples, though, was, "If your brother or sister sins, go and point out their fault, just between the two of you. If they listen to you, you have won them over." Notice the care Jesus counseled about giving counsel that it should be *just between the two of you.* No gossiping among others first. Go straight with your counsel to the person who sins. Notice also that Jesus says that you will have *won them over.* Sin places persons outside of the kingdom's reach. Jesus next told the disciples that if the person would not listen, to speak with them again with one or two others. If they would still not listen, then to tell it to the church, and if they would not listen to the church, then treat them as a non-believer. Righteousness has to do with belief, and sin with non-belief.

His natural inclination was to ignore, overlook, or soften and explain away the faults of others. That inclination had served him well at many points in his life and in many communities, organizations, and relationships, which may have been why it was his inclination. He found it much easier to ignore others' faults. He wanted to get along with, even to be liked by, everyone. What did it matter to him if someone whom he knew and with whom he had occasional interactions was doing something harmful? As long the harm did not reach him, then he just felt better about ignoring it. Yet at the same time, he felt a little uneasy about that approach. In many instances, he saw harm coming from the behavior, just as others surely did. He might have been able to help the person prevent it and thus might even have been able to help others affected by it. As he grew closer to Christ and understood more of Christ's teaching, he also realized more fully that sin had broader and deeper consequences, eternal consequences. And finally, he heard Christ's words about his own responsibility for his sinning brothers and sisters. Maybe, he thought, he could find ways to give counsel without losing a friend. Indeed, maybe that was what Christ meant in part when he said not to condemn.

Rebuke those who sin against you. Luke 17:3.

So we are to give counsel, to show sinners their faults. Jesus then takes the instruction a step farther when he addresses what we should do when someone sins *against us*. Sin does have its targets, does have its effects. The faults that others show and the wrongs that they commit out of those faults can affect us directly and significantly, even severely. One might assume from Jesus's statement about turning the other cheek that Jesus would say to ignore it when others sin against you, but he does not. Jesus says that we are to *rebuke* those who sin against us. Doing so is probably far easier than showing a sinner faults that do *not* affect us. We may hesitate to interfere in another's life when their misconduct has no effect on us, but we are probably only too ready to interfere, to give our two cents, indeed to rebuke, when their misconduct does affect us. To rebuke is to admonish, even to scold, something that we would find it easy to do out of our indignation over whatever untoward effect with which the other's fault had burdened us. The rebuke, though, that Jesus permits us is probably not the stinging and wounding rebuke that we may want to give because at the same time that Jesus permits us to rebuke, he admonishes that we are then to forgive. The moment that the person whom we rebuke stops the offense, we are to forgive, no matter how often that person resumes the offense and we must rebuke again. We are in other words never to hold grudges. Speak swiftly and firmly against others' sins that

271

affect you, and then move on in forgiveness as soon as they stop. No taking pleasure in rebuking.

Jesus was teaching his disciples about how they should respond when they see others commit sins that affected them. He first explained that people would certainly sin, that things would surely cause people to stumble. He then cautioned the disciples to watch themselves so that they were not the ones to cause others to stumble. When something or someone else caused another to sin, though, and the sin was against one of the disciples, they were to first rebuke and then forgive the sinner whom the rebuke turned from sin. "If your brother or sister sins against you, rebuke them; and if they repent, forgive them," Jesus said. How often should the disciples forgive? "Even if they sin against you seven times in a day and seven times come back to you saying 'I repent,' you must forgive them," Jesus instructed. The disciples' amusing but understandable reaction to this difficult instruction was to ask Jesus to increase their faith. When someone goes wrong in a harmful way, don't ignore it, Jesus was telling his disciples, and instead rebuke them, but also quickly forgive.

He loathed giving rebukes and was so thankful that he had so few to give. He knew that he preferred to avoid conflict, knew even that he would sometimes let things go too long and too far before giving a rebuke that he knew that he needed to give. Yet the more that he reflected on his responsibility to others, the more that he realized that his feelings about giving rebukes were not so important. What was important was that the person whom he owed a rebuke received it promptly, clearly, and firmly, with just as clear an invitation to correct the sin and move on as if the proverbial slate were clean. He did the offender no favor in avoiding a warranted rebuke. All that he was doing in those instances was facilitating the other's sin. Giving the rebuke might cost him a friendship for a short while, perhaps longer. It might make him uncomfortable and embarrassed, even stressed and depressed. But he was saving the offender something greater by turning the offender from sin. He had seen another give rebukes to others and had seen how much good the rebukes had done them. He prayed for the courage to rebuke swiftly and surely, and then prayed even harder for the courage to repeat the rebuke as often as necessary and to forgive just as often. Better to be

272

the watchman and call out the sin than to sleep through the watch and let both the watchman's and sinner's soul burn.

1.13 Sinning

Be clean inside. <small>Matthew 23:26.</small> *Do not entertain evil thoughts.* <small>Matthew 9:4.</small> *Do no evil.* <small>Matthew 7:23.</small> *Stop sinning.* <small>John 5:14.</small> *Cut off your hand if it causes you to sin.* <small>Matthew 18:7.</small> *Leave your life of sin.* <small>John 8:11.</small> *Do not do the devil's desires.* <small>John 8:44.</small> *Do not walk by night.* <small>John 11:9.</small> *Do not look at another in lust.* <small>Matthew 5:28.</small> *Avoid anger.* <small>Matthew 5:22.</small> *See your sin before showing others theirs.* <small>Matthew 7:5.</small> *Choose what is better.* <small>Luke 10:42.</small> *Do not set aside the commandments.* <small>Matthew 5:19.</small> *Obey the commandments.* <small>Matthew 19:17.</small> *Understand the word.* <small>Matthew 13:23.</small> *Cleanse the sinner.* <small>Matthew 10:8.</small> *Drive out demons.* <small>Matthew 10:8.</small>

The topic of the prior section, judging, and the topic of this section, sinning, bear close relationship. Judging implies discernment between right and wrong, moral and immoral, while sinning implies unwillingness to follow, comply with, and submit to the judgment. Each of the prior dozen sections addressed a positive activity about which Jesus instructed, like learning or teaching, or serving or working, all good things. The topic of this last section on activities about which Jesus instructed, sinning, is obviously a negative rather than positive activity. The prior dozen sections show that Jesus had much to say about how to go about doing good things. He counseled many good works, even though some of his instructions were prohibitions to *not* do certain things within those generally good works. This section though collects the many things that Jesus said about how to avoid a negative activity, how to avoid sin. Jesus said as much about how to *avoid* sinning as he did about how to *accomplish* any of the above positive activities. One lesson we should thus draw from the abundance of his counsel on how to avoid sin is that *not* doing can be just as important as *doing*. Proscriptions can be just as important as prescriptions. As we go about our days, we should be just as conscious to avoid certain things as we should to do certain things. Listen to Jesus on how to avoid sin.

Be clean inside. Matthew 23:26.

We do have a sort of inside and outside. For better or worse, one of the marks of maturation is the ability to construct and manipulate a façade visible to others and different from our instinctual reactions and interior dialogue known to and experienced by ourselves. Children say what they think, feel, and see. Adults hide thoughts, feelings, and insights inside, sharing only what they want others to see. We usually have little problem keeping the outside, the façade, clean. Vanity is a powerful inducement to propriety. We want others to think well of us, and so we turn our good side out, harboring the things that we do not want others to see. Inside, we hold tight to those things that satisfy our base instincts of appetite, desire, pride, jealousy, and greed. Too many of us fail to realize that God sees those things on which we dwell, that we value, hold, repeat, and mull inside. To God, our inside is just as or more important than our outside. God discerns and values the heart and soul, not the white-washed outside. Putting a good face on it may fool our neighbor or acquaintance for a little while but never fools God. We should care as much or more about what we are doing inside, how we are maintaining our interior life, as what we show on the outside. Sin is not merely what we do. Sin can include that on which we dwell in our hidden world inside. Rid yourself of sin from the inside out.

Jesus was teaching the disciples and crowd about sin through what we know as the *seven woes* of the religious leaders. The religious leaders were often Jesus's target or teaching foil, although in many cases their sins were probably things in which members of the crowd engaged all too often, too. His admonition to love and pursue justice, mercy, and faithfulness, for instance, was not just for the religious leaders but for all. One could readily say the same thing about his next admonition having to do with getting or staying clean inside. Jesus began this next woe saying, "Woe to you, teachers of the law and Pharisees, you hypocrites! You clean the outside of the cup and dish, but inside they are full of greed and self-indulgence.

Blind Pharisee! First clean the inside of the cup and dish, and then the outside also will be clean." The religious leaders were unclean inside, filled with greed and other sin, so that nothing that they did to clean up the outside ceremonially made any difference. Jesus said that if they would only clean the inside, then their outside would be fine without any of the pomp and circumstance. They would not need to cover up their sinful interior with a showy exterior. Being free of sin has to do with the condition of one's inside, not so much one's outside. The outside may look clean, but the inside is what counts.

His position brought to his attention things about people that others did not necessarily know. The difference between the genuine condition of people, all broken and filled with imperfections like the rest of us, and the way in which they projected themselves to others was thus more evident to him than the differences were to most others. Most probably did not see it, but he did. Yet he also reckoned that he saw only a tiny bit of others, the rest of the defects hidden deep inside. He also knew that his condition was no different. He had no illusion that he was any more pure than anyone else, which was such a big part of why he held so tightly to the promise and Spirit of Jesus. He didn't like the thought or experience of sin filling him any more than he liked the thought of it filling others. He knew that what was inside would eventually come out and that the only route to cleanliness was to clean from the inside out. He wanted the righteousness and holiness of Christ, which he knew was only available to him through Christ rather than any program, principle, or other pursuit apart from Christ, and would only express itself as Christ's Holy Spirit dwelled within him. The blood of Christ would cleanse him, and the Spirit would act and speak through him, he hoped and prayed, for he knew what would otherwise reside within him and make its way out. He had no illusions that he could bluff or act his way into the kingdom. God would see through him, and so he was hoping that all God would see was the image of his Son Christ.

Do not entertain evil thoughts. Matthew 9:4.

In another account, Jesus made the point clear that to clean one's inside means not to entertain evil thoughts. Plenty of evil thoughts are around to entertain us. Thoughts that if acted on would lead to harm to others are especially pernicious. What business have we in thinking ill of others? Anything that makes out of another an object of manipulation, desire, or destruction is malignant, corrupt, and evil. Thoughts that degrade and destroy oneself are also evil, whether those thoughts involve greed, arrogance, pride, narcissism, or other corruption. Think of your thoughts projected before a righteous judge, and you will get the picture. Realizing that God knows your thoughts should make you think differently if your thoughts include any degree of entertained evil. Stimuli trigger thoughts, and we do not control the stimuli. We should not condemn ourselves for thoughts occurring briefly to us. On the other hand, we must not *entertain* those thoughts, meaning to dwell on, expand, and enlarge them. The particular kind of evil thought, though, with which Jesus is most concerned is thought denying that Jesus is the Son with the Father's authority. Consider the following account illustrating how Jesus perceives and addresses the thoughts of others.

Jesus crossed the lake in a boat to his hometown. At his arrival, several men brought to him a paralyzed man who laid on his mat before Jesus. Jesus saw the faith of the men who had brought the paralyzed man to Jesus for healing and so forgave the paralyzed man, preparing to heal him. Teachers of the law nearby muttered to themselves that for Jesus to forgive was blasphemy unless of course Jesus was God. Jesus though knew their thoughts and so turned to them saying, "Why do you entertain evil thoughts in your hearts?" Muttering does no good. God reads the mind and sees the heart, no matter one's efforts to hide it. Jesus then explained to the muttering religious leaders that he did indeed have God's authority to forgive. To prove his authority, he turned back to the paralyzed man telling him to get up, meaning that Jesus had just healed him, and to take his mat home, which the man promptly did. The miraculous healing filled the crowd that had gathered with such awe that they praised God.

She was frustrated at herself for how often her mind returned to the same thinking that had so disturbed her in the first place. The thought had not started as an evil thought, she was pretty sure. At least, it was at first not obviously one of those deadly sins to avoid. Yet she could see that in short order the thought had connected with something in her that probably had to do with her pride, ease to take offense, and other familiar imperfections. She felt as if she could not put the thought out of her mind. She also felt as if she didn't *want* to put the thought out of her mind. The thought satisfied something within her, scratched one of those itches that she knew she shouldn't be scratching. The whole thing of entertaining this destructive thought was so much like trying to let something heal that badly needed to heal for all the harm it was doing to her and those around her, even while she wanted badly to keep picking at the wound so that it would *not* heal. Part of her didn't want the wound to heal because her pride was gaining something from it. While she searched for some solution, the realization gradually came to her that she just had to stop dwelling on the thought. The more she did so, the more she acted out on the thought in ways that she knew she should not be acting. She had to put the evil thought out of her mind, she decided. She would fill her mind with Christ, she resolved. And so she went back to memorizing favorite passages of the Bible.

Do no evil. Matthew 7:23.

The next admonition after not to entertain evil thoughts is a natural and readily understandable one, which is to do no evil. We may think it more difficult not to think about evil than not to do evil. Controlling our thoughts may indeed be more difficult than controlling our actions, especially if one thinks only of the fleeting thought that stimuli produce instinctually. Yet be careful assuming that thought must precede action when the subject comes to evil. Some of us sometimes may not think much about evil but may still readily do evil. While many evil acts may well begin with substantial thought, planning, and deliberation, evil acts without much thought certainly occur. Indeed, listen carefully to the confessions of those who surprised everyone by committing some serious deliberate wrong, and in some cases you hear surprisingly little deliberation. It seems like sometimes, people do evil acts almost spontaneously. You may recall a wrong of your own that way that it seemed to spring from your heart and hands as naturally as getting out of bed in the morning. The point is that Jesus's admonition not to do evil has its own place and value beyond his admonition not to think about evil. Neither dwell internally on evil nor let your hands do evil. Watch just as much where your feet take you and what your hands do there as you watch, to guard against doing evil.

Near the end of his Sermon on the Mount, Jesus distinguished false from true disciples based on whether or not he knew them or were instead evildoers. Jesus's distinction can be troubling. In it, he clearly looks beyond what people say about him to what they do, specifically whether they are evildoers. He begins the account by saying that many will come to him calling him Lord and saying that they drove out demons and performed miracles in his name. Yet Jesus says that they will not enter the kingdom, when he tells them instead, "I never knew you. Away from me you evildoers!" To enter the kingdom, a disciple must know Jesus and not be an evildoer. Jesus followed this lesson by telling the disciples the story of the wise and foolish builders. Those who put his words into practice are like the wise who build on the rock, while those who ignore his words are like the unwise who build only on sand. Only houses built on the rock survive. The disciples and any others who wish to enter the kingdom must build on Jesus. Jesus must know them, and they must follow his words rather than be doers of evil.

He at first thought it odd that he would need to learn so much about sin. Wasn't it all just a matter of knowing right from wrong? He at first had no sense of sin's subtlety, of the nefarious ways in which evil works with which he would need to become familiar. Soon, though, he came to appreciate how knowing the way that sin works was essential to avoiding it. For instance, he sensed that evil was at work both in his mind and in his body or actions through it. Evil certainly pressed in on him, occupying or trying to occupy his thoughts, trying to distract, condemn, depress, entice, and destroy him. He knew that resisting evil was in large part a mental and spiritual battle. Yet he also saw how evil could so easily flow from actions, almost mindlessly. The mind had to keep a check on the body, or the body might just do something evil that the mind had hardly contemplated. He learned that the two, body and mind, mind and body, worked back and forth, and worked together, to either solicit and embrace evil or conversely to resist and overcome evil. While he had at first thought that growth in faith meant learning more about good works, he finally came to acknowledge that it also meant learning more about the ways and wiles of evil.

Stop sinning. John 5:14.

Jesus's admonition to stop sinning strikes a different chord than his instruction to do no evil. The two instructions may have different connotations or meanings. To sin is to disobey God, to act outside of and contrary to the will of God as expressed by the words, embodied by the actions, and communicated by the Spirit, of Jesus. One can imagine much sin in any life given the spiritual knowledge and maturity, and the devotion, that remaining constantly or consistently, or even frequently, in the will of God takes. Jesus's admonition to stop sinning seems then a call to dwell on and remain within the will of God, a call to devotion, something both profound and subtle. Some may think of sin as simply drinking, cussing, and other carousing, perhaps also lying, cheating, and stealing, but sin can be anything outside of the will of God. Jesus may at times and in ways be less concerned with the carousing including the obvious evils than with our unwillingness to dwell on and in the will of God, with our unwillingness to attend and adhere closely to the words of Jesus, that is, with our sin. Yes, do no evil. Stop the lying, cheating, and carousing. But also draw near in devotion to God so that you stop sinning.

Jesus had instantly healed the man laying by the pool, who for decades had been an invalid. Jesus had first noticed the man by the pool, asking him if he wanted to get well. The man had replied only indirectly that whenever he tried to get into the pool at the rare moments that the pool appeared to have its renowned healing capacity, others beat him to it. Jesus generously took the man's reply to mean that he did wish the healing that Jesus had just offered him and so told the man to get up and walk with his mat. The man did so, healed. Jesus found the man again later after the religious leaders had rebuked the man for carrying his mat on the Sabbath. When Jesus found the man at the temple, Jesus first reassured the man that he was well again, no longer an invalid. Jesus then told him, "Stop sinning or something worse may happen to you." The account gives no direct indication of the sin that the man had apparently been carrying other than what one might draw from his few words and the event itself. Perhaps his failure to recognize Jesus and respond directly and affirmatively to his invitation for healing was the man's sin, a failure in witness and faith. In any case, the man learned Jesus's identity in this second exchange and so told the religious leaders that Jesus had been the one who had healed him on the Sabbath.

The thought daunted her that anything outside of the will of God was sin. Whenever she had thought of sin, which was probably not often enough, she had thought of it as those seven deadly things that one learns to avoid. *Sin* had such a strong negative connotation that she tended to associate it with the most obviously reprehensible acts. Thus although she fully accepted the litany that she was a sinner in need of God's mercy and grace, indeed in need of Jesus as her savior, she didn't think of much that she did as actually being sinful. Then came her reflection on sin as including anything outside of the will of God. She thought of how many things she did that, while not *rank* sin of that deadly sort, were nonetheless probably outside of the will of God, things that Jesus's instructions and actions in no clear sense sanctioned and may instead have in relatively clear ways prohibited. She wanted then to stop sinning. She wanted to remain constantly and consistently in the will of God. She didn't want her life to become some sterile set of duties to fulfill, yet she definitely wanted the fullness and richness of God's kingdom, which she believed to mean that she needed to stop sinning. She needed to devote herself to the words, obey the instructions, and accept the Spirit of Jesus.

282

Cut off your hand if it causes you to sin. Matthew 18:7.

Well, okay, this one is going to be hard. Many say that Jesus taught in hyperbole, with dire warnings of things like being thrown into the sea with a millstone around the neck, suggestions of strange conditions like having a log in one's eye, and offers of fabulous powers like moving mountains. His admonition to cut off your hand or foot if it causes you to stumble so that you don't end up in eternal fire may be one of those instances of hyperbole. Jesus may have used exaggeration as a teaching tool to gain the attention and activate the minds of his listeners, and impress his words on their memories. If so, then his instruction to cut off a hand or foot that causes sin definitely conveys how serious Jesus was about not sinning. How though do hands cause us to sin? The implication is that the things our hands do can be sinful, whether to steal, cover up and defraud, weigh out short measure and cheat, or the like. Our feet can also cause us to sin, carrying us places we ought not to go, where we do things we ought not to do. The connection between sin, doing with the hands, and going places with the feet, may be an important part of Jesus's instruction as if to say, *watch closely what you do* and *watch closely where you go*, for with the hands we do and with the feet we go. Yet even as we construe Jesus's exaggerated instruction as teaching hyperbole, we might also at least consider the possibility that in the choice between eternal life and eternal fire, Jesus was not exaggerating but quite serious. We would then have to understand what he meant about losing hand or foot.

Jesus was teaching his disciples about the kingdom of heaven, a frequent topic of his instruction. They had asked who among them would be the greatest in heaven. He had answered that those who enter the kingdom of heaven must be like little children, taking a lowly position here. Those of low position here are great in the kingdom, Jesus explained. Jesus then warned the disciples not to cause children to stumble, for those who do face terrible punishment. Jesus then cautioned the disciples not to let their own hand or foot cause them to stumble, telling them, "If your hand or your foot causes you to stumble, cut it off and throw it away. It is better for you to enter life maimed or crippled than to have two hands or two

283

feet and be thrown into eternal fire." Notice that in the way that Jesus gave this caution, he indicates that *entering life* would come *after* cutting off the offending hand or foot. To enter life is to enter God's kingdom. No sin enters the kingdom. Those who enter the kingdom have acquired the identity of Christ who has no sin. Not to enter the kingdom, not to gain eternal life, means eternal fire. Perhaps, then, the cutting off of hand or foot is not merely Jesus emphasizing avoiding sin but more so represents leaving sin behind after having taken Christ's image. One enters the kingdom whole of body but washed of sin, having denied hand and foot any impulse other than to serve Christ.

Everyone, he presumed, struggles with sin. Sin tempted Christ himself, not that Christ ever had any sin in him. He was conscious of his own struggles, which he took to be a good rather than bad thing. Shame indeed, he thought, if he had no sense of his own tendency toward sin, no sense of struggle. Of course, he knew others who struggled more openly and obviously, some of whom had serious drug, alcohol, or gambling problems, and who had been in and out of rehab centers, and in and out of jail or prison. Yet he had learned not to put their struggles on any different level than his own, as if they had more of a problem or more of a battle than he had. He knew that sin was everyone's struggle, and he wanted not to decamp from the struggle, not to let down a guard that he was absolutely sure he must keep up, not to give any sin any opportunity or foothold. He also knew or suspected that his sin would look every bit as rank to God as anyone else's if he did not have the complete cover of the blood of Jesus, if he had not taken the image of Jesus in just the way that would cause the Father to welcome him into the kingdom. He rather preferred his two hands and two feet to one of either, but he also wanted the Father to see only the hands and feet of Jesus when looking at his hands as he sought to enter the kingdom.

Leave your life of sin. John 8:11.

To not entertain evil thoughts, to not do evil, and then to stop sinning, requires each of us to some degree to leave a life of sin. As one learns what Jesus instructs, one also realizes the degree to which one has been living a life of sin. What you or I thought was just ordinary living, what everyone does, nothing particularly wrong or immoral, gradually comes under Jesus's instruction to look like what it actually is, which is sin. We then face a choice: do we continue in the life of sin that we have established, given that the life is our life, our custom, our normal, or do we instead leave that life of sin for a new life that we will gradually need to construct under the guidance of the Holy Spirit? To stop sinning requires following new paths, building new patterns, forming new relationships, and practicing new habits. Sin is not merely a momentary event, a one-off wrong, or even a string of connected events that constitute wrong. Sin is more a way of life, a way of thinking, acting, and living. Sin seeps deep into one's character and soul, wraps us in its own skin, and forms in us its dark and hating heart. Turning from doing evil is not alone like striking out down a new path as much as it is leaving behind an old life in favor of a new life. The way to treat sin is not with sandpaper, file, or chisel, removing a little here and there. Leaving sin requires starting over with new birth and new life.

Jesus was teaching in the temple courts again, this time in the early morning, when the religious leaders dragged in a woman caught in adultery. The leaders, using the occasion as a trap for Jesus, asked if he would sanction stoning the woman as the Law of Moses commanded. If Jesus said no, then he would have undermined the Law, while if he said yes, then he would have undermined his message of forgiveness. Instead of answering, Jesus bent down to write in the dust with his finger, but the leaders pressed him again and again. So he stood up just long enough to tell them that those without sin should be the first to cast a stone. He then stooped again to write in the dust with his finger. He had caught the leaders in their own trap, for none could claim to be without sin without themselves contradicting the law. They slunk away one by one, starting with the oldest, until all were gone. Jesus then turned to the woman, asking her whether any now condemned her. She replied that none did. "Then neither do I condemn you," Jesus replied, adding, "Go now and leave your life of sin." Jesus would not condemn her. He would instead direct her to go. Yet she

285

was nonetheless to leave the life of sin that had momentarily made her the leaders' tool to try to trap Jesus.

He could easily look back in his life to things that he knew today were then sin but that he did not then regard as sin or did not care then deeply enough about avoiding. He took no pride in those former things, which some seem to do, although the disclosures that they share may just be reminding themselves and others not to return to that life of sin. Teaching by bad example can be a good thing. Whether to his shame or credit, he was less likely, much less likely, to share examples of his prior sin. His very gradual spiritual maturation, the closeness that he increasingly felt to Christ, and the gradual but eventually profound changes in his thinking and behavior that resulted, nonetheless convinced him that he had previously led a life of sin, whether comprised of petty or serious offenses. He was glad that he had left that life of sin, and he was certain that he did not want to return to it. It held no attraction whatsoever for him. Yet he also recognized that the Spirit was still at work within him, that he likely still dwelt in sins that he was only beginning to recognize, and that still had sin-life to leave behind. He just wanted to hear more and understand more of what Jesus instructed, sanctioned, commanded, and expected. He wanted to leave all sin life behind, which he suspected would only ultimately have happened at his own death and resurrection in Christ.

Do not do the devil's desires. John 8:44.

Personifying evil presents a challenge for the modern mind. Parodies of those who do so, who accept the devil as tempter of sin, are easy, especially when the representations depict the devil as a mischievous minor red figure with horns and a long tail. Speaking of sin rather than simply mistakes or errors in judgment is hard because of the judgmental nature of the word. Sin seems both worse than error and more judgmental than mistake, and so we tend to avoid even using the sin term. Yet speaking of the devil as the father of sin can be much harder. Many barely believe that God exists. For those barely believing that God exists, believing that an opponent to God exists, particularly one so-often parodied as is the devil, is even harder. Supernatural beings are sensitive subjects, whether God, the devil, angels, or demons. We understand, accept, and embrace instructions, principles, and practices defining right and wrong, but hesitate to consider their personification, which may be odd considering that we in fact personify those principles and practices. We personify and act on belief. At times, we are like demons or angels, even labeling one another, particularly children but sometimes also adults, as such, particularly when our behavior becomes pronounced in either direction, as devils or angels. Jesus also describes persons as children of light or darkness, as children of God or of the devil. He particularly urges not to do the work of the devil. To conceive of the personality behind evil is probably no less a mental shift than to conceive of the Father, Son, and Spirit behind good. As we proceed in the struggle against sin, we should consider seriously the advantages in recognizing its promoter, in recognizing the enemy against whom we struggle.

Jesus had little opportunity left to speak and teach in the temple courts, as the religious leaders closed in on him. He told the gathered crowd that he was the world's light and that they would have the light of life by following him. The religious leaders interrupted saying that Jesus had no right to make such a claim. Jesus answered that he had his Father as his witness. The leaders denied knowing anything of this father of Jesus, while they claimed Abraham as their father. Their debate raged on, with Jesus pointing out to the crowd that the religious leaders were trying to kill him. Jesus confirmed his words by saying that he was speaking just what he had seen in the divine Father's presence, while the religious leaders were following and doing the works of their own fallen father, the devil, who bears only illegitimate children. Jesus finally told them directly, "You belong to your father, the devil, and you want to carry out your father's desires." Jesus went on to describe the devil as a murderer and liar. The reason that the religious leaders did not recognize Jesus's words as from the Father was that they did not belong to God, Jesus explained. They belonged instead to the devil and were doing the devil's work in seeking to silence and even to kill Jesus.

The experience shook him to such a great extent that he could recall it many years later. He had watched this person close to him

287

struggle mightily for a long time on several fronts including with relationships, security, illness, meaning, and purpose, but also with mental illness, severe depression, and thoughts of suicide. Communications with this person were routinely difficult as he gave a listening ear to the person's rambling and profane tirades, while trying gentle guidance, support, and counsel. Lately, the person had clearly been in decline. He remembered where he stood and how he felt when he took this particular call. During the monologue, for at this point the person was no longer able to listen to any counsel, the person's voice switched back and forth between the sweetly tender person whom he had once known and the raging, vicious, and periodically violent personality into which the person had slowly developed. The sweet voice, higher in pitch and so gentle, said that the person was losing contact and begged for help from the rage, but the raging voice, deeper and almost growling, swiftly silenced the sweet voice with threats of suicide and other despairing and violent actions. Back and forth the monologue went until the sweet voice was gone, leaving only the rage. He had heard before of persons having multiple personalities, which this communication seemed clearly to reflect. He had also heard of demon possession, which this communication just as clearly seemed to indicate. He prayed for the person's relief from both the personality disorder and the demon. Not long after, the person moved into a locked mental ward after a failed suicide attempt. Not long after, the person passed away in peace having acknowledged Jesus.

Do not walk by night. John 11:9.

The image of a night walk is powerful. At night, things do not look as they are. In the darkness, ordinary natural conditions can look extraordinary and supernatural, and thus scary. Not just night visions and appearances but also night sounds can distract and frighten. Try walking in a cemetery on an especially dark night. The hazards are not just fear and fright but also physical. How often and easily have you stumbled over a hole or stump, or had a tree branch catch your face, on a walk in the dark? Yet the same route in the daytime will look and be harmless. The same is also true about driving at night, when difficult-to-see obstacles in the road, and animals or people crossing the road, or misleading illusions, are far more likely than when driving in the daylight. Daylight walks, bikes, and drives are just far surer, safer, and more secure, than nighttime forays. Think then of the figurative meaning of walking at night. Walks at night imply an effort to conceal route, identity, and destination. Thieves walk, enter, and steal at night so as not to be detected. To act in secret is often to act with the intent of hiding and covering up the conduct accomplished in secret, as at night. The more that we operate in secret, as at night, to conceal our sin, the less that we see of the obstacles and dangers around us. When we find ourselves doing a lot of walking at night, we need to stop and come back in the daylight. Walk with the guidance and counsel of Jesus. Walk in the light.

Jesus planned his return to Bethany in Judea where his friend Lazarus was sick. One of those with Jesus cautioned him that the residents of that area had tried to kill Jesus, to stone him, the last time that he had visited just a short while earlier. They did not want him to go back to his death. Jesus replied indirectly that each day brings daylight. Jesus continued, "Anyone who walks in the daytime will not stumble, for they see by this world's light. It is when a person walks at night that they stumble, for they have no light." Jesus's literal meaning was plain and clearly true. Walking in daylight avoids stumbling over obstacles apparent from the daylight, while walking at night results in stumbles and falls over unseen objects hidden by dark. Jesus's figurative meaning may also have been apparent to the disciples. Jesus was walking in light, indeed as the light, avoiding or overcoming all obstacles. The disciples would also overcome all obstacles when walking in the light of Jesus. As long as they walked in the light of Jesus, they would have the vision of obstacles and strength to avoid them that they needed in order to continue. Jesus then explained that he must return to Bethany to raise Lazarus, who had died. This walk in the light would result in miracle resurrection, as do all such walks with Jesus.

The realization took a while, but gradually he came to see the power of omniscience. God sees all, even that, and especially that, which we attempt to conceal, he soon learned. The problem is that we do not see all that we attempt to conceal, that we do not see the hazards to us when we are concealing things. He saw others learn this lesson that the cover up is worse than the offense. He saw that when others try to act in secret to hide offenses, the offenses hurt them far worse. So he soon adopted as a guide that everything he did he would do as if others were observing it because in fact God was observing it. He felt that only in this manner would he be walking in God's light. He wanted no more of walking in any darkness where he could not see the pitfalls. If something was coming at him that would cause him to stumble, then he wanted to see it in Jesus's clear light. He might then have a good chance of avoiding it. In the world of many hazards in which he seemed to operate, he felt that he needed all of the light that he could get.

Do not look at another in lust. Matthew 5:28.

Jesus concerns himself with the heart, not merely the conduct that flows from the heart. The Ten Commandments list fundamentals of obedient faith including to have no other gods, not to make idols of other things, not to take the Lord's name in vain, to honor the Sabbath and also father and mother, and then not to murder, commit adultery, steal, bear false witness, or covet. One can with a little circumspection follow each of these proscriptions, avoiding each of the actions that the commandments prohibit. We would indeed likely find it easy not to kneel, literally kneel, to another god, or not to prop up, literally, a physical idol, or not to swear using God's name, again literally swear out loud. Yet Jesus taught that literal compliance, outward compliance, mechanical and formal compliance, with God's commands is not enough, is not the point. The commandments intend that we pursue the pure hearts, clean minds, and saved souls that produce sound outward actions. Jesus reflected this goal, this concern, in several ways but did so most memorably using the command not to commit adultery. While the commandment may sound like simply avoiding the physical act of intimacy with one to whom one is not married, Jesus instructs in addition that no one should look at that other in lust. To look and lust is to commit adultery in the heart. Attractions are natural, and appearances stimulate, but do not pursue and amplify the thought. Guard your eyes and in doing so guard your heart.

Jesus had told the crowd that had followed him up the mountainside to hear his Sermon on the Mount that he had not come to abolish but to fulfill the law including the commandments. He then started addressing some of those commandments, taking each one to a deeper level than his listeners had previously imagined, illustrating what he meant by his statement that he had come to fulfill the law. He was not simply interested in formal compliance but rather heart compliance. Indeed, his Spirit would write the law deeply and naturally on the hearts of those who accepted him so that they would obey the law when barely even knowing it. As he addressed some of the commandments, Jesus soon reached the command not to commit adultery, one of the Ten Commandments. Here, too, as in the case of other commands, formal compliance, meaning in this instance not to have physical intimacy with one to whom one was not married, would no longer be enough. Jesus said instead, "But I tell you that anyone who looks at a woman lustfully has already committed adultery with her in his heart." Jesus was not changing the command but deepening it, extending it to the heart that God intended it to reach. Sin was no longer simply avoiding the lust-fulfilling act. Sin now included mentally pursuing and contemplating the act to satisfy that same lust.

He knew, just as anyone knows, the attraction of images, whether live, print, or virtual. Fortunately, he had long ago learned the value of avoiding the attraction, of not pursuing the look. Of course, he knew especially that the cautionary practice included not looking at others of the opposite sex or indeed of any sex in lust. Yet an equally valuable and perhaps more interesting thing that he discovered was that the practice also held true for other looks, like looking after material things that might satisfy his natural acquisitiveness in greed, or looking after fashions that might satisfy his natural vanity, or looking after prestige that might satisfy his natural pride. None of these things were particularly easy, especially at first. Eyes wander naturally, and the stimuli that they observe naturally trigger responses arising from attributes, including corruptions, that lie deep in the heart. He found that observing his own eyes, tracking what his eyes followed, was a worthwhile discipline that enabled him to examine his own heart. In time, he found that he had much less interest in looking at fancy cars or clothes, attractive people, or any other particular thing. The stimuli and their temptations remained but held less and less interest for him. The discipline further seemed to bring the gradual comfort, ease, and contentment of a purer heart.

Avoid anger. Matthew 5:22.

Formal obedience, in the nature of avoiding the outright commission of sin, would certainly include not committing murder, just as one of the Ten Commandments states. Do not murder. Yet Jesus points us beyond that formal obedience of simply not murdering, to curing the heart condition that would promote murder and other violence against persons. The root of violence against persons lies in hatred for them. When the heart hates, the hands prepare for violence. When the heart harbors anger toward another, the mind naturally plans their demise. If we lived in a world that carried out every thought of the mind or inclination of the heart, then we would likely see an extraordinary degree of violence. We still see extraordinary violence enough. The world is hardly a peaceful place. Frequent undisciplined expression of the evil heart is exactly Jesus's point. The heart must be pure, or the actions will be impure out of the prompting of the heart. Anger involves denying another value, worth, and right to exist. Counsel and rebuke help others reform and change course. The commandment not to murder, with its extension not to harbor anger toward another, does not prohibit showing another that other's wayward ways. Anger though implies that the other should not merely reform behavior but should no longer exist. Recognize what anger is, and avoid anger. It does no one any good.

When addressing how the members of the crowd who listened to him on the mountainside must obey the commandments in a new and deeper way, Jesus first used as an example the command not to murder. Likely, few of the members of the crowd who listened to Jesus, and none of the disciples, had actually killed anyone. They were even less likely to have committed murder, an unjustified and premeditated killing, not in military action or self-defense, which the law of any civil society would condemn. This commandment *not to murder* should then be the easiest of them to obey, those who heard Jesus may well have previously thought. Yet Jesus quickly corrected that misreading of the commandment not to murder. While they had heard the commandment not to murder and that murderers would face judgment, Jesus began before adding, "But I tell you that anyone who is angry with a brother or sister will be subject to judgment." Jesus further explained that the person who does even so little as uses a term of contempt for another, such as calling another a fool, runs the risk of facing the fires of hell. They must instead resolve differences quickly, avoiding all anger and its expression in contempt.

Anger, he knew, just as anyone knows. He felt that he had more than the usual allotment of patience. He was often and generally slow to anger, quick to forgive. He also had the habit of not harboring offense or insult. He knew what it meant to unduly scratch an itch and tried, usually successfully, to avoid doing so. If certain people and their personalities, dispositions, or situations annoyed him, then he knew well enough how to avoid them and not think so much about them as to allow his annoyance to turn to anger. Yet once in a while, something would just seem to catch him, shake him, and anger him, something that he had not quite anticipated and so had not quite managed to avoid. He had no illusion that acting out the anger, letting off steam so to speak, would help resolve and remove the anger. Rather, acting out the anger inevitably made those situations far worse for others and for him without really getting at the root of the anger. While avoiding anger did not really seem to get much easier, he learned from the commandment that he must not justify the anger when it caught him up. To the contrary, he must refuse it all justification, must condemn and reject it, even as he struggled to substitute for anger the proper patience, counsel, understanding, insight, or other recourse. Knowing what anger really is, what its expression intends and entails, was at least a first good step. He hated and resisted anger, knowing what anger made of him and intended for others.

See your sin before showing others theirs. Matthew 7:5.

For many of us, seeing one's own faults, indeed one's own sins, is so much harder than seeing the faults and sins of others. The subjectivity that we each experience, centers of our own tiny universes when Jesus centers the great universe, requires a strong corrective. We actually have a choice to look only at others while seeing only through our own eyes or instead to also and primarily look at ourselves taking the perspective of others, particularly of Jesus. We can turn the mind's eye on our own conduct, sin, and faults, which is what Jesus instructs. We will undoubtedly remain subjective in our perspective, for we continue to see things through our own eyes in the frame of our own experience and interests. Yet committing to turn the mind's eye on ourselves, and holding fast as far as able to Jesus's universally sound and objective perspective, gives us the hope of seeing and correcting our own sin before pointing out the sin of others. No one likes those who constantly find fault in others. We each harbor plenty of sin for others to discover and point out. The one who constantly finds fault in others, though, is likely one who exhibits just as much or more fault as the ones who are the target of the criticism. Seeing one's own sin has greater value than seeing the sin of others. We probably do more for others by reforming ourselves than we do by urging their reform upon them. Lead by example, by showing, rather than telling. Turn your microscope on yourself, and turn it away for the greater part from others. You may find more than specks to correct in your own condition, even as you see plenty to correct in others.

Jesus sometimes displayed a wonderful, even humorous sense of absurdity in the memorable way in which he taught profound truths. Jesus's instruction must to a degree have been entertaining to crowds, just as it must also have been informing, convicting, and life-changing. Such large and diverse crowds probably would not have followed Jesus so readily and earnestly if his instruction had not captured the minds and entertained the emotions of his hearers. The Sermon on the Mount in all of its breadth, topicality, familiarity, and profundity is of course the prime example. The Sermon on the Mount's log-in-the-eye lesson is likely among the best of examples of the exaggerated fashion in which Jesus sometimes seemed to teach, although one must take care not to mistake literal meanings as exaggeration. Jesus was cautioning others not to judge others, or God would judge them. He then told the crowd, "Why do you look at the speck of sawdust in your brother's eye and pay no attention to the plank in your own eye?" Jesus continued the parody by describing how the judging one would offer to help the judged one remove the speck when the judging one still had a plank in the eye. The crowd might have howled in delight at his humor, although might also have been silently spellbound or convicted in chagrin. Jesus's point remained that his hearers should see their own large sin before pointing out the tiny sins of others.

She sensed how a critical spirit undermined relationships, and so she fought the good fight to avoid it. Some people just seemed to have more than a word or two of criticism for everything and everyone. She didn't want to be one of those people. She sometimes found conversations with those especially critical acquaintances to be attractive invitations to join in the criticism. On its surface, criticism of others appeared to be a powerful inducement to agreement and even friendship between the criticizers. She worried though that the minute the other left and spoke with another that she would then be the criticism's target. She realized for that reason that criticism was not such a trustworthy friend after all, even if criticism made occasional short-term allies. She also saw how direct criticism affected the one criticized. She appreciated counsel, guidance, and even correction. She knew that in certain cases she had the obligation to give counsel, guidance, and correction, just as she hoped to receive it from others in appropriate situations. Yet she also felt that she had plenty to work on in her own condition, a truly ripe labor in fixing her own faults and reducing her own sin, before being quick to fix the faults of others. May God bless me with a critical eye for myself and forgiving spirit for others, she prayed.

Choose what is better. Luke 10:42.

The challenge of addressing sin is not only a challenge but also an opportunity. Addressing sin is not only dealing with negatives but also with positives. Sin occupies the heart, mind, hands, soul, and spirit. As Jesus's instructions and Spirit diminish the influence and effects of sin, the preoccupations and activities of sin, in one's life, opportunities arise to dwell and act on things that are better than sin. Some think of sin's attraction as if sin were in fact satisfying, when sin does not satisfy. To give in to sin is not to prosper, not even to enjoy one's destruction. Rather, giving in to sin is choosing a deadly and despairing course, a lonely and desperate demise ending a difficult life. Sin presents itself as a carnival of fun, when the presentation is itself a lie. Satisfaction and blessing in life arise from things other than sin, from pursuing and obeying Jesus. When we choose what is better than sin, and indeed choose Who is better than sin, we gain life. We should not treat the question of sin alone as avoiding evil but should also treat it as a question of choosing good. To choose good is to reject evil. To reject evil is to choose good. We have only so much to occupy in natural life. Occupying that time with sin means not occupying it with something better. The blessings and rewards that Jesus offers, the fruits of his righteousness, are incomparably greater than the enticements of sin. One really has no comparison to make. The point of Jesus's instruction is to consider the choice, consider that you have a choice and are making a choice, a choice for the better even if you believe only that you must rid your life of sin. Indeed, choose Jesus over anything, even things that occupy and distract you from him while not looking quite like sin.

Martha had invited Jesus into her home knowing that she would have to busy herself with preparations to host him properly. As Martha worked hard at those preparations, each of which she felt was quite necessary to honor such a distinguished guest as Jesus, Martha's sister Mary sat adoringly at Jesus's feet attending to every word that he said. Before long, Martha resented that Mary was not helping her with the preparations, as many hosts or hostesses might naturally resent another member of the household not contributing to guest preparations. Finally, Martha asked Jesus directly whether he cared that Mary wasn't helping her. Martha then told Jesus to tell Mary to help her. Jesus answered, "Martha, Martha, you are worried and upset about many things, but few things are needed — or indeed only one. Mary has chosen what is better, and it will not be taken away from her." While Martha felt that she had no choice but to prepare her house, and while Martha let worry over it and her lack of help upset her, Mary had chosen simply to attend to Jesus, the better One whom no one could take away from Mary.

Every day was a series of distractions from other things that seemed more important. Some distractions were major and others minor. Some were urgent while others just needed attention at some point. The energy that dealing with the distractions required to some degree kept him going. As a result, when he wasn't distracted frequently and when his energy lagged, he would go looking for distractions to reenergize him. All the while, he continued to feel that he was ignoring more-important things even if he was not always able to discern those things. Over time, though, he realized that some of the distractions were not distractions at all. They were precisely the activities that showed the care and concern that Jesus expected of him. When he was doing those things, particularly in service of needful people, he was serving and attending to Jesus. Other things, though, he began to realize were true distractions, things to which he should give little or no attention. He knew that in those instances, he needed to choose what was better, meaning things that reflected the instructions and drew the appreciation of Jesus. He began to see that day-to-day success was not only a matter of expending substantial energy but also of prioritizing it to apply to the better things.

Do not set aside the commandments. Matthew 5:19.

While avoiding sin may require leaving a sinful life behind and struggling against formidable demons and devil, on the other hand avoiding sin sometimes requires as little as not consenting to wrong action, not deliberately setting aside the commandments. Sin sometimes comes not as a way of life or temptation but as an invitation. Jesus instructs us to say no to the invitation. Indeed, we have the opportunity and thus the responsibility to evaluate courses of action as others propose them. Each day presents us with choices.

Some of those choices do not even require action on our part. They may only require consent, approval, or even after-the-fact ratification. Sometimes, sin simply knocks at the door, awaiting an invitation in. Other times, sin may not come through the front door but try a side or back door, not even waiting for an invitation. When sin enters by the side or back door, one has then to refuse consent. Do not let sin simply take over, inducing or implying your consent. Make judgments, especially about what would or would not be sin if you were to entertain the proposed or ratify the ongoing action. The moment that you recognize wrong action, reject it rather than consent to it. Do not consent to wrong action, and you will have gone a long way toward reducing your involvement in sin. Do not set aside what you know to be Jesus's instructions.

The authority with which Jesus spoke and taught, and the fresh way in which he seemed to approach instruction, must have confused some as to whether he was teaching them something new and different from the old commandments. Jesus made the answer clear in his Sermon on the Mount, saying that he had not come to abolish the law or ignore the prophets but to fulfill the law and prophecies. To emphasize the point, Jesus told the crowd that not the smallest letter or stroke of the pen will disappear from the law until everything for which God meant it Jesus has accomplished. Jesus thus answered a most-important question regarding behavior and sin, which was that commandments like not to murder or commit adultery were still in place, indeed meant more than ever. The consequence of Jesus's fulfilling rather than abolishing the law was that the members of the crowd should follow the commandments closely rather than setting them aside bit by bit. Jesus told the crowd, "Therefore anyone who sets aside one of the least of these commands and teaches others accordingly will be called least in the kingdom of heaven, but whoever practices and teaches these commands will be called great in the kingdom of heaven."

It had finally come to that point, and frankly, she was glad of it. She had for a long time accepted some behaviors on her part and among some of her acquaintances that she had first suspected were errors in judgment and had only later come to realize were small but clear sins. After realizing the error of her ways, she had at first sort of explained them away as too small to be worth addressing particularly insofar as changing them would likely have required disrupting certain well-established practices and relationships. Better not to be too righteous, especially among friends. So for a time she continued in those practices. Yet her sense that they were wrong and that she should not be engaging in them grew instead of waned. She thought that by ignoring them her conscience would subside, when instead her sense that they were undermining her and her friends grew stronger if not day by day then season to season. She first abandoned one practice, the one that she regarded as slightly more offending, and then saw to abandon another. In the end, she realized that she just could not consort with sin of any kind or degree, could not allow herself that undue liberty. She even wondered whether sin had degrees. While not wanting in any way to turn prudish and unpleasant, she just decided to keep all of the commandments, to stop her own sin wherever she sensed it. Although in plenty of instances she was still unsure about the specific qualities of certain behavior, when she saw sin, she was going to stop it.

Obey the commandments. Matthew 19:17.

Many think of Christians as do-gooders, as well they might. Christians and others have plenty of good to do. One finds little harm in committing to doing good works and then applying oneself diligently to them. Indeed, we should all make and carry out that commitment. Yet many make the mistake of believing that good works are the entry into the kingdom of heaven and that one must therefore earn one's way in through the accumulation of merit. Jesus once corrected a young man who appears to have thought so, as the following account shows. Good works bring a reward, no question. Doing good works here can store up treasure for oneself in heaven, where real treasures abound. But entry into kingdom life involves obedience, not good works covering up and somehow cancelling out disobedience. We do not gain entry into kingdom life based on a ledger showing that the plusses just barely or even substantially outweigh the minuses. Entry requires obedience to God's commands. Entry requires the One who kept all the commands, the

One who is Jesus. We do well to do good works. We do better to adhere closely to Jesus's instructions, to obey the commandments just in the way that he taught us to obey them, with the Holy Spirit's sensitivity and the heart of Jesus.

Jesus had just left a place where people had been bringing little children to him to bless. As he passed on from there, a rich young man, one who had great wealth, approached Jesus with a question, the rich young man whom another section above has already described. In this gospel account, though, the rich young man asked Jesus what *good thing* the young man must do to get eternal life. Jesus replied, "Why do you ask me about what is good? There is only One who is good. If you want to enter life, keep the commandments." Notice that Jesus named no good things, no good works. Jesus's reply instead appears to indicate that doing good things is not the answer for kingdom entry, for entry into life. Rather, Jesus replied that *keeping the commandments* is the key to life, a key that we know one finds through the instruction, life, and Spirit of Jesus himself, the only perfect Commandment Keeper. Despite Jesus's direct answer, the young man had another question, specifically, *which* commandments. Jesus then replied not to murder, commit adultery, steal, or lie, and also to honor father and mother while loving your neighbor as yourself. Jesus's answer still did not satisfy the rich young man, who asked Jesus what else the young man lacked if he had kept all these commandments since he was a boy. As the prior section also recounted, Jesus told the young man to sell all his possessions in exchange for treasure in heaven, which Jesus knew that the young man would not do.

She liked the thought of following rules in part because she loved order and organization. Chaos, disorder, and confusion bothered her, annoyed and frustrated her for all of the waste, carelessness, and distraction that she saw in them. She preferred following the rules and wanted others to do so also. On the other hand, some rules she discovered that she could just as well do without. She could see that some rules had gravity to them, generality and fundamentality, while other rules were clearly just conventions, practices adopted out of convenience or necessity but bearing no moral content or eternal consequence. Indeed, that distinction grew to her in its importance. Some rules were more than mere rules and instead more like commandments. They were principles of first order, things to which one tried constantly to adhere even if they didn't always tell you precisely what to do or not do in any one instance. She thought of them as guide stars, not just recommendations because they instead had the real sense of must-do command, but still just distant enough that she could not seize upon them, apply them with certainty, and thus control them, in all the circumstances in which she might have wanted to do so. She liked that they were rules that she could not control but to which she had to listen and attend, and which she wanted very badly to obey. God give me the discernment and strength to obey the commandments, she prayed. She wanted to see the King who had issued them, in his kingdom.

Cleanse the sinner. Matthew 10:8.

The above sections show that we have much to learn from Jesus about how to treat our own sin. Jesus may also have given us instruction to cleanse other sinners of sin. Of course, one does not exactly cleanse oneself of sin in the sense of absolution, any more than one could cleanse another of sin in that same sense. Only God absolves sin, and God does so through the redeeming sacrifice of Jesus when accepted and embraced by the sinner. Yet we can carry the word and life of Jesus to others. We can wash others with the words of life, letting the Word absolve those others of their sin. Just as we bear responsibility to be watchmen over sin, to let our spiritual brothers and sisters know of transgressions so that they may turn again to Jesus for guidance and redemption, so too may we accept responsibility to carry the gospel, the good news of the redemptive work of Jesus, to others and in doing so take part in their cleansing from sin. Someone else brought news of Jesus's sacrifice and redemption to us. We can and should share that good news with others. Everyone needs cleansing from sin. None can enter the kingdom carrying sin with them. Cleansing from sin is just as important as, or indeed more important than, avoiding sin in the first place. None other than Jesus has avoided all sin. All require

301

cleansing. Not all have heard of its availability in Jesus. Carry the message of the good news, and let others join you in your cleansing.

When Jesus sent the twelve disciples out still early in Jesus's public ministry, and blessed them with his authority to heal, he also gave them specific instructions. Those instructions included not just to heal, even to raise the dead, but also to "cleanse those who have leprosy" whom they would meet along their way. Leprosy was a skin disease then, just as it remains a skin disease today. Scriptural references to leprosy, scholars tell us, we should read also as references to other skin diseases of the day. Yet to read Jesus's instruction here as simply a reference to physical skin diseases might be to read the instruction too literally. Indeed, Jesus told his disciples to *cleanse* those who have leprosy, which might be odd considering that leprosy was and is a disease *of* the skin rather than a deposit *on* the skin that one might be able to wash away or otherwise cleanse. In its biological meaning, leprosy requires healing, not cleansing. All the cleansing in the world won't make leprosy go away. Jesus may thus have been referring to both the literal skin disease and also to something else that one would hope to cleanse, which in this sense would be sin. The same might also have been true of Jesus's instructions to heal, that it also bore a connotation of spiritual healing rather than just physical healing, and to raise the dead, that it also bore a connotation of giving Jesus's spiritual life to the spiritually dead. That Jesus was telling the disciples to cleanse those whom they met of their sin seems quite plausible, a worthy instruction that we might hope to follow bringing others the word, life, and Spirit of Jesus.

She had a heart for helping others deal with past wrongs probably because she had a strong sense of relying herself on Jesus for forgiveness and redemption. She knew as an intellectual matter that everyone engages in sin and that everyone accordingly needs forgiveness and redemption. Yet she also saw that some had a more-acute sense of the need for forgiveness than did others. She like anyone could point to specific wrongs in which she had once engaged and for that matter could even point to a few recent ones. She didn't really feel that she had a worse record of sin than others, although then again she would have been perfectly willing to accept that judgment if anyone had the basis to make it. She neither

302

counted herself better nor worse than others because relative judgments were unimportant. She only felt acutely that she needed Jesus's cleansing, and because she felt that need acutely, her heart went out to others having the same feeling. Or more accurately, her heart went out to others who had the feeling of need for cleansing but who did *not* yet have Jesus's cleansing. If she had any ministry that she valued more than any other, then that ministry of cleansing the sinner, of carrying the cleansing word and redemptive action of Jesus, was her ministry. She could count a few instances when she had those ministry opportunities, but she also prayed for more of them. While she knew intellectually that God would accept her under the blood of Jesus, she nonetheless sometimes felt that the only way that she could truly hold fast to her own salvation from past sin was to help others find their own cleansing.

Drive out demons. Matthew 10:8.

While the label we should each hesitate to apply to others, any of us have probably seen someone from whose bad behavior, poor demeanor, poorer personality, and strained relationships, we could imagine as being demon possessed. Anyone would find difficulty drawing lines between and among mental illness, mental disability, personality disorders, and demon possession. Perhaps few if any should profess special ability to do so. Who wants to attribute demon possession to another? What possible good could come from doing so? On the other hand, if demons possess others, then humane persons should prefer their ousting. Who would want anyone possessed by a demon? When we see others struggle in their spirits, struggle in ways that suggest a fight over internal control of thoughts and actions, as most of us have probably experienced ourselves in some instance, we should desire to give them aid in the battle. Jesus instructs to drive out demons. The effort is not one that any should attempt to undertake of their own initiative, but any should welcome the opportunity to carry the Spirit of Jesus to any such battle. Bring Jesus's word and Spirit to those who suffer internally, and don't mind too much if someone wants to recognize it as driving out demons.

Another instruction that Jesus gave to his twelve disciples when he sent them out to heal the sick and raise the dead early in his public ministry was to "drive out demons." The gospels include accounts of Jesus driving out demons, in which he promptly restored to sanity those who had previously been unable to think and express themselves clearly or control their violent and harmful actions. The evidence of demon possession that those accounts give include things like violent seizures and raging, harmful to both the one possessed and those nearby like family members, area residents, or caretakers. In those accounts, demon possession might require chaining the possessed, avoiding the possessed, or supervising the possessed closely. Demon possession was in other words a terrible condition, extremely hard on the possessed and often nearly as hard on others. The gospels also suggest that driving out demons was no easy matter, including accounts where the disciples or others were unable to drive out demons, leaving the work to Jesus. Jesus nonetheless gave the disciples that authority and expected them to use it effectively.

They had seen some unusual events together in their times and travels. This one was surely one of them. The details of it they would not care to share with others, particularly those who did not understand and speak openly and comfortably of things involving the spirit. Some things were better left unsaid, even if not unaddressed. That addressing of spiritual things was the central lesson that they drew from those unusual events, especially from this prime example. Some conditions, they learned, were so much of the spiritual realm that only the spiritual realm could address them, indeed only the Spirit of Jesus. But for that Spirit, they could not have imagined themselves having any part, large or small, in the proceedings to which they were occasional witnesses. The proceedings themselves were so unusual that they might not have given much credence to them. Yet they also saw the healing results, those remarkable results giving that credence. They just left it at that. They had glimpses into things about which they had no appetite to learn more even while they were very glad for those who found such remarkable relief through them. Sin, they decided, is formidable. Bring the big guns when needed.

2

Relationships

While knowing what Jesus said to do and not do, that is in terms of *actions,* would give anyone a great start on entering into and living within God's rich kingdom, that start might be only a start, maybe half of what we need to dwell richly in Christ in kingdom bounty. Jesus also spoke often and profoundly not just about actions but about *relationships.* We both *do* and by doing *become,* our doing and becoming then inevitably involving relationships. For instance, in believing, confessing, praying, and obeying, we become a Christian, meaning that we have a relationship with Christ. In making the covenant of marriage, we become married and have a relationship with a spouse. If the union results in children, we become a parent and have a relationship to children. Because life inevitably and so thankfully involves relationship, and because the quality of those relationships has so much to do with preparing us for entry into kingdom life, Jesus gives us many instructions on relationships. We need his instructions, need especially to follow those instructions, to enter the kingdom anticipating just and lasting reward there. We cannot have poor or non-existent relationships with the Father, Son, and Holy Spirit, and yet expect welcome in the kingdom. We cannot have poor or non-existent relationships with others, and expect any special reward. Listen carefully to Jesus on relationships, and commit to following his instructions faithfully.

307

2.1 God

Seek God's Kingdom. Luke 12:31. *Do not test God.* Luke 4:12. *Serve God only.* Matthew 4:10. *Do the will of God.* John 4:34. *Give God your fruits.* Luke 20:10. *Belong to God.* John 8:47. *Hear what God says.* John 8:47. *Commit your spirit to God.* Luke 23:45. *Recognize God's coming to you.* Luke 19:44. *Love God with everything.* Luke 10:27. *Praise God for healing.* Luke 17:18. *Obtain God's praise.* John 5:44. *Ask God to send you.* Matthew 9:38. *Put God's word into practice.* Luke 8:21. *Do what God says.* Matthew 21:29. *Do what pleases God.* John 8:29. *Obey the word of God.* Luke 11:28. *Show God's work in your life.* John 9:3. *Hold to God's commands.* Mark 7:8.

The primary relationship in any life, whether the person living that life recognizes the relationship or not, is with God the Father. Relationships certainly affect us and others even when we do not recognize the relationship, indeed in some cases especially when we do not recognize the relationship. If the judge orders your attendance at a court hearing and you fail or refuse to recognize the judge, then you will find police officers hauling you before the judge on a bench warrant. If you refuse to recognize your child, then the state will force you to pay child support, and the child will stand a far greater likelihood of incarceration, homelessness, abuse, depression, and suicide. Relationships matter whether you care for them or not. No relationship matters more, and nowhere will your ignorance of the relationship affect you and others more adversely, than relationship with God the Father. We must, as his word says, first accept that he exists and then discern that he rewards those who pursue and obey him. Listen to what Jesus says about relationship with God the Father, knowing that no relationship matters more.

Seek God's Kingdom. Luke 12:31.

The authority of its king is what defines a kingdom. A kingdom has no more-central definition than that a king rules it. Indeed, a kingdom is only as large, and is every bit as large, as the extent of the king's authority over it. A kingdom is that realm within which the king's edict rules. In a kingdom, the subjects who populate it obey the king, or they will find themselves cast out and in a different kingdom. One cannot dwell long or fruitfully within a realm without obeying the authority of the one who rules it. Yet in what other kingdom would one want to dwell than God's kingdom? Most of us have yet to find an earthly ruler to whom we are fully glad in all respects to submit. We might obey many different rulers, finding most of them reasonably acceptable, if the extent of the rule had primarily to do with distant things and Constitution or Bill of Rights restricted the rule. But if the ruler had complete authority over us, over our goods, life, and welfare, as is the case in a true kingdom, then we would find no suitable ruler-king other than the perfectly just God to whom we submit in the kingdom of heaven. While we tend to think of the kingdom of heaven as something we hope with Christ's blood to enter after death, Jesus spoke repeatedly of the present availability of the kingdom. We should act *now* within the realm of God's authority as Jesus informs and instructs it, and benefit *now* from the rule of the King.

On more than one occasion involving large crowds of listeners, Jesus spoke warnings and encouragement, about worry and watchfulness, and on other subjects, all relating to the kingdom of God. The kingdom was a central theme and subject for Jesus, one to which he addressed many comments, cautions, and instructions. In one example repeated in more than one sermon in accounts in different gospels, Jesus cautioned against running after things that we think we need, such as food and drink, rather than pursuing God's kingdom. In one gospel account, Jesus concluded that lesson on not worrying about earthly things with the admonition, "But seek his kingdom, and these things will be given to you as well." Seek his kingdom *first*, Jesus was saying to his listeners, and you would receive the *other* things after which you run. Prosperity, peace, and provision come not by their direct pursuit but instead through pursuit of the kingdom.

He kept thinking about this subject of the kingdom of God about which Jesus taught so often and so much. The thought of entering the kingdom after death was something he could grasp, indeed on which he had long reflected. Yet the thought of entering the kingdom now, of living this present life under the authority *and within the realm* of God, was something different. He wanted to live in that flow of God's authority. If he didn't have to do so, then he didn't want to wait until his earthly demise to think and behave after death as he would hope to do in God's kingdom. If entering the kingdom now was indeed possible, as Jesus seemed repeatedly to suggest, then he definitely, earnestly, wanted to do so. Reading Jesus's words carefully, over and over, he also began to see how doing so might just be possible. He would need to set aside a lot of old habits, especially old thought processes. In fact, he would need to set aside an old life. But he was more than ready to do so. He decided to devote the better part of his days and energies seeking that kingdom now rather than waiting for future life.

Do not test God. Luke 4:12.

God is reliable. God makes many promises, gives many assurances, all inviting reliance. We should trust and rely on God more so than we trust and rely on anything or anyone else, for instance, our own understanding. We may barely understand what is going on around us, and yet we can trust that God knows and that God plans for our prosperity, as long as we rely on him. God's promises and providences reassure us about provision, plans, prosperity, peace, comfort, salvation, and other great things to which we should look forward in anticipation, and after they occur, look back in gratitude. Yet sometimes we do not see the past providences of God. At other times we lose faith in his future providences. Jesus cautions us not to test God in those times. To test God would be for us to create an artificial circumstance in which we expect and in essence demand that God perform his promise. In testing God, we would attempt to command his performance rather than trust in hope and faith that he will perform. God commands us; we do not command God. To test God is to demonstrate a lack of faith rather than to demonstrate faith. God does not appreciate and reward lack of faith, nor does he appreciate the created commanding the Creator. Do not test God.

Jesus fasted in the wilderness for forty days after John baptized him in the Jordan River. The devil tested Jesus during those forty days. The first test had to do with hunger that the devil urged Jesus to turn stone into bread but with Jesus replying that man does not live on bread alone. Persons live instead on the word of God. In the second test, the devil invited Jesus to worship the devil in exchange for the world but with Jesus replying to worship and serve the Lord God only. Persons must worship and serve none other than God. In the third test, the devil urged Jesus to throw himself from the highest point of the temple so that God would send his angels in rescue. Jesus replied, "It is said: 'Do not put the Lord your God to the test.'" While God promises many things, persons should not challenge God with tests to prove those promises. Jesus's refusal to test his Father ended the devil's tempting of Jesus in the desert. The devil left until another better time, when he might again attempt to tempt Jesus.

She felt that she needed a sign from God, reassurance about something that was so critically important to her, and not just to her life and circumstances but rather to her faith. She prayed, but she prayed gently and only once, for that sign. In her prayer, which became a long prayer, she reassured God that she hoped, trusted, and believed that he had done as he had long promised. She told God that she would continue to trust and believe even without the sign for which she asked him. She reassured God that she was not going to doubt him over this promise whether or not he sent her that sign. As she meditated, reflected, and prayed, she realized and reassured God that her asking for a sign was not because she doubted but because she trusted and only wished to celebrate his providence and promise with him and with others. She wasn't absolutely sure that her reassurance was true, but she wanted her reassurance to be true. She did want to celebrate with God that he had done as he had long promised. She reassured God that the doing of this so-important thing would not have been for her but for the one for whom God would have done it. She was not being selfish, she told God, but self-less, thinking only of the other for whom she hoped and trusted in God's promise of salvation and resurrection with Jesus. She was asking God nothing for herself but for the other, except that this sign would be for her, a reminder and evidence that God saves, Jesus saves, that life eternal is the reward for need, acceptance, acknowledgment, relationship, and obedience. She prayed only once and then waited. And the sign came.

Serve God only. Matthew 4:10.

Whether we realize it or not, we do choose whom and what to serve. Sometimes we serve our employer, other times our family, and at other times ourselves. Sometimes we serve money, other times our recreation or pleasure, and at other times our pride. One hopes that we do not serve evil, in openly pursuing things that are obviously wrong. Yet that we serve something or someone is inevitable. Jesus's instruction to serve God only is thus at once both admonition and opportunity, both proscription and prescription. We are to serve God and not to serve others. To serve is to support, aid, assist, or devote oneself to the other. To serve God does not mean to abandon family or employer, or even to abandon some degree of comfort or pleasure. Indeed the opposite is true. By serving God, we provide and care for family more and better than we otherwise would because God expects us to provide and care for family. By serving God, we work for employers more engagingly and productively because God expects us to work as if we worked for God. The employee who works for an employer as if working for God will make a very good employee. We should not hesitate to serve God, and to serve God only, because in doing so we give our best service to all to whom we genuinely owe it.

Two gospels give accounts of the devil tempting Jesus during his forty days fasting in the wilderness. In the first account, described in the prior section, the devil's last tempting has to do with testing God. Jesus refused to test the Father on his promise to send his angels to save him. About three years later, in the hours before his crucifixion,

Jesus would once again refuse the tempting, once again decline to ask the Father to save him from what he would face because Jesus knew that the Father would act in his time and plan exactly as he had promised. Resurrection and the salvation of humankind would be Jesus's reward for his trusting rather than testing God. The other gospel account of Jesus's tempting in the wilderness, though, makes the devil's last tempting a different tempting. The devil took Jesus to a very high mountain to show him the splendor of the world, offering it to Jesus if he would only bow in the devil's worship. Jesus replied, "Away from me, Satan! For it is written: 'Worship the Lord your God, and serve him only.'" Jesus would serve God only, and instructs us to serve God only.

Some things that he did for others, say, for his employer, he did not particularly value or appreciate doing. Not all work carries obvious meaning. Much work is repetitive rather than creative, he knew, and some of that repetitive work seems not to bear much relationship to the welfare of anyone, he felt. He appreciated that work requires showing up, being consistent, and fulfilling roles that while not plainly meaningful on their own nonetheless contribute in some small and barely discernible way to the overall welfare of the organization and its customers, clients, or constituents. Not surprisingly, though, he found little incentive to pursue those duties and roles, just as anyone else would find little incentive. He didn't appreciate drudgery, especially when his employer or the others whom he was serving in doing the drudge work didn't even necessarily know that he was doing it. Yet he had learned that credit with an employer, customer, client, or other person is not the important measure of service's value. Indeed, he had committed to serve God only. God saw everything that he did, whether or not others saw it. If God wanted him doing drudge work, then he would do it more than willingly. He would do it happily, earnestly, with the most skill and ardor with which he would do any work, even more creative, satisfying, and apparent work. With his commitment to serve God only, the tasks that confronted him and required his attention, whether at work or elsewhere, began to take on equal value and meaning. Everything was important because he was serving God in doing it.

Do the will of God. John 4:34.

To serve God, and to serve God only, one must discern what is within God's will, what God desires, plans, and values. One does not serve God by doing things that God does not desire, plan, or value. To serve God requires discerning what is God's will and then doing that will rather than doing something other. Although the Old Testament tells us a great deal about God's nature and will, some might still claim that discerning the will of God would be mystifying if we did not have the instructions, words, actions, and model of Jesus. We study, accept, and follow Jesus's instructions in order to do the will of God. What Jesus says to do and not do directs us in the will of God. Who, after all, is Jesus but the Son of God, One who speaks nothing other than what he hears from the Father and who when we see him, we have also seen the Father? We have the clearest of instructions and examples, the best possible insight into God's will in having the gospels record the words and actions, and reflect the character and will, of Jesus. One needs only do as Jesus said to do and did, in order to act within the will of God. Imagine the excitement that we should hold for doing the will of God, then grasp that opportunity to enter the kingdom with him.

Jesus had tired of his travels back to Galilee from Judea through Samaria. So he sat by a well while the disciples went into town to buy food. While waiting at the well for the disciples to return, Jesus met a woman who came to draw water. When he asked her for a drink, she remarked that she was only a Samaritan with whom Jews usually did not interact. Jesus nonetheless offered her his living water that, he said, would well up into eternal life if she accepted it from him. In their conversation, Jesus also disclosed that he was the long-awaited Messiah, a message that she carried back to her town. The disciples, though, were surprised on their return that Jesus would even talk to a lowly Samaritan. They urged Jesus to eat, but Jesus declined, saying that he had food about which they knew nothing. They saw no food, but Jesus clarified, "My food is to do the will of him who sent me and to finish his work." God feeds those who pursue his will, doing his work.

She had heard of the modern, kind of-sort of New Age concept of living in the *flow*. Indeed, while she rejected anything New Age that she found inconsistent with the Ancient of Days whom she followed, she nonetheless appreciated that things of God, the things that God asks, expects, and requires of us, living in and through his kingdom, might be somewhat like keeping within the *flow*. God is not simply a force, field, or energy, she knew. God is instead a Father, Son, and Holy Spirit, three persons in one. God's will, though, might feel like a special path or power, she at least hoped. The plans and purposes of God, he will accomplish. To work within the will of God, then, should be at least somewhat like working within constantly succeeding plans and purposes, she thought. God's plans and purposes are also wholly beneficial, she knew. God acts for good, not evil. So she reasonably felt that working within the will of God should be like working for the most-beneficial good of God, herself, and others. She did not expect everything to work like clockwork. She knew that God could work through human shortfall and failure just as effectively as through human effort and skill. Miracles were certainly possible. She was willing to do as she discerned he would have her do, even if doing so felt or looked difficult or unproductive. Yet she also felt that doing the will of God should feel a lot like that thing *flow*. None of the things that Jesus said to do or not do sounded or seemed awkward, backward, or strongly counter-intuitive. They instead seemed like one gloriously integrated God-centered flow.

Give God your fruits. Luke 20:10.

The image of producing fruit is so satisfying, even compelling. Have you ever walked in an orchard or vineyard heavy laden with the impending fruit harvest? The sense of bounty is so great that in our metaphors we often use the image of *bearing fruit*, pursuing *low-hanging fruit*, and enjoying the *fruits of one's labors*. We all have time, we all have capacity, and we all have some skill and resources, even if the relative amounts or degrees of each differ fairly widely among us, except that God may value each of those things differently than we do including equally among us. In any case, with investment and labor, we each produce a harvest. To some of us, our harvests look meager, while to others, the harvest looks plentiful, even though again God may value our harvests differently than we do including equally among us. No matter our harvest, we should dedicate it to God who owns our orchards and vineyards. We work his lands, not our own or another's. The fruit we harvest from his lands may also be a different harvest than what we first think of as a harvest. We may think of our harvest as cash in a paycheck or bank account, as market share earned, as satisfied clients or customers, or even as homes and furnishings, things that we hold and consume. God may instead consider our fruits to be loving and caring relationships, feeding the hungry, visiting the prisoner, and carrying word of his Son to those who do not know him. Whatever vineyards God has leased you in which to work for a harvest, be sure to give him the fruits rather than take them for you. If you do so, then he will return to you what you need. If you don't do so, then know that he will come for his harvest.

One day when Jesus was teaching in the temple courts and sharing with the people his good news, the religious leaders asked him what authority he had to do so. Jesus knew that they were trying to trap him, and so instead of answering, he asked them what authority they thought John had to baptize. The religious leaders could not answer without either rejecting John whom the people respected or endorsing John's baptism of Jesus, which they didn't want to do. When they refused to answer, Jesus also refused to answer their question. Jesus then turned to the people to teach them the parable of the tenants, as follows. A vineyard owner rented his vineyard to some tenants who, after harvest, refused to give the vineyard's fruit to the servants whom the owner sent or even the owner's son. The tenants beat the servants and killed the son, thinking that they could then own the vineyard. But the owner would then come, kill the tenants, and give the vineyard to others, Jesus concluded. The religious leaders who overheard the parable knew that Jesus was speaking about them. They had not given God the fruit of his vineyard, and now they were going to kill God's Son.

317

She felt far too frequently that the world valued too little the harvest that her labors produced. While others earned their daily appreciation and weekly paychecks from employers, she voluntarily looked after sick, hurt, elderly, or disabled family members, neighbors, and friends. While others trained for marathons, triathlons, and fun runs where crowds would cheer them on for ribbons and other recognition, she kept her home and yard, and helped keep the homes and yards of others. While others served on boards and councils building their resumes and getting their names and photographs in the media, she did the quiet volunteer work that the boards and councils governed and mandated. Whatever she produced in her daily labors, which were plentiful labors, was an intangible rather tangible harvest. She could not point to a bank account, resume, website profile, or even photo album as evidence of the fruits of her abundant labors. Yet she also knew that she wasn't working for the world, surely not for the world's recognition. She was working for God and bringing him his fruits, things that she hoped and had good reason to believe that he appreciated more than the world appreciated. She had to admit that she had some days when she wanted to keep some of those fruits or pursue other fruits that the world seemed more to value. But she had decided long ago to keep bringing God his fruits. After all, she knew that he was more than returning the blessing.

Belong to God. John 8:47.

An early step to serving God, doing the will of God, and giving God the fruits of one's labor, is first to belong to God. When we say that an object *belongs* to someone, we mean that a person owns the object. By *ownership*, we mean a bundle of rights that include possession, right to use and enjoy, and right to exclude others from use. Ownership above all implies control of the thing owned. For a *person* to belong to someone must today have a slightly different connotation than ownership because people do not own one another except in slavery, an arrangement we rightly reject. The connotation of slavery, though, or at least of being subject to an all-powerful master, made more sense in biblical times when slavery was more prevalent and also makes more sense when concerning God to be the master. If we are slaves to anyone, then we are slaves to God. Indeed, many of us would gladly accept slavery to God, being utterly subject to his beneficent will, rather than enslave ourselves to our desires or to others. Yet setting aside this uncomfortable question of one owning another, even God owning some of us, we can still accept the weaker connotation of *belonging* as in belonging to a club, team, alliance, or group. If some do not completely submit to God as a slave would submit to an owner or servant would submit to a master, then one hopes that all would at least accept to aligning themselves with God. Belong to God and no other.

Jesus had disputed at length with the religious leaders, first over who Jesus was, and then over whose children the religious leaders were, whether the devil's children or God's children. Some had believed Jesus, while others had not, even though Jesus was simply telling the truth. Jesus kept asking those who did not believe him why his language was not clear and why they were unable to hear him. He was telling them the truth. Why didn't they hear and believe? Jesus answered his own question, saying, "Whoever belongs to God hears what God says." Jesus was telling the religious leaders that they must belong to God. They must *be* God's people before they would hear God. Jesus was making clear to the religious leaders who did not hear and believe him that they never would hear or believe him until they belonged first to God. Those who belong to God hear, understand, and accept God's words. Those who do not belong to God, reject God's words even when God's words are always true. Truth does not necessarily determine belief in truth. Believing truth first requires belonging to the right side, to God's side.

Although the thought first struck him as odd and made him a little uncomfortable, the more familiar that he became with it, the more willing he was to accept and commit to it. He ended up loving the idea of being servant or even slave to God. He had few reference points, certainly none within his direct experience, for the concept of being a slave or even for that matter a servant. He admitted to himself that he might really have no clue what servitude was truly like. He had no delusions that it had anything romantic about it, certainly not when the master was anyone other than God. He would not submit to be a slave to an employer, schedule, program, image, or any other institution, person, or thing, other than God. He wanted not to even think about those other possibilities, although he suspected that at times he *had* been a slave to things or others. Yet in the end, he was still quite willing, almost eager, to entertain the thought of belonging to God, even of being in servitude to God, and only because God was no ordinary master. While legend might say that the slaves of Solomon lived better than many royals of other realms, God must be the only master whose servitude would vastly improve the station of any who undertook it. The meaning that meant most to him, though, was not his improved station in servitude to God. He wanted God to know him, recognize him, save him, give him place in his kingdom, and give him eternal life with his Son, no matter in what low station that fellowship left him. He would be a doorman in the kingdom over a god or priest in any other kingdom. If he *belonged* to God, then God could not reject one who was his.

Hear what God says. John 8:47.

So one must first belong to God in order to hear and accept God's words. Yet one then has to go ahead and *hear* those words. Belonging is great as far as it goes because it opens the heart and mind to earnest listening. One must then take the next step not just of letting the voice of God pass through one's ears but to actually consider, comprehend, evaluate, and incorporate the meaning that the sounds convey. When Jesus says first to belong to God and then to *hear* God's words, he means more than to let the voice of God become audible. After all, the words of Jesus are certainly available to us in the Bible, in the media airwaves, in the messages of ministers and the words of acquaintances, family members, and friends. The kind of hearing to which this teaching refers, though, is not simply to be within earshot of those words. Hearing in this meaning instead entails active consideration, believing and accepting consideration, of those words. Scientists must begin with the willingness to consider the evidence, much like the willingness to believe what they may learn. The scientist who refuses to consider the evidence is not a scientist at all. The scholar who refuses to consider the content of the text, refuses to accept even the possibility that the text represents truth, is not a scholar at all. Hearing requires of anyone, not just faith believers, active and open consideration of the evidence and its meaning. We must hear the words of God ready to consider and accept their meaning. Without hearing, we are lost to his desires and will. We cannot discern his will and serve him accordingly without hearing his communication. Hearing requires the disposition to learn, understand, believe, and follow.

Jesus had spoken to the religious leaders so many times, sometimes as he moved from place to place teaching the crowds, other times as part of those crowds, sometimes as they listened to him teaching in the temple courts, and at still other times in their homes at their invitation. That the religious leaders did not hear, understand, and believe was remarkable after they had heard Jesus so many times in so many settings. Jesus had already told them this time, in a long and difficult teaching that he directed at the religious leaders, that they did not belong to God. They had given themselves over to one another and to impressing, intimidating, controlling, and manipulating the crowds. Jesus then repeated himself and elaborated, "The reason you do not hear is that you do not belong to God." The religious leaders must *hear* Jesus, not just let his voice pass over them, but *comprehend* what Jesus was saying so that the truth of his words would begin to appear to them and they would then accept those words as sound. They did not belong, and so although they heard his voice, they did not consider and incorporate the meaning of his words.

He had long heard preaching here and there, in passing through radio or television channels, in film, and in parody. He had also long known of the Bible text. He had even once read the Bible as literature and history in the manner that a secular school presents it. He had read that Bible cover to cover, although the secular version that the school had supplied for reading had deprecatory commentary introducing each book, and the version had omitted many books, particularly the letters of the Apostle Paul. So he had heard the voice of God, read the words of Jesus. In doing so, he appreciated their

321

profound nature set within both history and the supernatural or divine. He also appreciated the impact that these words must have had on many and the distinct literary quality that they represented. He also sensed the magnificence of their historical breadth, a single book collecting much more than a millennium of history woven into a single progressive theme. Yet without the Spirit of God fully within him, not yet within him, not yet baptized in the Spirit and belonging to God, those words passed through and out of his mind. He had read the words without hearing them, read the words without considering their truth, read the words without fully coming to grips with the person and truth of Jesus. But others prayed for him that he would face and come to know Jesus, and when he had, the words took their proper hold, settled in his mind, and informed his spirit.

Commit your spirit to God. Luke 23:45.

The moment comes for each of us when our bodies give out, leaving only our spirits to contend with what remains of life. Jesus urged and instructed us repeatedly to enter God's kingdom, to pursue and accept eternal life. Yet he also demonstrated that which we must do at the last moment of natural life when all that remains is our spirit. We can and should serve God when our bodies are able. We should discern and pursue God's will, and should in doing so belong to God as a servant belongs to a master, concerned only for his concerns and doing only his will. At the final moment, though, when we have no more to do because we have no strength for doing, we must then know and trust that God will accept our spirit. We must commit our spirit to God, entrust him with our spirit life and its resurrection in Jesus. We may even commit our spirit *and body* to God earlier, while still in good natural health as we live, breathe, and do God's will through the temple, energy, bounty, and blessing of our natural body. The moment will still come when we have no natural body to commit but only spirit. Plan, commit, and expect then to turn your spirit over to God as Jesus did. Do so in godly confidence and joy that you enter God's presence in heaven.

Jesus stood before the council of religious leaders at daybreak, after Jesus's arrest and a night of mocking and beating by his guards. The religious leaders first condemned him before leading him off to the Roman leader who held the government's authority for executions. That leader sent him to another leader who ridiculed and mocked him before sending him back. The Roman leader wanted to release Jesus, but at the religious leaders' urging, the crowd demanded that the Roman leader condemn Jesus, which he did. Soldiers scourged Jesus cruelly before leading him out to the hill where they crucified him with two criminals. One of those criminals berated Jesus, while the other asked Jesus to remember him in heaven, the latter one to whom Jesus promised paradise with him that day. Darkness then gathered as the sun stopped shining, even though the hour was noon. The sun remained dark for the next three hours as Jesus suffered his last on the cross. A mysterious tearing of the temple's curtain that had separated the people from the temple's inner place occurred as Jesus came near to dying. Jesus finally called out in a loud voice, "Father, into your hands I commit my spirit," those words his last breath.

They shared less and less fear of dying, and more and more anticipation of joining Jesus in God's glorious heaven. They had been close to each of their parents in their passing, had held the hands and stroked the foreheads of each parent as each parent lay about to die or breathing their literal last breath in dying. They held little doubt any longer that the human spirit is far more than the electrical impulses that were right then ceasing in the natural minds of each passing parent. One cannot locate the human spirit or even human consciousness in the brain or any related biological structures. The spirit resides in some condition and location other than cell or tissue, chemical reactions, or electrical charge. God, they knew, would resurrect their parents' natural bodies as new temples for their parents' surviving spirits, their parents having given their lives to the care of the only One who could save them, Jesus Christ. They knew that they had one last commitment to make, one that they did not fear, indeed one that removed all fear, which was to release their own spirits to God.

Recognize God's coming to you. Luke 19:44.

So much of how one thinks about faith has to do with, well, how one thinks about faith, as in *am I doing this or that right?* The pursuit of righteousness and obedience seems at one level to involve that constant introspection that enables one to shape behavior and thought, to believe and to act accordingly. Committed introspection, examination of one's beliefs and practices, and study of and meditation on God's word are all good, indeed necessary. Yet the project of holiness is not all on us. We have a loving and pursuing God at hand. We do not know him as the Hound of Heaven for nothing. We do not so much catch God as God catches us. In any reading of Jesus's words to learn the attitudes, approaches, practices, habits, and acts that will form and mark our obedience, we must also realize that Jesus through his Spirit constantly informs and guides us. The key is to recognize the moments when God comes to us. Many saw and heard Jesus, even witnessing his many miracles. Many believed, while many did not. Many who saw and heard him recognized that they were seeing the image and embodiment of God, Emanuel, as the incorporeal God with us, God deciding to reveal what he looks like in person. Others pretended or decided that they were seeing nothing other than a deluded criminal, one whom the secular authorities must execute lest the lunatic destroy the established religious order. Recognize when God comes to you. Even while you pursue obedience to Christ's word, model, and person, appreciate also that Christ pursues you.

The crowds thronged Jesus as his disciples led him toward Jerusalem in triumphal procession, mounted on the donkey colt that stepped along the cloaks that the crowd had strewn on the road. Having witnessed so many of his miracles, the crowd was shouting hosannas, calling Jesus the king that had come in the name of the Lord. Some of the religious leaders told Jesus to rebuke the crowd of believers because surely Jesus was not the Messiah whom the crowd was proclaiming. Jesus refused to do so, instead telling the leaders that the stones would cry hosannas if the crowd fell silent. As he neared Jerusalem, though, Jesus began to weep not only over its imminent demise but that it of all places had failed to recognize the

King who would have given it peace. Jesus warned of the army that would encircle the city, kill its people, and destroy its structures, none of it having been necessary. Jesus said, "They will dash you to the ground, you and the children within your walls. They will not leave one stone on another, because you did not recognize the time of God's coming to you."

He was aware of the possibility of a God visitation. He knew others who spoke after that fashion that God would visit them, whether through words, events, persons, dreams, or maybe even apparitions. He did not discount those visits when others described them. If God visitation was what they perceived, then more power to them. Let the visitations bless them. On the other hand, he did not want to be imagining God, seeing God where God wasn't, attributing to God events, dreams, or visions that were not God's but were instead his imagination. He resisted delusion, and especially self-delusion, even while his sense, confidence, and insight grew that God could visit, might visit, and perhaps even wanted to visit. Events not appropriate to describe here ensued that convinced him of God's willingness to come to anyone who accepts him. One thing that he felt that he learned from those events was that this wondrously loving God will come in just the manner that the person is most prepared to accept him. To some, that manner might be through words, to others through events, and to others through dreams, visions, or persons. The important resolution to make is to welcome the visit. Recognize that God will come even to you, as long as you prepare heart, mind, and senses to recognize, accept, and embrace him.

Love God with everything. Luke 10:27.

The ancient scripture that Jesus affirmed as the way to eternal life is to love God with all of your heart, soul, strength, and mind. Scholars, commentators, and message-givers have fruitfully parsed that great command, distinguishing heart from soul, soul from strength, and strength from mind. Indeed, we could learn much from such parsing. To love with one's heart has a slightly different meaning than to love with one's soul or strength or mind. Love can be a heart thing, or love can be a soul, strength, or mind thing. To love with the heart implies emotion, passion, spontaneity, and openness. To love with the soul implies meditation, reflection, and depth. To love with strength implies vitality, discipline, and commitment. To love with the mind implies thought, reason, and rationale. Yet the command simply says to love with all of those things, whatever their distinctions are. By distinguishing among those things, we do not necessarily gain in our understanding and commitment if, as the command says, we are to love with all of them. We should instead be sure that we love with every aspect of each of them. While scholars and message-givers who so fruitfully parse the distinctions among heart, soul, strength, and mind might rightfully object, one might do nearly as well by simply loving God with one's all. Give Him everything you've got. Hold nothing back, nothing at all.

The law expert was testing Jesus, which was never a good idea. He should have learned from Jesus, not tested him. Experts, though, can have hard times recognizing greater expertise than their own and thus have hard times learning. The heart leads the mind and mouth. Jesus likely knew the expert's testing rather than discerning heart well before the expert spoke. In any case, the law expert began by asking Jesus what he must do to have eternal life. Jesus threw the question back on the law expert by asking him what the Law said and how the expert read the Law. "'Love the Lord your God with all your heart and with all your soul and with all your strength and with all your mind,'" the law expert quoted the Law back to Jesus, while continuing with the command to also love neighbor. "You have answered correctly," Jesus replied, adding, "Do this and you will live." The law expert should have stopped there because Jesus had answered, showing him the way to eternal life. Yet the law expert wasn't there to learn from Jesus but instead to justify himself. The expert soon got a hard lesson, a difficult parable in answer to his next question testing Jesus. Setting aside the other lesson that the expert needed from Jesus, we should not miss that Jesus answered the expert's question, telling him how to receive eternal life by loving God with all he had.

He was still plumbing the depths of the great command to love God with everything one has. At one level, as he initially felt, the command seems so simple as to be almost trite. Well sure, everyone should love God with all, he readily agreed. Yet how much can one learn from a statement as broad as that? Give me some detail, he somewhat felt. Still, as he reflected further on the command, and read and heard various commentators and message-givers on it, he began to see in the command much greater subtlety and depth. He knew some people who only seemed to love God with the head and not so much with the heart. Indeed, he knew some times of his own when that limited head-love was probably his own case. He also knew other people who seemed to love God with only the heart and not the head. They had a passion for God but not much thought or reason to go with it. He knew still others who had heart and head for God but not much strength, and others who seemed to lack the deep soul response to God. He could see after these reflections that he had much with which to love God, several different capacities. He knew, too, that he wanted to devote each of them, all of him, to God. He wanted to love God with everything and now knew that to do so, he needed his heart, soul, strength, and mind involved.

Praise God for healing. Luke 17:18.

We have the liberty and also Jesus's instruction to recognize, receive, and serve God, do his will, and love him with everything that we have. As our creator and redeemer, and showing his fathomless love, God certainly deserves these things from us. One more thing that he expects and warrants, not yet mentioned, is our praise. Praise is in one respect a perfectly natural thing and in another respect an odd thing. We naturally praise one another, praise events, praise circumstances, and even praise the weather. We each appreciate and even need praise, while knowing that others want and deserve it. Giving praise is easy for us and probably healthy for us, almost surely healthier than whining, criticizing, and complaining. On any account, as the creator of the universe, author of life, only good, and love itself, God most certainly deserves our praise. If natural reason and response were guiding us, if for instance God were our literal neighbor blessing us so gloriously, then we would be singing God's praise with every breath from dawn to dusk. The odd thing for us in praising God is not finding the reasons, which are infinite. The obstacle to our praise may instead be that we don't recognize that God appreciates it. We don't see God as intimate, God as friend, God as person, or God as neighbor. He is so much that we praise him so little. Don't make that mistake that others have made. God is a person, a deeply caring person who cares about your praise, especially when healing, as the following account shows. Give God praise for every blessing, and then give special acknowledgment for his healing.

Jesus was heading along the border of Samaria on his way from Galilee to Jerusalem, preparing to enter a village. At the village's edge, ten men with leprosy called out to Jesus from a distance, begging that Jesus, whom they also called Master, would have mercy on them. The lepers were making an extraordinarily insightful acknowledgment of who Jesus was while also making an extraordinarily faith-filled request in asking for his mercy. Jesus responded in generous kind, telling the men to go present themselves to the priests, meaning that he would have healed them of leprosy by the time that they arrived. Yet only one of the ten men whom Jesus had miraculously healed bothered to come back to thank Jesus. That one man, who was only a Samaritan and not a Jew apparently like some others, threw himself at Jesus feet while thanking him and praising God. Jesus asked, "Has no one returned to give praise to God except this foreigner?" Jesus then graciously confirmed the man's healing, acknowledged that his faith had been the cause, and bid him go on his way. Jesus expected praise to God from all those whom he healed, perhaps especially those Jews who professed faith in God.

Praise, she concluded, was a learned behavior. For a long time, she had given little thought and less effort to praising God. That time might have been many years or maybe as long as decades. Logically, she knew that she had many reasons, indeed endless reasons, to praise God. Logically, she knew God as a person who was familiar with her, even close to her. She managed to praise her friends and family members but somehow didn't find the forms and expressions to praise God, not with anything like the frequency or form that she logically believed that he would deserve. She had no strong first-hand impression of what praise to God might look like. She had not seen others praise God in ways that she might adopt. She had no pattern, no model, no mentor, no training in praise, which might sound unnecessary but she actually would have found quite helpful. Then she found a body of believers that seemed to know all about praise. They had so many free and full forms of praise, some quiet and some loud, some active and others reflective. She saw spontaneous dance and heard praise both shouted and whispered. Above all, she saw the constancy of praise, pleasure in praise, and freedom in praise. In those constant small and large celebrations, she found her own form of praise, time of praise, and passion for praise. She knew that the God who listens was pleased.

Obtain God's praise. John 5:44.

Even while we praise God unstintingly, we should also know that God is generous with his own praise when we give him grounds for that praise. Glory, grandeur, brilliance, and wonder are unusual things in the world, although usual things with God. God holds such magnificence that glory abounds around him. Our praise of him simply joins a chorus of resounding praise, giving us proper place among many equal celebrants. We should be very glad that the universe resonates with his glory because the world would be a dismal place without it. When we praise him, we make our part of the world a little brighter, banishing the darkness, and entering bit by bit the kingdom lit by his glory. The wonder then is that he allows his glory to shine on us. When we love and accept his Son, that Son whom the Father loves like he loves us, the Father can do no less than beam his appreciative light on us like a shining smile. God praises those who know and follow his Son. As brothers and sisters in Christ, we are somehow able to catch and hold this glory of the Father's love for his own Son. God grants us ground to seek his praise through pursuit of his Son. We each have a love-bucket to fill, one that only God can fill, indeed one that he designed for only his

329

Son to fill. He is fine that we make it our ambition to seek his praise, even as we praise him. Direct yourself to obtaining God's praise, not the praise of others whose praise your love-bucket can never fill.

Jesus had shown the religious leaders how they had rejected him when they had every scripture, sign, miracle, and other evidence instead to accept him. He then explained further *why* they were rejecting him. Jesus explained that while he does not accept glory from men, the religious leaders accept glory *only* from men. Because they did not have the love of God in their hearts, they would not accept Jesus, even though they accepted any other person who came in their own name. The religious leaders were making the whole show about who was who among persons rather than who was God. As long as the religious leaders were looking only for acceptance and praise from one another and other persons rather than from God, they had no chance of recognizing Jesus, giving God due glory, and gaining praise back from God for their witness. Jesus summarized, "How can you believe since you accept glory from one another but do not seek the glory that comes from God?" The religious leaders should have been seeking the glory that comes from God rather than seeking the acknowledgment and praise of others.

As earnestly as he pursued every duty, he had never had a strong sense of fulfillment, surely not a sense that God had any praise for him. He felt at a loss, certainly, because wasn't God all about duties? So went his line of thinking for quite a long time until Jesus gradually turned his heart, not away from duties but toward the One for whom he worked. He first realized that the duties were not really the point. Duties, he learned, were only like signposts pointing to the One whom he should intend to serve. Indeed, the duties hardly told him what to do. They only gave general guides for various behaviors at various times. When he did his duty, he wasn't really sure that his duty he had actually done. He reached the point that he thought God might even be playing games on him, making up duties for him to perform only to have the duties undone. His frustration over not gaining any strong sense of meaning or fulfillment over completing one duty after another over and over again gradually turned him back to Jesus's instruction. Somewhere in Jesus's words, he captured the sense that God was interested in glory, was concerned with notice, and desired praise. And somewhere in Jesus's words, he learned that God would praise those who accepted and loved his Son. So he decided not to work simply to finish one duty after another. He decided to work for God's praise, particularly by seeking after, obeying, and loving his Son. His turn was a small turn, not like turning around and going back but instead like going on a little farther. The difference, though, was profound. For the first time, he gained a strong sense of God's glory.

Ask God to send you. Matthew 9:38.

God has much work yet to do saving souls through the blood and redemption of his son Jesus. The work with which God is most concerned, the work in which he is most invested, is to save lost souls. God loves the lost soul. Losing another lost soul gains God no glory, no honor. Every soul gained is another witness to testify to God's glory, while every soul lost is one less witness. God will leave the ninety-nine saved souls to reach the one lost soul. Saving souls is so important to God that he gave his only Son, the life of his only Son. Any who would believe in the Son would live eternally in the kingdom, praising God's glory. Knowing how important the saving of souls is to God, Jesus instructs us to ask God to send us to carry Jesus's good news to lost souls. God wants us involved in the work of his Son saving souls. God delights in our salvation but then wants the saved to carry his Son's life and word to the lost souls yet to save. God knows how many lost souls remain for saving. We know how many lost souls we see among the many people with whom we have daily contact. God wants us involved in their salvation. He wants us invested like he is invested. He wants us to ask him to send us on that work that his Son advances in redemption and God completes in resurrection.

Jesus went from town to village to town, teaching and preaching the good news in the synagogues and healing all the sick whom he encountered, until he had been to all the towns. News of Jesus's miracles and authoritative teaching must have spread because crowds would gather wherever he went. Each time a crowd would gather, Jesus's heart would go out to the members of the crowd because they looked to him like lost sheep without their shepherd. He wanted everyone to know the Good Shepherd. So he told his disciples to look at the great harvest of souls before them and notice how few there were to gather that harvest. He wanted the disciples to enter and work in the harvest field of souls. Jesus told them, "Ask the Lord of the harvest, therefore, to send out workers into his harvest field." Jesus would send the disciples into the harvest field and, after sending the disciples, would commission more workers to go out into the plentiful harvest fields. He wanted willing workers who would ask God to send them out to reach and gather lost souls.

He never figured that he was much of an evangelist, as he knew that others called the role. For a long time, he considered that he would never make an evangelist because he had no particular capacity to preach. The few times that others induced him to speak words of faith to any small gathering, he had felt no call, power, or authority, and had seemed not to produce any special notice or result. He marveled at and admired the oratory, emotion, power, and moving effect of recognized evangelists, no doubt. He was just as far from any such figure as a personality could get. For a long time, he kept telling himself these things even as he regretted that he had not answered God's call to carry the word of his Son, the good news of Christ's salvation, at least not carried it as he saw others do so. Yet one day he realized that he shouldn't be examining himself, evaluating himself, questioning and judging himself. If, as he vaguely and at times even acutely felt, he should be evangelizing, then he should be asking God to make him an evangelist. Other than the preachers he had seen moving crowds, he had no clear idea of what makes a good evangelist except that he had heard that evangelism takes many personalities and many forms. So he prayed for a call and harvest. And God began to show him fields in which he was already sowing and the harvest God was preparing him to help his Son reap.

Put God's word into practice. Luke 8:21.

To hear God's word, truly listen to it and consider it, is of course key to understanding it, evaluating it, and accepting and incorporating it. Yet acceptance of God's word does not end one's responsibility. Rather, we are then to put God's word into practice. To put words into practice means to do more with them than just understand and accept them. Putting words into practice means acting in ways consistent with them, letting the words make a difference in the choices, directions, initiatives, and other activities that one undertakes. Words do influence us. If someone says that some place is giving free goods or services, then we may well change our agenda and itinerary to take advantage of the offer. If we learn from a report that something is particularly bad for us, perhaps a food, substance, or material, then we avoid it. If we learn that some health practice is particularly good for us, then we adopt it. We listen to words all of the time in ways that change our actions. The point then is that we should not just listen to God's word and agree with it. God's word is for action, not merely for agreement. Putting God's word into practice means something distinctly greater to Jesus than does simply agreeing with it. Consider the unusual context in which Jesus spoke so directly about putting God's word into practice, and the unusual, even compelling, way in which he expressed the positive consequence of doing so.

After the Sermon on the Mount, Jesus traveled about his home region teaching the word of God to whoever would listen, often using parables but also teaching directly without his hearers having to decipher the parables. The crowds grew in response to his message. Indeed, the crowds grew so large that when Jesus's mother and brothers came to see him, they could not get close enough to Jesus, could not get into the place where he was teaching, in order to get his attention. One gospel account relating the incident gives no clear indication of why Jesus's family wanted to see him. Another account, though, indicates that his family came out of concern that the religious leaders were calling Jesus crazy, out of his mind, and possessed by the devil. They came to take charge of him and put a stop to his craziness because they thought him out of his mind. Someone in the crowd told Jesus that his mother and brothers were standing outside the place where he was teaching, wanting to see him. Jesus was not about to submit to his family's charge and stop sharing his message. He replied instead, "My mother and brothers are those who hear God's word and put it into practice." Ancestry, bloodlines, and heredity do not matter. Those who heard God's word *and put it into practice* would be Jesus's family.

She liked the thought and exercise of putting God's word into practice. Her knowledge of the Bible had grown, although of course she felt that she had much more to learn. Yet as much as she was appreciating her growing knowledge of Jesus's words and instructions, she had a greater interest in actually doing something with it, doing something about it, seeing that the words made a difference in her life and especially in her actions. She had always had a fine sense for hypocrisy. She didn't want to be a hypocrite. She didn't want to hear and agree with God's word, and call herself a Christian and follower of Jesus's instructions, but then be doing the same things that everyone else who didn't know, agree with, and commit to follow God's word was doing. She wanted to put God's word into practice. As she realized her commitment to act consistent with God's word, she began to identify some of her activities that indeed looked like they were godly practices but also a few other activities that didn't look quite so godly. Those insights gave her the opportunity to increase the godly practices and decrease the other practices. The distinctions were not always so clear. Some activities just didn't seem to have any special relationship to God's word, while other activities very clearly did have that relationship. She loved the thought and initiative of following the godly practices. Doing so gave her days whole new meaning.

Do what God says. Matthew 21:29.

Putting God's word into practice can be as simple as doing what God says to do. Jesus makes a special point of illustrating that the words one uses are not as important as the actions one takes. We may call ourselves Christians, but if we do not act as Christians should, then what we call ourselves makes little difference. Jesus also makes a special point of illustrating that who we are is not as important as what we do. We may not carry any rank in society, may even carry some public disrepute, and yet if we do as God says, then how negatively society may regard us makes little difference. God concerns himself more with actions than with intentions, more with performance than with promises to perform. When we see something that God says to do, we should *do* it, not talk a good game about doing it. Talk is cheap. Actions matter. Consider the following parable in which Jesus lauded those who actually do what God says to do, no matter who they are or what they may have said that they will do or not do.

Jesus was teaching in the temple courts at a time when the chief priest and elders came to him, challenging the authority by which Jesus taught. Because they would not answer Jesus's question about John baptizing Jesus, Jesus refused to answer their question about his authority. Instead, Jesus told them a parable of two sons. In the parable, the father told the first son to go work in the father's vineyard. "'I will not,'" Jesus quoted the first son as saying, adding, "But later he changed his mind and went." Jesus explained that the second son agreed to go but then did not. Jesus then asked the chief priest and elders which son did what the father wanted both sons to do. They of course answered that the first son had done as the father wanted. What the mouth says is less important than what the feet and hands do. To disagree but then act in agreement is better than to agree but then *not* act in agreement. Jesus then told them that tax collectors and prostitutes were entering God's kingdom ahead of them because they had believed what John had said and done regarding Jesus's baptism, while the chief priest and elders had not believed.

He had in small respects reached a point where he might rest on reputation rather than fully do as God says to do. His witness had over the years been sufficiently consistent, and his service sufficiently constant, that neither seemed fresh, original, or new. He felt that he had some time ago discerned much of what God said to do and had then gone ahead and done it. Of course, he knew that he had much else that he *could* do, knew that God had not relinquished all expectation for him, and knew that he might yet have significant and even new things to do. Yet the nagging thought occurred to him more often than he wished that when the question came to godly witness, action, and service, he had *been there* and *done that*. The

335

thought concerned him, indeed nearly frightened him. Why should he presume that he had done anything just as God had said? How did he of all people know the mind of God? Wasn't this attitude precisely the kind of thinking that leads to big words, a puffed-up sense of self, arrogance, and *inaction*, when God concerns himself instead with *action*? He decided not to entertain the thought of slowing down, of talking the good talk but not taking any action. He decided instead that God might be showing him that he needed a fresh ministry, a new call to action. He had unbroken fields that he had not plowed. He needed more than ever to *do* what God says, no matter what respite his words or small reputation might gain for himself among those who shared his work and commitment.

Do what pleases God. John 8:29.

In saying that he *always* does what pleases his Father, Jesus gives us yet another way to pursue and appreciate what it means to hear God's word, serve God, belong to God, do God's will, put God's word into practice, and do as God says. Each of these actions implies, overlaps, and supports the other. They may be saying the same thing several different ways or involve successive activities that build on one another, or both. Yet Jesus spoke them, instructed them, and urged or implied them in these different forms and in different contexts and circumstances. When Jesus added that he always does what pleases the Father, Jesus gave us another reason, a motivation different from the other motivations. God is a God who feels or experiences pleasure, perhaps even desires pleasure, or whom in any case Jesus can please. Jesus would not have said that he always does what pleases the Father if the Father was one whom Jesus could not please. That Jesus could please the Father at least implies that we could please the Father, too, especially by pleasing and glorifying the Son. The gospel accounts strongly indicate that Jesus experienced pleasure, even took pleasure in the responses and actions of those who trusted and relied on him, believed him, and honored and praised him and his Father. Far too many likely believe that God is a distant entity or force that has no experience of pleasure and whom we can certainly not please. Jesus instead showed his passion for pleasing the Father, whom we should also seek to please.

In one of his many intense encounters with the religious leaders, Jesus made a special reference to pleasing the Father. Jesus had told the religious leaders that he was going away to a place that they could not follow because they would instead die in their sin. Some wondered if Jesus was about to kill himself. Jesus repeated that if they did not believe that he was the Messiah, then they would die in their sins. They asked Jesus directly who he was, and while telling them that he had already told them, he repeated that the Father had sent him to say just what the Father told him to say. Jesus explained that they would not realize who he was and what he was saying until they had lifted up the Son of Man, referring to his crucifixion. Jesus then repeated, "The one who sent me is with me; he has not left me alone, for I always do what pleases him." Jesus always does just what pleases his Father. While Jesus did the Father's service and spoke exactly what he heard from the Father, Jesus had pleasing the Father in mind as his goal and purpose for being.

She adored the very thought of pleasing the Father. She knew that not everyone has an earthly father whom they could imagine pleasing or especially whom they would love to please. She also knew that many do have a special earthly father. She counted herself extremely fortunate to have been among that number, loving to please her earthly father. That privilege of loving and pleasing her earthly father may have been why she so loved the thought of pleasing her heavenly Father. She made a fine distinction here, though. She was actually not at all sure that she really did please the Father, even if she knew that she so much wanted to do so. She hoped that he was pleased. She thought often and deeply about what would please him. She wanted him to be pleased. But she didn't quite have the confidence that she knew his desires well enough that what she chose to do for him was what pleased him. She wished that she had the mind of Jesus who knew the Father's thoughts so completely and who did and said nothing other than what the Father desired. Then she realized, she *did* have the mind of Jesus, carried to her by the Holy Spirit. The Spirit was constantly informing her, guiding her into what the Father desired. She knew that she had the Spirit because she wanted so badly to please the

Father. She figured that no one who wanted to please the Father as badly as she did could be entirely outside the influence of the Spirit. Everything that she did that increased her love to please the Father, including each prayer and praise, each witness for Jesus, each act of worship, and each act of service, must be an act informed by the Spirit. She had begun to understand the glory of the Trinity.

Obey the word of God. Luke 11:28.

Jesus had yet another way of putting the sense of hearing God, doing what God says, pleasing God, and serving God, a slightly different sense that he spoke in a different context. In a setting in which Jesus had just performed a miracle healing, some in the attending crowd had nonetheless murmured that he was in league with the devil, while others challenged Jesus to do another miracle. The following account describes Jesus's specific rebukes and responses, but the instruction Jesus simultaneously gave was to *obey* God. Now clearly, to obey God is to do what he says. Yet Jesus's instruction to do what God says, accounted above, bears a slightly different meaning than his instruction here to obey God. Odd as it may at first sound, one can do what another commands either out of obedience, which is what Jesus instructed here, or for other reasons and motivations. One might, for instance, hear the command but decide to do what it says simply because one believes it in fact to be beneficial, perhaps only to oneself. Or one might hear a command and do what it says not to obey the one who commands but to disobey and spite another. Hearing and doing a command is not precisely the same as obeying it. Jesus instructed not just to do what God says but also to do it out of obedience. We do well to do what God says. We do better to do what God says *out of obedience to God.* Consider and appreciate the context in which Jesus gave the instruction to obey God.

Jesus had just driven a demon out of a man who was mute, enabling the man to speak. While Jesus's miracle healing amazed the crowd, some in the crowd murmured that Jesus was invoking the devil to drive out demons. Others tested Jesus to show them a sign from heaven, as if the miracle were not enough. Jesus lectured them that the devil would not drive out his own demons. They should know that God was driving out the demons and that the kingdom of God was upon them. Jesus continued his teaching until a woman called out that Jesus's mother was blessed for having given Jesus birth. Jesus replied, "Blessed rather are those who hear the word of God and obey it." The crowds continued to increase in size, and so Jesus continued his teaching. He warned that their current generation was wicked, more so than earlier generations that had listened to their prophets. Now a greater person and event was here, Jesus told them about himself and his own coming, but they do not even listen to that greater sign. They should have heard the word of God and obeyed it.

He realized, fortunately not too late at least by his own measure of lateness, that he had been doing as God said, as Jesus instructed, but only when he thought that doing so was a good idea. He had been doing more of what God said to do, and for that progress he had reason to be pleased, he thought. But then he realized that he was only doing so when he discerned and concluded that the command was sensible, rational, and beneficial. He was in effect deciding whether to do as God said rather than simply obeying God. He had early been impressed with the sensibility of what Jesus said to do and not do, which was part of his attraction to Jesus and his teaching. He just felt that doing as Jesus said made practical sense, made him better at what he did and better for whom he did it. But well into his program of self-improvement, he had realized that self-improvement programs are not God's desire and intent. God could tell him something that his own judgment did not especially approve, something that he could not confirm would improve his performance, position, or standing. Here was where he realized that God wants obedience more so than performance. God wanted him obeying more than just doing. God was not impressed with performance simply when it coincided with his own judgment. God wanted him putting his judgment aside in favor of obedience. And he was increasingly prepared to do so.

☦

Show God's work in your life. John 9:3.

We seem always at the ready to show the work that we have done for God, whether the service we have provided to the poor, or the meals that we have delivered to the shut-in, or the songs that we have sung in his praise. Jesus instructs us to do God's work, and we also have his urging to let his light in us shine. Doing God's work is a great privilege and great pursuit. Yet Jesus also has something to say about letting God's work show in us. The question is not all what we have done for God, or not even primarily what we have done for God. The point is often what God has done in us. God works miracles in us. He takes our blindness and gives us not just sight but wisdom and insight. He takes our deafness and helps us not just hear but understand and accept. He takes our disability and enables us not just to walk but to do good works. God creates us and gives us life and breath to show his glory, not to marvel at ours. While we do God's work, serve God, and please God, we should also *display* God's work in us. We should see what God has made of us, and when we see, tell others what God has done.

Jesus had left the temple grounds where he had taught, until disputes with the religious leaders had nearly come to violence. The religious leaders had been furious at Jesus's claims that God was his Father and that they, who claimed to be sons of Abraham, were liars. Jesus had even told them that he had been around before Abraham a millennia and a half earlier. The religious leaders were so angry at Jesus that they had picked up stones to stone him. But Jesus had slipped away with the disciples in tow. As Jesus walked along, he encountered the blind man whom the disciples thought had sinned, or whose parents they thought had sinned, causing his blindness, as a prior section recounts. Jesus corrected them, saying instead, "This happened so that the works of God might be displayed in him." He then healed the man's blindness, indeed displaying God's works in the blind man. The blind man then took the first occasion to tell those who asked that Jesus had healed him. The blind man thus displayed God's work in him, showing that God had given him sight.

She had the strongest sense, lately, of God having done some very good work in her. That sense did not mean to her that she was something very special, at least to anyone other than God. Instead, the sense that she had was that she had *not* been anything special, indeed, had been something and someone somewhat messed up but that God had done something special in her nonetheless. He had taken several flaws in her that she had assumed were intransigent, immoveable, permanently stamped in her character and soul, and had either hidden or removed them. These defects not only she but others also knew. Indeed, she had the odd sense that God found important that others knew of her flaws, the things that he had hidden or eliminated in her. She almost felt as if he might not have removed them if others had not known, felt almost as if by removing those things from her he was doing so to display his work in her, show his glory. Of course, she felt immensely grateful for his work in her. She was greatly relieved not to have to deal with those haunting and depressing defects at least for the present time, while hoping that he had healed her permanently. Yet the very special thing to her was not so much that she was healed as that God had decided to display his works in her. She was utterly glad to have been his vessel, his conduit, his stage for his good works. She delighted that God was the show, even while she had an understudy role.

Hold to God's commands. Mark 7:8.

God concerns himself with how we hold to his commands. Jesus instructs to *hold to* God's commands while letting go of other things that are merely human traditions. The sense of *holding to* things is a helpful illustration. Our obedience can in theory be transactional, doing the right thing one rule at a time. Yet obedience should soon become less of a transaction, one rule at a time, than a habit and practice. We should reach the point that we don't so much decide to obey moment by moment as *hold to* commands, embrace them, and make them ours. To hold to a practice is to grab it with gusto, knowing that it is right. To hold to a command is to make the command less *his* or *theirs* and more *ours*. We should reach the point that we walk alongside God in happy obedience, grasping and holding his commands close to us *like they were ours, too.* Holding to God's commands relieves our relationship with God of his disapproval. God accepts us because of Jesus's sacrifice. God holds no offense against us when we have the covering of Jesus. Yet to be in Jesus's embrace, to be trusting and relying on Jesus, must have some effect on us. We make it a more difficult case to claim the protective covering of Jesus while outright disobeying what he teaches. Relationships benefit from respect. When we hold to God's commands, we show him the regard that we have for Jesus, showing him that our commitment comes from our heart and is more than mere lip service. See in the following account how Jesus illustrates this instruction.

The religious leaders and law experts had come all the way from Jerusalem to observe Jesus. They noticed that the disciples did not ceremonially wash before eating. The religious leaders and law experts consistently observed not only that ceremonial practice but many others including ceremonial washing of pitchers and cups. The religious leaders challenged Jesus, asking why his disciples were violating the traditions by eating with defiled hands. Jesus quoted Isaiah in reply that the leaders' hearts were far from him. They were worshipping vainly, only giving God lip service, and instead following human rules and traditions. Jesus summarized, "You have let go of the commands of God and are holding on to human traditions." He gave them the example of how they broke one of the Ten Commandments to honor father and mother. They had the people instead deny their parents support in order to follow a tradition of purportedly devoting that support to God. He said that he could give many other examples of how they were nullifying the word of God with their traditions. They would have done better to instruct the people to follow God's commandments.

He finally had, as the scriptures themselves say, taken a certain delight in God's commands. No question, they had seemed quite foreign to him at the start. They were so out of time, so ancient, so of another era, especially in the way that the Old Testament presented them in its historical and cultural context. He at first could hardly imagine them really translating to today. Of course, many of them made great sense, like not stealing, murdering, or even coveting. But others made less sense in this modern, secular age, he definitely felt,

342

like having no other gods and not making any idols. Really, he thought, who had other gods or idols to follow? He didn't see anyone in his neighborhood worshipping Asherah poles or erecting altars to Baal. Jesus, though, gave the old commands fresh cast. He could see from the way that Jesus presented them what the heart of the old commands meant. They made more sense even for today, in the way that Jesus taught them and was showing the people how to live them out. And then the Apostle Paul's explanations seemed so modern, so in tune. He could see from Paul's letters how many people today did indeed follow other gods and make many idols of things, indeed, how he had been doing so, too, in his own misguided way. As Jesus reflected them, God's commands made such fundamental sense. In the end, the commands lost for him their last bit of seeming oppressiveness and instead looked more like delightful liberty. Even more strangely, the traditions that he had unwittingly been following began to look like oppressiveness. He loved this God even in his commands, especially in his commands, to which he now was learning how to hold fast.

2.2 Jesus

Believe in Jesus. John 11:26. *Know Jesus.* John 8:19, 14:7. *Respect Jesus.* Luke 20:13. *Come to Jesus.* Matthew 11:28. *Love Jesus.* John 14:21. *Feed on Jesus.* John 6:57. *Confess Jesus as God's son.* Matthew 16:17. *Do not deny Jesus.* Luke 22:61. *Acknowledge Jesus before men.* Luke 12:8. *Follow Jesus.* Mark 8:34. *Praise Jesus.* Luke 19:38. *Honor Jesus.* John 5:23. *Remain in Jesus.* John 15:4. *Watch for Jesus's coming.* Luke 12:37. *Do not be deceived about Jesus's coming.* Luke 21:8. *Make room for Jesus's words.* John 8:37. *Listen to Jesus's voice.* John 10:16. *Remember what Jesus told you.* Luke 24:6. *Build on Jesus's words.* Matthew 7:24. *Hold to Jesus's teaching.* John 8:31. *Do not reject Jesus's words.* John 12:48. *Take Jesus's yoke.* Matthew 11:29. *Come to Jesus for rest.* Mark 6:31. *Urge Jesus to stay with you.* Luke 24:29. *Recall Jesus's death.* Matthew 26:38. *Lose your life for Jesus.* Mark 8:35. *Accept anyone Jesus sends.* John 13:20. *Stand by Jesus in trials.* Luke 22:28. *Serve Jesus.* John 12:26. *Do what Jesus commands.* John 15:14. *Do what Jesus did.* John 14:12. *Feed Jesus's sheep.* John 21:17.

The prior part shows Jesus instructing that relationship to God the Father is paramount. We know as this part shows, though, that relationship to God the Father comes through the Son. God's grand architecture gave us the incarnate Son so that we would know the Father. We have Jesus so that we know what the Father looks like, says, and does. God gave us the incarnate Son as his image, knowing how much we need, value, and rely on images. The Christian witness is not a theoretical but a practical and historical witness. To the Christian, matters of faith are not philosophical or speculative, not imagined and intellectual, but authentic, solid, substantive, and real. This part on what Jesus instructs about our relationship to him is longer than the other parts because everything else including our relationship to the Father depends on relationship to the Son. Get this part right, knowing, understanding, recalling, and following

345

what Jesus says about relationship to him, and you will likely have gotten all else right. Get right relationship to Jesus. Got Jesus?

Believe in Jesus. John 11:25.

Jesus instructs in the following account, which is among the most moving of all the gospel accounts, that we must believe. Believing in Jesus involves more than accepting him as a historical figure whose words the gospel accounts record accurately. Some do not even believe that Jesus ever actually lived, but the question of his natural existence is not the significant issue. Belief in Jesus must entail not only believing that he lived and taught as recorded but also that he had the divine Son-within-the-triune-God status that he claimed. Fine, believe that Jesus walked the ancient lands teaching until his crucifixion. You have made a start, believing *of* Jesus. Believe also, if you will, that Jesus performed miracles. You have made progress, believing *more of* Jesus. Yet the deep belief, that which Jesus instructs and requires, is that he came as the incarnate God, the One, as Messiah. To believe *in* Jesus is to believe that when one saw, heard, and touched him, the Son, one had also seen, heard, and touched the Father. To believe *in* Jesus is to accept that he is divine, that he is divinity, he is God.

While Jesus disguised in parable or indirection some of what he said about himself, he also on occasion told exactly who he was and what he was about. On one such occasion, Jesus had headed to the home of Mary and Martha to raise their dead brother Lazarus. While Mary stayed in the home waiting in faith for Jesus, Martha had come out to meet Jesus. When they met, Martha told Jesus that her brother would not have died if Jesus had come but that she knew God would still give Jesus whatever he asked. Jesus replied simply that her brother would rise. Martha thought that Jesus meant that Lazarus would rise at the resurrection in the last day, as many Jews believed. Jesus corrected Martha, saying, "I am the resurrection and the life. The one who believes in me will live, even though they die; and whoever lives by believing in me will never die. Do you believe this?" Martha replied that yes, she believed that Jesus was the Messiah, the Son of God. Shortly later, Jesus order the stone moved away from the entrance to the tomb in which Lazarus had lain dead for four days. Martha objected that Lazarus had been dead four days, and his body would have a bad odor. Jesus admonished her once more that if she believed, she would see God's glory. After a brief prayer, Jesus called the resurrected and living Lazarus out of the tomb.

Because she had grown up among people who believed in Jesus, she too had at first believed. Yet the moment came in her life, as that moment must come in every life, when she had to decide about believing on her own rather than because her people believed. Her moment came, as it does for many others, when she left her people for a time to join a community of people unlike her own. Her new people were not so very unlike her own people except that they were not a close community of believers, indeed not a close community at all. They were instead a collection of individuals from many other communities, thrown together for only a time. Her new people, this loose community of unlike others, had not formed around beliefs or affinities, at least not their own beliefs and affinities. They instead were together with the more-or-less professed goal of adopting the beliefs and affinities of others. Those beliefs that their resident leaders professed were decidedly not beliefs in Christ, were instead largely antithetical and opposed to Christ. For no one does not believe in Christ without being opposed. As she explored this loose new community while watching its other members survive, thrive, or founder, she gradually decided that a community without Christ is not her community. She gradually committed, or recommitted, to her belief in Christ. And when she had committed again to her Christian faith, her faith in Christ as the only true God had deepened. She believed in Jesus.

Know Jesus. John 14:7.

If a first step in relationship with Jesus is to believe that he exists and then to gain and accept an understanding of his divine status, then a second step must be to get beyond that head knowledge to a familiarity or acquaintance with Jesus, to *know* Jesus rather than just believe in him. To know someone implies familiarity, acquaintance, and maybe even friendship or at least fellowship. To know *of* someone would imply only knowledge of their identity and perhaps their reputation. But to *know* someone rather than merely know *of* someone implies something more like frequent presence together, as in belonging to the same group, team, cause, or initiative. To know someone certainly implies at a minimum that one would recognize that person if they were to appear. One cannot claim to know another and yet not recognize them. Jesus's instruction to know him, though, means more to us than just knowing the Son of Man who walked and talked on earth. Jesus instructs that we must know him if we are to know the Father. Only by knowing Jesus can we know the Father. We have no image of the Father, no presence of the Father, no path to the Father, without knowing the image, presence, and path of Jesus. Knowing Jesus is the critical step to knowing the Father. Know Jesus because to know the Son is to know the Father.

At the Last Supper, Jesus had just told the disciples the hard things to come. He then comforted them that he was preparing a place for them and would return for them to take them to that place with him. Jesus urged that the disciples knew the way to the place where Jesus was going. Thomas, ever the doubter, told Jesus that they had no idea where he was going and so had no idea of the way to join Jesus there. Jesus corrected Thomas, saying, "I am the way and the truth and the life. No one comes to the Father except through me. If you really know me, you will know my Father as well." Jesus wanted the disciples to know Jesus, to *really* know him, meaning to know his Son relationship to the Father and know that Jesus was thus the way to the Father. Jesus then added that the disciples did know the Father and had seen the Father, for indeed, they had seen and known Jesus, the Son and Christ. Philip, still not understanding Jesus, asked Jesus plainly to show them the Father. Jesus repeated that because they had seen Jesus, they had seen the Father. Jesus had no one else to show, no other Father. He then explained exactly who he was in the Father and the Father in him, doing the Father's works and speaking only the Father's words.

In her deepening faith, she found that she was doing something more than simply knowing *of* Jesus or even believing *in* Jesus. While she felt that she had made such great gains in believing in Jesus, she had begun to realize that she was getting to *know* Jesus, not just know of him but truly to know him as one knows an acquaintance or, better yet, a friend. She had not anticipated that her faith would grow from belief to acquaintance, although she was more than delighted that it had. She was enthralled. The sense that the Holy Spirit was constantly conveying to her was that she could have, and indeed for moments at a time already did have, the presence of Jesus, the Spirit of Jesus, as her companion. That sense was not yet strong. She suspected though that it would grow. She began to believe that she might someday actually walk with Jesus in constant communion. For now, though, she was exploring this sense of actually *knowing* Jesus as one knows a family member or friend. After all, she thought, they conversed in prayer, didn't they, she and Jesus? Prayer was no longer merely a petition signed and sent off to a distant government. Prayer was beginning to feel just like that, like a comfortable conversation with an acquaintance who wanted to hear more from her. She knew Jesus. He had acknowledged and accepted her acquaintance, as of course she should have known that he would.

Respect Jesus. Luke 20:13.

To believe in Jesus and to know Jesus are foundational steps in relationship with Jesus. To know someone, though, is not necessarily to respect them. When Jesus adds that one must respect the Son, he helps us take the next step beyond belief in Jesus and knowing Jesus to something closer to the kind of reverence that God deserves and commands. To respect a person is to appreciate, venerate, and commend that person to oneself and others. We have respect for those whom we consider to be worthy, worthwhile, valuable members of a faith, organization, community, party, or fellowship of which we are a part. Respect connotes admiration, loyalty, trust, and confidence. To respect another invites reliance on that other for leadership, governance, stewardship, production, performance, guidance, or other things of value. Respect implies that the person holds attributes that will contribute to the community and has a character of integrity that one sees what one will get. When we respect Jesus, we hold Jesus up in honor to others, promote Jesus's name and cause, and even follow Jesus ourselves. We need to respect Jesus after believing and knowing him. While Jesus instructs us to respect him, Jesus has, of course, everything to respect. If he had not given the instruction, then we would find cause and character in him nonetheless to respect.

Jesus was in the midst of telling the parable of the tenants, already recounted in a prior section, when he may have revealed another attitude that his listeners should have toward him. The parable of the tenants was the one in which a vineyard owner rented the vineyard to some tenants who beat and sent away the owner's servants when the owner sent the servants to collect a portion of the harvest as rent. Jesus continued the story, quoting the vineyard owner as saying, "'What shall I do? I will send my son, whom I love; perhaps they will respect him,'" just as the Father had sent Jesus to represent him. In the parable, the tenants killed the son rather than respect him as the owner expected, just as the people to whom God sent Jesus would soon kill Jesus rather than believe, know, and respect Jesus. Jesus then explained to the people listening including the religious leaders and law experts that the stone Jesus that they were rejecting, in the same way that the tenants rejected the owner's son, was the cornerstone. They were falling over the stone, which would soon fall on and crush them, just as the vineyard owner would kill the tenants. One who does not respect the Son does not respect the Father.

He had grown so in his admiration for Jesus. Every chapter in Jesus's life, every step, challenge, and event, taught him to respect Jesus more not only for who he was and what he was doing but for what he had to go through to accomplish it. Jesus had such unfathomable strength and character. No one who was not both God and man could have accomplished what Jesus accomplished, he had long ago concluded. His first impression of Jesus had been more like *right time, right place*, as if anyone who had the insight that Jesus had could have taught as Jesus taught, and maybe even could have consented to his own demise as Jesus did, indeed as Socrates had in a much different manner before him. Yet as he learned more about the events of Jesus's life including the forty-day fast, the long conspiracy for his murder, the large crowds thronging him wherever he went, the religious leaders harassing and trying to stone him, and then his arrest, trial, crown of thorns, horrific scourging, and even more horrific crucifixion, he could no longer imagine anyone other than Jesus even beginning to accomplish what Jesus accomplished. Jesus's perfect composure, his ready answer for every challenge, his feeding thousands from virtually nothing, his walking on water and calming storming sea, and then his constant outlook for miracle healing and raising from the dead, all set Jesus so far apart from anyone who ever lived, that his regard for Jesus grew beyond respect to exaltation, just what God warranted.

Come to Jesus. Matthew 11:28.

Jesus's invitation and instruction to come to him goes beyond belief in, knowledge of, and respect for Jesus. To come to Jesus is to submit to his attraction, to approach him and participate with him. One can know another from afar and respect from afar, but then one has the invitation and opportunity to move toward the other, to come to them accepting the invitation, and even to pursue. Although loving God, Jesus nonetheless stands apart from us. He is not mist, air, or force. He does not seep into us like radioactivity or permeate our pores like vapor. He instead gives us an invitation that we can refuse but should not refuse, an invitation to move toward him, move with him, join him in his loving work. Although his invitation he clearly initiates, rather than us inviting ourselves, still our movement toward him is our work, reflecting our interest, acceptance, and willingness. We must act, we must move, we must respond even as he initiates. Simply believing, knowing, and respecting does not end or consummate the relationship. Relationship with Jesus involves movement together, coming to join him as he moves, loves, and works.

Jesus reached the point of denouncing the towns in which he had performed many of his miracles because not even the miracles had caused their residents to turn away from their sin and to Jesus. Other towns, towns not known for their religious populations and instead known for their commerce or corruption, would have confessed their sins and turned to him, Jesus said, if they had seen the miracles that

Jesus had already performed in these unrepentant towns so well known for their religion. Yet Jesus praised his Father even for having hidden the truth from these supposedly wise and learned people while showing the truth to those who were not known as wise and who were instead more like little children in their lack of sophistication. Whatever the Father wished, Jesus was glad to see and do. Indeed, Jesus explained, the Father had committed everything to the Son who was the only one to know the Father other than those to whom the Son revealed the Father. Jesus said, "Come to me, all you who are weary and burdened, and I will give you rest." Jesus had a yoke for followers to wear, but his yoke was light, and he was gentle and humble of heart. Anyone coming to Jesus would find their souls finally at peace and rest.

She had heard the old gospel choir sing of coming to Jesus so many times. Yet something triggered in her a new sense of urgency about the slow but certain movement toward Jesus as she listened to the swaying rhythms and plain words of the familiar song. This opportunity to come to Jesus was not like joining a club or making an important new friend, she had learned from the song. This movement to Jesus was not even merely opportunity, she was now convinced. It was instead a life's work, she knew, the course of any well-lived life, indeed the course of life itself, of all history. Jesus drew persons, causes, movements, and things, even drew time, in fact drew all thought, spirit, and matter to him as surely as things are capable of movement, capable of being drawn, she had learned. The only things that do not come to Jesus, she suspected, are those that will themselves away from him, take the contrary course, and pursue false gods. She had finally reached a vision nearer the magnificent character and prime place of Jesus in the universe. He was drawing her to him, drawing her even now into the kingdom, and she was willingly coming along. She would join the eternal dance coming to Jesus.

Love Jesus. John 14:21.

To come to Jesus then must ultimately be to love Jesus. One can come to a person in grief, struggle, request, protest, or complaint. The kind of coming to Jesus that Jesus instructs and expects, the kind of relationship that he intends, is one of love. Those who come to Jesus must come in love, to love Jesus as Jesus loves a disciple. While Jesus showed his willingness to love all when he sacrificed his life for any who would come to him, his love is for those who love him. Jesus chases the sinner but catches the lover. The Father loves Jesus because Jesus loves the Father, does nothing other than what the Father does, and says nothing other than what the Father would say. Love is reciprocal. Indeed, one loves Jesus by obeying Jesus, as the Son loves the Father by obeying the Father. One who loves Jesus does not reject Jesus's command. One cannot simultaneously love and disobey. To disobey is to reject, which is to not love. Love is to accept Jesus's command. Jesus tells us much, instructs us much. Those who love Jesus listen, respect, and obey, and Jesus loves them back and shows himself to them.

At the Last Supper, Jesus was now telling the disciples of how he would ask the Father to send the disciples the Spirit of truth as an advocate to help them. The world would neither see nor know the Spirit, but the disciples would know the Spirit because the Spirit would be in them, just as Jesus would be in them. Jesus would leave the world as if dead, but he would in fact be alive. While the world would not see Jesus, the disciples would still see Jesus who would be in them just as they would be in Jesus. They would love one another, Jesus loving the disciples and the disciples loving Jesus. Jesus then repeated what he had said that began the discourse on the Spirit that whoever keeps his commands is the one who loves him. Indeed, the Father will love the one who loves and obeys Jesus. Jesus explained, "The one who loves me will be loved by my Father, and I too will love them and show myself to them." Obedience and love, intertwined together, one showing itself the other. Jesus would love the ones who loved him and would show himself to those who loved him.

The world spoke to him of love in a different way than Jesus taught him about love. The way that the world valued and characterized love seemed most to involve close and intimate interludes of pleasure, he reckoned, brief passionate pursuits to satisfy sensual desires. By contrast, Jesus's love seemed to him much more to involve close and intimate obedience, not in brief but in extended passion, not to satisfy momentary sensual desires but to grasp eternally fulfilled life. The world's love was sensual, self-seeking, and inward, he was learning, but Jesus's love sensitive, encompassing, and aware. The world's love required knowing what one desired and would never fulfill, he had surmised, but Jesus's love required knowing what he desired and what he would always fulfill. The world's love depended on the mood or whim of the other, he knew, while Jesus's love depended only on one's own willingness to obey Jesus in love. Jesus gave everything he had in love for him, he had long known, while the world gave in love only what it wished for itself. He had once thought that obedience was a high price to pay for love, when he had first heard Jesus's words speak of it. He had since learned that obedience to Jesus is hardly any price at all to pay, indeed an utter privilege and honor to pay, in exchange for a love having inestimable worth.

Feed on Jesus. John 6:57.

Love for and obedience to Jesus mean so much, as Jesus's prior instruction made so clear. They mean that Jesus would love back, and that those who loved and obeyed would live in Jesus and Jesus in them. They would know the Father through the Son, for the Son loved and obeyed the Father, and the Father loved the Son who obeyed. Jesus extended his teaching on loving him and living in him even farther, although that extension was among his most difficult of teachings. Jesus said that we must feed on him, which taken in its figurative meaning one could understand and accept. We feed on food, literally, but figuratively we feed on words and concepts, even on images and sensations, each of which can occupy and enliven us in parallel fashion to the way that food occupies and enlivens us. In that latter sense, Jesus's words, his teachings, and his image and identity can feed us, occupy and enliven us. Yet in his teaching, Jesus said not only that his followers would feed on him but that they would eat his flesh and drink his blood, statements to which his hearers objected as a veritable impossibility. At the time that Jesus gave the teaching, he had not yet shared the Last Supper with the disciples and thus had not yet performed the first Communion with them, when he indicated that the broken bread that he offered them was his broken body he was about to sacrifice for them, and the wine he offered his blood poured out for them. We do eat his flesh and drink his blood in the sacrament of Communion that he gave us. His teaching was hard at first because it was not complete. We commune with Jesus by eating the broken bread and drinking the wine poured out in remembrance of his ultimate sacrifice for us. Indeed, we feed on Jesus.

Jesus was giving the crowd that had followed him across the lake one of his more-difficult teachings. He had described himself as the living bread come down from heaven. He had told the crowd that whoever eats this bread will live forever. While the crowd would have known the Old Testament story of manna from heaven, and might well have understood Jesus to be referring to that manna when speaking of bread, Jesus elaborated that the bread from heaven was *his flesh* that he would give for the life of the world. Jesus's reference to his flesh unsettled the crowd, whose members immediately began to question among themselves how he could possibly give his flesh to them to eat. But Jesus rejoined that unless they ate the Son of Man's flesh and *drank his blood*, they would have no life. They must eat his flesh and drink his blood to have eternal life, Jesus continued. Jesus added, "Just as the living Father sent me and I live because of the Father, so the one who feeds on me will live because of me." Jesus repeated that he is the living bread that came down from heaven, not the manna. Their ancestors ate the manna and died, but they would live forever if they ate Jesus's bread. Even the disciples agreed that this teaching was a hard teaching.

She watched as the believers moved forward in groups, making circles around which to pass the broken bread and wine poured out into goblets. As she watched, she could just hear the celebrants' quiet voices saying *body broken for you,* and then *blood poured out for you,* over the music that was just starting. This moment was one of her favorite times of the services, indeed of any time of the weeks, months, and years. The music would slowly rise as the circles of celebrants ebbed and re-formed until the last congregants had taken

355

communion. At some point just before the last circles had concluded and the music had grown to its joyous peak, time seemed to stop. Jesus seemed then to be present, more present than at any other time, at least any other time when she was in a group with others, for she had quiet times, alone times, when he was quite near, indeed was within her. Time seemed to stop as the band rose in timbre and the people stood to sing and celebrate one last time. Time seemed to stop, she realized, because everything but timeless celebration must stop when the King of Kings is near. The kingdom was indeed near.

Confess Jesus as God's son. Matthew 16:17.

Believing in Jesus, knowing Jesus, coming to Jesus, loving Jesus, and feeding on Jesus are at once overlapping and progressive states. We do seem to grow from stage to stage even as we embrace all at once. Loving and feeding may be last or first, while believing and knowing may be first or last, or any may be in between. Each description that Jesus gives us of relationship to him has its own meaning and common meaning with other descriptions. To confess Jesus as the Son of God, which is another instruction that Jesus gives us about our relationship to him, has its own distinct clarity. When one confesses, one admits or acknowledges, indeed more so, one comes clean or owns up. Thus to confess Jesus as the Son of God is to do more than acknowledge *Jesus's* role, status, and position, although it is also to do that. In calling Jesus the Son of God, we exalt him to the divinity of his Father, that the two are One, making the Trinity when one adds the Spirit who is love between them. Yet in *confessing* Jesus as the Son of God, we own up to something not just about Jesus but also about *ourselves*. We come clean in the sense of submitting to his redemption. Jesus, meaning literally *he saves*, bears a unique role as the Savior God. When we do as Jesus instructs, which is to confess Jesus as Savior God, as *our* Lord Savior God to whom we submit, we own up to our need for salvation. The criminal gains pardon only through confession.

When Jesus and the disciples had traveled far to the north, Jesus stopped to ask the disciples who they thought he was. They first

356

talked about who others had thought Jesus was including his cousin John the Baptist or the ancient prophet Elijah. Jesus insisted, though, asking them who *they* thought he was, not who others thought he was. Simon Peter answered directly that Jesus was the Messiah, the Son of the living God. Jesus replied to Simon Peter, "Blessed are you, Simon son of Jonah, for this was not revealed to you by flesh and blood but by my Father in heaven." Jesus then explained that he would build his church on this rock of confession, giving confessors the keys to the kingdom of heaven. Although he told the disciples not to tell anyone yet that he was the Messiah, he had blessed those who would call him the Son of God. Jesus wanted his disciples to know who he was and to say who he was. He had told them their reward for confessing that he was the Messiah, the Son of God. That reward was no less than the greatest reward of entry into the kingdom of heaven.

He had a fascination for the kingdom of heaven that only seemed to grow. He was not one to live solely for the future. He certainly looked forward to the promise of eternal life after his natural demise. Indeed, he earnestly desired that future, which relieved him of all confusion over natural death. Yet his fascination with the kingdom of heaven did not have so much to do with his future but with the present. Jesus seemed to say repeatedly that the kingdom was near, present, and available to those now living, not just those resurrected after natural life. He had the sense from much of what Jesus said that he was supposed to live in the kingdom of heaven now, not just in the future. Jesus clearly said that he was the way, the path to the kingdom, but he sometimes spoke of that entry into the kingdom in the present tense. He had long confessed Jesus as the Son of God. He had every confidence that Jesus would do as he had promised in the future. But he wanted all that Jesus would do now, too. He wanted to obey and confess, and enter the kingdom as soon as the kingdom would have him.

Do not deny Jesus. Luke 22:61.

Relationship to Jesus does not end when one has believed in Jesus, known him, loved him, drawn near, fed on him, and confessed that he is the Son of God. The world has a way of putting us into situations that challenge our confession, cause us to draw away from him, and feed on other things. Once we lay hold of Jesus, we must build and maintain the courage, develop the resolve and resilience, to keep hold of him in the face of challenges. We must not deny Jesus after having confessed him. We must not go back on our word, turn back to old ways, and give up on his promise. Probably, both large and small things can cause some to do so. A change of place, a move out of a close community of believers, can cause a loss of faith support and gradual eroding of commitment until the moment comes when denial seems natural, appropriate, convenient, or necessary. A situation, event, or loss may seem to compel a denial when we are unprepared to hold fast to and defend our confession of faith. One close to us, perhaps a spouse, parent, child, or friend, may turn us away from Jesus. A fellow believer or body of believers may even do so unintentionally out of misunderstanding, offense, and hurt. Even a troubling doctrinal point can undermine a confession. No matter the large or small cause, Jesus warns us against denial even as he predicts denial and stands ready to reinstate.

After arresting Jesus in the garden, the officers of the temple guard took Jesus to the house of the high priest to stand trial. Peter followed at a distance, stopping in the courtyard outside the house where he warmed himself near a fire. Three different people recognized Peter as a disciple of Jesus at different times through the night as Peter waited outside while Jesus stood trial. Each time, Peter denied that he even knew Jesus. The third time that Peter denied knowing Jesus, a rooster crowed. From inside the house, Jesus turned and stared at Peter, who could just see Jesus. Peter just then remembered that Jesus had said to Peter, "Before the rooster crows today, you will disown me three times," after Peter had insisted that he would follow Jesus to the end. Realizing his faithlessness and fear, Peter went away weeping bitterly, while the officers of the temple guard blindfolded, mocked, and beat Jesus through the night. After his resurrection, Jesus would restore Peter, giving him special commission to feed his sheep.

Years later, he still remembered moments when he had opportunities to confirm his confession of faith in front of non-believers but had not done so with the conviction that he had wanted to show. He had not exactly denied his faith on those occasions, but he had also not shown the excitement that he felt about Jesus and had not spoken of Jesus in the manner that might have excited his listener. He had intended on those occasions to speak respectfully, not to boast or say something canned or trite. He had meant to politely acknowledge the comments that had invited confirmation of his confession without turning the conversation back to a challenge to his questioners. Yet somehow, in retrospect, he felt that he had inadvertently belittled his confession and in doing so not shown the respect due his incomparable savior Christ. He also felt that he had missed an opportunity to promote the faith of his questioners. He prayed that Christ would forgive and reinstate him for what was probably an offense, although he hoped not a severe offense. He also committed to do better with the next questioners. Looking back over the years since then, he felt that he had indeed done better in clearly confirming his confession of Christ on those periodic occasions where a non-believer asked him something direct about it. He had begun even to think that his more-confident confessions might through the Spirit's action have some effect on his questioners. Perhaps Christ held hope for him yet, he laughed.

Acknowledge Jesus before men. Luke 12:8.

Jesus does more on this subject of speaking about him with others, than just instruct us not to deny him. He does not just give us the negative proscription against giving up our faith when around others. In another gospel account, Jesus also gives us the positive prescription to *acknowledge* him before others. Staying neutral among non-believers is not an option in relationship with Jesus. One cannot pretend not to either accept or reject Jesus and yet still please God. Right relationship to Jesus means acknowledging Jesus not just before God but before others. As to other relationships, secrecy might be acceptable or even expected. You might belong to an organization or club that had no interest in you sharing your membership, or work for an employer that didn't care whether others knew. Yet God must see at least in part the value to him of our faith, as residing in our testimony about him when speaking with others. Apparently, from Jesus's prescription to acknowledge him before others, faith in Christ cannot be a secret thing and yet be an effective thing. His prescription is clear enough that we should simply follow it, although we can also imagine why we must share faith. When we openly acknowledge Jesus when among others, we glorify God. When we openly acknowledge Jesus, we give others the opportunity to learn of Jesus and accept his saving grace.

As the crowd of many thousands gathered to listen to Jesus, so large of a crowd that people were trampling over one another, Jesus spoke first to his disciples. The religious leaders were after them, Jesus explained, so that the disciples must be careful what they say even in private. Yet they should not fear the religious leaders, Jesus added. Their only concern should be for what God thinks of them. God decides the fate of their souls, not the religious leaders. God would protect them. Jesus continued, "I tell you, whoever publicly acknowledges me before others, the Son of Man will also acknowledge before the angels of God." Jesus added that whoever denied him before others, he would deny before those same angels. As he prepared the disciples to carry his message, Jesus knew that they would face situations in which acknowledging Jesus could cost them heavily right up to costing them their lives. God though would save their souls.

She never had a real problem sharing her faith among others who did not hold it. She knew that others did have that problem, and she could see why they would. Others seemed to her to have more concern for their place within groups that were not faith-based communities. In some instances, co-workers at secular employers comprised those groups, while in other instances the groups were social, recreational, cultural, or intellectual. In each case, the groups might have included Christians or might not have, but they were secular communities. How members of those groups would regard a Christian, especially a professing Christian, was at best uncertain. In some instances and probably most instances, the confession of faith in those groups would at least violate a group norm and could result in effective expulsion. In the case of some employers, confession of faith could result in job termination. She too had a concern for how others regarded her. She also wanted to be a valued member of certain groups. Yet when she thought of it, the groups that she valued were all faith-based groups, gatherings, or communities. She was not sure that her choice had been intentional, but she simply did not belong with any special commitment to any community that was not a Christian community. Confession of faith, acknowledgment of Jesus, was simply no concern to her. Confident in her faith, she did not hesitate to speak of Jesus with anyone individually, and rightly or wrongly, for better or worse, she kept her commitments to faith groups. She hoped that she always acknowledged Jesus.

Follow Jesus. <small>Mark 8:34.</small>

To love and feed on Jesus implies another activity describing right relationship with Christ, which is to follow Jesus. Jesus said clearly to follow him. To follow another suggests agreement, support, and being part of the other's mission or program. Jesus described this following as becoming his *disciple*. A disciple is one who follows another closely in order to become like the one followed. A disciple is like a very close student, a student who wants to take on the character and personality of the teacher. One sees students fall into the thrall of charismatic teachers, although that immature thrall is not the same as becoming a disciple. True, a disciple shows extraordinary devotion, living close by or with the teacher, becoming a part of the teacher's own small circle within which the goal was to make more teachers like the leading teacher. To become a disciple, though, is not simply to fall under the charismatic spell of the teacher but is instead an intentional process in which teacher and disciple agree on sound terms that the teacher is worthy of emulation. Jesus invites disciples. He encourages that we follow him on a figurative journey, a spiritual journey, a God journey, and the journey of our own souls.

Jesus had been telling the disciples of his coming rejection by the religious leaders and his execution, but that he would rise again in three days. As he spoke, Peter interrupted him, pulled him aside, and tried to tell Jesus that rejection and execution could not be the course. But Jesus pulled away from Peter and, rebuking him, told him that he was thinking only of human concerns rather than the mind of God. Jesus knew God's plan and needed the disciples to see and acknowledge it so that they could later explain and carry it to the masses. Jesus then called the nearby crowd to him and began again to teach. Jesus told the crowd, "Whoever wants to be my disciple must deny themselves and take up their cross and follow me." Those who tried to save their own lives would lose them, while those who gave their lives to Jesus would save them. Anyone who wanted to save their soul, who wanted eternal life, must follow the way of the cross. They must live for Jesus and eternity rather than show their concern only for their natural life.

He knew that he had become an ardent follower of Jesus. He knew from the time that he spent thinking about Jesus, reading about Jesus, and talking about Jesus. He knew from the way in which he saw his life through the perspective Jesus shared with his disciples. Not many others necessarily knew the lengths to which he pursued Jesus, but a few knew some of those lengths. He had a hard time telling what they thought of his discipleship, whether they respected it or not, because none reacted too directly toward him. He knew that a few others probably did not respect his ardency for Jesus, while some others probably did. He was not too concerned with their reactions, though, other than wanting them to become disciples, too. If they had chastised or mocked him for it, then he would have turned gently away and back to Jesus, he knew. He was not a fair weather friend of Jesus but a disciple. He had considered the cost and decided Jesus was worth it, worth anything. He hoped that he would not lose friends or lose the respect and confidence of co-workers or others. But he was ready to lose a few and maybe, he hoped, ready to lose all. He wanted to be more like Jesus and less like himself. He knew he had to follow Jesus in order to do so.

Praise Jesus. Luke 19:38.

Praise is something that we know, although the concept takes on slightly different meaning in faith settings. We praise so many things. We praise the evening meal, the coffee or other drink, the weather and its temperature, and the sunrise or sunset. We praise the cook or chef, the mail carrier, the neighbor, the schoolteacher, and the mayor. We even praise the pastor and worship leader. Jesus, though, suggests that we should also praise him, indeed, that if we don't praise him, other things, even inanimate things, will praise him. Praise in the spiritual setting has a different dimension than the ordinary praises we give to others, whether people or things. Praise of Jesus, praise of God, reaches the root of all things, nearly as Jesus suggests in saying that in the absence of our praise, the inanimate would praise him. The universe that is God's creation often appears to have the capacity to praise God for its creation, through the wonders of its size, power, intricacy, and magnificence. So too, the creature who is God's creation has opportunity and obligation to praise the creature's creator. For us not to praise Jesus is like the script ignoring its author, the film ignoring its director, or the orchestra ignoring its conductor. The conductor gets the applause first, not just the audience's applause but especially the applause of the orchestra's members. Praising Jesus is so elemental an act as to be fundamental.

Jesus had sent two disciples ahead to make arrangements for his entrance into Jerusalem during festival week. They would find a donkey colt that no one had ridden whose owner would permit them to take it to Jesus for his triumphal entry. The crowds that had built and followed Jesus throughout his three-year public ministry had now swelled into a crowd of disciples lining the road to welcome Jesus into Jerusalem. As Jesus rode the colt along the road into the city, the crowds of disciples spread their cloaks out for him to ride over in honor. Whole crowds praised God for the miracles Jesus had performed and sang out that blessed is the King who comes in the Lord's name. The religious leaders told Jesus to rebuke his disciples for their blasphemy in calling Jesus the One who comes in the name of the Lord. But Jesus replied, "I tell you, if they keep quiet, the stones will cry out." If his disciples did not praise him, then all creation would praise the coming King Jesus.

363

She delighted in praising Jesus. Her greatest praise was in church, where she loved to raise her hands, sing loudly, and shout out, even as she danced and clapped. Sure, she felt some embarrassment, but she didn't care about the embarrassment. She cared more for praising Jesus. And the more she praised, the less embarrassed she felt. Her concern was how *he* felt about her praise, not how others regarded it. She was appropriate and orderly. She didn't want to interfere with others in their own forms of worship. Yet given any opportunity, she wanted to be a part of praising her King to whom she owed all. Her praise, though, was not limited to church services. She would sing in the car when alone, sing on her walks, and even give silent praises to him when in gatherings and not otherwise occupied with the proceedings. She had friends, some of them elderly church mothers, whose praise for the King she especially admired and from whom she had learned new praises. She saw praise as a response of her heart but also appreciated that she could learn praise from others. Indeed, one of those church mothers taught her a special praise that she valued as much as any other. One day she saw the church mother get her finger pinched painfully in a door. As the mother grimaced while shaking her finger exaggeratedly to withstand the intense pain, she said with special emphasis, *thank you, Jesus.* She then always remembered to praise Jesus for all things, not just in joyous celebration.

Honor Jesus. John 5:23.

To give honor to another is to recognize that the other has standing, authority, and character consistent with the norms of the community in which one gives that recognition. Honor involves commendation, generous and affirming words lauding the conduct and status of the one honored. We honor leaders in particular, although we also honor those who lead by their words and actions without necessarily having the status of a leader. We honor fathers and mothers for their tireless fulfillment of those special roles. We honor employees who put forward special effort or who have served the employer loyally over a long time. We honor team captains when they retire and valedictorians when they graduate. To decide to give honor, though, involves more than quantitative criteria. One does not get honor simply for putting in one's time. Honor involves fitness, integrity, and character, a moral judgment as well as a judgment of strength, endurance, and performance. Jesus says quite clearly that we should give him honor just as we honor the Father because the Father has entrusted him with judgment about to whom to give life. Indeed, Jesus makes clear that unless we honor him, we do not honor the Father.

On one of those occasions when the religious leaders were trying to persecute Jesus for healing on the Sabbath, Jesus explained to them that his Father was always working, and so he would always work with his Father. Jesus's explanation did nothing to change the minds of the religious leaders. Indeed, now they had another reason to persecute Jesus who was not only breaking the Sabbath but calling himself the Son of God. The religious leaders understood that to call himself the Father's Son meant that Jesus was saying that he was equal to God. If Jesus was not God, then calling himself God's Son would be blasphemy, another violation of the laws over which the religious leaders considered themselves guardians. Jesus corrected the religious leaders again, saying that he was doing nothing by himself but only doing what he saw the Father doing. Indeed, Jesus told them that the Father had entrusted all judgment to the Son "that all may honor the Son just as they honor the Father." Jesus continued that anyone who does not honor the Son also fails to honor the Father who sent the Son. Jesus had much more to tell the religious leaders about his authority and the honor due him.

Together, between the two of them, and when they spoke with others, they always spoke about Jesus in ways that gave him honor. They never questioned him, doubted him, or complained about his commands to one another. They never made offhand comments about him or did or said anything about him while around others that might give those others reason to think that they did not utterly respect and honor Jesus. They shared that much respect for him, indeed had that much holy and healthy fear for him, that they just would not let a word pass their lips that sounded like they were denigrating or profaning him. When others used his name cavalierly or even profanely around them, they cringed, hurt inside, and tried

365

when they could to guide and correct the offender. They realized together that they had this constant solicitude for him, to ensure his honor, because they had his Spirit in them and they dwelled in his Spirit. Their honor had not so much to do with a rule or convention but rather with his presence. Who after all would dare to offend a friendly ruler, the King of kings, in his own presence?

Remain in Jesus. John 15:4.

We are interior beings. We dwell mentally, emotionally, consciously, and subliminally in thoughts and imaginations of people, places, and things. We set our hearts on things, think about them, anticipate them, turn them over in our minds, and amplify them, until we can almost experience them before they happen. The things on which and in which we dwell may be upcoming meals, meetings, vacations, achievements, or ambitions, or they may be relationships with family or friends, neighbors or enemies, supervisors or subordinates. We just have a way of devoting ourselves through our interior lives and inner conversations. Jesus says to remain in him, meaning one presumes to stay connected to him, to dwell on his Spirit, reside in his words, and contemplate his character and image. To remain in Jesus may be to devote our interior lives to him as we devote our exterior actions to the things that others require of us. To remain also suggests not to leave him, suggests that one who has already dwelt in him should continue to do so. We remain in a person when we know and love that person so intimately that we live in that person's virtual presence. Jesus expects us to abide in him, live in him, dwell in him, and so remain in him.

Jesus had already taught much at the Last Supper, and he would have much more to teach. He wanted, though, to give the disciples an image of how to remain close to him, connected to him, and productive of the works that he desired from them. Jesus began by calling himself the *vine* and his Father the gardener. This image must have meant much to the disciples who would have been quite familiar with the many local vineyards. The Father cuts off branches of the vine that do not bear fruit, Jesus explained. The Father then prunes every branch that does bear fruit so that it will bear more fruit from the pruning, Jesus continued. Jesus must have wanted to be sure that the disciples understood the meaning of his image of the vine, its branches, and the gardener because he then explained it in clear terms. Jesus continued, "Remain in me, as I also remain in you. No branch can bear fruit by itself; it must remain in the vine. Neither can you bear fruit unless you remain in me." The disciples were the branches. They had to stay connected with Jesus, had to remain conscious of and committed to his teaching, and had to welcome, receive, and hold his Spirit. The only way that the disciples would produce the fruit that the Father sought was through Jesus.

She increasingly abided in Jesus, dwelt in him, reflected on him, and lived through him. She had the strong sense not only that she was already connected with him but that she needed to remain connected. All was well and good that she had believed in Jesus, come to Jesus, and loved Jesus. Yet she wanted and needed so much more than spiritual stages, spiritual achievements. She wanted and needed a moment-to-moment presence, a habituation to Jesus that made her a part of him. She felt that without a constant connection to him, she would not produce in her life that which he desired and she desired for him. She had clues about how to remain in Jesus, and she pursued those clues gently, quietly, but resolutely. She found that she needed or benefited from quiet reminders, quiet moments, small practices and habits that reinforced her thinking about him, not just learning from him but, more so, drawing from him, like she was simply a small branch. She was much happier being a branch in Jesus than she had ever been as a weed of her own, she laughed to herself. She never wanted God to cut her off from Jesus and knew he never would. Pruning, though, she could take because she wanted to produce his fruit.

Watch for Jesus's coming. Luke 12:37.

Jesus came once and will come again, we know. Jesus says that we should watch and be ready for his coming, indeed to be working on his behalf when he returns. The kind of work that Jesus expects is of course kingdom work. Kingdom work is at its root work that serves the King. We serve Jesus when loving and praising him, surely. We also serve Jesus when caring for the sick and poor, sheltering the homeless, and visiting the prisoner. Another implication one draws from the gospel account in which Jesus tells the parable of the watchful servant is that kingdom work involves feeding the kingdom's other servants. We serve Jesus when we are teaching others about Jesus, supporting their faith, and encouraging their discipleship. These are the things that we are to be doing when Jesus returns. Because we do not know when he will return and only know that he will return when least expected, we should be doing these things as a matter of course and routine, now. We do not obey Jesus when we set aside kingdom duties as if we need not watch for his return. We obey Jesus when we continue and persevere in kingdom duties.

Sometimes Jesus taught the crowds, while other times he taught only the disciples. Jesus had turned to his disciples to teach them more after having addressed the crowd. He had told the crowd of thousands warnings, encouragements, lessons, and parable. The disciples, though, he told not to worry. Calling them *little flock*, he said that the Father would provide for them and protect them so that they could work for treasure in heaven. Jesus wanted them to earn that treasure, being sure that their hearts were not on earth but in God's kingdom. Jesus then told them to be *dressed ready for service*, for the Master was coming. The disciples should be ready to act for the Master's benefit the moment that he comes. Jesus continued, "It will be good for those servants whose master finds them watching when he comes," especially because no one knows that moment. Those who are ready to serve the Master, the Master will serve as reward. But again, Jesus warned, the Master will come when least expected. The disciples must watch for the Master to come. Peter asked Jesus whether this parable of the watchful servant was only for the disciples or for everyone. Jesus answered that the faithful servant is the one who feeds the Master's other servants. That faithful servant the Master will give charge of everything as reward.

She had developed a keen sense of watchfulness, perhaps not fully as keen as it could or ought to be, but yet far more than she had once known. Life had for a long time seemed to be an endless playground largely for her own designs. Oh, sure, God had made the playground, but the playground was now hers, and she enjoyed it richly as she hoped he wanted her to do. Yet over time, she had learned more of his expectations of how she used her time, what she made of her life in this place, and what he wanted her to be doing. She learned more about Jesus's return, which she anticipated quite gladly, but about which she had previously known nothing. She learned that she needed to be doing kingdom work, not merely enjoying the playground, when he returned. She learned more of what kingdom work entailed, whom she should be visiting, whom she should be encouraging, and what might be her reward. She heard of predictions of Christ's return, which she learned to ignore. The cautions that she learned about his return were that he would come unexpectedly and that she had better be working. She was going to be ready, that was for sure.

Do not be deceived about Jesus's coming. Luke 21:8.

While we watch for Jesus's coming, standing dressed and ready for service, we must not let others parading as prophets or events that look particularly bad deceive us as to his coming. Predicting his coming will not be that easy. Things may look bad, even very bad at times, so bad that we might assume that Jesus's coming is near. We may also suffer persecution of the kind that makes us think that end times are near. Look what the world has endured in the past century. How often might our ancestors have reasonably thought that the world was ending? What events do we see now, or how often might we see events soon and in the future, that look just as apocalyptic to us as the world wars, genocides, nuclear bombs, and natural disasters of the past century looked to our parents and grandparents? Think of the plagues and revolutions of prior centuries. Many have predicted end times, many have seen what looked like end times, and yet none of these earth-shaking events presaged Jesus's coming. We still have his good work to do, his kingdom work to do. Jesus says both not to worry and not to let things deceive us. We are to stand, work, and watch. Only the Father knows the time.

Jesus had been watching people put their gifts into the temple treasury and had taught the disciples about how God values the nature and quantity of giving. Some of the disciples pointed out the beautiful stones adorning the temple and the gifts piling up for God. Jesus told the disciples in effect to ignore human adornment of a human artifice because others would soon tear it all down. Jesus's statement must have startled the disciples, who asked when the destruction would occur and what would be the sign of the destruction's coming. Jesus said, "Watch out that you are not deceived. For many will come in my name, claiming, 'I am he,' and, 'The time is near.' Do not follow them." Jesus told them that the earth would see wars, earthquakes, and famines, but only after others had put them in prison and brought them before kings to testify about Jesus. Despite all of these things, Jesus reassured them that they would live if they only stood firm until the end.

He probably had as strong of an apocalyptic sense as did others, maybe even a little stronger. Sometimes, he felt that the worldwide news, and particularly social media, was just better at getting the disasters, terrors, and revolutions in front of us quicker and in more-graphic fashion than previously. He certainly felt that he knew more of what was going on in the world, more quickly, than he had ever known. Yet the news seemed undeniable that things were getting worse, whether one considered natural or manmade disasters. Who had ever heard of a tsunami or ever imagined radioactive clouds spanning the globe while nuclear waste washed into the ocean? Who had imagined terrorists killing thousands by flying jets into office towers or conducting ritual beheadings and crucifixions? One week, jungle bandits kidnap, rape, and enslave hundreds of schoolgirls. Another week, a crazed dictator arms submarines with nuclear-tipped ballistic missiles. Another week, an earthquake kills thousands while causing a deadly landslide down the world's tallest mountain. New deadly epidemics, new genocides, social upheaval, and political revolutions all made the news only to have other disasters push them aside. In all the uncertainty, terror, and horror, he kept thinking of Jesus's return, judgment, and peace, even as he knew that Jesus himself had warned that his return was unpredictable. He would not let the news deceive him, but he would keep doing kingdom work while watching for Jesus's coming.

Make room for Jesus's words. John 8:37.

Jesus's instructions, though often simple, are also always profound. They require more than small adjustments. They require in many cases a completely different way, a completely new way, of seeing things. For a person to accommodate and incorporate his instructions often takes more than making small adjustments. It takes throwing out old ways of thinking entirely and starting anew. Jesus's way is so distinct, so different, so revolutionary that it takes a new mind and new heart to receive it. One cannot just continue on with old practices based on old thinking, and presume to have understood and followed Jesus. The great truths are not difficult to accept because they are arcane or complex. They are difficult because one must empty the mind of falsehoods that contradict them. To truly follow Jesus, to really incorporate what he proposes and commands, takes emptying the mind of old interpretations rather than building his new instruction on those old things. With Jesus, one cannot hold to old comforts that are only limited and temporary comforts rather than the whole and eternal truths Jesus offers. Jesus says that we must *make room* for his words, meaning that we must be willing to accept the truth of what he says *in full* even when and especially when it will contradict falsehoods to which we have long clung.

Jesus challenged even those religious leaders who believed some of what Jesus had said to make room for more of what he said, to prepare to accept the full truth rather than just part of it. He kept urging them to hold to his teaching so that they would know the truth, which would then set them free. Every time that he pushed them onward in their understanding, though, the religious leaders pulled back without seeing that Jesus was the fulfillment of their old ways. They kept ending up in conflict with Jesus because they clung to their old interpretations. Jesus knew that their problem was that they were not willing to open their hearts and minds to him in a way that they could receive his word. They did not have the will to take in his word. Jesus said to them, "You are looking for a way to kill me, because you have no room for my word." Jesus explained that he was telling them what he had seen from the Father, but they were instead still following what they had heard from their father. They were not pursuing Jesus but following and trying to impress and control others. Jesus finally told the religious leaders that they were following the devil, who is a liar.

He found that he had to unhook from a lot of what he had assumed that he knew or had assumed had value in knowing. He had to let go and nearly start over. Like everyone does, he had slowly constructed meaning out of the world, gradually adding layer after layer of the world's wisdom as he matured. That construction included not just getting along in the world, seeing how it operates, taking its lumps and bruises, but also reading, researching, investigating, and examining. The traditional sources that the world offers, historical, philosophical, psychological, and educational, had given him a place in the world and a set of principles by which to act. Yet in Jesus's teaching, he found that he could not simply add it like another layer over what the world had taught him. Every time that he tried to layer Jesus's teaching on top of some principle or practice of the world, things simply did not work. He could not follow both the world's teaching and Jesus's teaching. He had to make new room in his mind and heart to lay a new foundation on Jesus. He had to work up from the bottom of his heart and depths of his mind. He could not mix the holy with the common. He needed to start over with Jesus.

Listen to Jesus's voice. John 10:16.

Jesus had many things to say to his disciples and has many things to say to us. The number of his instructions, their subtlety, their simplicity, and their profundity, all invite us, draw us in, and challenge us to move forward in our understanding. Their invitation is not to intellectual mastery but to a kingdom, God's kingdom. That invitation to a new place may be why we must start over in new birth, as the prior section suggests, making new room for Jesus's words. Once we open the new mind and heart, then we must listen to Jesus, truly listen to him, hear his voice and sense his living presence in his words and instructions. We do not simply grow smarter in listening to Jesus, we grow freer, entering a realm in which more good things are possible than we can hope or imagine. Jesus has so much to say, offering us so much to attain, that we must begin with an open mind and heart to receive it but then listen to him with concentration and even courage. To listen to Jesus, to really hear Jesus, takes a courage that many do not immediately have and may not actually wish to possess. Yet Jesus says that we must listen to him, really listen to him, so that we can then follow. He charts a different path. Listening to the world will not lead you up the path into the kingdom.

Jesus was coaching and challenging the religious leaders once again, this time using a parable of the Good Shepherd and his sheep. The religious leaders would not understand the parable at first, until Jesus made it clear to them. He told them first that everyone must enter the sheep pen by the gate rather than climbing over the enclosure the way that thieves do. The shepherd opens the gate for the sheep that know and trust the shepherd's voice. Sheep run from a stranger's voice but follow the shepherd's voice. Jesus then explained the parable to the religious leaders, saying that he is the gate and the Good Shepherd who calls believers to him so that they may enter eternal life through him. His followers know his voice, which is how they follow him. He lays down his life for them. Jesus told the religious leaders that he had other followers whom they did not know among the Jews, adding, "They too will listen to my voice, and there shall be one flock and one shepherd." Jesus's teaching was so clear, and he had healed so many, that some of the religious leaders believed even while others called him mad.

As often as he had read and heard Jesus's words, he was just beginning to listen to them in the way that he was realizing that he needed to listen to them to understand and accept the truth that they conveyed. The experience was a bit like hearing new strains in an old tune, strains that one had never before realized were there. Or it might have been like realizing that one had long misunderstood the meaning of a certain word, with the correct definition opening a whole new meaning to an old and often-read text. Whatever the case, he was so glad to have begun to develop this new capacity to listen. He felt that he had almost missed the opportunity, almost let the words close off to him because of their familiarity, when they still held such profound truths that he had not yet grasped. That sense of near-miss, of nearly having given up on the pursuit without having discovered such important truths, convinced him that Jesus's words were likely inexhaustible in their capacity to inform him further, to enlarge his spirit through the advocacy of the Holy Spirit conveying Jesus's imprint. He would continue to listen to Jesus until he saw Jesus in his kingdom.

Remember what Jesus told you. Luke 24:6.

We make room in our hearts and minds for Jesus's profound instructions, and we listen for his voice so that we can follow his deep meaning. We must, though, in that process recall Jesus's words to mind. We have to *remember* what he told us, what we read, what others told us about him, his Good News, and the deep things that he told us about the kingdom. Memory is such an important attribute and capacity. Those who lose the ability to remember lose a part of them and with that loss lose memory of others. Recall is an equally important habit and practice, one in which we pull back into our minds the critical words and teaching of Jesus. If we learn Jesus's instructions but then do nothing with them, then we gain little or nothing. To do something with Jesus's words, we must recall them, mull them, and turn them over in our minds, until they convince us to change our outlook and actions. Some of us are memory masters, recalling whole Bible books and passages. Others of us make little or no effort to remember, no attempt to master. Those who remember and recall live a different life because of that mental activity. Those who do not remember and do not recall live the same lives unaffected by what they once heard. Remember what Jesus told you.

Jesus had told the disciples at the Last Supper to share the cup of wine, and to give thanks, break bread, and share the bread, in remembrance of him. He had told them and the women who were with them of his coming arrest and demise but also of his resurrection. The awful events that ensued, including Jesus's trial, scourging, crucifixion, and burial, had nonetheless so shaken and scattered the disciples and the women that they had forgotten his words, forgotten that he had explained to them that he must die and rise again to take them and other believers with him into the kingdom. They were to have remembered him, remembered his words and instructions, but they did not do so. Then the women went to the tomb on the third day with spices for the body. But when they reached the tomb, it was empty. They still did not remember until two men in gleaming clothes suddenly appeared, saying, "He is not here. He is risen! Remember how he told you, while he was still with you." Only then did the women remember Jesus's words, rushing back to the disciples and others to tell them what they had witnessed, the gleaming men had reminded them, and what they finally remembered.

She had accomplished something that she had never thought of her doing, never really thought that she had the talent or capacity to do. In the end, all it had taken was commitment. Well, of course it took practice, dedication, discipline, and long rehearsal, but each of those things grew out of her simple commitment to memorize a book of the Bible. She chose a somewhat shorter book, although not the shortest book. She chose a favorite book every verse of which seemed to her to carry special meaning, rather than a book distant to her and difficult for her. Still, over time, not too much time, she had memorized the whole book to the point that she could repeat it verse by verse, chapter by chapter, to others. She also found that she could pull back verses and passages when events or circumstances triggered their recall. She could complete references to the book that others made, where they didn't recall the full verse of passage. While these abilities encouraged her, most of all she felt encouragement and confidence in the way in which the memorized verses popped up in her mind to guide, counsel, warn, and support her. She was remembering Jesus much more often than she had previously, even though she had always loved him deeply. His words were coming back to her more often, and with those words, his presence was gracing.

Build on Jesus's words. Matthew 7:24.

Jesus encourages us to think of his words as the foundation for our actions. He wants us to build on his words, expects and instructs us to put them into practice so that what we do becomes an expression of his words. What we do with our time and talents becomes like building. We either build a sound structure using our time, skills, and resources on things that Jesus instructs and values, or we waste time, skills, and resources on things that are so meaningless and outside of Jesus's will that they do not withstand the first test. Words, especially Jesus's words, can be the foundation for action. Indeed, one may not overstate the case to say that words are always the basis for action. Without words to guide and justify our actions, the actions are only impulses, like satisfying thirst or hunger. The kind of purposeful action that defines a person and life are actions that words stimulate, guide, and promote. Organizations adopt and publish missions because words guide actions. Individuals adopt missions whether they define them or not. Know your life's mission. Base your life's mission on the life of Jesus as Jesus expressed in his words. Build a sound and lasting, indeed an eternal, life.

Toward the end of his long and spectacular Sermon on the Mount, Jesus had warned against false prophets who came in sheep's clothing. He had also warned against false disciples who were always calling out to the Lord but not doing the Lord's will. Jesus explained to the crowd that when those false prophets who did not do his will came to him to enter the kingdom, he would chase them away as evildoers whom he never really knew. Everyone must build on the words of Jesus, doing the work that Jesus expects and instructs. Jesus summarized using an analogy, "Therefore, everyone who hears these words and puts them into practice is like a wise man who built his house on the rock." When the storms came, Jesus continued, that house did not fall because its owner had built on the rock. Wise builders build on the words of Jesus, while foolish builders hear his words but build on other things, Jesus told the crowd. They don't put his words into practice as they should.

He had read Jesus's words so often that he hoped that he was putting them into practice, building on them, making something of sound foundation that would last. He hoped, but he wasn't sure, and hoping, he decided, wasn't enough. He wanted to ensure as best he could that he was indeed building on Jesus's words rather than simply letting them pass playfully through his mind, entertaining himself with them, and then neglecting them when he went about his daily business. How, though, could he truly build on Jesus's words? The thought occurred to him again that he might get to the point where he was in such constant communication with Jesus's words, so constantly aware of them in his interior dialogue, through which he navigated the world, that he could at any moment draw on Jesus's words to justify his action. He supposed that to build on Jesus's words would mean something just like that. He could of course not literally build on Jesus's words because words were only blips on a page, sounds uttered from the mouth and gone again, or fleeting thoughts in the mind. If words were so temporal, ephemeral, and temporary, and building implied the opposite, something solid and lasting, then he needed the words to be almost constantly in mind. The words must guide enough of the actions to constitute building. He thought that he might have found a clue to true building.

Hold to Jesus's teaching. John 8:31.

The practice of building on Jesus's teaching finds a close companion in the practice of *holding to* Jesus's teaching. We find several ways to describe adherence, each description overlapping with the meaning of another while also extending that other meaning. Building accumulates. We first lay a foundation and then the first course followed by more courses until the structure takes shape. *Holding to* a teaching has a slightly different connotation of grasping and refusing to let go. Things intercede that might encourage us to let go of Jesus's teaching, whether those things are doctrinal dispute, misunderstandings, and maybe offenses caused by other believers. Even as we build, we must hold on to the teaching on which we build. We might otherwise begin to build on Jesus's teaching but then gradually let go of his teaching to take hold of some other teaching. We see people doing exactly that, even prominent preachers who somehow begin to let go of Jesus's teaching in order to follow the teaching of other practitioners, principles, and practices. They build with a little from Jesus, a little from Buddha, and perhaps a lot from themselves, which in the end is not to build on Jesus at all. Why they let go is sometimes a mystery, other times not so mysterious. In the end, the reasons don't matter. We must not let go of Jesus's teaching but instead grasp it like the hammer with which we build.

Jesus was speaking more openly and deeply to the people, calling himself the light of the world, and speaking of standing with the Father. The religious leaders were challenging many of his words but especially these open and deeper teachings. For the religious leaders, lessons and parables were one thing, but profound truths expressed clearly rather than hidden in parable were another thing. Jesus explained that he was leaving, that he was going to the Father, and that until then he spoke only what the Father taught him to say. When they realized that Jesus was referring to his death, some speculated on how he might die, even by his own hand perhaps. Jesus corrected that the religious leaders would *lift him up*, referring to his crucifixion. These deep and challenging lessons caused some to believe Jesus, while others rejected him. Jesus then told the Jews who believed him, "If you hold to my teaching, you are really my disciples. Then you will know the truth, and the truth will set you free." He was urging the believers not to let go of his teaching but to hold to it, whether through challenge, fear, or contradiction.

She loved when the kids sang the song to *oh no, you never let go,* through the calm and through the storm, oh, no, Lord, you never let go of me. The song seemed to her to have two possible meanings. She even guessed that the kids saw both meanings. On one hand, the song seemed clearly to be saying that Jesus would never let go of the children who sang the wonderful song so joyfully, with such energy and verve. Jesus does not let go. Even when we give up our faith, he remains faithful. The children seemed to welcome that sense of security in Jesus that he would never let them go through a storm without him, the children all likely being familiar with storms of one kind or another. The world is just as fearful to children as to adults, she knew. Yet on the other hand, the song seemed to encourage the children that they should hold on to Jesus, that *they* should never let go of *him*. She felt in watching the children sing the song that the children needed to proclaim to themselves and others that they were also going to hold on to Jesus, just as Jesus held on to them. That mutuality, that love affair, that joyous embrace, she realized, was what she so appreciated about the song. She knew that every child she saw singing it would face great challenges, some incidental to their faith but others directed to destroying their faith. She hoped and prayed that they would indeed never let go.

Do not reject Jesus's words. John 12:48.

One might think that Jesus's instruction not to reject his words goes without saying, given all that he said about listening to him, building on his words, and holding fast to those words. Yet Jesus did also say not to reject his words. His giving the proscription *do not,* along with the prior prescriptions to *do,* gave Jesus an opportunity to explain why not to reject his words and what would be the consequences of doing so. Holding fast to Jesus and building on his instructions leads to eternal life. What happens to those who do not hold fast, do not believe, and do not build? Jesus explained that when one rejects his words, one rejects him and rejects his Father. Jesus does not, on his own, of his own accord, impose the consequence of rejecting him. Rather, Jesus made clear that he came to save rather than to judge. Yet Jesus made equally clear that the Father has a judgment to make at the last day. The Father gives us plenty of time to accept rather than reject Jesus's words, generally right up until our last breath, although we do not always know, indeed often do not know, when that least breath will come. But the judgment will come, and the judgment is to bar entry to the kingdom. With banishment from the kingdom comes loss of eternal life. Rejecting Jesus's words leads to condemnation and eternal separation from Father and Son, God in Christ.

Jesus had performed so many miracles that all should have believed in him. Fortunately for them, some did believe. Jesus reassured those in the crowd who believed him but were also afraid of the religious leaders that they believed the Father when they believed him. Indeed, he told them that they saw the Father when they looked at him, also telling them that he was the light who removes believers from darkness. On the other hand, Jesus told the non-believers in the crowd that he would not judge them. He did not come into the world to judge but to save, he reminded them. Jesus continued, though, with these ominous words, "There is a judge for the one who rejects me and does not accept my words; the very words I have spoken will condemn them at the last day." Jesus continued by explaining that he was only speaking his Father's words, the Father who had commanded him to say those words. Jesus reassured his listeners that he was only speaking the Father's words because he knew that those who followed them would receive eternal life.

She had never rejected Jesus's words and never expected to do so. She knew a little about despair. Most of us do. She had suffered as many suffer. The kind of suffering that scared her most was of course mental suffering, depression, darkness, and despairing of a future. Physical pain certainly hurt and had its own effect on one's outlook on life. But for her, and she realized probably also for all others, the thought of hopelessness, meaninglessness, a world without love, comfort, or beauty, was the worst kind of suffering. The awful darkness of that world was a large part of why she would never reject Jesus. That dark world was the world without Jesus, without God, without faith, hope, and love. That dark world certainly existed. Many, she suspected, landed and remained there. Yet she also knew that the bright world of Jesus, the light world of the kingdom, existed just as certainly and that many had entered and remained there. She was bound for the light world. Jesus had banished the darkness from within her. All that she had to do was not to reject Jesus and instead to continue to accept and hold onto Jesus. She was never going to let go. She had far too great a fear for unending darkness.

Take Jesus's yoke. Matthew 11:29.

Few probably think of taking the yoke of one whose teaching they plan to follow. Jesus's analogy would have been fitting for the ancient Middle East crowd to whom he preached. Beasts of burden, oxen that plowed the fields and pulled the carts necessary for farming and commerce would have been common. Oxen were effective beasts of burden, highly effective, perhaps like having a tractor and combine, and transport truck, all in one today. Oxen were only effective, though, when they took the yoke that made plowing or pulling a cart possible. Oxen without a yoke would have been virtually useless, a liability, another mouth to feed with little or no productive capacity. The yoke was the key to usefulness, or more accurately, *willingness to accept the yoke* was the key ingredient because the yoke was simply a widely available piece of equipment, while the willingness to accept the yoke was an attitude, disposition, or capacity. Oxen broken to the yoke had a value that unbroken oxen or rank oxen that had rejected the yoke did not have. The difference between an ox broken to the yoke and one not broken or, worse, not breakable, could be vast difference. Some masters gave their oxen a heavy yoke, hard work in hard soil or heavy carts up steep hills, while other masters knew how to make the yoke lighter, to break the soil at shallower depths in stages or to distribute the load across other carts and trips. Oxen yoked hard would rebel or breakdown, while oxen yoked light would work easily, live long, and prosper. When Jesus says to take his light and easy yoke, he means that following him is a lot easier work than following hard masters like money or government, or impossible masters like pride and jealousy.

John the Baptist's disciples had just left Jesus to return to John in prison to tell him the good news of Jesus's miracle works. As was so often the case, a crowd had been around Jesus as Jesus had spoken to John's disciples. When John's disciples left, Jesus turned to teach the crowd beginning with John's role as a herald to Jesus. Jesus then explained that John's preaching had not caused the towns to repent, nor had the towns repented in witness of Jesus's miracles. Things would not be good for those towns on judgment day, Jesus warned, including for their wise and learned. Jesus praised the Father for revealing truth instead to the little children whom the Father had entrusted to Jesus. The Father had entrusted all things to Jesus, whom only the Father knows, Jesus said, adding that only he, the Son, knew the Father unless the Son chose to reveal the Father to others. Jesus ended by urging the crowd, "Take my yoke upon you and learn from me, for I am gentle and humble in heart, and you will find rest for your souls. For my yoke is easy and my burden is light." Jesus wanted the members of the crowd to let him guide them, let him work them in the easy and light way that the Lord works his servants.

He had a good sense from his experience with animals of what breaking to the yoke meant, and he was more than ready for Jesus's yoke to break and guide him. He had seen rank animals and so had known their danger, liability, and uselessness. Indeed, he had broken rank animals, seeing the difference that breaking meant to them. To break an animal to the work for which its owners bred or bought it is not like breaking a tool or piece of equipment. Break equipment, and the equipment is useless. Fail to break the animal, and the animal is useless. Break the animal to the work for which its owner bred it, and the animal is not less well-off but is instead much better off. The animal is more relaxed, happier if animals experience happiness. The animal puts on the weight and muscle that it should, sleeps as it should, and rises to work again as it should. Working animals nearly seem to take pride or at least satisfaction in their work, provided that their master is a kind and thoughtful master. He knew that he would never want to be the animal of a cruel master. Yet he knew just as well that he would indeed like to be the animal of the Good Master. He would take Jesus's yoke in a heartbeat, to have the Master's gentle hand, meaningful work, and constant care and guidance.

Come to Jesus for rest. Mark 6:31.

The world goes at a fast pace, and sometimes we go even faster. The energy and excitement of many opportunities, challenges, and demands keeps us going fast and faster. Technology and social media add new stimulation and new demands. With smartphones, emails, and multiple forums for texting, anyone can reach us anywhere and at any time, and they don't hesitate to do so, even as we do the same with them. Even when we go away for breaks, those whom we leave behind expect frequent posts and updates, and we are only too glad to provide them. The challenge that the frenetic pace of life creates is that we don't find opportunities for deep reflection. We cannot get long perspective because the immediate is constantly at hand. Life races by without the moments of solitude and rest that we need to focus on the important things. Finding solitude and rest requires clear intention. They don't just happen on their own. We must make them happen. Jesus instructs that we come away with him for solitude and rest. He knows that we need those moments. He also knows that the moments are not so much in the unoccupied time as they are in the relationship with him. We cannot find unoccupied time. We always have something with which to occupy ourselves. And so we must occupy ourselves with him, find rest in him, and reflect deeply with him to gain our peace and contentment. We must take solitude and rest in Christ, not in the world, which gives no solitude or rest. The world keeps us busy so that we do not dwell in Christ, and so we must intentionally come to Jesus for rest.

The disciples had done as Jesus had asked. Jesus had sent them out with the authority to heal, and they had done so, healing many sick people and casting out many demons in Jesus's name. Jesus had sent them out to preach repentance and carry the good news, and they had done so. The disciples went so many places and were so successful that Jesus's name became even better known. King Herod even heard about the disciples' work. King Herod was the the local ruler who had beheaded John even though the king knew John to be a righteous and holy man. The disciples returned to Jesus to report all their good work preaching repentance and healing the sick. As was so often the case, so many people were crowding around Jesus and coming and going that they had no peace, could not even rest or eat. So Jesus said to the disciples, "Come with me by yourselves to a quiet place and get some rest." Jesus wanted the disciples to restore themselves alone in rest with him. They got in a boat to head alone to a quiet place, although the people saw where they were headed and ran ahead to meet them there.

She was finding increasing need in her life for peace and solitude. She had grown up seeking stimulation, occupation, and activity. She had nearly hated the quiet times, resented the quiet times as if they meant that life was passing her by and leaving her behind. Now, she had all the stimulation that she needed, and then some. She had too few gaps in her busy schedule and too many demands. She had no natural times of peace and rest. When she did have a quiet moment here or there, she found herself way too ready to occupy those quiet moments with the things that kept her busy at other times, way too ready to pick up the technology or busy herself with chores and recreations. She sensed that she needed something positive, something that she could *do*, in order *not* to do. She understood now the attraction of meditation, of concentrating on little or nothing, in other words of concentrating on *not* concentrating. Yet where she was beginning to find more peace, more positive rest and contentment, was in Christ. Her times with Jesus, dwelling on his word, thinking of his life, thinking of his actions in her life, were more restful than doing nothing. She was beginning to find rest in coming to Jesus, and she knew that doing so was good for her soul.

Urge Jesus to stay with you. Luke 24:29.

Jesus's words come to us at different times. Something reminds us of his life, his teachings, his presence, and we dwell on him for a time. At those times, he seems to talk to us through his words and teachings. We gain a sense of his strength, courage, love, joy, and comfort. We might be traveling or doing mindless chores as we dwell on his words, and he seems to move right along with us, accompany us to where we are headed. Yet then, we arrive at our destination or complete our chore, and he prepares to leave, to move on just as we seem ready to move on. At those moments of departure, we face an opportunity to invite Jesus to remain. More than merely invite him to remain, we may *urge* him to remain, strongly entreat him to remain. When we do, he may accompany us into our meeting or on to our next chore. His words and teachings may remain in our minds and hearts as we pick up the next activity, begin the next part of our day. Jesus need not only accompany us through quiet moments or interludes, through our periods of rest or solitude. He may also join with us in the fray, weaving his words and teaching into the activity of our busy nights and days. Urge Jesus to stay with you after he has visited with you. He makes the best companion at all times, not just in-between times.

The two men walking on the road to Emmaus had been going over and over the sad events of the prior week that had culminated in Jesus's crucifixion and the empty tomb discovered just that morning. Just then, Jesus came up to join them, although the two men did not recognize him. When they shared with him what they had seen and heard that prior week involving Jesus, he explained to them what the scriptures said about him, about the Messiah, as they walked along to the village where the men were headed. When they reached the village, Jesus looked as if he was going to continue on. But the two men didn't want Jesus to leave them, and so they urged him strongly, "'Stay with us, for it is nearly evening; the day is almost over.'" Jesus more than complied with their request. After going into the village to stay and eat with them, he actually gave them communion, breaking bread, giving thanks, and sharing it with them, before disappearing from their sight. They realized only then that they had been walking and talking with Jesus.

He had a gnawing sense that he had been leaving Jesus behind. He had good times with Jesus's words, teachings, and Spirit, times of study, meditation, prayer, reflection, and praise. Yet those times always ended and sometimes ended abruptly, too abruptly, as if he need not have made such a stark demarcation between Jesus time and other time. The gnawing sense that he had developed had to do with this division in his life, as if he occupied two worlds not concurrently but consecutively, switching back and forth between the two worlds, entering and leaving God's kingdom. Maybe, he thought, that was the way all believers behaved, the way that things had to be. But his gnawing sense was instead that he was making an error, a gross error, in his conduct and thinking. He did not need to occupy two worlds. He could, he felt, somehow remain in the kingdom throughout his days. Maybe what he needed to do, he realized, was to urge Jesus not to leave when his solitude times were done. Maybe Jesus was leaving only because he knew that he was

385

not welcome to accompany him further. He decided to give inviting Jesus, urging Jesus to continue on and stay with him, a strong try.

Recall Jesus's death. Matthew 26:38.

We rightly focus on Jesus's instructions and teachings. He gives us so much guidance and insight, so much encouragement and counsel, in such profound commands. We should dwell on those teachings, listen to him, follow him, serve him, and carry his message to others. At the same time, though, Jesus may appreciate that we recall and recognize the sacrificial and redemptive meanings of his trial, crucifixion, and death. Jesus's crucifixion is a difficult aspect of Christianity for many, as indeed it should be. The difficulty though should not lie in the constructs of sacrifice and redemption, the meanings of which should be clear enough. We are naturally and frequently corrupt in our hearts, minds, and behaviors. We have no getting around that corruption other than through Jesus's making it up to God for us, giving God his perfection and image in place of our corruption. Instead, the difficulty with Jesus's death that we should face and feel, even frequently, involves how horrible his death was that a perfect man should die in such an unimaginably painful and shameful way. Of course, only such a profound and profoundly disturbing sacrifice could give us any approach to a perfectly holy God. These things we should recall, perhaps often. Why else would we have the following account of the way in which Jesus suffered in prayer facing his death, while wanting the support of his closest disciples? Recall Jesus's redemptive death, even as you recall and celebrate his redemptive resurrection.

Jesus had taught the disciples at length at the Last Supper. They had ended the meal and teaching by singing a hymn together before walking out to the garden Gethsemane on the nearby Mount of Olives. Jesus was about to pray in great earnest to the Father over his impending arrest and trial, and horrific scourging and crucifixion, for which he would need supernatural strength. To pray in such enormous sorrow and trouble, Jesus told the other disciples to sit in one part of the garden and then took aside three of his favorite disciples Peter, James, and John, to a corner of the garden. Jesus told the three of them, "My soul is overwhelmed with sorrow to the point of death. Stay here and keep watch with me." Jesus wanted his disciples with him, keeping watch, supporting him, accompanying him, as he faced and contemplated his horrible but strangely necessary death. Jesus then fell to the ground in prayer. But when he rose, the three were sleeping. He woke them and repeated that they must keep watch with him. Jesus prayed again, but the three disciples fell asleep again. Jesus just returned to prayer while the disciples slept until the officers came to arrest him.

He thought of Jesus's death from time to time. He had seen, heard, and read many highly moving, frightening, and even stunning representations of its strangely glorious awfulness, although he kept coming back to the Bible descriptions, which on their own communicated the event's profundity. The awfulness of scourging and crucifixion is fairly obvious. Its strange and mysterious magnificence in this one instance of course had for him to do with Jesus's unique historical and universal mission. God permitted it and Jesus accepted it as the only possible plan of redemption. God must voluntarily give himself up, sacrifice his Son, in the most ignominious death possible in order to create a path for us back to him. Given God's holiness and our corruption, no other sacrifice would do, could do. In his modest Christian walk, he knew this deepest truth and embraced it wholeheartedly. One of the ways in which he had learned to embrace it was to recall Jesus's death. The garden story of the sleeping disciples reminded him that he needed to recall it, needed to know how deeply Jesus had suffered in separation from his Father, even if only for a time until his resurrection. He hoped always to remember the crucifixion so that he would always recall the glory of the resurrection.

Lose your life for Jesus. Mark 8:35.

Jesus lost his life for us, gave his life away to save us in that glorious sacrificial redemption. Jesus gained his Father's eternal glory and assumed his glorious resurrected body by giving away his life at his Father's command. While we understand and accept, indeed embrace, Jesus's sacrificial redemption, what are we to do in return or imitation? How are we to follow Jesus in his taking up the cross? Jesus instructs that we take our own cross, that we carry our own cross for him so that he can reward us with eternal life. To carry the cross symbolizes life sacrifice. Condemned to crucifixion, Jesus carried his own cross, as far as he was able and then with the help of another, to the hill where it took place. When he instructs that we also carry our own cross, he urges that we give up our life in favor of the life that he has for us. We need not construe Jesus's instruction to mean that we will have no life while we carry our cross giving up our own. To the contrary, while giving up our own life, we assume the eternal life that Jesus supplies for us. Some things we cannot achieve by their direct pursuit. If you want a fulfilled life, as we all do, then you must give up pursuing it through your own designs in order to accept Jesus's designs, in which event you will have more life than you could have imagined.

Jesus had just spent time alone with the disciples, when before the other disciples Peter had acknowledged Jesus as the Messiah, Jesus had predicted his death, and Jesus had rebuked Peter for discouraging him in pursuing God's plan. Jesus then called to him the crowd that, as usual, had been waiting to hear more of Jesus's teaching. Right after the momentous events of Peter's confession of Jesus as the Messiah and rebuke by Jesus for discouraging Jesus's sacrificial death, the disciples might have expected that Jesus would have an especially important teaching for the crowd, as indeed he did. Jesus began by telling the crowd and his disciples that those who wished to be his disciples must *take up their cross* and follow Jesus. Some in the crowd might have wondered to what cross Jesus was referring, although others would have known well the Roman practice of making the condemned carry their own crosses to crucifixion. Jesus made his meaning clearer by continuing, "For whoever wants to save their life will lose it, but whoever loses their life for me and for the gospel will save it." Jesus indeed expected sacrificial following, giving up one one's life, but he also promised eternal life as reward. As Jesus explained to the crowd and disciples, what good does one do holding onto the world but losing one's soul?

She had learned quite well the lesson of not too much pursuing her own life but instead laying down her own life to carry her cross to receive the life of Jesus. While this teaching of Jesus was a little difficult for her to explain to others, she had learned it from her own experience. She had at times pursued her own life. She knew what self-pursuit was like, as we all do. Those times had not been happy times, not been fulfilling times, and not been safe and growing times. In retrospect, she could see that those times had been the opposite, times of despair and stagnation. She had so much wanted to do good deeds and do well for herself that she had thought that pursuing those things would lead her straight to them. Wasn't life that simple, to, as they say, grasp and live life to the fullest? Yet life had not been that simple. She had been making a good bit of a wreck of things through pursuing her life. So she finally tried living the other way, living for Jesus. She set aside her own designs while listening to the designs and purposes that Jesus might have for her. She found that giving up her life in some respects meant getting it back for the first time ever. She wasn't really sure how that switch even worked. She couldn't give a logical or psychological explanation for it. But Jesus's teaching was proving remarkably true. She was gaining from him a life that she nearly had not imagined, a life that seemed to fit her more than any that she *had* imagined.

Accept anyone Jesus sends. John 13:20.

While the Bible is our source and the Holy Spirit our guide, we learn of Jesus's words and teachings, and his intentions, from and through many. Jesus says to accept anyone that he sends because by doing so we accept him and his Father. Jesus's instruction may have to do with the incorrect way in which we sometimes judge authority. When we do not know the source of authority, we look for authority's trappings, the things that might indicate to us that we have found the source. We might look for famous or recognizable names, or big and important-sounding titles, or multiple degrees and certifications, or memberships and associations. We might look for the charismatic personality, the special voice, the special effects, or the special forum or theatrics. Jesus recommends none of these things. He did not anoint a university or accredit a program to carry the one true message. Rather, Jesus says to accept *anyone* whom he sends. When Jesus says instead to accept anyone rather than only the special one, the recognized one, or the one whom everyone agrees has the proper interpretation, he may have been warning us against looking to the trappings, the popularity, the formal recognitions, and telling us instead that he communicates through the humble and unexpected. Jesus may send us a seminary professor or an illiterate. Jesus may send us a rich magnate or a pauper. He may send us a corporate chief executive or a custodian. Whomever Jesus sends us, we should accept. We should be looking to the one who sent the messenger, not the gold tray on which the messenger carries the message. Distinguish messengers based on who sent them, not how they look carrying the message. Accept those whom Jesus sends, not others.

Jesus had washed the disciples' feet in that demonstrative act of service at the Last Supper. He then explained that they, too, would receive God's blessing if they acted as servants in the way that Jesus had taught them to serve. The evening then took an odd twist that the disciples likely had not expected. Jesus said that not all of them would receive that blessing. He was not referring to all of the disciples but only those he had chosen. Jesus reminded the disciples that the scriptures said that one who had shared his bread would turn against him. Jesus told them that he was warning them of his betrayal so that they would believe that Jesus was who he was. Jesus said, "Very truly I tell you, whoever accepts anyone I send accepts me; and whoever accepts me accepts the one who sent me." Jesus wanted the disciples to welcome anyone acting with his authority but to know that one of them would not do so and would instead betray him. John wanted to know who, which one would be the betrayer. Jesus told John to watch for a sign, which Judas Iscariot promptly fulfilled, leaving the disciples to arrange with the religious leaders for Jesus's arrest late that same evening.

He had once given fairly substantial weight to the reputation, education, experience, membership, and other status of the ones from whom he learned, but no longer. Jesus's teaching had changed all of that giving credit where credit seemed from the package to be most due. The more he learned of Jesus's teaching, the more that he found that he was looking right through the reputation things, the trappings of credibility, the associations and networks of which the author, speaker, or instructor was a part, and looking instead to the source of the message that they were conveying. He was holding Jesus's message up, letting Jesus's teaching measure everything, even when the content had the endorsement of the most impressive institutions or personages. If the message conveyed was not rooted in Jesus, if Jesus had not sent the messenger, then he was simply no longer interested in accepting it. He no longer cared at all for the weight of the messenger's reputation, the messenger's degrees and certifications, or the reputation of the publishing house or conference sponsor promoting the message. If the message carried Jesus's words, conveyed Jesus's life, represented Jesus, then he was accepting the messenger because he was accepting Jesus. If the message didn't carry Jesus, then he was rejecting it and looking for another Jesus messenger.

Stand by Jesus in trials. Luke 22:28.

We draw constant strength and courage from having Jesus stand with us, teach us, guide us, and instruct us. We know that through him we can do all things. We know that in our weakness he becomes strong and that we have only to stand in the gap in faith for him to pursue and prevail in his cause. Yet Jesus stood trials of his own and recognized and appreciated those who stood with him in those trials. One might even go so far as to say that Jesus continues to stand trials, although trials of a very different kind than the trials that preceded his condemnation and crucifixion. No one crucifies Jesus again. His redemptive sacrifice and resurrection are finished and completed works. Faith won, and everything else lost. Still, struggles in faith, trials of faith, challenges to truth, go on all around us. Jesus works through the Holy Spirit in those trials. Some of us stand with Jesus in those trials even today. Others of us step aside or take a seat. In commending the disciples and rewarding them with a kingdom for having stood by him in trials, Jesus may also be telling us today to stand by him in today's trials. His resurrection and victory are no longer at stake, but the salvation and resurrection of others remain at trial. Stand by Jesus in trials, whether his or your own trials, or the trials of others.

Jesus had just completed his first communion with the disciples at the Last Supper. He finished by telling the disciples that one of them would betray him, likely a shocking revelation. The disciples began disputing who would betray Jesus and then who was the greatest among them. Jesus stopped their arguing, instructing instead that the greatest among them would be their servant, just as Jesus had been their servant. The disciples might have needed encouragement at this low point in the already-long and difficult evening that would soon grow much more difficult. So Jesus told them, "You are those who have stood by me in my trials." The disciples had stood by Jesus while few others had done so. Because they had stood by Jesus in his trials, Jesus told them that he was conferring on them a kingdom in the same way that his Father had conferred on him a kingdom. By conferring on the disciples a kingdom, Jesus told them that they were then to eat and drink at Jesus's table in his kingdom. Jesus was giving the disciples great standing and riches even while cautioning them that they were to remain servants to Jesus, one another, and others. They only needed to stand by Jesus in trials. Emboldened, Peter told Jesus that he would accompany him to prison and death, but Jesus cautioned Peter that Peter would deny Jesus in trial that very night.

She had faced trials of various kinds, as everyone does. Her trials she felt were not worse than the trials of others, although nor were they any easier. Trials are trials, difficult for whoever must face them. That's why we call them *trials*, she thought. She very much felt now that Jesus had stood by her then in those trials, even when she didn't fully know then of his presence nor appreciate then the difference that he was making to her in drawing her through and out of those trials. What she was still exploring today, though, was her capacity and commitment to stand by Jesus in trials. She was glad that *he* stood by *her*, but she also wanted him to be glad that *she* stood by *him* in his trials or the trials of others. She figured that he didn't really have trials of his own these days, having withstood the test of the greatest trials ever the night of his crucifixion. Yet she also figured that he stood trial of a different kind in the battles of faith that went on all around her every day. The trials were not over his outcome, which God long ago assured in his resurrection. The trials were instead over others' outcomes as people and circumstances challenged their faith. She figured that was the kind of trial in which she could stand by Jesus, trials of her own faith, trials of Jesus's truth, and trials of the fate of others. She wanted Jesus to appreciate that she had stood by him. She might, she realized, even receive a kingdom.

Serve Jesus. John 12:26.

Prior sections addressed Jesus's admonitions to be a servant, serve others, serve all, and serve others as Jesus serves us. Service to others is obviously important to Jesus. Jesus described several different forms of service such as healing the sick, providing shelter to the homeless, and visiting the prisoner, and then described great reward, indeed a kingdom, for that service. Yet Jesus also gives us a slightly different instruction about service that relates to our relationship with him. Jesus tells us not only to serve others and serve like he serves but also to serve *him*. Jesus speaks about *his servant*, telling us that to be *his servant*, we must follow him in order to *be where he is*, which of course would be true of any servant. What servant serves effectively from a distance? To be Jesus's servant requires proximity to him. We must remain close to him. Then, to be his servant requires that we *do* what he requires of us. We are not just to be near but to be active in his support, to carry out his wishes as a servant carries out the wishes of the master. Servants obey, and we are to be obedient to Jesus's wishes as a servant would be obedient to any other master. We must listen for Jesus's desires and be near enough to him to fulfill those desires.

Jesus had made his triumphal entry into Jerusalem during festival week to the acclaim of great crowds that had gathered on the testimony of those many who had seen Jesus raise Lazarus from the dead. Seeing the great crowds giving Jesus such acclaim, the religious leaders accelerated their plot to kill him. People who had come to worship at the festival from as far away as Greece were asking to see Jesus. In reply, Jesus said that the hour had come for his glory. He spoke of the need for the seed to die in order that it produces many other seeds. He repeated that people must reject their lives in this world if they wanted to receive eternal life by following and serving Jesus. "Whoever serves me must follow me; and where I am, my servant also will be," Jesus told the crowd, adding, "My Father will honor the one who serves me." Those who serve Jesus receive his Father's honor. Distressed then from facing his crucifixion, Jesus called out to the Father not to save him, because Jesus had come for this very purpose, but to glorify the Father's name through him. Just then, a voice rang from heaven that the Father had glorified his name and would do so again. Some in the crowd mistook the voice for thunder, while others attributed the voice to an angel who had spoken to Jesus.

He felt himself a servant by nature. At least, he liked to serve, even if the idea of a literal servant was odd in the modern context in which he lived and acted. He admitted that he probably would not like to be an actual servant, but still, the act of serving satisfied something in his nature or commitments. The only thing that troubled him from time to time about serving was that he might serve the wrong person or cause. He didn't want to serve evil but rather serve good. Distinguishing between the two, between good and evil, was sometimes easy but other times harder. That distinction was where he had grown to so much appreciate Jesus's command to serve *him*. As long as he served Jesus, he had no reason to worry about persons or causes. He had found a light, a guide star, an attitude, and an approach for service. In each setting in which he served, whether working, volunteering, caring for family or friends, or just in simple acts, he only needed to think of Jesus. As long as he was near in his thoughts and heart to Jesus, as long as he was following the instructions and commands of Jesus, he was fine with whomever or whatever he served. God would act in many people and causes among which he need not worry too greatly about distinguishing as long as he was following and serving Jesus.

Do what Jesus commands. John 15:14.

Jesus urges us to do as he says, specifically saying to obey his commands. At times, Jesus appears to give lessons, at other times instructions, and at other times warnings and cautions. Because of their generality and lack of specificity, some of the things that Jesus says may sound less like commands than observations or maybe recommendations. Yet Jesus is the authority, the King of kings, the Lord of lords, the Alpha and Omega, the First and Last. We have no basis on which to treat what Jesus says as anything other than or less than a command whenever what he says has a hint of *thou shall* in it. Jesus commands. He does not suggest, advise, or recommend. What then may surprise some is that Jesus conditions his love and approval, and indeed his friendship, on obedience to his commands. Some today define love as an unconditional attribute, something that one ought to do no matter what the other, the one loved, does. An unconditional-love approach may be appropriate in some other relationships, but unconditional love is not the way that Jesus defines our relationship with and to him. Jesus loves those who *obey* him. In Jesus's way, love is not solely or primarily an emotion or sentiment but instead a criterion-based action. Similarly, some today define friendship as a relationship without judgment. Judgment-free friendship may be appropriate in some relationships but not in our relationship with and to Jesus. Jesus instead defines friendship as appropriate only for those who do what he commands. In Jesus's way, friendship is not an unconditional gift but instead a criterion-based status. Jesus's love and friendship is robust and mature, even tough and strong, if you prefer, not sentimental. Do as Jesus commands, and he will shower you with love and friendship.

Jesus had spoken at the Last Supper of the vine and its branches and about the disciples' need to remain in him. He urged the disciples to keep his commands so that they would remain in his love, just in the way that Jesus kept his Father's commands and so remained in his Father's love. Jesus told the disciples to keep his commands because he wanted the disciples to share his joy, to have Jesus's joy in them. Jesus was offering them something very different from a harsh master looking only for arm's length obedience.

Instead, Jesus said, "You are my friends if you do what I command. I no longer call you servants, because a servant does not know his master's business. Instead, I have called you friends, for everything that I learned from my Father I have made known to you." By telling the disciples just what the Father had told him, Jesus was making friends of the disciples, a friendship fostered on obeying Jesus's commands, just as Jesus fostered the love of his Father by obeying his Father's commands. One does not love without obedience, just as one is not a friend without obedience. Jesus wanted the voluntary love and friendship of the disciples submitting to light-giving and life-giving commands, not grudging obedience to harsh commands.

He had no problem with commands, with obeying authority. Indeed, he knew that he probably needed authority and especially authoritative commands, whether for cultural, personality, or even hereditary reasons, into which he had no insight and cared for none. He just respected properly constituted authority, particularly when that authority was giving beneficent commands. When he had first studied and followed Jesus, he had immediately seen that Jesus often spoke as a commander spoke, which had surprised him because *commander* is not the image that secular culture or even faith culture usually gives Jesus. Yet Jesus seemed to him to be giving commands right and left, even if he was not necessarily expecting the disciples, crowds, and religious leaders to carry them out promptly. Indeed, the opposite seemed true that Jesus, while clearly a commander of unprecedented insight, power, confidence, courage, and authority, fully did *not* expect many others to carry out his commands, indeed seemed to expect and predict that only a very few would do so and mostly only after his extraordinarily un-commander-like demise. And so as he studied Jesus and grew closer to him, he discerned that Jesus was the Supreme Commander who, save for his many miracles, had momentarily, and completely voluntarily without any coercion or necessity other than the necessity of accomplishing his strangely wondrous missions, relinquished much of his command. He, at least, was going to turn his obedience to Jesus, obeying everything that he could discern and construe as a command.

Do what Jesus did. John 14:12.

Jesus's admonition to do as he had been doing, or to do what Jesus would do, makes such perfect sense that the admonition is a well-worn slogan. We ask what Jesus would do, and then we go do it. Jesus is our model. If his admonition to do as he did makes a good slogan and if that slogan makes a good handy formula, then we should appreciate the convenience and clarity of the admonition turned slogan turned formula. Do as Jesus did. We need only have a good knowledge of his plans, intentions, and actions, and then generalize, specify, or construe those actions into our own circumstances. Of course, knowing how to do what Jesus did presents a considerable challenge that we meet by first believing Jesus and then studying and serving Jesus while listening to the Holy Spirit. Do-as-Jesus-did is anything but a formula. It instead implies many things including primarily a very close relationship. Yet the wondrous thing about that admonition to do as Jesus did, and that relationship with Jesus on which doing so depends so deeply, is that Jesus did not merely say that we would do as he did. He further predicted that those who believe in him will both do the works that he was doing *and even greater things*.

At the Last Supper, Philip had wanted Jesus to show the disciples the Father. One hears Jesus's disappointment in his response to Philip that Philip still did not know him after such a long acquaintance. Jesus had to tell Philip and the disciples again that Jesus was in the Father and the Father in Jesus. When they saw Jesus, they saw the Father. Indeed, because the Father lived in Jesus, the Father was doing his work in Jesus. Jesus told Philip and the disciples that if they couldn't believe Jesus's words that the Father was in Jesus that they should believe the Father's miracles through Jesus. Jesus could not do the miracles he did without the Father doing those miracles in him. Here, though, Jesus turned the teaching in a way that might have surprised the disciples. By believing in Jesus, the disciples would do the works that Jesus had been doing. Indeed, Jesus took it one step further, saying, "Very truly I tell you, whoever believes in me will do the works I have been doing, and they will do *even greater things* than these, because I am going to the

Father." Jesus would no longer be on earth to do his good works directly. The disciples would remain to do even greater things, carrying the teaching, healing, and salvation of Jesus around the world.

She like everyone else had long heard the phrase *what would Jesus do* and of course seen a few of her friends or others whom she knew wear the WWJD bracelets. She respected the idea and the people who pursued it. Indeed, she counted herself among those fortunate people, even if she didn't wear the bracelet. Her challenge, though, was not so much in remembering to ask the question *what would Jesus do*. Her challenge instead was the challenge that she suspected others had, even those who wore the bracelets, which was actually discerning what Jesus would do in each situation when she thought again of answering that fundamental question. She often wondered what Jesus *would* do. She wasn't asking herself that question in disrespect for Jesus or for the question. She was instead honestly asking herself how she could possibly discern, or how she best and most consistently discern, what Jesus would do in any given situation. She knew that the answer lay in part in knowing what Jesus *did* when *he* faced various situations and then also in part in knowing what Jesus *said to do* as to various situations and relationships. She thought of this question over and over, what *would* Jesus do, until she decided to make a thorough study of it. She wanted to be able to answer that most-important question and then do as the answer indicated. She wanted *what would Jesus do* to be more than a slogan.

Feed Jesus's sheep. John 21:17.

One gospel ends with the touching account of the resurrected Jesus restoring Peter after Peter's denial of Jesus during Jesus's trial. During Jesus's conversation with Peter, Jesus admonished Peter successively to feed Jesus's lambs, take care of his sheep, and feed his sheep. Whether or not the slight differences in Jesus's three successive admonitions to Peter are consequential, their general implication seems clear. Jesus instructs us to feed and care for those who follow Jesus. Jesus's reference to his sheep would naturally mean Jesus's followers. Jesus had told parables of the shepherd leading his sheep by the sound of his voice. Jesus is the shepherd, and we are his sheep. When Jesus instructs to feed and care for his sheep, he must mean more than to provide literal food, drink, and shelter, although he may also mean that. He very likely means to share his word with those who would follow him. The food and drink with which Jesus was most concerned were his body and blood, and his words leading others to eternal life with him. We are to teach, exhort, instruct, guide, and counsel those who would follow Jesus, using Jesus's words, sharing his gospel message. Feed Jesus's sheep with the words of Jesus.

After his resurrection and first visits to the disciples, Jesus had appeared once again to a group of the disciples on the short of the Sea of Galilee. The group had fished at night without catching anything. As they returned to shore in the early morning, Jesus had called to them from the shore to throw their nets out one last time on the boat's right side. The disciples did not yet know that Jesus had given them the advice, but they tried anyway, catching an enormous haul. John just then realized that Jesus had been the one to call out. Peter jumped into the water to rush to Jesus at John's startled exclamation. On shore, Jesus had bread for them and a fire ready to cook some fish for breakfast. After they ate, Jesus asked Peter, who had denied Jesus during Jesus's trial just before his crucifixion, whether Peter loved Jesus. Peter answered that he did. Jesus then told Peter to *feed his lambs.* Jesus asked Peter again whether he loved him, and when Peter said that he did, Jesus answered again *take care of my sheep.* Jesus asked and Peter answered a third time, after which Jesus said, "Feed my sheep." After speaking to Peter about his end, Jesus told Peter to follow him, which he did, as did John. The gospel account ends saying that Jesus did many other things, so many that the world would not have room for the books they would fill.

She had a very soft place in her soul for sheep, for the funny, timid, wooly animals to whom Jesus often referred. Her family had taken a photograph of her holding a lamb on her grandparents' farm when she was young. In that photograph, she is struggling to clutch the long lamb as it slides from her arms, but even as she struggles to

399

hold the lamb up, a huge grin spreads across her face with her eyes half-closed in pleasure. Other than those few times on her grandparents' farm, she did nothing with sheep either growing up or when an adult, even though for a good time she worked on farms, just not on farms that had sheep. She saw sheep from time to time on nearby farms just enough to confirm that, in addition to being very timid and easily frightened, sheep were easily misled and not very smart. In other words, she learned that sheep were a lot like us. She also learned, as Jesus's parables implied, that sheep indeed respond only to their shepherd, to one whom they know and trust, which is probably necessary for their survival, given how acutely limited they are in their understanding and interpretation of their surroundings. Somehow, this combination of insights and experiences led her to the point of seeing Jesus's gospel message more through the sheep perspective with which Jesus instructed Peter than any of his many other perspectives. Indeed, she could not read the gospel account of Jesus's restoration of Peter without weeping over its perfect blend of the essential with tenderness.

2.3 The Holy Spirit

Receive the Holy Spirit. John 20:22. *Stay in the Spirit.* Matthew 25:4. *Wait for the Spirit's power.* Luke 24:49. *Never speak against the Holy Spirit.* Matthew 12:32.

We know much from Jesus's instruction about the relationship that we must maintain, may maintain, and have the privilege and impossibly grand opportunity to maintain, with the Father and Son. How perfect, and yet perfectly surprising, God's plan was to enter the world that he created and governs through an incorporeal Son. And how necessary, and yet necessarily awful, God's plan was to sacrifice his Son to save that world from the corruption that entered with our will to choose evil over good. How mysterious, and yet mysteriously comforting, then, is God's plan to inform us of his plans and purposes through the Holy Spirit present in the flame-intense love between Father and Son. We know far less of the Holy Spirit than we know of the Father and Son. At least, Jesus tells us much less about the Holy Spirit than about the Father and about how to relate to him, the Son. We should not, on the other hand, make the same mistake that the crowds, the religious leaders, and even the disciples so often made with Jesus and the Father. When we read about Jesus, learn about Jesus, hear about Jesus, and see Jesus, we also know the Holy Spirit. The Holy Spirit is, like Jesus is in relationship to the Father, all of Jesus and of the Father, three in one. The mystery of the Trinity is one that this inquiry cannot in the least address. All we have to do here instead is to listen with care to the little that Jesus taught about the Holy Spirit, knowing that we have much more to learn about the Holy Spirit from the life and image of Jesus.

Receive the Holy Spirit. John 20:22.

Jesus's instruction to receive the Holy Spirit is at once among his most striking, attractive, mysterious, and even perplexing statements. In his earthly ministry before his crucifixion and resurrection, he had rarely referred to the Holy Spirit and only once clearly spoke at some length of the Holy Spirit in ways that the disciples might well have then readily understood. On the other hand, the disciples and others had several demonstrations of the Holy Spirit both during Jesus's three-year public ministry and after Jesus's crucifixion and resurrection. The most striking early demonstration of the Spirit would have been the Spirit's descent on Jesus like a dove from heaven as Jesus rose from the water at his baptism, marked by the Father's words proclaiming Jesus his Son. The signal post-resurrection demonstration of the Spirit was of course at Pentecost when the Spirit's flames descended on hundreds who instantly witnessed for Jesus in many languages. These and other demonstrations framed Jesus's explanation at the Last Supper that his Father would send the Holy Spirit as the Advocate for all that Jesus himself had attested. Jesus explicitly said to receive the Spirit, when in the following gospel account Jesus gave the Spirit to the disciples in another manner. We have this extraordinary privilege of welcoming God's Spirit into us, into our hearts, minds, and souls, to inform us of kingdom things, of God's workings. Thus our relationship to the Spirit is of critical concern in our ability to hear and follow Jesus. Receive the Spirit, just as Jesus commands.

The resurrected Jesus surprised and overjoyed the disciples when he first appeared to them shortly after his resurrection. The disciples were still hiding in a large room with the door locked for fear of arrest by the religious leaders. That morning, the third day after Jesus's crucifixion, one of the women had visited Jesus's tomb, seen it empty, and then encountered Jesus outside the tomb, mistaking him at first for a gardener. Revealing himself to her, Jesus had told her to go tell the disciples that he was ascending to the Father, his God and their God. She had rushed back to the disciples with the news that she had seen the Lord, only to have Jesus appear to the disciples, too, that very evening. Jesus showed the disciples his scarred hands and side, telling them that peace would be with them and that he was sending them as the Father had sent him. Jesus then breathed on them, saying, "Receive the Holy Spirit." He then told the disciples that if the disciples forgave anyone's sins, those sins are forgiven, adding that if the disciples did not forgive, then those sins are not forgiven. Jesus then left as he had come. Thomas, who was not with the other disciples when Jesus had appeared, joined them later, refusing to believe what they had told him. A week later, Jesus appeared again through the locked door, showing himself to Thomas, who then believed. Jesus said that those who did not see him but believed nonetheless, God would bless.

He had the sense of the Spirit's indwelling from time to time, although he rightly questioned any too-direct sense of someone who after all was Spirit rather than substance or form. He had once even asked a wise pastor whether the Spirit had a body or form as Jesus had body, form, image, and identity. The wise pastor had said of course the Spirit has form and image, indeed precisely the body, form, image, and identity of Jesus. Hadn't the Spirit descended onto and into Jesus at his baptism? Hadn't Jesus breathed on the disciples to convey the Spirit out of Jesus's own body and form? While these explanations helped him grasp that the Spirit was indeed one in the divine Trinity, one with the Father and Son, and helped him accept that the Spirit was a person rather than some emotion, force, principle, material, or gas, he nonetheless left room for the Spirit to be whomever the Father and Son wished. He welcomed, indeed treasured, the Holy Spirit. He hoped that the Spirit dwelt richly in him. He hoped that the Spirit was speaking constantly to his mind about Jesus and the love between the Father and Son, but he would still leave to God just how and where the Spirit resided and acted.

Stay in the Spirit. Matthew 25:4.

Once having received the Spirit of God from Jesus, we must remain in the Spirit through study of God's word. While stating anything certain relating to the Spirit may be difficult or lead to contention, the conclusion seems reasonable that we do not simply receive the Spirit once and then forever retain the full power and presence of the Spirit without respect to our continuing beliefs, practices, and habits. Again, while certainty over things of the Spirit is probably not available to us, the conclusion seems reasonable and apparent that just as our devotion to Jesus may grow or wane, the Spirit's power and presence in us may also grow or wane. A special parable that Jesus told the disciples, recounted below, appears to confirm these tentative conclusions. Studying God's word renews the Spirit within us. God's word feeds the Spirit, who anoints the reader's mind to draw insight, meaning, and courage from the words of Jesus. We must not only *receive* the Spirit but also *remain in* the Spirit. Make commitments and follow practices that help you stay in the Spirit and the Spirit stay in you.

Jesus hinted in the parable of the ten virgins about staying in the Spirit after receiving the Spirit. In the parable, one of several parables and lessons that Jesus gave to the disciples on the Mount of Olives late in his public ministry, ten virgins, five foolish and five wise, went out to meet the bridegroom. The five foolish virgins took lamps but not oil. "The wise ones, however," Jesus continued, "took oil in jars along with their lamps." The bridegroom came very late, not until midnight. The wise virgins trimmed their lamps to see and welcome the bridegroom, but the foolish virgins missed the bridegroom while they were going to buy oil. The bridegroom took the wise virgins into the banquet, shut the door, and later refused to open it for the foolish virgins who finally returned with their oil. Jesus ended with the parable's lesson to *keep watch* because no one knows the day or hour of the bridegroom's arrival. Many interpret the oil to represent the anointing of the Holy Spirit and believe the bridegroom, of course, to represent Jesus. Jesus implied to the disciples that the wise study God's words, receive the Spirit, and remain alert and prepared to recognize and welcome Jesus. Jesus also implied that the foolish do not study God's words but instead relinquish the Spirit, lose faith, and miss the coming of Jesus.

She had, she admitted, competing views of what it meant to stay *in the Spirit*. She had known others who were always speaking of Jesus, who seemed at every turn in their lives to be thinking about Jesus and in some sense reflecting him to others. They reflected Jesus to others in the many church, mission, and service activities to which they devoted their time and energies but also in the frequent testimonies that they gave about Jesus in their activities that did not so obviously center on church, mission, and service, such as in their illnesses, families, schooling, or workplace. She believed that these individuals, so soaked in Christian faith and so outwardly confessing and professing, were likely remaining *in the Spirit*. On the other hand, she knew others whose outward lives were less obviously devoted to Jesus but who nonetheless carried a quietly powerful Christian witness. These individuals had church homes but did not so plainly live in the church and breathe witness to Jesus as her outwardly professing acquaintances seemed to do. She still believed that these quiet Christians were likely remaining *in the Spirit*. They still discerned and interpreted events and relationships through the gospel message, and still did some church work, much Bible study, and lots of quiet service work. Both the outward and inward Christians she knew were also deeply concerned about, and in their very different ways effective at, helping the Spirit and word of God bring others to Christ. In the end, she hoped that she fell somewhere between the two groups, outward and inward, but no matter where she fell wanted to be sure that she remained enough in God's word to feel the powerful presence of the Spirit.

Wait for the Spirit's power. Luke 24:49.

To receive and remain in the Spirit should produce some sense and effect of one's possessing the Spirit's power. Jesus said so. After years of instructing the disciples, and then after the tumultuous, frightening, and amazing events of Jesus's crucifixion, burial, and resurrection, Jesus gave the disciples one last instruction. When the teacher is Jesus, one might be wrong to give any one instruction more weight than another. Just because Jesus's admonition to wait for the Spirit's power was his *last* instruction may not mean it was any *greater* instruction than any other. Yet effective teachers follow a rule of primacy and recency. They start and end with the most important points. Jesus had said little about the Holy Spirit until the Last Supper, when he had for the first time been perfectly clear that the disciples would receive the Advocate, the Holy Spirit, from the Father, after Jesus ascended to the Father. His last instruction, though, coming after his resurrection and just before his ascension, was that the disciples should wait for the Holy Spirit's power. That instruction, that last command and invitation, is a special one, no doubt. The disciples would have known from the Old Testament that special things happened when the Spirit briefly came on certain ancient figures, whether judges, kings, or prophets. Now here was Jesus promising again that *they* would receive the Holy Spirit and, with the Holy Spirit, the Holy Spirit's extraordinary power. This, the disciples must have realized in such great anticipation as to approach ecstasy, was *going to be special*. Perhaps you know now, if you hadn't already known, how the disciples would turn almost instantly from cowards hiding behind locked doors into fearless witnesses almost gleefully confronting the most fearsome adversaries whom the disciples knew would kill them. Wait for the Spirit's power.

It would according to one gospel account be his last teaching, last instruction, and last command to the disciples before his ascension. Jesus had startled, frightened, and amazed the disciples with his appearance after his crucifixion and his burial in the tomb, even though the women and the two men who had walked to Emmaus with Jesus had already told them of his resurrection. To convince them that he was alive and that he was Jesus, he had both to show them his scars and eat a piece of broiled fish in their presence. Then opening their minds, Jesus taught them yet again how he and the events that had just occurred fulfilled the scriptures. As witnesses to these things, they were now to preach repentance and forgiveness to all nations in his name. Then Jesus gave them that one last instruction, following hundreds of prior instructions. Jesus said, "I am going to send you what my Father has promised; but stay in the city until you have been clothed with power from on high." His Father had promised the disciples the Advocate, the Holy Spirit, who just a short while hence at Pentecost would come in the sound of a roaring wind and in the form of many flames descending on the heads of many believers.

He was naturally timid, he and everyone else knew. Every circumstance of his life seemed to have contributed to and amplified his naturally cowardly disposition. Some of it was genetics, his small size and slight frame taking after his spritely and timorous grandmother. Some of it involved the not-so-cowardly and instead overbearing disposition of his parents, dominating him into submissiveness. Some of it was his place within his family under cousins and siblings whose many artistic talents and interests further hid what little aptitude and identity he might have claimed if anyone had been listening. Some of it was his own fault that he was too ready to succumb, turn away from challenges, hide, and hope no one noticed. Yet for all his timidity, yes all of the inherited, environmental, claimed, and developed defects, he somehow found a voice, developed a skill, heard a calling, formed a ministry, and gained the standing to represent Jesus. Although he accomplished very little else, what he accomplished in that respect would have shocked anyone who knew him, who knew his origins, certainly any family member but also many old teachers, neighbors, friends, and enemies. He was equally certain as anyone else would have been that a small miracle had happened in his accomplishing anything, no less so many things. The only difference in their view would have been that he knew to a certainty of his mysterious power's source in the Holy Spirit. He had waited for the power of the Holy Spirit.

Never speak against the Holy Spirit. Matthew 12:32.

Jesus said in many ways and contexts that he came to forgive rather than to condemn. He demonstrated the depths and lengths of his salvation mission, in forgiving the thief on the cross next to him. One can plainly live a fruitless life, one devoid of witness to Jesus, and yet at the last moment still gain entry through Jesus to God's kingdom, indeed into the paradise that Jesus promised the thief that very day of their death by crucifixion. Such is the wonder of Jesus's saving mission. Jesus himself said that a person could commit every kind of sin and still gain entry into God's kingdom. Nonetheless, Jesus at one point warned that although one could even deride Jesus, at least for a time, without losing hope of the kingdom, one must not speak against and reject the Holy Spirit, the consequence of which is never to receive forgiveness. One cannot deny the only one, the Holy Spirit, who leads persons to Jesus, and still reach Jesus. Jesus was likely not suggesting a formal offense, words against the Spirit, for which God decides never to forgive even when a person accepts Jesus. Rather, Jesus was likely instructing that those who reject the Spirit never confess Jesus because the Spirit is the only agent for inducing confession. The context of the following account, involving religious leaders who rejected God's Spirit while calling the Spirit's work the work of Satan, supports that interpretation that we need the Spirit to accept Jesus. Do not reject the Spirit because you will then inevitably reject Jesus. Remain in the Spirit, and you will remain in Jesus.

Jesus had healed the blind and mute man so swiftly and miraculously that some in the attending crowd wondered aloud whether Jesus might be the coming of the Son of David. The religious leaders who heard the comments scoffed that Jesus was healing by demon power, not God power. Jesus rebuked the religious leaders, pointing out that demons do not do God's work, and that if God's Spirit was doing this healing work, then the kingdom of God had indeed come. Jesus added that people are either with him or against him, none staying neutral. People either do Jesus's work or work against Jesus. As to the Spirit of God, Jesus told them that every kind of sin God can forgive, except that God does not forgive blasphemy against the Spirit. Jesus added, "Anyone who speaks a word against the Son of Man will be forgiven, but anyone who speaks against the Holy Spirit will not be forgiven, either in this age or in the age to come." The religious leaders could insult Jesus, but they had better not insult the Holy Spirit. Jesus ended the rebuke by saying that they would have to account on judgment day for every word they spoke, and that their words would condemn them.

She had heard of the unpardonable sin and, like most others who had heard of it, worried whether she had committed it. The sin, she knew, involved speaking against the Holy Spirit. So she tried to think of any moment that she could recall when she had criticized the Holy Spirit. As hard as she tried, she could think of none. She thought that she had probably foolishly taken the Lord's name in vain long ago, maybe even on more than one occasion, if not quite so profanely as she had heard others do, then at least obliquely. Yet she remembered that the Bible passage about not blaspheming the Spirit said at the same time that one could still receive forgiveness for speaking against Jesus. She would have guessed so even if the Bible had not said the latter because so many people did come to Jesus after having rejected him, as the thief on the cross had even done, the one who joined Jesus in paradise. In the end, though, she decided that the warning against blaspheming the Spirit was probably not a formal warning but rather a substantive warning. A slip of the tongue was not the point, she was pretty sure. Jesus looked at the heart. As long as she never spoke vile condemnations of the Holy Spirit out of her heart, as the religious leaders had done comparing the Spirit to Satan when Jesus condemned them, which of course she was miles from ever doing, then she figured she would be alright. She still had Jesus's pardon because she still had the Spirit who first led her to Jesus.

2.4 Yourself

Lose your life. Luke 17:33. *Do not love your life.* John 12:25. *Hate your life.* Luke 14:26. *Do not seek to please yourself.* John 5:30. *Deny yourself.* Matthew 16:24. *Do nothing on your own.* John 8:28. *Give up everything.* Luke 14:33. *Take your cross.* Matthew 10:38. *Carry your cross.* Luke 14:27. *Enter by the gate.* John 10:1. *Enter by the narrow door.* Luke 13:24. *Do not look back.* Luke 9:62. *Repent for the kingdom.* Matthew 4:17. *Repent or perish.* Luke 13:5. *Repent at preaching.* Luke 11:32. *Repent and believe the gospel.* Mark 1:15. *Be perfect.* Matthew 5:48. *Walk in the light.* John 12:35. *Weep.* Luke 6:21. *Weep for yourself.* Luke 23:28.

Your next most-important relationship after relationship with the Father, Son, and Holy Spirit may well be relationship with you, meaning the way that you think about yourself. Jesus had much to teach, command, and instruct about how one thinks about one's own nature and status, position and privileges, and rights and responsibilities. How we each behave depends a lot on how we think about who we are, who or what we hope to become, what is important to us, what others owe to us, and what we owe to others. Frankly, the world is not all about us, at least to anyone other than ourselves. Yet each one of us is important to God, again so important that God gave his Son for each of us, no one of us more than another of us. And of course, we are or tend to feel important to ourselves. We each have only one life to live, and that life is *our* life, not someone else's life, except that we each have great opportunity to lay down our life for God. We cannot live another's life, although we sometimes try, and others cannot live our life for us, although we sometimes want them to or they sometimes try. Listen then to what Jesus instructs about how you should think about and live your life. Develop an ear and sensitivity for how you think about yourself.

411

Lose your life. Luke 17:33.

The first relationship that one might assume toward one's own life is to lose it. Jesus's admonition to lose one's life is certainly arresting the first time one hears it and then several times thereafter. How, after all, does one lose one's own life? Isn't life instead a matter of pursuing and finding one's life as secular culture so strongly and effectively promotes today? Jesus clearly said that the way to gain one's life is to lose it, while the way to lose it is to try to hold onto it. While his message initially seems counter intuitive, on deeper thought it makes great sense. Each of has only limited imagination for what we might do and accomplish. Really, how far can any of us see into our future? God has no such limitation. He sees things for us and brings things to us of which we are capable even if well beyond our imagination. When Jesus says to lose one's life, he very likely means to lose one's life to God who will return the unique life for which he made each of us. Another problem with holding onto one's own life, beyond a lack of imagination, is that we naturally skew our vision for our own life toward ourselves. If God fulfilled only what we dreamed for ourselves, we would live highly narcissistic lives, more self-involved than we already are even when we try instead to commit our lives to God. We will always remain self-involved because, after all, we only lead our own lives. Committing one's life to God's care and feeding, rather than grasping and pursuing it on one's own, is our only hope for gaining real and eternal life rather than artificial and deadly life.

According to one gospel account, Jesus made the same or very similar statement twice in different settings through different lessons. In the later of the two accounts, occurring late in Jesus's public ministry, the religious leaders had asked Jesus when God's kingdom would come, as if its coming was an event external to them. Jesus corrected them that the kingdom is not something to stand back and observe. One wouldn't be able to point it out, to say *here it is* or *there it is*. Instead, Jesus explained, the kingdom of God is right in our very midst, as if it to say that the kingdom was in the air or atmosphere in and around us. Jesus then turned to his disciples to remind them that life was just going on normally when the great flood came for which only Noah had prepared. The same was true when fire and sulfur rained down on Sodom, after only Lot and his family had fled and escaped. Jesus said the same remained true right then for the disciples, although it would not be flood or fire but God's revealing of the Son or Man. Jesus reminded them not to look back at their old lives as Lot's wife had done, losing her life because she had not looked forward with the rest of her family to new life. Jesus said, "Whoever tries to keep their life will lose it, and whoever loses their life will preserve it." The disciples must persist in their new kingdom life with Jesus, leaving their old life behind.

While he knew others who would resist, even strongly resist, the idea of giving up their lives, he immediately understood the great value of the instruction. Those others whom he knew would insist on pursuing their own lives would, he also believed, not end up with the lives that they desired. Well, they *would* end up with the lives that they desired, but those lives would *not* be what they had thought they would be. Their lives would certainly not be all or even nearly all that they could have been, he knew from having observed those lives. They would instead in the end be lonely lives, in certain ways even desperate lives, lives that did not warm, embrace, and fulfill the one who lived the life or those who lived around them. Their lives would miss the one great connection that everyone needs for a life to be worthwhile, meaning fulfilled in the grand cosmic and eternal sense. Every life, he believed from experience, observation, instruction, and conviction, had the capacity for divinity, to reach, touch, and connect with the one Forerunner and Creator of all things, who is not only the First but who will be the Last and Forever. To him, to lead a life without accepting that Creator's invitation is not simply to lead a less-desirable life, not simply to lead a life that is something less than all that it could have been, but rather is to *waste* a life, *throw away* a life. To live one's life grasping to one's self-pursuits is to die rather than live, to accept momentary illusions for eternal reality. He had no special confidence that he was in fact living for God rather than for himself. Indeed, he strongly suspected that he was not much if any more successful than others in getting past his natural self-determination. But he knew that he had made that commitment and was going to follow through on it, God help him.

413

Do not love your life. John 12:25.

Jesus gives a closely related but slightly different instruction when he says not only to lose your life but not to *love* your life. The insight with this instruction not to love one's life may be that loving one's life is precisely the obstacle to losing one's life to God's better designs. Knowing that eternal profound life is available to us at Jesus's invitation, why would we choose anything else? The answer may lie again in our limited vision, but this time not our vision for what we want but for what we *have*. When we love our present life, including the small or large satisfactions, achievements, comforts, and securities that it brings, we begin then to lose vision and appetite for a life that we could love much more. Let's face it: some lives bring great present outward satisfaction. Cue here the many images of the pleasures and privileges of the extraordinarily rich and famous, although we also know that quiet lives of simple solitude can bring great satisfaction. Yet even the ones living those rare lives of extraordinary public fame and material riches, or those almost perfectly ordered and peaceful lives of quiet solitude, have not achieved a fraction of what Jesus offers us in eternal life in God's kingdom, not the tiniest of fractions. Infinity has no partial measure. No slice of time compares to eternity. Enjoy what God gives you, but do not *love* it as if it was your own and only life. Do not let love for your present life become an obstacle to receiving eternal life in God's kingdom.

Jesus was teaching for his last public time at the festival in Jerusalem. He of course knew that his hour had come and also knew that he must further prepare the disciples for his departure. So Jesus interrupted as the disciples continued to bring worshippers to Jesus in their usual efforts trying to manage the crowds and support new believers. Rather than accept more curious visitors, Jesus told the disciples that his hour had come. He explained that a seed must die and fall to the ground to produce the many seeds for which God intended it. Jesus then said something similar to what he had said before but with an emphasis that may have surprised the disciples.

"Anyone who loves their life will lose it," Jesus said in a familiar refrain, but added, "while anyone who hates their life in this world will keep it for eternal life." The disciples must *hate* their lives in this world in order to keep their lives for eternity in the kingdom. Jesus then acknowledged to the disciples that his own soul was troubled at the thought of his impending death, as their souls must also be troubled. But he also said that he would not turn away from the Father's desire for him because he had come out of the Father's desire. The Father's voice thundered down from heaven in affirmation.

She loved her life in small ways, indeed in some large ways. Oh sure, her life had challenges like any life has challenges and not just small challenges but rather bigger challenges. She actually felt that her life was large, privileged, and blessed while at the same time and in its own way limited and difficult, just the way that she imagined most others felt even if she also knew that every life was quite different. She would not have traded her life with anyone, although her life had problems, annoyances, challenges, and issues that other lives did not have and that she would have readily given up if given the opportunity. Yet she still had so many small and warming conveniences, pleasures, supports, comforts, friendships, and fellowships that in all, she knew what Jesus meant that one could love one's life. She could fairly easily love her life, just as she could see that many others could love their lives, indeed *did* love their lives. Still, she knew that she did not *really* love her life and should not really love her life, against which Jesus had after all clearly admonished. She knew what small shift her outlook need only take toward loving her life and also knew what the outcome of that small shift would be. She discerned that the moment that she started to love the pleasures with which God blessed her more than she loved God that those pleasures would capture her, diminish her love for God, and then dissipate themselves into meaningless activities. She knew that her life must remain rooted in eternity if it was to have any value to her, to others, and to God, at all.

415

Hate your life. Luke 14:26.

To hate one's life is an extraordinary instruction, one that probably bears careful reading. In so saying, Jesus probably did not intend us to become the kind of chronic, downcast, immature whiners and complainers that we sometimes are. We need to count blessings, not count insults, offenses, and indignities. To hate one's life must not mean to find everything wrong with one's life and then express those shortcomings loudly and frequently to others. Jesus must instead have meant something much more like what the context suggests, which is that we must see that his life, the life that he gives us back for giving up our own, would naturally make us feel revulsion for anything less. We must stop desiring any life or relationship as if it could possibly compare favorably to life and relationship in Jesus. We must instead see it in contrast to Jesus's life and relationship as repulsive, as loathsome. We should and do love parents, spouse, children, and siblings. Only when the question turns to pursuing those relationships *over relationship with Jesus* should we instead see those relationships, and any other, as distasteful. When instead we turn fully to Jesus and Jesus gives us eternal life, we may once again embrace life and relationship in and through him in complete love and without speck of hate revulsion, dislike, distaste, or loathing. Loathe life until you receive Jesus, and then celebrate life with and through him.

Jesus had been traveling from town to town, eating in homes into which the religious leaders or others invited him, and teaching wherever he went. Large crowds began not just to form wherever he stopped but also to *travel with him*, indicating indisputably how transformative his message was to those who heard and received it. Today, we consider and sometimes accept Jesus's invitation to walk with him, largely considering his offer to invite and involve our figurative acceptance. Then, people in droves were *literally* leaving their everyday lives and activities behind simply to walk with, watch, and listen to Jesus. The spectacle must have been extraordinary, the opportunity even more so. On one of those occasions when a large crowd was walking along with Jesus, he turned to the crowd, evidently as they still walked along, to teach and warn about the sacrifice that comes with true devotion to Jesus. Jesus first said to them, "If anyone comes to me and does not hate father and mother, wife and children, brothers and sisters—yes, even their own life—such a person cannot be my disciple." One wonders whether some in the large crowd stopped to think of having to hate their own life, and maybe even stopped following and turned away from Jesus. Jesus then added that they must count the cost of following him, like a builder counts the cost of constructing a tower or a king counts the cost of going to war. He concluded the sobering lesson with the statement that those who did not give up everything to follow him could not be his disciples. Discipleship required hating one's life.

Jesus's instruction to hate one's life presented a new challenge for him. His problem was not so much that he loved his life. He liked some things about his life but not others. He knew that in many ways he led an extraordinarily privileged life like so many other first-world lives are extraordinarily privileged. His challenges were mostly first-world challenges, meaning that individuals living outside first-world circumstances would not have regarded them as significant challenges or even as challenges at all, instead likely as privileges. As comfortable and secure as his life was, and as blessed as his life certainly was, he still did not feel any strong urge to pursue and preserve it. He could at least say with some sense of commitment that he would be only too happy to lose his life in favor of a life with Jesus, whatever life Jesus had for him, even though he also suspected that his commitment and willingness to lose his life were not as strong as he could make it sound. Nonetheless, his problem was not so much in *not loving* his life as it was in *hating* his life. What did hating his life even mean? As he kept thinking about it, he decided that he must be surer than he had previously been that he not hold to those first-world privileges. He must in some sense activate his guard against loving privileges by actually *disliking* them. Maybe the lesson he should draw, he concluded, was that actively disliking and denying privilege was acceptable, even right. He could do more than make *not loving* his life a theory. He could practice active dislike of the specific things to which Jesus may have been referring when instructing to hate a life. His challenge then was to discern those things to hate, and in privileges, he already had a target.

Do not seek to please yourself. John 5:30.

The admonition not to seek one's own pleasure probably has a much deeper meaning than we give it. On its surface, it might seem merely like a wise warning against a sort of deadly narcissism, like seeking *too much* pleasure undoes a person. We might think for instance of drug abusers and alcoholics killing themselves in pursuit of addictions. Yet in the following gospel account, Jesus intimates a deeper meaning than that secular wisdom. God the Father, and Jesus the Son, have life *in themselves* whereas we draw life only from them. We obviously do not have life *in ourselves*. We cannot on our own raise ourselves or anyone else back to life after death. We are finite and natural beings only when we are without God and his divinity, inherent life, and eternity. Thus when we seek to inject life into our own lives, pursuing fulfillment of life's natural pleasures, we are attempting the impossible. Because we cannot without God infuse life into our lives, we cannot without seeking God create, sustain, and satisfy desires for pleasures. If we were inherent beings, beings with innate life, not sustained from the outside but supernaturally alive from the inside, then perhaps we could create, sustain, and satisfy our desires for our own pleasures, although query how deeply unsatisfying such an inward life would probably be. But doing so is impossible given our limitations without the life God grants us and sustains in us. We must not seek to please ourselves because we cannot do so.

The religious leaders were already after Jesus early in his public ministry, particularly for healing on the Sabbath. In response, Jesus gave them an elaborate teaching on why he acted as he did perfectly consistent with the Father's wishes. He told them that he could do only what his Father wished. Jesus would raise the dead just as the Father raises the dead, Jesus told the religious leaders. Jesus would do so because just as the Father had life *in himself* rather than from another source, so too, the Father had given Jesus life *in himself* making him capable of raising the dead. Jesus told the religious leaders to set aside their amazement at what he had just said. The time was coming, he told them, when the dead would indeed rise, the do-gooders to eternal life and the evildoers to condemnation. Jesus concluded that part of his long lesson saying, "By myself I can do nothing; I judge only as I hear, and my judgment is just, for I seek not to please myself but him who sent me." Jesus was not seeking to please himself in accepting the Father's life and using it to give life to others. He instead sought to please only the Father who sent him.

She wrestled some, as she saw others wrestle, with the question of pleasure versus denial. She had long believed that God offered simple pleasures to show the good of his creation. She didn't want to refuse what God offered and in doing so take an unholy pride. She understood not to pursue and indulge pleasures, and few or none would have accused her of doing so. She knew others who seemed to pursue, in fact did pursue, pleasures to a much greater extent than she ever might have done, but she made sure not to judge anyone because they, too, might be simply accepting and enjoying gifts God gave to them. On the other hand, she had friends who denied themselves pleasures even when those opportunities to enjoy the pleasures had arisen on their own or perhaps even with God's action. In some instances, those persons would speak with some apparent satisfaction and possibly even pride at their having denied themselves a certain indulgence. She wondered whether God saw any difference between satisfaction that people drew from enjoying pleasures and satisfaction that people drew from denying themselves pleasures. In the end, she decided that she needed simply not to seek her own pleasure, in just the way that Jesus instructed her, and that she would then be able to enjoy whatever pleasure God offered or accept whatever lack of pleasure circumstances arranged. She would simply not *seek* pleasure.

Deny yourself. Matthew 16:24.

Jesus's admonition to deny oneself came in the midst of a statement that actually had three instructions within it. The first instruction was to deny oneself, then to take up one's cross, and then to follow Jesus. A prior section in the part on one's relationship to

Jesus has already addressed Jesus's instruction to follow him, the last of the three instructions in his statement. A subsequent section addresses his instruction to take up one's cross. Here, though, consider his instruction to deny one's self. Hating one's life and not seeking to please oneself, which are both addressed above, may each seem a lot like denying oneself, and perhaps they are. Jesus may have been saying the same thing in multiple different ways, as may any effective teacher. Repetition and paraphrasing are helpful tools in instruction. One may need to hear the same thing multiple times to begin to grasp, recall, and apply its meaning. On the other hand, hating one's life is not precisely the same as denying oneself. One could hate one's life but still accept oneself for all the hating. People often enough do hate what they nonetheless desire to do and in other ways hate their lives but continue to pursue those very same lives. Doing so may be like the proverbial definition of insanity, which is to do the same thing expecting different results. Yet actually denying one goes beyond merely hating the status quo. Denying one implies *not* doing as one did before or wants to do presently. Consider saying *no* to some of the personal pursuits to which you too often say yes. Especially, deny that sinful part that seeks corrupting pleasures.

More than one gospel account tells the matter of Jesus first extolling and then rebuking Peter. Jesus had of course blessed Peter for acknowledging that Jesus was the Messiah, the Son of God. Yet no sooner had Jesus proceeded to teach the disciples about the Son's coming death at the hands of the religious leaders then Peter had lost Jesus's momentary favor by rebuking Jesus that he must not die. Easy come, easy go, a reader might think. Peter had only to change his stance from acknowledging Jesus as the Savior to rebuking Jesus over God's plan for salvation, to lose Jesus's favor, indeed for Jesus to reply to Peter, *get behind me, Satan.* Peter should have kept God's concerns above human concerns, Jesus had told Peter. This exchange had been the one that led Jesus to his triple instruction, "Whoever wants to be my disciple must deny themselves and take up their cross and follow me." Taking a cross and following is not enough. Denial of self was part of Jesus's criteria for discipleship.

Although he thought at first that denying his own self would prove difficult conceptually, not to mention psychologically, biologically, and emotionally, he did soon find ways in which he could regularly do so. Sometimes the denial had to do with stopping thinking about food or drink, about which he knew that he thought far too often. Anyone feels hunger and thirst, but he realized that he had been thinking about food and drink even when not hungry or thirsty. At other times, his denials had to do with stopping angry, prideful, or other corrupting thoughts. He realized how those sinful parts of him could so easily destroy the sensitive and God-seeking conscience that he hoped to foster and develop. At still other times, his denials had to do with setting aside frivolous diversions reading, watching, or doing things that had no redemptive value that he could determine. He realized how he would attempt to justify those diversions to himself in various ways that were not in any sense credible justifications. Soon enough, he had developed a small practice of denying himself that indeed seemed to be addressing Jesus's instruction. The conceptual part solved, he then set to the harder part of persevering with those small denials.

Do nothing on your own. John 8:28.

Admonitions not to pursue one's own life, and instead to hate one's life and to deny oneself, together paint a clear enough picture that we are ineffective as governors of ourselves. The implication is that we need life from without, from God, for our lives to fulfill their purposes. Yet while Jesus often taught in parables and with lessons having disguised meanings, he also often left little to doubt. The remarkable thing about Jesus's statement about needing God to direct us is that he used *himself* as an example. Jesus did not simply say that *we* should do nothing on *our own*. Rather, Jesus said that *he* does nothing on *his* own, instead doing only what the Father taught him. Jesus asks us nothing that he would not do first. He instead asks us to do as he does. Jesus does nothing on his own without the Father. We should do nothing on our own without the Son. We are so ready to act, so ready to take a proverbial flyer, try things out, go our own way, without waiting for God no less looking for God's leading. We want to lead and hope that God follows. Jesus instead

421

dwelled in the Father, doing only as the Father wished. We should do likewise, waiting for the leading of the Son.

A prior section emphasizing that Jesus had said that he spoke only what the Father taught has already recounted the gospel account in which Jesus said, "When you have lifted up the Son of Man, then you will know that I am he and that I do nothing on my own but speak just what the Father has taught me." Jesus had been addressing the religious leaders in a contentious discussion about who Jesus was. Jesus of course had said that he was from God, from above, while he had chastised the religious leaders that they were from below. They were of the world, while Jesus was not of the world. They would die in their sins if they did not believe him, Jesus concluded. Notice, though, that in saying that he spoke only what the Father taught, Jesus had first said that he *does nothing on his own*. Like effective teachers will do, Jesus had gone from the general, doing nothing on his own, to the specific, not even talking on his own. The religious leaders should have done likewise. Indeed, many believed and did so, as the gospel account recounts.

She had learned over quite some time that tending to things that God had plainly given her to do was fine, indeed excellent, while taking initiative on her own without God's leading was hazardous, indeed sinful. In retrospect, some of the lessons had been hard. She had seen only later that she had rushed ahead in her own plans without much or any thought, reflection, or prayer. She had not deliberately set about to align her thinking and plans with his. She had not reflected on what Jesus commanded to see if those commands warranted what she had thought. She had not felt the Holy Spirit's leading, had not had a believing friend confirm her plans, and had not had a verse, parable, or passage infuse her initiative. She had instead just sort of rushed into something because she could, or because she wanted to, or sometimes even because she couldn't and didn't want to. Looking back, those things had been so hard and unfruitful. She wanted to do nothing other than what God purposed and sanctioned. She had no particular plans of her own but increasingly saw ways in which God might be acting and leading.

☩

Give up everything. Luke 14:33.

Giving up everything is certainly a striking approach toward managing one's own impulses. Even after reflection, this straight-forward instruction of Jesus's seems as clear as it sounds. Jesus expects us to give up everything, leave behind everything and everyone, to follow him. We must not hold back on anywhere. Jesus does not say that giving up everything for him will leave us with nothing. Indeed, Jesus often said the opposite that we gain only by losing, that we receive God's blessing only by giving God service and glory. Jesus also does not say that when we give up everything to follow him that he will take us somewhere we would not like to go to do something we would not like to do. One suspects that God has taken people who gave up everything for him, far from where they began, to do things that they had not imagined, with aptitudes that they did not think that they possessed. Yet one also suspects that God has taken people who gave up everything for him, not far at all, to do things that they had often done, with aptitudes that they knew that they possessed. God moves one halfway around the world while leaving the other right at home. God calls us to minister far afield or in the home field. He asks us to use new skills or old skills. He keeps some poor and makes others rich, and keeps some obscure and makes others famous. When we give everything up for him, he takes everything from some of us but leaves everything with others of us. Jesus commands that we give it all to him. Give it all to God, and he promises to give you far more, immeasurably more, back. And the greatest gift that he returns to us is him, in his kingdom, eternal life.

A section above recounts the gospel account of Jesus turning to the large crowds that were traveling with him to warn them to count the cost of doing so. Jesus did not want to suffer fools gladly. His mission was instead to make them wise in the way of the Lord in order to save them. He demanded and then drew out maturity in his followers. Part of that instruction involved the two examples of the builder counting the cost of constructing a tower and the king considering the cost of war. In the builder's case, Jesus said that no one would want to lay a foundation and then be unable to finish it because everyone would then ridicule them. Jesus didn't want fools following him only part way before quitting after making a mess of things. In the king's case, Jesus said that any king taking ten thousand into battle against twenty thousand would first consider whether he could win or should instead send a peace delegation. Jesus didn't want builders who quit leaving half-built structures or kings who sent peace delegations for half-way terms. His followers, his builders and kings, must be ready to go the whole way, to finish and win at all costs. Jesus concluded saying, "In the same way, those of you who do not give up everything you have cannot be my disciples."

He looked in his closet at the clothes hanging there, while he thought of Jesus's command to give up everything. The command made him wonder briefly whether he had too many clothes, nice clothes, comfortable clothes, fitting and fun clothes. He resolved to remember that life was not about clothes and to remove from his closet and donate especially any unused or little-used things. He looked in his garage and driveway at the vehicles his family used regularly and resolved to consider prayerfully any next vehicle purchase. His identity did not depend on what vehicle he drove. He looked at the several pairs of shoes by the door and resolved that he would wear them out before thinking of buying any others. Life was not about cool shoes. He thought of his job and career that, while they provided well for his family, he resolved to relinquish the moment that God gave him a different call. He thought then of his family and its pets with the love that he had for them but even there resolved to turn instantly away from them and to God when God should call. He took no pride in any of his resolutions because God would have him leave behind that pride, too. He was not sad over giving things up and leaving things behind but instead glad at looking ahead. Until then, he would act responsibly toward everything with which and everyone with whom God entrusted him as he followed Jesus.

Take your cross. Matthew 10:38.

To take one's cross, as Jesus instructs, implies a formidable undertaking in the development of one's disciplines. The cross to which Jesus was undoubtedly referring was the cross that the Romans used for crucifixion. To *take* one's cross had equally obvious meaning. The Roman protocol was for the condemned to carry or drag the cross from the place of condemnation or subsequent scourging, or wherever the cross was otherwise stored, manufactured, or available, to the place of execution by crucifixion, much as Jesus had done so far as he was physically able. The condemned prisoner took the cross on which the prisoner would shortly die a horrible death. Jesus may in other words have been telling his disciples that their devotion to him would in fact lead to their literal crucifixion, as it did in the case of Peter whose crucifixion Jesus prophesied and as it may also have done for the other disciples as tradition holds. The cross is less often an executioner's tool today, although extraordinarily, it remains so, or is once again, in rare places today. For us today, Jesus may well have intended that in following him with our own cross, we would be accepting his crucifixion as due sacrifice and his resurrection as our redemption. We must have Jesus's blood to have his resurrection. Yet in secular usage today, to *bear one's cross* carries a much less imposing meaning, as if to bear one's sorrows or other burdens but certainly not to proceed to one's slow and painful execution. Jesus could conceivably have intended something more like this modern meaning of cross bearing that we must accept the indignities thrust upon us for having followed Jesus, although that interpretation seems too much to relieve the historic event and salvation process of its necessary and extraordinary weight of glory.

According to different gospels, Jesus at least twice told the disciples to take up their cross and follow him, in different contexts, once after Peter had acknowledged Jesus as Messiah but also at an earlier time when Jesus was first sending out the twelve disciples. Of course, Jesus may have told the disciples the same thing several or many times. Effective teaching bears repeating. The two times that the gospels record Jesus telling the disciples to take their cross, they record him saying it in a slightly different form, once in the triple instruction referred to in a prior section to deny self, take cross, and follow. On the other occasion, when first sending the disciples out to heal and teach, Jesus had first given the disciples basic instructions on where to go, what to do, and how to conduct themselves. He had then warned them of severe resistance but also encouraged them not to fear. Jesus had then explained that he came not for peace but division. That point that his teaching would even divide families led Jesus to say that only those who love him more than family members are worthy of him. Jesus then added, "Whoever does not take up their cross and follow me is not worthy of me." Jesus wanted the disciples to carry a cross behind him on his journey.

He had for quite a while fully appreciated and gladly accepted the work of Jesus on the cross. He understood God's extraordinary plan for salvation. He knew and confessed the depth of his sin and need for Christ's sacrificial redemption. He thought that he had every appropriate appreciation for the meaning and the power of the cross. Then one day, the verse that a disciple must take up one's own cross to follow Christ caught his attention. He had probably read the verse a dozen times, maybe two dozen. He had always construed it as he believed that many others construed it, which is that following Christ can be difficult, inconvenient, embarrassing, and burdensome. One may have to change some things, give up some things, and even lose the respect or fellowship of some others. Having been a Christ follower for quite a while, though, he had gotten over any strong sense of what taking one's cross might really mean beyond those initial uncomfortable stages of Christian witness and profession. Then the verse arrested his attention, and he began to meditate on it. Maybe he had been misreading it all those times, all those years. Maybe he had unintentionally stripped Jesus's instruction of its power and core meaning. Maybe in taking one's cross, one was both accepting something far deeper and, solely through the authority and power of Christ, accomplishing something far greater.

Carry your cross. Luke 14:27.

Carrying one's cross is a powerful way to think about one's own character, approach, and disciplines. Actually, among the several gospel accounts that mention Jesus's teaching about believers taking up their crosses to follow Jesus, only one of those mentions *carrying* one's cross rather than simply *taking it up*. Perhaps the distinction between *taking up* and *carrying* a cross is of no import whatsoever and instead only a recall, recording, copying, translation, or interpretation issue. One supposes, though, that distinctions can be drawn. To take up a cross may be to grasp and lift it and maybe even shoulder it, while to carry it would be to move it from one place to another *after* having taken it up. Figuratively, then, one could take up one's cross, declare oneself a Christian, and ask and receive God's forgiveness. Yet to *carry* one's cross seems a different act not only physically but figuratively. What more does one accomplish by carrying one's cross than by taking it up? What happens in the course of one's cross transport? Interestingly, Jesus not only took up his cross but also carried it, and yet then required another's assistance to complete the carrying. To carry one's cross may indeed be more fully to participate in, benefit from, and *serve through* Jesus's redemptive work in sacrifice and resurrection. Discipleship may be deeper than salvation. While the thought could be purely speculative, the possibility exists that carrying one's cross may allow Jesus to do greater work in one's soul and spirit, preparing one for more effective witness and service.

In the several gospel accounts in which Jesus spoke about taking up one's cross and following him to be his disciple, he once spoke the phrase a little differently and not to his disciples but to large crowds that were in fact following him. As a prior section recounts, Jesus may have been discouraging the foolhardy from continuing to follow him, as he explained that they must hate family members and their own life in order to follow him. Jesus then added, "And whoever does not carry their cross and follow me cannot by my disciple." Notice here that Jesus referred to *carrying* the cross rather than simply *taking* it up. As previously mentioned, the crowd members would have known exactly what Jesus meant about carrying the cross from the Roman crucifixions that they must have observed or about which they would certainly have heard. Crowd members would likely also have known of the Roman practice of having the prisoner bear the cross to the place of execution. Jesus would do so, although his collapse along the way required the Roman guards to conscript Simon of Cyrene to help him complete the impossibly arduous effort,

427

particularly after Jesus's brutal scourging. After addressing the crowd about *carrying* their cross, Jesus then gave the examples of the builder counting construction costs and the king considering the probability of prevailing in war.

She felt that she carried various crosses, perhaps like the Apostle Paul bore something untoward, even though undisclosed, for which he prayed multiple times for relief even while persevering. Her crosses were in some respects terribly weighty, deep things that seemed to break and even condemn her, just as anyone who looks deeply enough in their soul will find such things. She didn't often *feel* that way that others had equally crushing crosses, although she knew logically that it was likely true. Knowing that others bore crosses didn't in any case relieve her burden. The odd thing was, though, that she realized that the only reason that she bore the cross was because she had the conscience with which Jesus had blessed her through the Holy Spirit. She only had the weighty cross to bear because of the sensibility she had from the teaching and Spirit of Jesus. That source being the case, Jesus seemed to be bearing the cross for her, just as Simon of Cyrene had for a little way borne the cross of the collapsed Jesus. The cross-bearing dynamic was strange and mysterious, but she felt that the deeper that she grew in Christ, the heavier her cross became, and yet the more he carried it for her. By taking her cross as Jesus instructed, she was at once deepening her sense of her own sin, her appreciation for Jesus's sacrifice, and the lightness of her being in the salvation and kingdom of Christ. She held nothing but wonder for the power and glory of Christ's ongoing work in her through the cross.

Enter by the gate. John 10:1.

As we think about ourselves, which again we in one way or another do pretty much constantly, we develop ethics or attitudes about how best to proceed. At some point in one's life, risk and adventure may seem appropriate, while at other points the safe route may seem the only warranted way to proceed. At one point, we may want to throw off restraints and strike out on our own, while at other points we may prefer to submit or even succumb to every ordinary rule or restraint. At other points, shortcuts may seem necessary or attractive, while at other times in life we may prefer going the long, slow route. You may know persons who are always quick to jump at opportunities but others who are always considered in thought, persons who are impulsive and others who are deliberate, or persons who think they always know and others who think they never know. While telling how much these ethics, attitudes, and dispositions influence our actions may be difficult, the possibility exists that they influence us heavily at all times. When Jesus instructs to enter by the gate rather than climb in, he refers to himself as the gate into the kingdom, Jesus as the way, truth, and life. Our kingdom access is only through Christ. We have only one gate in. Yet Jesus may also in some sense be instructing us in an ethic, attitude, or disposition toward our own actions. We cannot live kingdom life thinking that after the gate closes, we can later climb our way in. Each day, at every moment, we must be following the Great Shepherd in. Develop a gate-entering attitude. Stop trying to climb in.

A prior section on listening to Jesus's voice recounted the parable of the good shepherd and his sheep that Jesus told to the religious leaders. Jesus had said that the sheep listen only to the shepherd's voice, not the voice of a stranger. Sheep run from strangers but follow the shepherd through the gate into the safety of the sheep pen. Jesus began that parable, though, by cautioning against trying to get into the sheep pen by any other way. Jesus said, "Very truly I tell you, anyone who does not enter the sheep pen by the gate, but climbs in some other way, is a thief and a robber." Jesus continued that the one who enters by the gate is the shepherd, while the gatekeeper opens the gate for him. When the religious leaders did not understand Jesus's parable including whom the figures represented, he spelled its meaning out that *he* is the gate for the sheep. Jesus was clearly saying that he was the way into the kingdom. God saves anyone who enters through Jesus. While many rejected his teaching, even calling him raving mad, some in the crowd listened and believed. They recognized that Jesus's parables were sensible rather than crazed as further confirmed by his healing miracles. Crazed men don't open the eyes of the blind, the believers concluded.

429

Over the span of several years, he realized from the disciplines that he gradually drew and adopted from the teachings of Jesus how much and how often he had been trying to do things halfway. He had never really thought of himself as if he was always trying to take shortcuts, do it his own way, get by with half-baked actions, and cut corners. He had instead believed that he was as complete, considered, thoughtful, thorough, disciplined, and resolute in his actions as anyone else. Yet at the same time, he had recognized some individuals who just seemed to be far ahead of everyone else in doing things the right way, in turning square corners. They seemed not to care that while they went methodically about following every appropriate practice and discipline, others were instead making swift and easy work of things, and in doing so seeming to get ahead. Indeed, the square-corner individuals were rare. Everywhere else he looked, he could see people cutting corners, which was in large part why he thought he was doing just about as well as everyone else. Nearly everyone else was actually not doing so well in the square-corners department. Then, he met and studied Jesus. Jesus was not cutting corners, and he was not tolerating those who do. He was instead demanding from his listeners that they follow him if they were to enter the kingdom with him. He told parable after parable about those who get lazy, ignore the cost, or try to take shortcuts. None of them were getting in. He decided to stop cutting corners. He was going to follow Jesus in through the gate and stop trying to climb in late.

Enter by the narrow door. Luke 13:24.

Jesus repeatedly invites us to enter God's kingdom. One could have no greater personal goal than to do so, especially if one's motivation was to reside with and glorify the King for eternity. Jesus clearly approves the goal of entering the kingdom, making that entry a compelling way to structure one's commitments, habits, and practices. Get the right attitude and approach toward entering the kingdom, and you get most other things, perhaps all other things, right. So each of us should be especially interested in what Jesus says about how to enter and who will enter. One of his answers to that question had to do with entering through the *narrow door*. The point of the narrow-door image seems to be to emphasize that one has only one specific route into the kingdom, which is through the narrow door. Yet the context that Jesus then gave around his instruction to enter through the narrow door is important. The parable in which Jesus gave the narrow-door instruction makes two things reasonably clear. First, the owner of the narrow-door house must know the one who expects to enter. If you don't know Jesus, or more to the point, if *Jesus* doesn't know *you*, then don't expect entry. Second, the owner of the narrow-door house welcomes those who enter through the open door *before it closes*. The door might not be quite so hard to squeeze through if you enter before the owner closes it. Walk now with Jesus, developing his close acquaintance. Enter the house now while he holds the door open for you, or be sure that Jesus holds you as a very close and trusted acquaintance if you intend to try entering later.

Jesus taught in the towns and villages each time that he headed to Jerusalem. On one of those times, one of his listeners along the way asked him a question that many today would also ask, which was whether only a few would receive salvation. Jesus answered with a narrow-door parable that seemed to confirm the questioner's suspicion, although perhaps not for the reason the questioner suspected. Jesus began, "Make every effort to enter through the narrow door, because many, I tell you, will try to enter and will not be able to." Jesus continued that the owner of the house would close the door, leaving people standing outside knocking to get in. The owner, Jesus said, would send them away because he didn't know who they were or where they were from, and only knew that they were evildoers. The parable was thus especially instructive as to the qualifications for entry into the kingdom. The questioner may have assumed that few getting in would have to do with God setting a standard that the many commoners in the crowds who followed Jesus could not meet. Jesus's parable clarified instead that few getting in would be solely because they didn't know Jesus and kept doing evil. Jesus ended the parable with what his questioner might have felt was an encouraging conclusion that in the kingdom the last may be first and first last.

She thought of the parable often, had seen compelling pictorial representations of it, and had even dreamed of it. She had the strong impression of Jesus at the door, holding the door, considering whether to close or open the door, and just generally examining her. In those dreams, representations, and impressions, Jesus didn't seem to be looking *at* her as much as *in* her. He seemed to be gauging her heart rather than her looks, measuring her intimacy rather than her effort. She realized in her meditations on the narrow-door parable that acquaintance, closeness, familiarity, and relationship seemed most to be his measure, certainly not anything that she planned to do, presently did, or even had done. He was not reviewing her resume or portfolio, not asking any questions of her whether she could answer with the right doctrine, not inquiring into her memberships and associations. He was instead seeing if he *knew* her in the way that a father, brother, husband, or friend would look to recognize her. While she often felt close to Jesus when praying, worshipping, and studying the Bible, in her meditations and dreams on the narrow-door parable she did not yet have the strong impression that Jesus was recognizing her. At first, the thought disturbed her. But then she realized that the parable, or more accurately the Holy Spirit speaking through the parable, was guiding her, not rejecting her. She simply needed to continue to attend to her relationship with Jesus so that he would at her time throw the door wide open for her.

Do not look back. Luke 9:62.

Jesus instructed that once one begins kingdom work, one must not look back to old matters. Kingdom work makes a clean break with the past. Looking back to old matters makes one unfit for kingdom service. The meaning of Jesus's admonition against *looking back,* especially in the context in which he gave it, seems reasonably clear. Work is all about moving forward, anticipating, planning for, and completing what needs to be done. To look back while working is to divert one's attention from the work to something behind one, something in the past that has already occurred but has no relevance to the new work that the person has yet to do. One who takes attention away from kingdom work in order to look back is not giving kingdom work the priority that it commands. Looking back rather than continuing on in kingdom service is treating the kingdom like less than all that it is. Indeed, to look back to say goodbye to family, as one to whom Jesus gave the warning was doing, ignores the priority of the kingdom family. To look back to a funeral, as another to whom Jesus gave the warning was doing, ignores the eternal life available in the kingdom. The impression that looking back leaves is that the person doing so does not have the heart in the new work. The heart remains back with the deceased parent or back with the old family. Jesus wants us yearning for kingdom work, kingdom life, and kingdom family, not for former matters. All things are new in Christ.

Jesus took other opportunities to warn and teach about the cost of following him, giving different instructions to three men who said that they intended to follow Jesus. A man walking along the road with Jesus claimed that he would follow Jesus wherever he went. Jesus replied to the man in a manner that likely discouraged him, in saying that while foxes have dens and birds have nests, Jesus could find no place even to lay his head. Jesus then told another man to follow him. When the man replied that he would first bury his dead father, Jesus told him to let the dead bury their own dead while the man instead proclaimed God's kingdom. A third man claimed that he would follow Jesus after first saying goodbye to his family. Jesus replied, "No one who puts a hand to the plow and looks back is fit for service in the kingdom of God." The gospel account does not identify as disciples these three odd men whom Jesus challenged. Jesus may have had many others make similar commitments when first encountering Jesus, his miracles, the crowds that followed him, and his transformative teaching. Jesus seemed to be saying to each, in different ways, that following him took a special kind of commitment. That Jesus challenged these three men may have indicated that he knew their lack of commitment.

Together, they thought little of their old ways. They had history together, events together, relationships together that went way back. If they had wished, then they might have devoted considerable time to old history, old events, old relationships, and old matters. Some people they knew did so. Some people they knew were always going back, scratching old sores, bringing up old relationships, trying to preserve and relive old matters. In their case, they had little appetite for doing so. While they had a few photo albums and a little memorabilia, what little they had was mostly boxed and ignored, even long forgotten. They just weren't trying very hard to remember the past. Indeed, they spent more effort trying to forget the past, not that the past had been a bad past, just that they were not particularly backward-looking people. They instead looked concertedly forward. They particularly looked forward to joining Christ. They were doing kingdom work from which they would not let the past distract them.

Repent for the kingdom. Matthew 4:17.

The concept of repentance bears a heavy religious connotation. Many would probably identify it, *repentance*, as the central attitude that one should maintain toward oneself. While to *repent* simply means to show course-changing contrition for past wrongs, few use that word in any context other than as the Christian practice of confessing and turning away in remorse from sin. Although contrition is healthy, and stopping intentional wrong is healthy, too, a secular therapist would probably rarely if ever use the word *repent*, at least not without risk of offense and in certain settings even some professional discipline. Although repentance might be healthy for anyone, believer or non-believer, the caution to reserve the word and action for faith contexts may be a good one. Jesus commanded repentance in different contexts and with different consequences. He did so, though, not for mental health or personal character but instead for kingdom purposes. Although Jesus gave sage counsel, he was not a secular counselor. He was and is the Savior. Indeed, he tied his first and consistent command to repent to *gaining the kingdom*. Jesus did not say to repent because doing so would make us better persons, although repenting certainly would. Jesus instead said to repent because the kingdom was near, implying that we would have access to the kingdom in the course and consequence of our repentance. Remorseful turning away from sin is not all that kingdom access requires. We need the blood and redemption of

Jesus. Yet Jesus linked remorseful turning away from sin to the kingdom's proximity. Repent for the kingdom because the kingdom is near.

According to one gospel account, the first thing that Jesus preached in his public ministry, after his baptism by John and Jesus's fasting and testing in the wilderness, was that the kingdom of heaven has come near. Actually, Jesus's first preached word, according to this gospel account, was to *repent* because the kingdom had come near. The passage first quotes Isaiah prophesying many hundreds of years earlier that the people living in darkness, in the shadow of death, would see the dawn of a great light out of the land by way of the Sea of Galilee. Jesus lived in that land, in Capernaum by the Sea of Galilee. Jesus was of course that great light who would shine in the shadow-of-death darkness. When Jesus heard that John the Baptist was in prison, he went first to his hometown of Nazareth in the Galilee region and then lived in Capernaum where he began to preach. In this gospel account, his first recorded preaching words were, "Repent, for the kingdom of heaven has come near." Indeed, the account states that *from then on* Jesus began to preach kingdom repentance.

He knew that sin has no place in God's kingdom. God could not tolerate sin. He could not bring his sin, of which he wished to have none but knew that he would have some, into the kingdom. No one can. One gains kingdom entry only through the sin-free Jesus. He had long thought, then, that he would have kingdom access only on natural death and supernatural life in Jesus, in that traditional way that many think about joining the Father and Son in heaven. The only body that he could bring into the kingdom, he assumed, would be his resurrected body. Yet here was Jesus saying to repent because the kingdom is all around us, he thought again. Jesus seemed to promise or imply kingdom access or at least kingdom nearness to the repenting believer. He knew that Jesus's blood was enough, but Jesus was still preaching remorseful contrition and turning away from sin, while suggesting that such repentance had something to do with kingdom nearness and maybe kingdom access. The thought made him more serious about repenting. He didn't want to live a naively carefree life in Jesus while sin kept him from present or future kingdom access.

Repent or perish. Luke 13:5.

Repentance has its extraordinarily positive consequence in gaining us kingdom nearness and access, as the prior section showed. Our constant attitude toward ourselves should be one of repentance. An attitude of repentance is the opposite of an attitude of arrogant self-justification. As often as we think of ourselves, we should be thinking repentance, thinking of turning in contrition away from the sin that dogs us. The kingdom is certainly worthy reward. Yet failure to repent has its corollary negative consequence. While Jesus preached repentance because the kingdom is available, at other times and in other places Jesus preached to repent *or perish*. We have no need of perishing. Jesus heals of sin those of us who turn to Jesus. Those who do not turn straight away from sin in remorseful sorrow, and do not maintain that contrite inner attitude that moves one ever farther from one's sin nature, will perish. The way that Jesus framed it, repentance is a life-or-death matter. Anyone who thinks that they can go on doing whatever they choose, no matter how obviously sinful, and then expect that Jesus will open the door to the kingdom for them, should consider carefully Jesus's instructions on repentance. Make repentance your primary attitude toward yourself, which from Jesus's instruction on repentance, appears to have much to do with letting Jesus save you. Repent, or perish.

Jesus had given a long teaching starting with his disciples before addressing the crowd of thousands gathered around them. Jesus had repeatedly warned against sin and exhorted godly righteousness in several lessons and parables. Near the end of Jesus's long teaching, some in the crowd began telling Jesus how the region's Roman ruler had executed some fellow Galileans, likely rebels against Roman rule. Those who pointed out to Jesus the other Galileans' executioner may have been indicating that *they* were not rebellious like those executed, although they may also have been bringing the ruler's atrocities to Jesus's attention, expecting Jesus to join in condemning either the rebels or ruler, or both. Jesus had none of it. Chastising those who had raised the subject, Jesus asked bluntly whether the Galileans whom the ruler had executed were worse sinners than any other Galileans. Jesus answered his own question with emphasis that the executed Galileans were not any worse. Jesus then brought the point home, saying, "But unless you repent, you too will all perish." Pointing at the sin and condemnation of others did those in the crowd no good. Jesus wanted their attention on their own sin, lest they too perish.

She was learning the power of contrition. During her studies on repentance, she had realized that she had two competing inner dialogues with herself, or if one prefers, monologues within herself. One inner voice justified things that she thought, said, and did, while frequently criticizing and in some respects condemning others. She learned to call it her *critical spirit*, although she knew that she could also call it her *arrogant* spirit. The other inner voice instead looked primarily to her thoughts, words, and conduct, finding wrongs and sin within them, while expressing remorse, sorrow, sadness, and deep regret for that sin. She called this inner voice her *repentant spirit*. Her repentant spirit called out to Jesus for forgiveness. When on the infrequent occasions that her repentant spirit turned its focus to others, she saw little other than unending grace in those others, not the corruption that her critical spirit would see. While she knew that the competition between these inner voices and the contrasting spirits that they represented was deadly serious for her present and future, whether she would enter the kingdom or perish, she nonetheless learned to take some amusement in how evident each voice was and how different they were. The key, though, was that she gradually learned how to silence the critical spirit, giving ever greater voice to the repentant spirit. Her motive was easy. Jesus, she figured, wanted it that way.

Repent at preaching. Luke 11:32.

Another disposition that we should each develop, in studying what Jesus says about how to regard ourselves, is to repent when listening to preaching. Admonitions to repent for the kingdom and to avoid perishing describe motives or reasons for repentance. Yet what should trigger and inform our repentance? Where do we find the insights, stimuli, and impetus for repentance? Jesus answers to repent when hearing preaching of God's word. Those who are soaked in their Christian faith may think, well, of course, preaching should inform and reform the congregant. Those who are not so conditioned to submit to a message-giver's God-inspired agitation, though, might not be so prepared to reform. One actually finds a great deal of *resistance* to, and contempt and sarcasm for, preaching of any kind, even and sometimes especially God-informed preaching. One should probably not even assume that regular churchgoers would be more likely to repent at preaching than would others. Indeed, in the following gospel account, Jesus pointed out that the biblical record shows the godless and corrupt much more willing to repent at preaching than the people of God. Let the Holy Spirit prepare your spirit to repent at preaching. Submit to, rather than kick at, the goads.

Jesus had driven a demon out of a mute man who then spoke. The crowd was amazed at Jesus's miracle healing powers, although some wanted Jesus to show them a special sign from heaven, as if miracle healing was not enough. Jesus instead gave them a lesson on the source of his power directly from God. During the lesson, a woman called out to Jesus that his mother was blessed for having given Jesus birth and nursed him. Jesus replied instead that the blessed are those who hear God and obey him. When Jesus saw that the crowds were getting bigger, he told them that their generation was wicked. They had asked for heavenly signs when they should instead have listened to preaching, particularly his preaching, like prior generations had listened and responded to preaching. Jesus even contrasted the growing crowd with those from ancient Nineveh who, though a violent people, had listened to the prophet Jonah. Jesus said, "The men of Nineveh will stand up at the judgment with this generation and condemn it, for they repented at the preaching of Jonah; and now something greater than Jonah is here." Jesus wanted them listening to preaching and changing their ways in response to it.

They had together heard so much preaching in so many different venues, styles, contexts, media, and forms, and had each read sufficiently deeply and frequently in the Bible and its commentaries, and participated in so many studies, that they felt fairly readily able to discern God-inspired preaching. They were always ready to draw from and submit to that preaching, although they also found that they had to guard against becoming preaching connoisseurs. As often and as deeply as they had listened to preaching, they knew that they might find it too easy to stand in judgment of the qualities of the message rather than let the message stand in judgment of the qualities of its hearers. They wanted to draw conviction from the message, not criticize and convict the messenger. They shared no sense that the many messages that they had heard, accepted, and applauded had relieved them of so much of their sin that they had little or no remaining sin to reform. Instead, they each retained the conviction to let preaching convict them. They would far rather leave a sermon in remorse over their condition than in remorse for having attended. They were not listening to preaching to judge it but to let God's word judge and turn them.

Repent and believe the gospel. Mark 1:15.

The prior sections show that Jesus had much to say about repentance. The act of turning remorsefully away from sin, especially when prompted by sound preaching, is clearly the attitude toward oneself that Jesus instructs, both for kingdom access and so as not to perish. Turning away from one thing, though, implies turning toward something else. No matter which way one turns, one still faces something. Jesus addressed this concern with yet one more instruction on repentance that when one repents of sin, one should simultaneously believe the good news. As we turn away from sin, we turn toward the gospel's cleansing sacrifice, life-giving resurrection, and God-embracing redemption. As Jesus said in another context, casting evil spirits from one's soul does little good if nothing replaces them and they come right back in. We are not empty vessels but vessels God made for God to fill. When in our repentance the Spirit empties our vessels of sin, we must affirmatively embrace Jesus's good news. Abnegation is fine as far as it goes. Repent, and be rid of sin. But affirmation is equally important. Repent and then believe the good news.

The account of Jesus's fasting and testing in the desert, John the Baptist's imprisonment, and Jesus's return to preach in Galilee, all appear in more than one gospel account. As a prior section shows, one of those gospel accounts had Jesus first preaching to repent because the kingdom of heaven is near. Another gospel had Jesus preaching to repent or perish, while another had Jesus preaching to repent at preaching. The disciples, crowds, and religious leaders could not have mistaken Jesus's concern over repentance. Jesus did not begin his public ministry as a sentimental pushover peacemaker with a naive message that God would forgive everything and forgive everyone. He instead came with a figurative sword, the word of God that challenged and divided. Yet in another gospel account, Jesus's first preaching did include the good news that repentance would bring. "The time has come," Jesus said, "The kingdom of God has come near. Repent and believe the good news!" Jesus's message was good news for anyone willing to follow it, bad news only for those who were not.

She was plumbing the depth of this good news-bad news tension in Jesus's preaching. The issue had snuck up on her. She had not really seen it coming. For years, she had been able to compartmentalize Jesus's very challenging, even dark exhortations against sin, warning of its dire consequences, from Jesus's incredibly attractive, resplendent invitations to the kingdom, extolling its extravagances. She had not thought of the two sides of Jesus's message as in any sense colliding. Sometimes, she thought of the dark side of sin, while other times she thought of the bright side of salvation. Back and forth she had gone, sometimes within a day's meditation, sometimes in seasons. Yet she had never quite put the two messages, one foreboding and other inviting, exactly side by side. The messages had always seemed separate, almost as if one could work on one at a time, which may indeed have been what she had been doing or trying to do. Now though, she realized that doing one was not doing the other, and doing the other was not doing the one. One only really turned away from sin by turning to Jesus, and one always turned to sin when turning away from Jesus. Likewise, one only really turned to Jesus when turning away from sin, and one always turned away from Jesus, when turning to sin.

Be perfect. Matthew 5:48.

One of the most extraordinary and surprising things that Jesus commanded was to be perfect, and not just in any perfection but with the Father's perfection. As an approach to oneself, the thought of being perfect as God is perfect is at once both inconceivably daunting and yet somehow perfectly sensible. On the one hand, one would naturally not expect to attain perfection. Indeed, *you've got to be kidding* seems a natural reaction because who possibly could? Perfection seems an impossibility especially with the corruption we harbor and then living as we do within the world's complex web. Success for those who attempt perfection would likely last less than five minutes before the thoughts, mouth, eyes, feet, or hands wander where they shouldn't. Yet on the other hand, why would Jesus ever set any other standard? One cannot really imagine Jesus saying instead *don't bother because you'll fail* or *just come as close as you can.* God may know our weakness well, but that knowledge doesn't mean he should accept it. Consider, too, the power and mission of the one who gave the instruction. Of course, on our own we would almost instantly fail, but everything is certainly possible with Christ. When Jesus breathes the Holy Spirit on his disciples, he doesn't do so to give our tarnish a slight burnishing. No less a one than the Holy Spirit resides within us, at least as long as we aspire to perfection. Imbuing us with that extraordinary aspiration may be part of why Jesus said to be perfect *as the Father is perfect* because the Holy Spirit might not abide without that redoubt within us. Aspire to perfection, and then let the Holy Spirit guide you to being the Father's kind of holy perfect. Jesus did it. With Jesus, you can and someday will do it.

Jesus's extraordinary instruction to *be perfect*, stated well into his Sermon on the Mount, came as the conclusion to a lesson on loving enemies, about which a section below says more. A key aspect of that lesson, though, was that Jesus said that by loving enemies and praying for people who persecuted them, his hearers would be children of their Father in heaven. If his hearers in the crowd wanted to be God's children, then they should love and pray for enemies. Jesus could have added that *they* would then be children as *he* was a child of the Father, he, Jesus, who loved God's enemies so deeply as to lay down his life for them. While he did not add that comparison, for which his hearers would not have been ready, his showing how his hearers could *become* the Father's children by loving and praying for enemies implies a sort of Son-like standing with the Father. That standing, after all, is why the Father would open the kingdom, only to his children, only to those who become like Jesus. Jesus continued on with the lesson by emphasizing that his hearers must do differently than do the pagans, who worship earth, nature, and many other gods, and who show love only to their own people. Jesus concluded the lesson saying, "Be perfect, therefore, as your heavenly Father is perfect."

He had once had an influential figure in his life who, while like any of us was very far from perfect, had nonetheless claimed perfection. The claim had come about almost incidentally, in one of those conversations that we all have that had begun entirely innocently but somehow turned to deep things too quickly for anyone to give considered thought. This person probably would not have made the claim to perfection had the person given it more thought. Much later in life, the person had quietly renounced the claim, or if not directly renounced it, then admitted that on at least one subject the person might at least have *taken the wrong approach*. Yet at the time, that was the claim that the person had made that the person had no faults, had committed no wrongs, and was blameless in all matters. Those who heard the claim and knew the person of course instantly appreciated that it was preposterous. They could have pointed to any number of major disruptions in the person's life that, while having several contributing causes, were due in large part to the person's large faults. They attributed the claim to the person's incapacity for productive introspection. Yet many years later, he who had the influence of this figure could laugh that Jesus had, after all, commanded perfection. He would not claim perfection, but he would aspire to it in order to give room to the powerful work of the Holy Spirit.

Walk in the light. John 12:35.

Another positive approach to thinking about oneself, different from but related to aspiring to perfection, is to walk in Jesus's light, as he once instructed. Anyone who has stumbled along on a moonless-night walk, especially in an unfamiliar area, knows what walking in darkness is like. Even a walk through one's own dark house can be disconcerting, stumbling into doorframes and furniture. The spiritual parallels that Jesus intends from his instruction to walk in his light are certainly apt. Jesus's model and instructions, his words and way, are spiritual light. We see clearly our spiritual path and its obstacles when we know Jesus's words and how they guide our course. When we don't have Jesus's words and don't have that guidance, our spiritual walk is aimless and obstructed by insurmountable obstacles. To lose an appetite for biblical study and counsel is to lose the light and path, and to undertake instead an aimlessly dark walk. Each day, our goal should be to walk in Jesus's light. He has cleared a straight path before us, making the hills low and our burdens light. Walk in his light.

Jesus had predicted his death to the crowd that was listening to him after his triumphal entry into Jerusalem. The voice from heaven, sounding like thunder, had confirmed that God would receive glory through Jesus. Jesus told the crowd that the voice some had just heard was for their benefit rather than his for Jesus knows the thoughts of the Father. Judgment was coming on the world, when Jesus's crucifixion would draw all to him. Jesus's profound statements caused confusion in the crowd, some of whose members wanted more explanation. "You are going to have the light just a little while longer," Jesus answered, continuing, "Walk while you have the light, before darkness overtakes you." Jesus then added that walking in the darkness would leave them without direction, not knowing where they were headed. They must instead follow him, follow the light. He concluded that they should also *believe* in the light, which would make them *children* of light. Jesus then slipped away to hide from the crowd and religious leaders. Many believed him, while many did not believe.

A greatly satisfying and encouraging change had happened for her over the few prior years. She had before then had a strong sense of aimlessness, as if she or something or someone else had cast her life adrift. She seemed to be going through motions without knowing why, without having any sense of the path down which those motions were leading. She felt as if she was following someone else's path or trying to follow the paths of several others all at once. In doing so, she felt that she was not on any real path at all, surely not one that was *her* path. That last sense of losing *her* path was the odd thing about her aimlessness. While she indeed felt aimless, she also sensed that somewhere she must have a path, a path that was her *own* path, unique to her and not some old path that many others had tread or even a new path that others had cobbled together for her to follow. Somewhere, she had her own path that God had made for her. Her convictions that God had made her and that thus only God could know her path were precisely what led her forward through her aimless times. Almost without knowing it, she had learned to walk in Christ's light. When the idea had first occurred to her that she was now walking in his light, it had seemed so simple as to be almost trite. Yet she had no other explanation for her new clarity and purpose, for her new energy and joy, certainly no *better* explanation. She was so glad now to be walking in Christ's light.

2.5 Others

Stay with the worthy. Matthew 10:11. *Welcome prophets and the righteous.* Matthew 10:41. *Gather and agree in Jesus's name.* Matthew 18:19. *Try hard to settle matters.* Luke 12:58. *Love one another.* John 15:17. *Love much.* Luke 7:47. *Do to others as you want them to do to you.* Luke 6:31. *Forgive.* Luke 6:37. *Forgive another's sins.* John 20:23. *Strengthen fellow disciples.* Luke 22:32. *Reconcile with others.* Matthew 5:24. *Do not burden others.* Luke 11:46.

Relationship to the Father, Son, and Holy Spirit, and then to ourselves, form a foundation for relating to others. Without right relationship to God, and then sound attitude about oneself, one stands little or no chance of healthy relationships with others. Good relationships, strong and healthy relationships, are two-way streets. One person feeds the other while the other nourishes back. Bring poor relationship with God and oneself into any other relationship, and you will drain rather than nourish the other. Everyone has acquaintances who nourish and acquaintances who don't. Relationship is the way in which we communicate and share the life, wisdom, and nourishment of Jesus. Reflect closely on your relationships with others, particularly those relationships with active believers, and you may notice the power that the Holy Spirit's witness to Christ brings through the relationship. Be a feeder of others just as you feed on the Spirit of Christ. Bring communion with Jesus into every relationship. Where two gather in his name, he is also present.

Stay with the worthy. Matthew 10:11.

445

One approach that Jesus instructs as to others is to reside, abide, or stay with the worthy. One readily suspects that Jesus does not by the *worthy* at all mean an elite class of privileged people. We are of course not to seek out those who would grant us special worldly privileges. Rather, the instruction in the context in which Jesus gave it, recounted below, strongly suggests that the worthy with whom we should abide are those who receive and respond affirmatively to Jesus's message. One might thus actually seek out and abide with those people whom society judges *not* worthy of society's worldly, status-driven approval, as long as those people are receptive to Jesus's message. When Jesus instructs to *stay* with the worthy, in the context in which Jesus gave the instruction, he meant literally to take room and accept board with them. We could, of course, do that from time to time. Yet accepting that most of the time, at least when near our own home, we will have provided already for our own room and board, Jesus may also mean simply to *spend time* with the worthy, to abide with them in fellowship around Jesus. This instruction has an obvious positive side to it that we would thus support the spiritual growth of the worthy and our own growth. The instruction also has a cautionary aspect to it that to abide with anyone else, with those who reject Jesus, could be to sow strife or endorse sin and lose faith. Go find the lost while staying with the worthy.

When Jesus sent out the twelve disciples on their first mission of proclaiming the kingdom's proximity and of healing, he would have known that they would need to find places to stay along the way. Jesus also knew that they would face decisions about where to stay, and so he gave them some instruction, saying, "Whatever town or village you enter, search there for some worthy person and stay at their house until you leave." Jesus then intimated what he meant by a *worthy* person. He told the disciples to give a greeting, consider from the response whether the home is *deserving*, and if so to let their peace rest on it. If the home's residents did not welcome them *or listen to their words*, Jesus continued, then they were to leave and not worry about it. A worthy person would thus be one who welcomed the disciples or listened to them. Jesus wanted the disciples residing among those who supported them or at least listened to them. If the mission was to proclaim the kingdom, then the disciples must find persons who would welcome the messengers or at least the proclamation. Jesus ended that part of his instruction by condemning the homes and towns that would not welcome the disciples.

She had struggled at times with the question of with whom she should be spending her time. Like anyone, she had friends whom she supported and who supported and encouraged her, on the one hand, and then on the other hand acquaintances who neither welcomed her nor seemed to draw much from her. As much as she enjoyed and drew from her friends, whose Christian witness fed her, she didn't want to miss Jesus sending her out to carry his good news of the kingdom. She seldom felt that she was actually on that mission and wondered whether she needed to be spending more time with those difficult acquaintances. As she kept reflecting over the years on the question of how she should be relating to others, she gradually sensed something from Jesus's instruction. No matter where she went or what she did, she definitely needed to keep entering others' homes, keep changing and expanding her contacts. Yet at the same time, Jesus seemed to be saying that she need not worry if some of those homes, even many of those homes, did not welcome or listen to her. As long as she kept trying, then she could take solace in Jesus's instruction to *shake the dust off* as she left. Indeed, shaking the dust off from those difficult encounters was just what she felt like. She didn't mind those encounters because she always hoped to find a welcome. But when she found no welcome, shake, baby, shake, she would laugh.

Welcome prophets and the righteous. Matthew 10:41.

Just as Jesus instructs with whom to stay when carrying the word of God, which is to stay with the worthy who welcome and listen, Jesus also instructs to welcome those who share and live out the word of God, that is, prophets and the righteous. Those who welcome prophets and the righteous gain their like reward. To welcome someone is of course to greet them with affirmation for who they are and what they do, and to invite them in for hospitality and encouragement. We could and perhaps should extend hospitality to

447

anyone, whether friend or foe, sinner or saint, believer or non-believer. Kindness can turn the heart of even a resolute foe. Yet we should especially welcome those who share and live out God's word. One might think that the primary reason for doing so is to provide prophets and the righteous with support and encouragement. Lord knows, they need it. But Jesus gives a different reason for receiving those who carry his word, which is that welcoming them welcomes him and his Father. One sure way that we have to get close to Jesus is to welcome those who represent him. Welcome prophets and the righteous for a very great reward.

In sending out the twelve disciples on their first mission to proclaim God's word and heal, Jesus shared with the disciples not just how they should conduct themselves but how others should conduct themselves toward the disciples. Jesus presumably did so in order that the disciples could help the people receive the disciples as Jesus would have them do. Jesus was not only teaching the disciples about others but preparing the disciples to teach others about them. In this instruction that Jesus gave the disciples to share with their hosts, Jesus first told the disciples that anyone who welcomed them welcomed him. The people who let the disciples stay with them on their missionary visits would be receiving Jesus along with the disciples. Jesus added that anyone who received Jesus in that way also received his Father. Jesus further described their reward, saying, "Whoever welcomes a prophet as a prophet will receive a prophet's reward, and whoever welcomes a righteous person as a righteous person will receive a righteous person's reward." Jesus then ended the lesson promising a *certain* reward for those who give as little as a cup of cold water to one of his disciples. In this way, Jesus showed his concern for how others would receive his disciples.

Together, they felt compelled to honor, support, and in some way celebrate special members of their faith community who seemed most and best to carry and live God's word. They did not want particularly to win favor among the religious leadership. Indeed, they made no special effort of honoring the most prominent and elevated. They hoped instead that they were acting out of genuine concern to support special ministers, elders, and missionaries. They just wanted support of the prophets and righteous to be one of their small ministries. So together, they periodically planned small banquets for those special individuals, where the two of them committed themselves to celebrating their guests' distinctive gifts, services, and ministries. Neither of them felt particularly gifted on their own in prophecy or righteousness. They were surely not prophets and didn't count themselves as peculiarly righteous. But they could certainly honor prophets and the righteous. They figured that by doing so, they just might receive a prophet's reward.

Gather and agree in Jesus's name. Matthew 18:19.

One way that we must relate to others, particularly to others who follow Jesus, is to agree on things that represent Jesus. Jesus instructs to gather and agree in his name. Getting together with other believers to celebrate Jesus honors God. Times of solitude can be productive, but we should not isolate ourselves too long from other believers. Fellowship among believers and especially corporate worship honors God. When we get together with other believers, we should commit our hearts, minds, and souls to agreeing on whatever we can and also to asking God who grants what two or more believers ask. While doctrine is important, and respectful discussion of proper doctrine is also important, disrespectful disputes over doctrine divide and destroy, particularly when the opportunity exists for agreement on some points and free celebration of a generous God. The Christian who can get along with no one, not even other believers, loses a great opportunity to have requests fulfilled and even to experience the presence of God. God comes in the midst of agreeing believers. Gather to celebrate Christ, and agree when you gather.

Jesus had taught the disciples several things about relationship with others, beginning by using the example of a little child. To enter the kingdom, they must be like little children, Jesus said. They must also not cause little ones to stumble and must also not despise little ones, he continued. The Father goes after every lost little one, Jesus added. Jesus then instructed about how to deal with sinning church members, starting with one, then two, and then the full body holding them accountable for reform. Jesus then said that if two believers agreed on earth that they should ask for something, then the heavenly Father would do it for them. Unity and agreement among believers is powerful, Jesus was telling the disciples, whose competition among themselves had triggered the lesson. Jesus added, "For where two or three gather in my name, there am I with them." Jesus is present when two or more believers gather to celebrate him.

They had never had any plans to move from one church to another. They doubted that many believers did make such plans, even though they knew that many did move. Rather, they had expected to be lifelong members of the first church that they joined together, where they each long had substantial roles in numerous ministries. Yet to their surprise, a time came when God seemed to move them to another church without their having had any strong desire to go. They seldom attributed things of that nature to God, not trusting their own sense of what was God's action and what was their action, but in this instance circumstances and signs seemed so to conspire that they both deemed the move a God thing. They felt the same about their new church as they each long held substantial roles in substantial ministries, and yet once again, before too long, God seemed to move them decisively to a new church home. In these mysterious moves that they had not planned and did not especially desire, the two things that seemed most clear to them were that they were to continue to gather with other believers and that they must agree with the other believers with whom they gathered. As long as they were fulfilling God's desire, they would follow him to any home.

Try hard to settle matters. Luke 12:58.

Jesus urges us to try hard to reconcile with our adversaries rather than requiring others to settle our disputes against us. While Jesus seems to urge a disposition toward peacemaking and commitment to agree, the context in which he admonished to settle disputes does not suggest that he was saying simply to give up and give in. Jesus probably does not want Christians to be pushovers, easily duped, coerced, or extorted. Rather, Jesus seems from the context of his admonition to have been urging that we see clearly what we owe others and then supply it. The disposition to agree depends on both self-insight and the ability to recognize the moral standard that we offend. Our adversaries can see quite readily the rights that we have denied them, but we tend instead to be blind to our offenses against others. Jesus wants us to judge for ourselves what obligation we owe others rather than force judges to judge against us. Holding out to see how much we can deny others until the judge forces our obedience is no way to treat others. When we find adversaries with claims against us, we should listen to them very carefully with an eye toward our own behavior and the right and wrong against which to judge.

Jesus had already taught so many lessons and parables, turning from the disciples to the crowd of thousands and back to the disciples. Then he turned to the crowd yet again to tell them about interpreting the times. Jesus first reminded them that they could readily predict the weather from appearances around them but then chastised them for not knowing how to interpret the times. How could they so easily see the weather coming but not see what was going on around them with others? How could they tell hot from cold and rain from dry but not right from wrong? Jesus urged them to judge on their own what was right rather than let a judge sentence them to prison. Jesus wanted them to settle their disputes responsibly, saying, "As you are going with your adversary to the magistrate, try hard to be reconciled on the way, or your adversary may drag you off to the judge, and the judge turn you over to the officer, and the officer throw you into prison." Jesus continued teaching as some in the crowd called other matters to his attention.

He didn't want to be a pushover and didn't believe that he was. He knew that conflict avoidance was his natural disposition, which most of the time seemed fine for his peacemaking, collaboration, and community roles and Christian commitments. He had enough roles to fulfill in which going along and getting along were just fine, the preferred attitude for those projects and initiatives. Yet everyone has their boundaries and limits, and everyone also has their responsibilities. He had other roles and faced other situations where he needed to advocate for one thing or another, one result or another, or often for one person or another. While he remained committed to advocating civilly and fairly, he knew that at times he must advocate zealously and that others expected him to advocate zealously, too. What he learned from Jesus's admonition to judge right from wrong and try hard to settle with an adversary was that he must not advocate just to be contentious. He must never cede to others his own responsibility to judge right from wrong. He could advocate firmly for right, but he must at the same time always be sure not to advocate for wrong and then to settle with an adversary the moment that the adversary was in the right. He must not fight for the sake of fighting even in arenas where doing so was the norm. He must not only judge right from wrong and act accordingly but also follow Jesus's resolution norm. He must always conduct himself not as a tool for conflict but as a moral actor, while preferring voluntary fair resolution over blood drawn.

Love one another. John 15:17.

Of course, the prime attitude, approach, and disposition toward relationship with others must be to love one another. Jesus could not have made his command, which was long his Father's command as are all Jesus's commands, any simpler than to tell us to *love each other*. To love another is to act for their wellbeing, to care about and for them when and where able. Love is active, as Jesus is active. Love is not emotion or sentiment but instead trusts, perseveres, and protects. Love seeks the other rather than the self, while demonstrating patience, kindness, and forgiveness. While love cares for the needs of others, love particularly cares for the *souls* of others, wanting every soul to enter the kingdom. Love thus means momentary sacrifice, as Jesus sacrificed, for eternal gain, as Jesus reigns. Yet what Jesus makes simple, our corruption will inevitably twist and make complex. Some will question *whom* they should love rather than loving all others, question *how* they should love rather than loving as Jesus loved, and misconstrue love as a self-feeding feeling or transaction. Some will condition love, limit love, and deny love to others. Instead, love one another as Jesus loved all others.

452

At the Last Supper, Jesus spoke about love, taught about love, and exhorted and admonished the disciples to love, unlike at any other time that the gospels recorded. An astute reader, one who knew Jesus, would have foreseen that Jesus must teach his disciples deeply about love, at his last and greatest opportunity. He began by telling the disciples that he loved them as the Father loved him. Love meant keeping his commands, he told them. Jesus wanted the disciples to experience his joy, he added. Jesus then told the disciples not just to love *him* but to love *one another* as Jesus had loved them. He then explained what real love is, which is to lay down one's life for a beloved friend. Jesus told the disciples that they were now his friends, those who did what he commanded. As friends, they could ask the Father anything in his name, and the Father would give it to them. Jesus concluded simply, "This is my command: Love each other." Jesus had much more to say to the disciples in prophecy, warning, and instruction, but Jesus's lesson on and assurance of his love must have meant everything to the disciples.

He felt that after much close study of Jesus's teaching, he had a proper biblical understanding of love and how that meaning differed from the world's love definition. He would need and draw heavily on that understanding. His long relationship with a couple of others had been rocky. They continually professed love for him while questioning his love for them. And indeed, they frequently showed him popular forms of affection that he did not always return. Yet he had remained steadfastly at their service and sacrificially generous with his funds through their many trials, while they were absent for all of his many fewer challenges. He had also quietly and consistently spoken to them of the love and saving grace of Jesus, while they remained steadfastly opposed to any salvation message, profaned the Lord's name in his presence, and denigrated the gospel message that he quietly shared, when they spoke about him to others. If he had not had Jesus's instruction about love, then he might have thought that he had it all wrong and that love was only outward shows of affection and happy sentiments rather than obedience to Jesus's commands, sacrificial care, and above all else, kingdom invitations.

Love much. Luke 7:47.

Just as Jesus tells us to love one another, he took another occasion to show that *how much* we love can take different degrees and that he appreciates those who *love much*. Many of us have known people who loved us and then known people who loved us much. We also know when we have loved others little and when we have loved others much. How far one goes to serve another, to give to another, to show respect for another, and to sacrifice for another, can all show how much one loves. Jesus, though, did more than exhort us to love much. He also showed what causes one to love more than another. We love more when we know that Jesus has forgiven us more and has done more for us with his unmerited sacrificial love. The deeper we know our fault, the more we know what Jesus gave up, and the more we know the depth of his forgiveness, the more we love in return. Jesus is the author of life and love incarnate. The closer we get to him, the more we love. The way that we should regard others is not simply to love but to love much.

The gospel account of the woman who wept on Jesus's feet, poured perfume on his feet, and wiped his feet with her hair is a very tender account. The woman had lived a sinful life, which was why she felt such debt to Jesus for his great forgiveness. The religious leader who had invited Jesus to the dinner where the event occurred questioned why Jesus had even let the woman touch him. So Jesus told the gathering a story of two debtors, one who owed ten times the other's amount. Jesus asked his host which of the two would love their lender more if the lender forgave both debts. The religious leader answered that of course the one who had received ten times the forgiveness would love more. Jesus then explained that the host had done nothing to clean Jesus's feet when Jesus had entered, while the woman had done so much. Jesus concluded, "Therefore, I tell you, her many sins have been forgiven—as her great love has shown." Jesus added that whoever God forgives little, loves little. Knowing that Jesus had forgiven her much, the woman loved much.

Each day, day by day, he knew a little more of his brokenness and corruption, knew more surely and remembered more often that he was wretched, pitiful, poor, blind, and naked. Each day, day by

454

day, he leaned a little harder on Jesus, repeatedly sighing Jesus's name in grief over his destitution. Each day, day by day, he knew a little more of Jesus's love, its potent, authoritative, and complete cleansing. Each day, day by day, he strove to give a little more of himself, his energy, mind, time, and actions, to Jesus, wishing more and more that he could pour himself out in the way that a certain woman, sensing her own moral destitution, had poured out perfume on Jesus's feet so long ago. He wished that he could wet Jesus's feet with his tears and wipe Jesus's feet with his hair as that woman had done so long ago. Each day, day by day, he was learning to love more, hoping that he would learn to love much. He knew that the only way that he would do so, the only way that his love would ever deepen, would be by deepening his conviction that he had such need of Jesus.

Do to others as you want them to do to you. Luke 6:31.

Jesus gave us what we know as the Golden Rule to do to others just as we would want them to do for us. The instruction highlights that we tend to live with a double standard, one standard for ourselves and a lower standard for others. Because we are each first responsible for ourselves, we do naturally provide and care for ourselves first and foremost. The Golden Rule's power lies in exactly that natural circumstance that we only control ourselves and so we first routinely think of ourselves. Under the Golden Rule, we need to transfer our natural concern for ourselves to unnatural concern for others. We need only ask what we would do for ourselves to know what we should do for others. While we properly ask what Jesus would do in this or that situation, Jesus tells us to ask what *we* would do for *ourselves* if we were in *their* situation. Jesus knew that we do the best for ourselves and, too often, the least for others. He wanted us adopting a different ethic to do the best for others just as we know how to do the best for ourselves. Jesus turned the power of our self-interest into regard for the interests of others, intimating a universal imperative that all have intrinsic worth.

455

Jesus had first told the disciples among the large crowd on the plain who among them God would bless and who among them God would show woe. Jesus said that God blesses the poor, hungry, weeping, hated, insulted, and rejected who follow the Son of Man, for the ancestors of those in the crowd had treated God's prophets just as poorly. Why must the people treat God's representatives so poorly? Jesus then gave the contrast that God will bring not blessing but woe on the rich, well-fed, laughing, and lauded, because the ancestors of those in the crowd had treated the *false* prophets in just that good manner. Why do the people celebrate God's enemies? Jesus then turned to the subject of how to treat one another, both those who love one another and those who hate one another. Everyone who heard Jesus was to do good to others and to pray, give, and lend to both friends and enemies. Jesus summarized, "Do to others as you would have them do to you."

She hadn't felt very self-involved until she began reflecting deeply on the Golden Rule. She had always thought of herself as reasonably well balanced when the subject came to thinking of herself or thinking of others. She had plenty of friends who seemed to regard her as supportive and encouraging. She had no sense that she was unusually isolated, thoughtless, or self-centered. She figured that she was probably about average or maybe a little above average in the time and energy that she spent doing small things for others that showed she was thinking of others. Yet as she reflected on the Golden Rule, she began to realize that being average had in a sense been her goal. While she had never really thought of it, she had probably been doing things for others out of a cultural norm, indeed, in order that others regard her as normal, or no, slightly better than normal. Funny, she thought, how she had never really given her care for others any solid basis, any clear thought. Jesus, she knew, had commanded to do for others as one does for oneself. She now had a basis in his command for acting and not just for average acts but for acts of deep love and regard. She had found in the simplest of rules a transformative ethic.

Forgive. Luke 6:37.

Another aspect of love, in addition to obedience, care, generosity, trust, and faith, is to forgive. To forgive is to excuse and release another from an obligation or claim that one has against them. Offenses, harms, wrongs, and other injustices committed against us give us rights against others for redress. The redress might include that the other stop the misconduct, renounce further misconduct, apologize, and repair the harm, replace the loss, or otherwise compensate so as to make the other whole. We have plenty of opportunity to make these sorts of demands on others, just as they have plenty of opportunity to make these sorts of demands on us. In the usual course of justice as we see it, a wrong creates an obligation giving rise to a claim and demand, leading to apology and redress. God of course could make the same claim and demand over the wrongs we commit and harm those wrongs cause. Yet God is merciful, so much so that he accepted the sacrifice of his Son to break the cycle of obligation, restoring us to God. Just as God is merciful, he expects us to be merciful. He forgives us as we forgive others. He breaks the cycle of obligation not merely to restore us to him but to cause us to show his mercy to others, to show others Christ, in order that he can also restore those others to him. Show mercy and forgiveness like Christ shows mercy, rather than condemn.

In Jesus's sermon to the large crowd on the plain, right after his Golden Rule lesson, Jesus gave simple rules about forgiveness. He had been speaking about loving both friends and enemies. His concern for enemies might have startled, confused, or made uncomfortable many in the large crowd. Yet Jesus immediately made clear that the Father is kind even to the wicked and ungrateful. Because the Father is merciful, Jesus explained, his listeners must also be merciful and forgiving. Indeed, in doing so, they will be the Father's children, Jesus told them, adding that they would then receive a great reward. Jesus continued, "Do not judge, and you will not be judged. Do not condemn, and you will not be condemned. Forgive, and you will be forgiven." Jesus had much more to tell them about giving generously to others and looking at their own faults before looking at the faults of others, but his message on mercy was crystal clear, that they must forgive in order to have God's forgiveness.

He found that forgiveness was easier with some than others. In some cases, he could forgive instantly, like nothing had even happened. Sometimes, forgiveness was easy because the wrong or harm was small, while other times forgiveness was easy because the person committing the wrong was a friend. Yet in other cases, he found forgiving to be hard. Sometimes, forgiveness was hard because the wrong or harm was large, while other times forgiveness was hard because the person committing the wrong was an enemy rather than friend. Of course, he didn't really think of anyone as an *enemy*, although at any one time, his life seemed to have at least one person who just seemed to want to make his life difficult. That person probably thought the same of him, he knew. He just figured that oil and water don't mix, personalities clash, strife takes root, and one finds the other person hard to forgive. In those fortunately rare cases when a person with whom he somehow couldn't manage to get along caused him some large harm from a large offense, he learned that forgiveness can still come in stages when it doesn't come instantly. Rather than grumble while waiting for an apology that he knew would not come, he would instead pray that God would treat the person well, even as he deliberately spoke well of the person to others. His prayers and speaking he may have forced, but in time, he always found that forgiveness came, his heart finally aligning with his commitment to forgive others that God may forgive him.

Forgive another's sins. John 20:23.

Jesus taught two similar but subtly different lessons relating to his command to forgive others. In his first lesson, addressed in the prior section, Jesus said to forgive others in order that God would forgive us. The context of that instruction suggested that Jesus was talking about forgiving others who commit some offense against us. Then, God would forgive us. Yet after his resurrection, Jesus gave a subtly different instruction with an importantly different consequence. Jesus's post-resurrection instruction was to share the

Holy Spirit leading to forgiveness of others' *sins*, meaning forgive their offenses against *God*, rather than to forgive others' offenses against *us*. The rest of Jesus's post-resurrection instruction also gave an importantly different consequence to our sharing the Holy Spirit leading to forgiveness of others' sins, which was that then God would have forgiven *their* sins rather than God having forgiven *us*. To ensure that we understand the difference between forgiving in order to gain our own forgiveness and sharing the Holy Spirit in order to gain *others'* forgiveness, Jesus added that if we do not forgive others their sins, do not share the Holy Spirit, then God would not have forgiven those others' sins. Share the Holy Spirit leading to acceptance of Christ and forgiveness of others' sins. Failing to do so may deprive them of God's forgiveness.

The resurrected Jesus had just appeared to the disciples on the first day of the week following his crucifixion. The disciples were then behind locked doors in fear for the religious leaders who had already condemned Jesus and might now condemn his disciples. Jesus had convinced the startled disciples that he was really present, not just an apparition. He had then breathed on them, telling them to receive the Holy Spirit. At that moment, having just granted the disciples the splendid Advocate, Jesus added a lesson, saying, "If you forgive anyone's sins, their sins are forgiven; if you do not forgive them, they are not forgiven." Well before his crucifixion, Jesus had already taught the disciples to forgive others in order that God would forgive the disciples. Now, though, after breathing the Holy Spirit on them, he was saying that when those others received the Holy Spirit and accepted Jesus's redemption, God would forgive those others. The disciples should now forgive not just to save themselves, to have God restore them, but also to save others who receive the Spirit, confess their need of Jesus, and have God restore them.

She had no hard heart about others' sins. While small sins annoyed her and large ones angered her, as they would anyone, she was still more than ready to have them accept Jesus and receive God's forgiveness. In this willingness, she knew that she differed from some others. She had acquaintances who were quite ready to condemn others without seeming to leave room for the Holy Spirit to work in those others that they might receive Jesus's redemption, God's mercy, and kingdom salvation. She realized that her willingness to contemplate and then accept that God would forgive the most-serious wrongdoers, the ones whose crimes make front-page news, cause serious harm or death, and lead to extended imprisonment, had taken years to develop. She had at first thought it impossible and later thought it improbable and uncomfortable. Yet as her faith deepened and matured, and she understood more of how God regards sin of any kind and who God gave up to redeem sin, in his very Son, she came to see the possibility and indeed the strong probability, no, the certainty, of salvation for anyone, no matter the degree of sin. She was ready to share the Holy Spirit with anyone who would accept Him, in order that they confess Christ and receive God's generous redemption.

Strengthen fellow disciples. Luke 22:32.

At a tender moment recounted just below, Jesus told his leading disciple that the disciple's faith would momentarily fail but that he would turn back to faith, and that when he did so he should strengthen the other disciples. The event embeds Jesus's instruction in such appropriate context for the trials that believers and disciples face today. We do gain faith, lose faith, and regain faith all over again. Few leading disciples have not fallen down or fallen back under some trial. Most, one might think all, have shown at least momentary lapses in faith. The lapses and recoveries do more than humble the disciple. They give the disciple a heart for strengthening others. Jesus commands us to pursue that inclination. When a fellow disciple stumbles, as we all do stumble, other disciples should be reaching out to that fellow with guidance, support, encouragement, and God's forgiveness, so that the disciple regains spiritual strength. Few things pain the heart more than to see or hear of a fellow believer facing the believer's own loss of faith. Indeed, Jesus may have given the instruction to strengthen other disciples in trials of faith because those moments are so hazardous to faith. Recovery may depend on another reaching out with strengthening support, love, mercy, and counsel. Let your heart break again for the trials of another in order that your heart lead you to strengthen the other for swift recovery.

At the Last Supper, the disciples disputed who among them would be the greatest, much as they had done on other occasion. Jesus once again corrected them that they were not to act like the godless who lord authority over one another while calling themselves benefactors. The disciples were instead to serve others while acting not like the greatest but like the youngest. Jesus used his own actions in serving others as example. He also said that because the disciples had stood by him, he was conferring God's kingdom on them where they would indeed join him in sitting on thrones at the table. They must be servants on earth while kings in heaven. Jesus then turned to the leading disciple Peter, saying that the devil had asked to attack them but that Jesus had prayed that their faith would not fail. Referring to Peter's coming denial of Jesus very late that same night, that is, to Peter's humbling failure in faith, Jesus added, "And when you have turned back, strengthen your brothers." Jesus wanted Peter, and likely each of the disciples, to strengthen one another in coming trials.

He shared the pain of others in his faith community whenever another member stumbled over trials because, like all other members of his faith community, he had also stumbled. He suspected that he heard of only a small fraction of those stumbles, which was as it should be, he felt. A body of believers should not entertain gossip. Yet a body of believers also has authority to guide and counsel its members, and responsibility to support and strengthen them, he believed. So in each instance in which the stumbling member was a close enough acquaintance of his to make communication appropriate, he would think and pray until he felt that he had just the right words to strengthen. Restoration in faith cannot be cavalier, he felt, especially when reading how firmly and yet also tenderly Jesus had treated Peter's falling away and restoration. We do not jump on and off the wagon so much as fall off and crawl back, humbled. Faith and its restoration are not cheap, he knew, thinking of Jesus's crucifixion.

Reconcile with others. Matthew 5:24.

The concept of reconciliation is a powerful one. We all want peace and reconciliation, for everyone to get along. The problem is that we tend to think first of what others owe us rather than what we owe others. We claim or demand a need for the *other* to reconcile to *us* rather than offering *our* reconciliation to *them*. Jesus though puts the burden on us to reconcile with others. He commands that we put aside for a moment our show of righteousness just long enough actually to *be* righteous, that is, to provide the apology, remedy, or reform that we owe others when we have done something untoward against them. We all offend. The question is not so much the number of our offenses as what we do about them. Our obligation is to offer reconciliation, to be the moving party, the acting agent who restores relationship by having made good the wrong, provided a make-whole remedy, and committed to reform. Others will owe us things, no doubt. Jesus though has us correct only our side of the ledger, what *we* owe *others*. Indeed, let others owe us much, for then their debt may be our reward in heaven, as Jesus gained all heaven's reward in carrying our debt. But let us owe others no debt, for we should want only reward in heaven.

In the Sermon on the Mount, Jesus had told the crowd of how God would bless them as the salt of the earth and light of the world. He had then cautioned them that he had not come to abolish the law but to fulfill the law, and that they should therefore follow every commandment. Jesus gave as an example one of the Ten Commandments, not to murder. He said that while the command is that anyone who murders God will be subject to judgment, he was telling them that anyone who gets *angry* with another, perhaps to their face calling them a *fool*, faces God's judgment. Jesus then told the crowd how to handle situations in which they had offended another. They would remember their offenses against others as they were offering their gifts to God at the altar. As the gospel account records Jesus saying, they would remember that a brother or sister *has something against* them. In those instances, they were to leave their gift in front of the altar and go address the situation before making their offering. Jesus then told them how to address the situation, saying, "First go and be reconciled to them; then come and offer your gift." In this way, Jesus told the crowd to reconcile with those against whom they have committed offenses.

She went through a period in her life when she took inventory of her offenses against and obligations to others. She was in no sense a frequent offender. Her offenses were no more frequent than the offenses of any other person who has the general respect and confidence of the great majority of their acquaintances. Yet everyone offends, and her conscience, aided by the Holy Spirit, had clear recall of at least a few of her offenses. She just reached a point that action became more important than conscience. She wanted a clear conscience, so far as she was able to clear it, rather than a guilty conscience. Indeed, she suspected that if she carried her guilty conscience much longer that it would no longer be guilty but would have disappeared as an informing organ. So one by one, she settled old scores that others had against her, meaning that she did what she believed most appropriate to make whole the persons whom she had once offended. She initially thought that it would be an arduous process, and in fact it did have its difficult moments. Not every transaction was successful. But in most instances, the person whom she knew had a claim against her had already forgiven her, unbidden. In those instances, her offer of apology and provision of remedy uplifted both her and the other person, showing them both to be acting within the command and will of Jesus.

Do not burden others. Luke 11:46.

Jesus gave one other instruction on how to relate to others about which strong believers should especially take note. Kingdom living is free and full within the life-giving commands as Jesus taught them. A life of obedience in faith is a rich life filled with creativity, affirmation, innovation, relationship, community, and possibility. One who disciples others should be finding natural and authentic ways to present kingdom life in that manner. Somehow, though, some would-be disciple-makers fail to do so. Presented in the wrong way, life-giving commands too easily become life-depleting restrictions. To some non-believers, faith life looks burdened, just as to some adherents, faith life feels burdened. The burdened may simply be misreading scripture and misunderstanding instruction. Unfortunately, some who share faith do so in ways that contribute to misunderstanding. Legalism is an easy substitute for careful counsel and insightful instruction but one that only creates burdensome misunderstanding. God made us to live obedient lives filled with reward and meaning, not disobedient lives filled with meaningless ceremonial rules, burdensome practices, and frequent punishments. Do not burden others in your faith sharing, counsel, and instruction.

While Jesus taught the crowds at length with tender, poignant, and even humorous parables and lessons drawn from everyday life, Jesus displayed no patience when addressing the religious leaders in their hypocrisy. No sooner had the religious leader invited Jesus into his home for a meal than Jesus was reciting woes against the religious leaders. What had triggered Jesus's admonitions was the religious leader's surprise that Jesus did not wash ceremonially. Jesus promptly showed the leader his hypocrisy that he was making a show of cleanliness without being clean by doing as God said. Jesus then gave example after example, ending with a statement that one of the attending law experts properly construed as an insult. Rather than back off his admonitions, Jesus responded with one more. Jesus replied to the law expert, "And you experts in the law, woe to you, because you load people down with burdens they can hardly carry, and you yourselves will not lift one finger to help them." Jesus didn't want the law expert weighing people down with ceremonial practices. He wanted the law experts and religious leaders lifting people up toward the kingdom.

He had made such a study of Jesus's words, commands, and wisdom that he worried for a time that he was reducing the life of Jesus to a set of wearying rules. He wanted to know and follow Jesus's commands but didn't want to lose the closeness, presence, and companionship of Jesus through the Holy Spirit. He wanted kingdom life, not law-induced death. So for a time, he set aside his studies of Jesus's words and commands, thinking that in doing so he might somehow gain a stronger sense of Jesus's presence and guidance. Yet instead, he seemed to drift in faith. Jesus became more of an image than a confidante, more of a satisfying symbol than the commanding King. So he picked up his studies again but this time trying to balance confidante with commander and relationship with rules. He realized in the process that close and trusting relationship with Jesus depends not just on general belief and acceptance but also on constant communication of desires and expectations, something that he knew to be true from other relationships. He could not study Jesus's instructions without also desiring Jesus's relationship, but he also could not desire Jesus's relationship without studying his instructions. He must pursue both, emphasizing relationship whenever words seemed to burden, and emphasizing words when relationship waned.

2.6 Family

Remain married to your spouse. _{Mark 10:7.} *Do not commit adultery.* _{Luke 18:20.} *Do not separate whom God joins.* _{Matthew 19:6.} *Honor your father and mother.* _{Mark 7:10.} *Tell family what the Lord has done for you.* _{Mark 5:19.} *Love Jesus more than family.* _{Matthew 10:37.} *Leave home and family for God.* _{Luke 18:29.} *Do not call any man* father. _{Matthew 23:9.}

Our priorities naturally begin with God and family. Others probably think of Christians in general as particularly devoted to family. Family members take special place in our relationships with others. We cannot, should not, and do not treat family precisely as we treat others. Those who do not adhere to the faith would rightly regard believers as strange if they did not have well-developed, sensitive, and supportive approaches toward families and family members. Indeed, faith can treat certain family relationships as sacramental, as an expression of the relationships between the Father and Son, and between the Son and the believer. Jesus, God's incarnation, certainly deliberately describes his relationship with God as the relationship of Father to Son, deliberately invoking that father-son family relationship. Jesus also certainly deliberately describes his relationship to the church and believers within the church as the relationship of groom to bride, deliberately invoking that husband-wife family relationship. Jesus could hardly have made family relationships more significant than to describe his own divine status and saving role in family terms. These and other family based biblical concepts, doctrines, and instructions tend to confirm that relationship to family is more important than any other relationship except for one's relationship to God. Listen then to how Jesus instructs us on his role and our role within the family, and our relationships with family members.

467

Remain married to your spouse. Mark 10:7.

The first relationship in any family is that of husband to wife, wife to husband. They may later become father and mother, creating another important relationship of parent to child, child to parent, but families form first with union of man to woman. The union may be formal or informal, of short or long duration, happy or sad, voluntary or arranged, but the biological imperative if not always the social one, too, requires that the union must occur in some way and fashion to fulfill the procreative function of family. Families of course have other important functions besides procreation, but a sustainable society must provide for procreation, and societies tend to do so through families, as God so provided in creation and Jesus confirmed in the following gospel account. God's command that husband and wife leave fathers and mothers to unite with one another would be enough to call marriage a sacramental union. When Jesus added that the two, meaning husband and wife, in marriage go from two to one flesh, he amplified marriage's sacramental nature. Jesus clearly regarded marriage as special, so special that no one should be a part of breaking a marriage apart, especially those who voluntarily enter into it and maintain it in safety and fidelity. Remain married to your spouse, and encourage and support others in doing so.

Jesus was traveling about the region of Judea, and crossing the Jordan River, with crowds of people gathering wherever he went. He had stopped to teach the crowd as he usually did, when some religious leaders joined them to test Jesus, as they often did wherever Jesus went. The leaders first wanted Jesus to tell them whether a man could divorce his wife. They may have chosen this question because they knew how popular Jesus had become among both men and women, and wanted either to catch Jesus speaking against the law or to make him admit to a law that women might find especially painful. Knowing that the religious leaders were testing him, Jesus turned the question back on them, asking them what Moses had commanded. They answered that Moses had authorized divorce. In this way, Jesus got the religious leaders to endorse the law so unpopular among women. Jesus then replied that Moses had so commanded knowing that their hearts were hard. Jesus also

468

reminded them that God had made humans both male and female, intending that they join together. Quoting the Torah's Book of Genesis, Jesus concluded, "'For this reason a man will leave his father and mother and be united to his wife, and the two will become one flesh.' So they are no longer two, but one flesh." Jesus was urging that individuals marry and remain married.

They shared a commitment to one another that they knew would not break. How can one break in two? They also knew that circumstances would test the commitment deeply, although they hoped not too frequently. Their experience was that the quality of each of their lives depended on the confidence of both of them in the totality of their commitment to one another and their marriage. Strangely, they learned that the quality of each of their lives had a nearly inverse relationship to the support that their lives generally gave to their marriage commitment. Put more simply, their experience taught them that challenges for either one of them, whether physical or mental or otherwise, meant stronger marriage commitment for both of them. They guessed that Jesus had meant as much when he had said that their two would become his one and that their marriage union was of a kind with his union with all believers, husband to wife like groom to bride church. The harder that life challenged either one of them, the more that they relied on one another in marriage and the more that their marriage meant to both of them. While every day they thanked God for their marriage, even on the hardest days of marriage, they had every faith and confidence that God would keep them together and that no one would drive them apart.

Do not commit adultery. Luke 18:20.

The common meaning of adultery is to engage in sexual intimacy with someone other than one's spouse. Jesus plainly instructed not to commit adultery. Adultery's damage can be psychological, social, occupational, financial, familial, epidemiological, and, of greatest concern, also spiritual. In its literal construction, the command is easy to judge when kept or not kept. No matter what a sinner might claim about certain sins just happening, sexual intimacy in its literal construction takes deliberate and elaborate action. One would know whether one had kept the command or not. Yet as a prior section shows, in commanding no adultery, no murder, and no theft, Jesus extended the commands' construction into questions of the condition of one's heart. To Jesus, the commands were not merely formal and legal but substantive, natural, and life-giving. One must commit no adultery in its literal meaning, which again, is easy to judge when kept or not kept. But one must also guard one's heart, preserving pursuit of the *thought* of intimacy for one's spouse. Marriage is sacramental, a divine union as well as a legal and social one. Sexual intimacy and procreation are incidents, privileges, and in certain instances and respects also responsibilities of marriage. Keeping the command in both its literal and heart senses rewards rather than constrains the believer, with greater intimacy and many other benefits both now and in the future. Obey Jesus's literal command not to commit adultery, while also allowing the Holy Spirit to shape the heart to the command's full power and depth.

Several gospel accounts record Jesus repeating or referring to the command, indeed one of the Ten Commandments, not to commit adultery. In one lesson, Jesus made the command not to commit adultery the first one of several of the Ten Commandments that he recited to the person on whom he was urging obedience. In reciting the no-adultery command first among the five commandments that he repeated to the person on whom he was urging obedience, Jesus took that command out of order. No adultery is the seventh of the Ten Commandments. Jesus recited it first before reciting the sixth command not to murder, the eighth command not to steal, the ninth command not to give false testimony, and the fifth command to honor father and mother. Neither Jesus's lesson nor its context indicate why Jesus recited no adultery as his first example of the great commandments, but his doing so could indicate some primacy either for the person to whom he repeated the commands or for us. Jesus told the rich young ruler who had asked what to do to inherit eternal life, "You know the commandments: 'You shall not commit adultery, you shall not murder, you shall not steal, you shall not give false testimony, honor your father and mother.'" In this account and several others, Jesus showed his concern that his hearers keep the command not to commit adultery. In another gospel account, he also showed how the keeping of this and other commands is not just a formal outward restriction but a deep matter of the heart.

Their worship and Bible studies together, their frequent sharing of growing faith, had many *individual* effects, but they both felt that the most profound or important effect had been on their marriage. They had always valued and protected their marriage. Yet without fully realizing it, they had probably at first done so more in the way that secular society and culture teach couples to value marriage than as Jesus teaches. They found much confidence and satisfaction in the *transactions* of marriage without yet fully embracing the *divinity* of marriage, its spiritual and devotional incidents. Because the transactions were satisfying, equal, and successful, they were happy. Jesus, though, showed them so much more. As they each confirmed and deepened their relationships with Jesus, they began to appreciate more fully what their marriage meant in its spiritual and devotional dimensions. Much of that progress they made individually, exactly as they should have done, because each had different things to learn about marriage's spiritual dimensions. But they also attended marriage retreats together and made other joint studies that brought them along together in their growing understanding of what Jesus's statement meant that they were not two but one flesh. In time, their marriage became a source not just of confidence and satisfaction but of authority and power beyond either of themselves. They were keeping the marriage commandment, and the rewards were multiplying.

Do not separate whom God joins. Matthew 19:6.

Jesus directed instructions to married persons to remain in marriages of safety and fidelity, and not to commit adultery in their course. Those instructions apply to married persons rather than the unmarried. Yet others outside the marriage nonetheless play roles in keeping marriages healthy and married couples safe, faithful, together, and happily married. In the gospel account recounted below, Jesus instructed others outside of marriage but who

471

nonetheless played important advisory roles to the married not to break up those marriages. Jesus does not want us to separate those whom God joins. A popular saying is that raising a child *takes a village.* Applying the same saying to marriages may be equally apt. Healthy marriages can require or benefit from a lot of outside support. We rightly focus on the individual responsibilities of husband and wife for the care and feeding of the marriage. On the other hand, we probably fail to recognize and appreciate the responsibilities of others outside of the marriage to support the marriage. Those responsibilities begin with the parents of bride and groom who must take care to let the two leave and cleave as one. But those responsible to support a marriage can also include pastors, faith-community friends, neighbors, employers, co-workers, siblings, and even older and adult children, not to suggest that young children are in any way responsible for the health or happiness of their parents' marriage. Certainly, to tempt and lure a married person away from a safe and faithful spouse for purposes of intimacy, work, recreation, or other attractions would offend the command not to separate husband and wife. To honor the full command, we might also take special care to support marriages.

As a prior section recounts, Jesus gave some religious leaders who came to test him a lesson in spouses remaining committed to marriage. Simply because Moses had permitted a husband to write a certificate of divorce ending his marriage to a faithful wife did not mean that husbands should necessarily feel free to do so. Moses had permitted the practice out of the hardness, not the righteousness, of their hearts. Jesus had explained that divorcing a faithful spouse in order to remarry could mean committing adultery in the new marriage. Yet Jesus may have embedded a corollary instruction in his lesson to the religious leaders on their legalistic misreading of the commands. Immediately after describing how male and female in marriage become one flesh, Jesus added, "Therefore what God has joined together, let no one separate." Notice that Jesus here did not simply address the responsibility of the husband or even of the wife. His instruction was to let *no one* separate a marriage that God had made. Jesus may have been, indeed was, addressing the religious leaders who may have been, indeed apparently were, promoting or at least supporting divorce in a legalistic misreading of the command.

Jesus was instructing the religious leaders, too, to get the command's natural and substantive meaning right.

He had a role, as many in today's society do, helping those who face divorce. Pastors, professionals, congregants, neighbors, family, and friends all have roles helping married couples remain married, separate, or divorce, he well knew. His role, though, carried with it specific responsibilities that he would have to fulfill to the extent that he was involved in helping separated and divorcing couples. At his first involvements, he more or less did as others in his role more or less do. Conventions are powerful in shaping practices. We do as others do. Yet he had a growing sense that he must align his involvement in helping married couples manage separation and either reconciliation or divorce, with Jesus's admonition not to separate what God had joined. Some would have questioned whether anyone could do so in the role that he played. Those would have washed their hands of any involvement, leaving the couples to struggle through without their help. He recognized that their choice not to get involved might have been the obedient one but felt otherwise as to himself. For a time, at least, he believed that within Jesus's admonition, in its natural and substantive heart sense, he could still play a protective role. He would certainly drive no couple apart. He might even be able to help some couples stay together. But he would for now, for a time, try to live out Jesus's admonition while playing advocating, mediating, guiding, counseling, and peacemaking roles.

Honor your father and mother. Mark 7:10.

The next family relationship, after relationship of husband to wife, wife to husband, about which one thinks, is the relationship to father and mother. As the following account reminds us, Jesus quoted and endorsed the fifth of the Ten Commandments, to honor father and mother, while rebuking the religious leaders for teaching otherwise. Honoring father and mother can mean several things, certainly including speaking well of them to their face and among others, but also to support, care for, obey in context, and show respect. The parent-child relationship is hierarchical, with parent responsible for the care and upbringing of child, and child responsible for obedience during that upbringing. The parent has authority over the child, not the child over the parent. The subordinate child owes obedience, honor, and respect, as attributes of authority. Parental behavior does not at every moment warrant the child's confidence. Parents certainly behave poorly at times including with respect to their parental responsibilities. Children often have cause for forgoing honor, especially in the case of things like abuse or neglect, but the command remains to find ways to honor within the limitations that every parent in some way reflects. The command to honor father and mother comes with the promise of a long life. Honor father and mother as Jesus commanded and as he demonstrated so perfectly in his own life.

The religious leaders and law experts, who followed so many religious traditions, had again come from Jerusalem to observe and question Jesus. The first thing that they noticed as they gathered around Jesus was that his disciples were not following their traditions, particularly the ceremonial washing of hands. So they questioned Jesus about the disciples' violation of their traditions. Jesus quoted Isaiah to them that they were worshiping God in vain. Their hearts, Jesus said, were far from God. They were letting God's commands go, following traditions instead, and teaching only human rules. Jesus then illustrated his point with specific examples, saying, "For Moses said, 'Honor your father and mother,' and, 'Anyone who curses their father or mother is to be put to death.'" But the religious leaders and law experts, Jesus continued, were nullifying the command to honor father and mother, by teaching that support for parents should go instead to devotions to God. The religious leaders were not letting them do anything to honor father or mother as the command required, Jesus rebuked them, adding that they do many other things the same way, putting their traditions above the commands of God. They should instead have been teaching everyone the command to honor father and mother.

He had faced his challenges, like any adult child who cares for and supports parents in their declining years. Some might say that he had faced larger-than-usual challenges, and to a degree that assessment might be true, but he knew that others had faced and would face far greater challenges than he did. The relative ease or difficulty of honoring parents in their later years is not the point, he had learned, indeed had learned the hard way. The point is to obey the command to honor father and mother. Certain parents at certain times can make obeying the command hard, but any command can be hard to obey at times, and again, the point was not the relative ease or difficulty of the command. His larger challenge was discerning just *how* to honor. What did *honor* mean when parents gradually or suddenly lose their fortune and finances, mental and physical abilities, and social sensibilities, when they are no longer fully or even partially responsible or at times even respectful? To honor, he learned, can mean to forgo or not to forgo, support or at times not to support, turn respectfully away but at other times turn respectfully back, but always to care, forgive, discern, and love as Jesus would do so. Honor for a parent, he concluded, has no formula but instead has a very big heart, indeed, the heart that a parent has for a very young and helpless child.

Tell family what the Lord has done for you. <small>Mark 5:19.</small>

Family members need encouragement and instruction in the Lord. We must, on the other hand, find sensitive ways to tell family about the Lord, for who are we after all when among family? What gives us such special place as to preach to family? Jesus encourages us to tell family what God has done for us including the mercy God has shown. God blesses, to be sure. Telling of blessings is a sound way to instruct in the way of the Lord. Yet telling of the Lord's mercies beyond and before blessings can be especially instructive. Think of a blessing as something that you have always wanted, and God provides it. Think of a mercy as something you have always feared, and God relieves you of it and forgoes it. Each of us has certain consequences that we unfortunately earn through broken ways on which we insist and corrupt actions we sadly pursue. Those consequences could be loathsome disease or other bad health, mental and emotional disabilities, anxieties and paranoia, broken and estranged relationships, lost jobs and reputations, financial burdens and legal liabilities, or even conviction and incarceration. The most upstanding and decent citizen can in all candor look back and see nearly any one or all of those consequences occurring to them with reasonable probability given life's vagaries and one's own small and large corruptions. Still somehow, someway, with miraculous relief, we manage to avoid many or all of them, or recover from them in short enough order that God's hand is evident. Thank God that we do not get all that we deserve. God is merciful. Conveying that mercy is a sensitive way of exhorting family members.

The Bible gives us a second account of the demon-possessed man whom Jesus healed, this second account in a different one of the four gospels. The gospels work in that way, sometimes two, three, or even four of them telling about what appears to be the same event but in some cases with slight differences among the accounts. Scholars tell us that those small differences help prove the gospels' reliability, accounting credibly for small differences in observation, viewpoint, memory, and communication. Mark's account of Jesus's healing the demon-possessed man barely differs from the account of Luke. In Mark's account, the awestruck townsfolk *plead* with Jesus to leave them rather than simply ask. More significantly, when the healed demoniac begs to go with Jesus, Mark's account has Jesus adding a little to his instruction, "Go home to your own people and tell them how much the Lord has done for you," including in Mark's account, *"and how he has had mercy on you."* Speaking of God's blessings is one thing, while speaking of God's mercy is another. Mercies also bless. Mercies also instruct. Jesus wanted the people to return home to their families and instruct about God's mercies.

Although most people, even those close to him, might believe that he had led a sufficiently protected and cautious life not to have experienced the profundity of God's mercy, to the contrary he understood quite well how far and how deeply God had extended him mercy. He found those mercies in every place from which he had come and everywhere he went. Things that he had said and done that could easily and naturally have caused very bad consequences by and large had not done so. Somehow, he had skated through intact. People, communities, and institutions had been patient and forgiving with him, when they might reasonably not have been, when they could have cast him out and cast him off.

Family members and long-term co-workers and employers had been particularly merciful in their long suffering of him. He had also avoided so many things that others had not avoided, events like accidents, injuries, illnesses, and disabilities, when his acts, habits, and practices were not qualitatively different than those who suffered them. He constantly felt as if he were just sneaking through, dodging so many consequences about which he could not in the least have complained if they had happened to him. This relief, he understood with great appreciation, was God's mercy. He assumed no right to any of it, instead attributing it fully to what it was, the desire of God to forgive and restore in recognition of his glorious Son. These mercies he regularly shared with his family, softening their hearts to anything else that he might say to encourage their faith.

Love Jesus more than family. Matthew 10:37.

One of the instructions that Jesus gave that probably surprises new readers or hearers as much or more than his other instructions is to love him more than family. We appropriately hold family values high and also highly value family relationships. We show great respect and sentiment for the love of spouse, parents, siblings, children, and grandchildren. To consider loving anyone or anything more than family takes careful thought, real hesitation. Yet we also know the proper order of things, expressed in the hierarchy of first loving God and then family, followed by allegiance to constitution, country, or other devotion. To love Jesus more than family is thus only to endorse what most already profess, whether they do so after or before careful consideration. The surprising thing about Jesus's instruction is instead that he contemplates that choosing to love him at all, choosing his salvation, will sometimes and perhaps often be the dividing point within families. We must then still love him first, love him more than family, even if doing so means for a time that we will lose family relationships. The instruction's challenge, though, may not be at all as great as it can at times seem because love for Jesus is at the same time the salve and saving grace for family relationships.

The *only* way that one can love family properly is to love Jesus more than family. One must first love Jesus before one knows what it means to love family.

Jesus was instructing his disciples about their first mission on their own. He had many instructions. Toward the end, though, he turned to the question of disputes within the family. Jesus had already told the disciples that some whom they met along the way would acknowledge Jesus while others would not, although he warned that those who did not acknowledge him, he would not acknowledge before his Father in heaven. Disputes between followers of Jesus and those who did not follow and obey Jesus would even divide families, Jesus also warned, even to the point of turning parent against child and child against parent. Family households would hold enemies. Yet Jesus's instruction to the disciples on this point of whether to follow him or submit to the contrary traditions or will of family members was clear. Jesus said, "Anyone who loves their father or mother more than me is not worthy of me; anyone who loves their son or daughter more than me is not worthy of me." Jesus did not counsel here to disrespect or reject parents or other family members but instead to love *him more* than family.

He felt a twinge of sadness or even irony that he had faced directly the question of whether to love Jesus more or less than extended family so often that it hardly troubled him anymore. He had long ago chosen Jesus, chosen to love Jesus more than family, as Jesus instructed. At the same time, he knew quite well that if he had not chosen Jesus, he would have been incapable in his love for family. While extended family members blew hot and cold in their relationship and regard for, and communication with, him, he had somehow instead, through the gracious work of the Holy Spirit, acquired equanimity toward his family members that sustained and balanced him. He felt able to respond when they needed him, communicate when they wanted him, and respectfully withdraw when not. More so, he felt that Jesus's instruction had given him sound basis on which to act in all of his family relationships. He hoped and prayed that they would someday find the same salvation and solace in, and receive the same counsel from, Jesus. He hoped above all that his quiet witness to Jesus, his steady demonstration of what Jesus does with a broken life, would draw his family members to Jesus. He knew fully what Jesus meant in loving him above family members.

Leave home and family for God. Luke 18:29.

Many households are faith households, while many other households are not. Many individuals who come to faith do so within faith households, while many others who come to faith do so in households not of faith. In that latter group are some newly committed individuals who must leave their households not of faith, if they are to maintain their faith or maintain their safety, finances, relationships, or sanity. Faith naturally divides followers from those who do not follow. Sometimes the division remains only spiritual, while at other times the division must also become physical. Sometimes, faith and no-faith cannot and even should not abide. Jesus recognizes the challenge that family members face leaving the traditions and confines of a household in order to follow him, to follow the one Christ. Jesus extends a reassurance that faith alive is far better than family dead. Those who accept Christ receive the kingdom, the rewards of which are far greater than a faithless household can ever offer. Yet those who leave a faithless household for the kingdom may also have done the one thing that will save the household by drawing its members to the kingdom. If necessary, or whenever appropriate to maintain faith and preserve order and peace, leave home and even family for God. Follow Jesus, and pray for the faithless household.

The disciples had made sacrifices to follow Jesus but of course had made much greater gains. At times, though, their sacrifices must have felt large to them. They had left families, friendships, hometowns, and occupations, and had faced hunger, cold, heat, and danger, for Jesus. The leading disciple Peter may have exhibited as much when he exclaimed to Jesus that they had indeed left all for him. The occasion was the moment when Jesus had told the rich young ruler to give everything to the poor because the rich find it hard to enter God's kingdom. His statement that the rich would find it hard evidently surprised his listeners, many of whom may have thought that the rich would find it easier. Someone had even asked Jesus then whom God could possibly save if not the rich. Jesus had only answered indirectly that God makes all things possible. That was when Peter had exclaimed that the disciples had left everything to follow Jesus. "Truly I tell you," Jesus had replied to Peter, "no one who has left home or wife or brothers or sisters or parents or children for the sake of the kingdom of God will fail to receive many times as much in this age, and in the age to come eternal life." Jesus had reassured Peter and the disciples that they would receive the far greater reward.

She of course felt a little odd about Jesus's instruction to leave home and family for God. She naturally put God over everything including home and everyone including family, even though her home and family meant a lot to her. The challenge that Jesus's instruction presented her wasn't so much to prefer God but to leave home and family. Did he mean really *leave* family? She could see that in some cases, with some people, he did likely mean to leave family, perhaps to travel to some distant land for missionary work, or to spread the gospel as a traveling preacher, or maybe even in certain consuming ministries, whether music, film, media, youth, or other. In any or all of those cases, she figured that leaving family might not mean abandoning spouse and children but instead not having a spouse or children. Or she could see that it might mean being away from family for a time or season. Plenty of individuals, she knew, left family to engage in military service, sports or entertainment careers, and other service and ventures. She, though, didn't see those major opportunities or obligations arising for her, whether in Christian ministry, artistic careers, or otherwise. What she did see was that in small ways, she needed at times to separate herself from family to join with God. Those times might be for prayer, study, meditation, or reflection. She could not predict when God would call her, but when from time to time she did feel his periodic call, she answered the call at least in mental and spiritual solitude from her family. In doing so, she hoped that she was obeying God.

✢

Do not call any man *father*. Matthew 23:9.

When Jesus instructed not to let anyone call another *father*, he did so in the context of the religious leaders loving to go around claiming titles and honors from the people. He may well not have been speaking at all about one's natural father but instead about leaders who claim to be *spiritual* fathers. In one respect, Jesus's instruction sounds easy to follow: just don't call a pastor or other religious leader *father*. Yet construing Jesus's command in that manner would only be a legalistic or formal construction. In substance, Jesus may also have meant not to treat any authority figure, whether a biological parent, religious leader, or secular ruling official, as a spiritual parent, when instead we have the Trinity, meaning Father, Son, and Holy Spirit in one, to be our spiritual authority. Jesus wants us to claim only the one spiritual Father in heaven and not to make spiritual fathers among men. Because we have one spiritual family that already has a Father, we don't need to recognize other spiritual fathers. Certainly, we learn much from wise scholars, pastors, study leaders, family members, and others. We should listen and learn much, and talk little. Yet if anyone, whether religious leader, biological parent, guardian, or other authority figure claims to speak over us for God, we should not accept them as substitutes for our spiritual Father who speaks to us through his Son and Holy Spirit. Use whatever terms of endearment for your natural parents that you wish, but call no one your spiritual *father*.

Jesus had once again rebuked the religious leaders by warning and teaching against their hypocrisy. He then turned to his disciples and the crowd that had gathered to hear him. Jesus told them not to act like the religious leaders and law teachers who did everything for show, to gain the attention and esteem of the people rather than to help the people and serve God. Jesus called the crowd's attention to how the religious leaders loved to be called *rabbi*, their religious father or teacher. Yet Jesus told the crowd not to let anyone call any of them *rabbi* or *teacher* because they had only one Teacher. Jesus added, "And do not call anyone on earth 'father,' for you have one Father, and he is in heaven." Jesus added not to let others call them instructors, either, because the Messiah was their one Instructor.

481

Jesus summarized that they must reject these honorific titles because the greatest among them must be their servant. God, he concluded, exalts the humble and humbles the proud.

She loved her father very much. He was kind, funny, gentle, patient, and well respected by others. More than that, he loved his daughter, she knew. She would have done for him anything that he asked and often did much for him even though he seldom asked much of anything. As much as they loved one another, as highly as she regarded him likely more than any other man, and as often as she expressed that regard to him and others, she nonetheless always held a little something back inside her that she knew was only for her one heavenly Father. Indeed, she reserved all for her heavenly Father, ensuring that he approved of whatever she gave to her earthly father. She sensed and believed that her heavenly Father fully approved of everything that she did for her earthly father precisely because she followed only the Father and Son on spiritual matters. When young, she had certainly looked in part to her father for spiritual instruction, as any child with a believing father should. Yet as she matured, she learned to look for herself to her heavenly Father, which her maturity taught her to do, although she also knew that her earthly father expected and approved. She had one Father, the same Father her mother and father had. Their first family was their spiritual family, all in one.

2.7 Children

Welcome little children in Jesus's name. _{Luke 9:48.} *Do not cause a child to sin.* _{Matthew 18:6.} *Let children come to Jesus.* _{Matthew 19:14.} *Humble yourself like a little child.* _{Matthew 18:4.} *Perceive God like a little child.* _{Luke 10:21.} *Receive God like a child.* _{Luke 18:17.}

Another relationship about which Jesus instructed much is our relationship with children. Of course, children are family members, and so what Jesus said above about family members could apply to children, too. This part separates out Jesus's instructions about children, though, because he had so much to say about children apart from what he instructed about families, and also because the children to whom we often relate are not our own. Put another way, Jesus taught not only about how we should relate to our children but also how we should relate to others' children, children who are not our own. Indeed in addition to instructing how to relate to children of our own and not our own, Jesus also instructed about how we should act, using children as the example. The child-like at heart will be pleased to know that Jesus made children an example for us. Jesus concerned himself greatly about children, about our relationship to children, and about the characteristics of children that we should preserve or redevelop within ourselves. Jesus's instruction about children warrants this separate section from the prior section on family. Consider Jesus's lessons, instructions, and commands on our relationship to children.

Welcome little children in Jesus's name. Luke 9:48.

483

Jesus said to welcome little children in his name. On one hand, his instruction seems easy and natural. Children are often playful, joyful, cute, entertaining, spontaneous, fun, silly, and energetic. Most of us have a soft spot for children. We even regard with suspicion those who don't like children and certainly readily condemn those who mistreat children. Who, after all, but an ogre doesn't like and welcome little children? Yet on the other hand, we for the most part really don't welcome little children especially when serious and weighty things of the soul and spirit are at issue. Children have their place, we too often feel. Their place may be for us to watch and enjoy when the subject is rest, relaxation, and play, *family time* especially, but definitely not study time, not spiritual time, not *Jesus time*, when adults should instead banish children to the nursery and playground so that study groups can parse the mysterious things of God. This banishing of children, though, seems to be the opposite of what Jesus instructed when saying to welcome little children *in his name*. As often as the disciples tried to shoo little children away in order to elevate themselves around Jesus, Jesus called the little children back to him and told the disciples to welcome them in his name. His doing so was not solely for the children's benefit but for our benefit, too. In the following gospel account, Jesus tells us the reward of welcoming little children in his name, which is that in doing so, we welcome him and the Father who sent him.

Jesus's prominence, the large crowds that thronged to hear and see him, must have tempted the disciples to consider their own prominence. The disciples knew not only that the crowds admired Jesus greatly and that Jesus had already accomplished great miracles but also that God destined Jesus for even greater. They also knew that Jesus had given them special roles as his disciples, brothers, and friends, and as recorders of his word, students of his teaching, and carriers of his gospel message. Their prominence naturally affected them, influenced their thinking, created in them certain expectations and attitudes. One of the ways in which their visibility among the crowds and proximity to Jesus affected them was to make them wonder who among them would be the greatest, especially when Jesus was no longer with them as he increasingly predicted. On one such occasion late in his public ministry when Jesus hinted at his departure, the disciples promptly argued about which of them would then be the greatest. Jesus brought a little child to his side, saying, "Whoever welcomes this little child in my name welcomes me; and whoever welcomes me welcomes the one who sent me." Jesus then made clear that the least among them would be the greatest.

As she went back and forth between the two churches, she noticed how differently the two congregations treated children. In one church, children seemed to be everywhere during the worship celebrations. They were asleep in the pews with their dancing, singing, and shouting parents. They were in the arms of their mothers singing in the choir. They were pulling at their daddies' shirttails as their daddies played their musical instruments. And the children old enough to play independently with friends were sneaking in and out of the balcony at the back. The older children had their own choir that sang at many of the celebrations, while other youth filled out a small orchestra also comprised of adults. She knew the conventions at the other church, though, where children were barely seen, never heard. Infants were not in their parents' arms or asleep beside them in the pews but in the nursery at the far end of the facility. Young children were in playrooms in the basement. Youth old enough to do so stayed home. She kept thinking of Jesus's exhortation to welcome the little children.

Do not cause a child to sin. Matthew 18:6.

After welcoming little children in Jesus's name, Jesus gives the corollary warning not to cause one of those little children to sin. Any person, whether informed in the faith or not, would recognize the hazards that adults cause to children, in abuse and neglect, and also through exposing children to drugs, alcohol, sexual indiscretion, and other adult dissipations. Sin, though, involves not just horrible crimes or rank dissipation but also turning away from Jesus and disobeying his commands. As we welcome and attract little children with our love for Jesus and love for them, we must ensure that we do not in any respect turn them away from Jesus or cause them to disobey his commands. We should of course show little children the love, concern, gentleness, and sensitivity of Jesus while providing for their needs. We should of course abstain from every crime or dissipation against them or in their presence, and about which they might hear and consider imitating. Yet we should also instruct them positively in the lessons, commands, and worship of Jesus so that they do not turn away from Jesus and break his commands. Jesus spoke in startlingly evocative ways about the horrible consequences of causing children to sin. From his alarming warnings, we should readily understand that facilitating our own corruption is one thing, and the corruption of another adult another thing, but the corruption of a child a terrible offense that God will punish.

Jesus had called over a little child to illustrate how the disciples were to behave in taking the lowly place to enter the kingdom in greatness. He had then told the disciples to welcome little children in his name. Jesus then turned the disciples' attention to their care for little children. He first warned the disciples not to cause children to sin, using a terrifying illustration of the eternal consequences of doing so. "If anyone causes one of these little ones — those who believe in me — to stumble," Jesus said, "it would be better for them to have a large millstone hung around their neck and to be drowned in the depths of the sea." He then repeated that while bad things must come to the world, things would go very badly for those persons through whom the bad comes. Better for those persons, Jesus said in another terrifying illustration, that they would cut off their hand or foot, or gouge out their eye, and yet enter heaven, than if they should cause such sin and so suffer eternal fire. Jesus was serious about how the disciples should treat little children in not causing them to sin.

She delighted in children. The world to her was just a little too weighty for her natural light spirit, indeed at times far too weighty. She truly felt of another world in the lightness and joy that her heart hid within her. Children revealed that lightness and joy. She could watch and laugh at children for hour after hour. Sure, they tired her out as they tire out anyone, even the strongest of moms and dads. Yet at the end of any tiring day with children, as she let her energy slowly return to her mind and limbs, she would not be down or depressed from the weariness but instead inwardly joyful for having spent the day with children. She would remember and recount to others all of the funny things that they did and said, the way that they encountered the world so openly and their little acquaintances and even their adult supervisors so freshly. She saw that they hid so few things and revealed so many. She saw far less of the guile and posturing that she observed in adults, indeed hardly saw any. The children didn't quite seem capable of adult manipulations and corruptions. Her heart grieved when she thought of the children slowly developing those adult habits that make the world so dark and weighty. She wanted no part of that aspect of their maturation. She wanted to help children remain children at heart, even as they grew to love more of Jesus.

Let children come to Jesus. Matthew 19:14.

To welcome little children in Jesus's name and then to be sure not to cause them to sin are two fundamentals in our relationship with children. Yet we really should be drawing children to Jesus, not just welcoming them and avoiding harming them when they come. Jesus demonstrated and instructed that he wanted children near to him. He placed his hands on them in answer to requests for prayer over them. Imagine the opportunity to have Jesus place his gentle, healing, Spirit-conveying hands on *your* child and pray over your child. Imagine how that event would forever change your child's life. Then go see that the touch, prayer, and blessing of Jesus will occur in your child's life and the life of every other child whom you can reach in your acquaintances. Even as he said to let the little children come to him, Jesus also warned specifically against hindering children in their approach to him. We should be bringing children to Jesus, not keeping children from Jesus. Jesus also told us why we should let children approach him, saying that the kingdom belongs to those who are like them. We should see the life-giving, life-transforming, kingdom destination of every child who comes to Jesus, and we should facilitate and encourage those contacts with the passion and urgency that those opportunities demand.

The crowds that followed, gathered around, and pressed in on Jesus included not just the disciples and other believers, the curious seeking answers or miracles, the sick seeking healing, and religious leaders looking to question and challenge Jesus, but also children. Before or after Jesus had taught, the parents or other guardians of the children would sometimes help the children forward to come near Jesus. On one of those occasions when the people brought their little children to Jesus, they specifically asked him to lay his hands on them and pray for them. The disciples, though, rebuked the people, apparently thinking that Jesus had more-important things to do than to attend to little children. Jesus quickly intervened to correct the disciples, saying, "Let the little children come to me, and do not hinder them, for the kingdom of heaven belongs to such as these." Jesus didn't want the disciples interfering with those who wanted the children to know, have the blessing of, and even learn from and follow Jesus. Jesus then placed his hands on the children just as the people had asked, in the sign of prayer and blessing. His work done, he then departed for another region.

She soon found that her delight in children had led her to a next step that she had not initially anticipated. She wanted these children not just to lighten her day and maintain their own joy and innocence. She also wanted those children to know Jesus. Indeed, she realized that living for the kingdom would soon become the only way that those children could preserve their joyful innocence. She knew that as they matured, just as she had matured, that life's challenges and temptations, and their own corruptions, would quickly weigh them down unless they had the hope, instruction, and love of Jesus. She wanted to help them learn about Jesus and grow close to Jesus so that they could enter his kingdom with the joy of children, no matter what their age. She had read and heard that the kingdom was for those who are like children, that entering the kingdom requires a child's faith, joy, and innocence. She wanted to see the day when those children in whom she took such joy had grown, as she knew that they must do, but see that they had retained Jesus's kernel of innocence, that very same kernel that she held and that carried her day by day toward the kingdom.

Humble yourself like a little child. Matthew 18:4.

Jesus not only teaches us how to treat children but also uses children to teach us about ourselves. Jesus makes clear that children have attributes and capacities that we should retain to enter God's kingdom. Children may have joy, they may have innocence, and they may be open, trusting, and without guile. God may find many things that children have in abundance but adults have abandoned or lost. Yet one thing that Jesus points to in particular about children that we should imitate and adopt is *low position*. Jesus's reference to a child's low position is of course humorous in one respect that children are literally small. Jesus is not saying that we should be literally small or physically inconsequential. Yet that children are not physically imposing or intimidating may nonetheless have something to do with Jesus's reference to their low position. Children find only low position in adult settings in part simply by fact of their small size. Watch adults greet one another with a little child also present. You will notice that the child gains attention only if an adult bends or stoops to take notice of the child. Children in those circumstances simply stand patiently by, not in any position to assert themselves into the conversation. Children have low position. God wants adults to assume low position even when they have the maturity and size to do otherwise. To take low position means having no need to call attention to oneself. Be humble and of low position like a little child.

As prior sections recount, Jesus had called a little child to his side to illustrate to the disciples how they were to conduct themselves in the kingdom of heaven if they wanted the notice of God. The disciples had been discussing who would be the greatest in the kingdom of heaven, presumably referring to which one of them, as they had argued on other occasion. Jesus had corrected them, saying in one gospel account that they must change to become like little children simply to get into the kingdom of heaven. Because entry into the kingdom requires a childlike reform, childlike attributes would also make them greater within the kingdom. Jesus pointed out one childlike attribute in particular, saying, "Therefore, whoever takes the lowly position of this child is the greatest in the kingdom of heaven." If the disciples wanted to be great in the kingdom of heaven, then they would need to take a child's lowly position. Humility marks merit in the kingdom of heaven.

He had many lessons in humility and more sure to come. God, he knew, apportions grace to each according to their need. Events and circumstances had humbled him so often that he figured God wanted him humble and had no room for any hint of pride and arrogance. He was of course fine with that frequent humbling, even if it never really came easily. He hated vanity and conceit as much as anyone, especially when he saw those attributes in himself. He wanted no part of his demeanor or conduct to reflect ego or entitlement. The challenge, though, was not commitment to humility but instead to learn the practices that would reflect it. He figured that few people actually get up in the morning intending to reflect arrogance. Instead, pride sneaks up on one, insinuating itself into little words, actions, and practices that if not kept regularly in check grow into pride's full-fledged forms of smugness, self-importance, and superiority. He found it hard, though, to discern and adopt practices of humility without those practices beginning to look like false humility and therefore more like pride. Trying to look humble when one is not simply does not work. He knew that he needed a deeper transformation, Jesus's transformation, indeed to become like a little child. Little children didn't act humble. They were instead simply of low position in which they acted comfortably and naturally. So he began moving through his days, as much as he could, as if in the low position of a child.

Perceive God like a little child. Luke 10:21.

Jesus suggests in the gospel account recounted immediately below that the way that we perceive God, the way that we see God, understand his instruction, and respond to it in kingdom power and authority, is the way that little children see things. On one hand, Jesus's assertion is surprising. Isn't spiritual insight instead something for seminarians and scholars? One might reasonably assume that to grasp proper doctrine takes a high level of understanding, to memorize and recall doctrine takes a high level of organization and synthesis, and to practice doctrine properly takes a high level of analysis and evaluation. If one thought so, then one would likely be wrong. Jesus says instead that God reveals these things not to scholars but to little children. Yet on the other hand, Jesus's assertion is not so surprising. Doesn't it seem that secular scholars, with all of their critical capacity and hardened learning, are the hardest to convince of the reality, historicity, authenticity, power, and immanence of Christ? Great scholars have of course been great believers. But they may first have had to set aside not their skill and appetite for learning but the hardened and incomplete or inaccurate knowledge that they had wrongly acquired. Try convincing an academic that the academic is wrong. Jesus may be saying that God reveals himself to those who have the open capacity to see someone who does not submit to prior knowledge because he is truth itself, a priori. Perceiving God like a little child may be the only way to know him because next to God, we are and will always remain very, very little children.

The seventy-two disciples whom Jesus had sent out, after having earlier sent out the twelve, returned to Jesus after finishing the preaching and healing work for which Jesus had commissioned them. They shared with Jesus their joy that even demons submitted to them. Jesus confirmed that he had empowered them to overcome the enemy and that nothing would harm them. Yet he cautioned that they should not be happy that demons submitted to them. They should not have been taking satisfaction in the power and authority that Jesus had given them. They should instead, Jesus corrected, have been rejoicing that God knew them in heaven. The gospel account, though, states that despite this correction or slight rebuke, Jesus was still *full of joy through the Holy Spirit*, presumably that the seventy-two disciples had understood, grasped, and deployed kingdom authority. Expressing that joy, Jesus then added, "I praise you, Father, Lord of heaven and earth, because you have hidden these things from the wise and learned, and revealed them to little children." Jesus evidently saw in the seventy-two successful disciples something akin to the faith of little children, the opposite of those attributes of adult weightiness that the supposedly wise and learned law experts must have exhibited in rejecting and testing Jesus.

He had an intellectual's challenge in coming to faith. His wide reading had given him an outlook that was in some respects more like a closed system, an *in-look* if you will, than like the open perspective and rational system for observation that it purported to be. What his secular reading had taught him would not serve him well in seeing the things of God. Yet something open, exciting, grand, sensitive, and discerning led him forward, some*thing* that he later learned to have been some*one*, the Holy Spirit of Christ who reveals the things of God. He followed the Spirit without yet fully knowing the Spirit and without yet fully have professed and confessed his great need of Christ. The Spirit nonetheless led him to Christ like a gentle Father leads a very small child. The Spirit seemed to take his tiny hand and pull it very gently along, letting him pause at every small diversion, but then gently tugging him again in the one way of Jesus's light. And so he came to see Jesus more and more clearly, and began to walk fully in the Messiah's great light. Even as he walked, though, he walked only as a little child. He had no pretense that he would ever be a great mind, great reader, or great scholar in the kingdom, which was perfectly fine with him, because he would far rather be a tiny child in the kingdom than a great scholar outside it.

Receive God like a little child. Luke 18:17.

Jesus's instruction to receive God like a child sounds so encouraging, even endearing. We easily picture children running and clinging to Jesus in all their delight and innocence. The image entirely relieves us of the burden of thought, reason, and rationale. All we need do is be like little children in our approach toward the kingdom. One need not even have any rationale or weighty doctrine for that approach, just simple acceptance, open heart, and ready trust and belief. Yet Jesus actually makes it not just an invitation but an *imperative* that only those who receive the kingdom like a child will get to enter it. It is not simply that we *may* receive God like a little child but that we *must* receive God like a child. We cannot literally turn back the clock to physically become a child again. Jesus says that we must receive the kingdom *like* a child, not *as* a child, although children may themselves enter the kingdom. Our opportunity and obligation is thus to display the attitude of a child toward the kingdom. What most marks the attitude of a child toward good things is that simple innocence, acceptance, belief, and delight. The children who scampered to Jesus to cling to him in delight were not doing so because their scriptural studies had confirmed that he indeed fulfilled the prophecies, nor because his own doctrinal statements were internally sound, nor even because of his miracle healings that might well have scared little children. They instead perceived a Person wholly without guile, whose charismatic love for everyone including children naturally attracted throngs. The children were willing to accept readily, openly, and wholeheartedly what adults also perceived but held too often at arm's length.

Crowds brought the sick, lame, and deranged to Jesus for miracle healing, so many healings that the crowds later lined the road to hail Jesus as the Messiah on his triumphal entry into Jerusalem shortly before his crucifixion. Yet people also brought babies, perfectly healthy babies, so that Jesus could place his hands on them in blessing. They also let their little children crowd around Jesus in delight. At one of these times, the disciples rebuked the parents for letting their babies and children distract Jesus. The disciples must have assumed that Jesus ministered only to adults, to the mature, perhaps only to those who would hear and assess his message intellectually and accept it by reason. Jesus corrected the disciples first by calling the little children to him and then by telling the disciples not to hinder the children *because the kingdom belongs to them*. The teaching might have startled the disciples because Jesus then emphasized, "Truly I tell you, anyone who will not receive the kingdom of God like a little child will never enter it." Imagine the disciples' consternation that as adults they had given up everything to learn from and follow Jesus, and yet now, Jesus was saying that the kingdom was for those who act like little children.

As much reading and study as she did of God's word, she nonetheless retained a child-like openness for whatever he had for her. She loved group Bible studies, especially when the program was organized and its leader consistently shared fresh insights. She liked to read Bible commentary including many different authors who shared their own insights. She loved reading and memorizing Bible books and passages, knowing the clarity and stability that the verses gave her. Yet for all of her reading and studies, she was not particularly interested in theories around scriptures and faith. While some of the authors she read were doubtless scholars holding doctorates in theology, she had little interest in theology and would not read theological texts. While she loved historical exegesis of the Bible texts because they placed the words of Jesus in such strong context, she had no particular interest in history itself, in things that had little or nothing to do with the Bible text. She also had no interest at all in comparative religion. For a time, these limits to her interest bothered her, especially when others around her devoted such energy to theological, ideological, political, historical, and other questions connected in some way with the Bible stories and text. But soon, she concluded instead that she wanted to retain a child-like love for God. If more-intellectual and more-theoretical studies would not help her love God like a child, then she was no longer going to be bothered by them.

2.8 Enemies

Love your enemies. Matthew 5:44. *Bless those who curse you.* Luke 6:28. *Pray for those who persecute you.* Matthew 5:44. *Do not resist an evil person.* Matthew 5:38. *Rejoice over insults.* Matthew 5:12. *Flee persecution.* Matthew 10:23. *Forgive those who sin against you.* Matthew 6:14. *Be merciful.* Luke 6:36.

The last relationship about which Jesus instructs much, one relationship not yet addressed directly in the sections above, is our relationship with enemies. That Jesus teaches so often and so much about how to deal with enemies might surprise some today, just as his instructions on enemies seem to have surprised many when he first gave them as recorded in the gospel accounts. Who, after all, really has *enemies*, at least on a personal level? And why, after all, should we care so much about them? Yet on the other hand, Jesus's instructions about enemies, or at least impressions about what Jesus taught about enemies, are at the same time relatively widely known today. Indeed, Jesus's instructions about enemies is in large part what feeds the caricature of Jesus in pop culture today as a peacemaker, unifier, wise man of love and nonviolence, and easy-going, anything-goes forgiving flower child of a man. Both impressions, either that enemies are an unfit subject for spiritual instruction or that Jesus just wants us to forgive and forget no matter the enemy or enemy's conduct, fail to do anything like justice to what Jesus taught. His instructions on relationship to enemies are not simply important additions as they are an integral part of the foundation for his other commands and teachings. Consider carefully what Jesus says about relating to enemies. How you relate to enemies may be just as important as how you relate to family and friends.

Love your enemies. Matthew 5:43.

Jesus's instruction to love one's enemies was profound at the time he first gave it, as recounted immediately below, and remains profound today. Many may think that they have no enemy, certainly no one coming at them with lance or sword, and so hardly need to attend to Jesus's instruction. In truth, we nearly all have enemies in the way in which we probably ought to construe the term and instruction. Enemies, one supposes, come in different forms, but what they have in common is that they oppose us. Who hasn't had a family member, neighbor, co-worker, fellow congregant, creditor, debtor, service provider, or other person or entity, oppose them in some manner? Given our large number of transactions and interests, modern society produces as many disputes as, or probably many more disputes than, ancient society. What Jesus said then applies just as much today. We do not ordinarily love those who oppose us. Indeed, we do everything but love those who stand in our way. *We* oppose *them*, challenging, belittling, and disputing their authority, credibility, fairness, right, and reputation, when none of these actions is loving. In this way, we make enemies when we don't even have them, when the people who oppose us may only be doing their jobs or protecting their own interests. Jesus's admonition to love one's enemies revolutionizes relationship. Hate and disrespect, conflict and opposition, are not options.

Jesus had reached the fullness of his Sermon on the Mount. He had begun with blessings, taught about salt and light, and the role of the law. He had addressed murder, adultery, divorce, and oaths. One can imagine his hearers in rapt attention at his authoritative instruction yet also somehow expecting more, expecting Jesus to reveal even deeper and broader truths ready for their application. Then Jesus's teaching, at once so sound and still somehow surprising, took another surprising turn as he began to address the crowd's treatment of their enemies. They might have thought that he would condemn their enemies for them, promising to bring fire and brimstone down on them, but instead he did not. Jesus began, "You have heard that it was said, 'Love your neighbor and hate your enemy.'" Here the crowd might have leaned forward for an endorsement of that conventional wisdom. "But I tell you, love your enemies," Jesus said instead, promptly offering the promise that they would be children of their Father in heaven if they did so. Could it be that the God who had alternately punished and restored Israel so often in its stubbornness would yet command them, indeed even permit them, to love one's enemies?

He finally admitted to himself first that he *had* enemies and then that he was not loving them. His admission took a long time, much longer than it should have taken. When he had first studied Jesus's instruction to love enemies, he had thought incorrectly that he really had none. Actually, though, he had many. His occupation, commerce, and society brought him into contact with many individuals who and entities that in one way or another disagreed with him, opposed him, diverted him, and obstructed him. Much time had passed before he was willing to admit to himself that these persons and entities, were his enemies within the meaning of Jesus's instruction, not that he should treat them as enemies but that they fell reasonably within the definition of enemies as Jesus's instruction probably intended. Indeed, he finally learned to recognize them as enemies within that definition because of the way that he felt about them and in some cases treated them, which was first to attribute all manner of negative attributes to them and then to disagree, oppose, divert, and obstruct them, just as they did him. Of course, he later realized that he was making himself *their* enemy. What he needed to learn was how to re-humanize them, to love them like a friend even if they seemed to him to be enemies.

Bless those who curse you. Luke 6:28.

In nearly the same breath that Jesus taught to love enemies, he also said to bless those who curse you. Some may not find much distinction between loving enemies and blessing those who curse us, and indeed, little distinction there may be. Yet Jesus said at once both to love enemies *and* to bless those who curse you. He thus may well have intended some distinction, some extension of his instruction to love, an extension beyond mere enemies to those who actively curse us, and an extension beyond mere loving them to the point of actively blessing them. To love in this context would seem to be to show undue affection for enemies, while to bless would seem to be to do more in the manner of positively approving and supporting them. Jesus seems to have appreciated that we might love enemies, show undue affection to them who are after all enemies, but yet in our hesitation to reward an enemy not go beyond mere love and affection to the point of blessing them. Jesus, though, instructs to do just that, to go beyond loving to blessing, even those who actively curse and vex us. Jesus is not in other words counseling mere toleration of passive enemies but approval of active adversaries. Something extraordinary is afoot in Jesus's counterintuitive treatment of enemies. The kingdom opens and operates on love, not conflict.

Jesus was teaching the large crowd on the plain in the manner after which he had given the Sermon on the Mount. After speaking to the crowd about blessings for the poor and hungry, and woes for the rich and well fed, Jesus turned as he had in the Sermon on the Mount to the subject of love for enemies. Yet while in the Sermon on the Mount, Jesus had spoken about loving rather than hating enemies, he had not said specifically, as he would say on the plain, to consecrate those who actively condemn them. On the plain, Jesus had begun nearly as he did in the Sermon, "But to you who are listening, I say: Love your enemies," and after another interjection, had continued, "bless those who curse you," before continuing on with more ways in which the crowd was to love, affirm, and approve of enemies. If someone slaps, then let them slap again, Jesus had said. If someone takes a coat, then give them your shirt, Jesus had added. Jesus wanted the people positively blessing their opponents.

He had learned that quieting his heart of the natural venom that conflict produced was not sufficient. He couldn't alone just tell himself to love his enemies when his head, heart, and emotions wanted to do the opposite. He had to find some positive way in which to direct his negative energy. Jesus had given him a clue in saying to *bless those who curse you.* So he decided to do so. Whenever he saw someone opposing him in a way that annoyed, angered, or rankled him, he would do what he could to set aside the negative inner dialogue and emotions. Yet he would also look for something positive to do for them. Sometimes, the positive blessing would be a kind word, recognition, lauding, or encouragement to the enemy or about the enemy to one of the enemy's friends. Other times, the blessing would be extension of a mercy or privilege, some small courtesy or gift, as unmerited as it might have been for an enemy. As he took these positive steps to bless, he saw in every instance that his anger and negativity toward the enemy subsided, sometimes well beyond the point of quiet toleration into respect and confidence. He had learned the power of Jesus's instruction not just to love enemies in sentiment but to positively bless those who curse you.

Pray for those who persecute you. Matthew 5:44.

To pray for those who persecute you, as Jesus also instructed, means to ask God that God would do for one's enemies as you would have God do for you. The Psalms and other books and writings give plenty of evidence of important figures praying that God would bring destruction on enemies, just as a reader finds examples of figures praying that God would bless family and friends. One can imagine God hearing the many overlapping prayers to bless friends and punish enemies, each side praying for them and against the other, until the prayers effectively cancel one another out. One has little way of knowing how God would resolve such competing prayers, particularly when prayers on both sides come from both the righteous and unrighteous. The conflicting prayers may sound to God like an unrighteous cacophony. Then imagine if a people, followers of Christ who listen to and obey his commands, instead united in prayers for all, both friends and enemies, simply for blessing. When Jesus instructs to pray *for* enemies, he does not mean to pray for their punishment. He instead means to pray that they would prosper first in their relationship to him and his Father and then in relationship to others including their praying enemy. The saying is that when one points a finger at another, several fingers point back. When one prays against an enemy, several prayers against may come back. Better to pray for both friends *and enemies* that all prayer would be for kingdom entry.

In his Sermon on the Mount, in the midst of his teaching about love for enemies, Jesus extended the teaching beyond loving rather than hating enemies. Right after saying to love enemies, Jesus added to "pray for those who persecute you, that you may be children of your Father in heaven." Jesus wanted the crowd speaking to the Father on behalf of their enemies, entreating the Father to do for their enemies as they would have the Father do for them. Many in the crowd had probably prayed to the Father that the Father would curse and punish their enemies. One wonders how few had asked the Father to forgive their enemies and even bless their enemies in the way that they would wish forgiveness and blessing. Jesus continued on that his Father shines sun on both good and evil, and brings rain on both righteous and unrighteous. Jesus concluded that part of the lesson saying that they were to love, greet, bless, and pray for all people, not just their people, so that they would be perfect as their heavenly Father is perfect. Jesus wanted them praying for their enemies.

Even as he learned to bless his enemies, those enemies that he had once thought that he did not have, he also learned to pray for those enemies. His prayers were initially strained, infrequent, and halting. He hardly knew what to pray because his heart was indeed filled with venom that he had hardly known was there. Yet gradually, as he learned the practice of praying for enemies, turning it from an infrequent event to a solid habit, he also learned how to pray for them, that is, for the same kinds of blessing for which he knew how to pray for family and friends. His prayers for enemies became less like, *Lord, let them see their errors*, and more like his prayers for anyone else. He learned to pray for enemies first, before praying for family and friends, sensing that God was hearing his prayers for family and friends better when he cleared his heart of venom for enemies and replaced that venom with prayer, that purging constituting a blessed miracle that God also returned.

Do not resist an evil person. Matthew 5:38.

Even when we love enemies, bless them, and pray for them, and our hearts toward them change accordingly, they may still remain enemies to us in their actions. One would be naïve to think that every loving kindness, every prayer, instantly melts every enemy heart. Love, blessing, and prayer change an enemy's heart, too, not just the heart of the one who prays, but the change of the enemy's heart may not be as quick or as thorough as the one who prays desires. Kindness and prayer may work more quickly when one's opponent acts out of natural interests over what both perceive to be limited opportunities or resources. Competition is natural and understandable. Prayer and generosity can bring competitors together in compromise. Yet the challenge that an enemy presents seems different when the enemy's motivation is not natural but *evil*. How does one respond to an evil enemy, not just one who opposes out of natural interests and responsibilities but who opposes and obstructs without natural cause? Jesus tells us not to resist an evil person. The instruction at first feels unnatural and sounds extraordinary. But one finds that evil can desire and thrive on conflict. Resisting an evil person gives the evil a foothold from which to work further evil. That foothold enables evil to draw down in struggle the resources and faith of the one who resists. Better not to resist an evil person over things that one can instead relinquish without losing one's faith. Pick your struggles wisely, and avoid struggling against evil over things having no kingdom consequence.

When Jesus began preaching about loving enemies, some in the crowd might have at first assumed that he meant only natural enemies, those whose interests were simply set against one's own interests, as in competition over limited land or resources. They might have found it hard to imagine that Jesus included *evil* persons in his concern. Yet in his message on the plain, right before Jesus summarized the theme with his generalization to love enemies, Jesus had already given specific instructions on how to treat those who injure, take, and offend, including the evil ones who do so. Jesus first reminded the crowd of the old way of taking an eye from the one who caused loss of an eye and knocking out a tooth of the one who knocked out a tooth. Jesus then said, "But I tell you, do not resist an evil person." He then said to let the one who slaps slap again on the other cheek, to give shirt to the one who takes cloak, and to walk a second mile with the one who forces the first-mile walk. Jesus did not want the crowd resisting those evil persons who must have their way.

At first, she felt the full weight of her opponent's opposition. She had been surprised at the opposition and not a little taken aback and even offended. She had not expected the person to oppose her at all and instead to support her. The surprise made her opponent's opposition all the more difficult with which to deal. Its unexpectedness undermined her confidence, caught her off guard, and made her question her own motives and actions. That questioning and her opponent's continued opposition, recruiting others to the opposition cause, began so to weigh on her that she could think of little else. The more that she tried to push back against opposition that seemed to her to have no rationale other than its own inward fury, the less energy that she had to care for other things that had real consequence. Her neglect of other things further undermined her confidence. She began to detect familiar symptoms of old depression. Then the thought occurred to her that she had taken the wrong approach in resisting. She had not really thought of her opponent as evil, but because the opposition continued to seem to her to be senseless, she decided to treat the opposition in the way that Jesus said to treat the evil person. She stopped resisting. As she did so, she slowly regained her composure to resume her other activities. She thought at first that letting her opponent proceed unopposed would have some major unfortunate impact, but it did not. She decided to watch more closely in the future for opponents whose opposition she should simply not resist.

Rejoice over insults. Matthew 5:12.

As the prior sections show, we can rationalize and make sense of the thoughts of loving, blessing, and praying for enemies, and not resisting evil persons, even though we need not rationalize those thoughts and should instead simply obey them as Jesus commands. Yet Jesus's instruction to *rejoice* over insults from those who persecute his followers takes a different mindset. Dutiful actions pursuing Jesus's commands, even difficult commands like loving enemies, makes sense from both an instrumental standpoint that following commands produces good and from the standpoint of submission to Jesus whether or not we witness or discern the command's good. Do as he says, hope for good, and obey in any case. But when Jesus instructs to *rejoice* over insults, he asks for something beyond dutiful obedience. To rejoice is to celebrate, even to exult, over an achievement, event, or occurrence. Few of us think of rejoicing over insults. Offense, injury, and retaliation are the natural reactions instead. Jesus, though, is clear that when the insult is because of belief in him, rejoice, don't retaliate. Let others heap insults on you for your following Jesus, and then simply smile back at them when they do. Those who insult you as a follower have just given you more to rejoice, more of a reward in the kingdom.

Jesus began the Sermon on the Mount with a list of blessings that we know as the Beatitudes. The Beatitudes begin with blessed are the poor, blessed are mourners, blessed are the meek, and so on, Jesus proclaiming kingdom access even to these downtrodden. His blessings would have uplifted and encouraged many among the crowd to whom he spoke, those in particular who would have had one or more of the attributes Jesus listed. His message must have meant much to those to whom and about whom he spoke because society did not value their attributes. Jesus was telling them that their rejection in the social and political hierarchy, and cultural values, and even within the religious hierarchy, meant nothing so far as kingdom access. Jesus ended the list of blessings, though, with special reference to the rejection that many would face because of their belief in him. Jesus concluded the Beatitudes saying that were blessed when people insulted and persecuted them, and said evil things against them, because of Jesus. He concluded, "Rejoice and be glad, because great is your reward in heaven, for in the same way they persecuted the prophets who were before you." Jesus wanted those among the crowd who followed him to rejoice over the insults of their enemies who were also enemies of Christ.

She had never been sensitive over her recognition of Jesus as Lord, never felt that she had to hide or protect it. She was fine with what other people thought of her love for Jesus, whether they liked it or not. She knew though that she had grown up in a family and community that did not challenge but instead supported her insight, wisdom, and discernment in relying on the Lord. She knew also that those challenges were out there in the broader world. Indeed, others' denigration of belief, commitment, truth, and faith sometimes crept in to her world, even if primarily indirectly as things that she heard but to which no one expected her to respond. Direct confrontation, insults, and persecution over faith just didn't happen much in her world, which was of course fine with her, she had always thought. Indeed, she had long felt that she was the wiser and better for it that she had chosen friends and community to nurture her faith and the faith of one another. Yet as she read again Jesus's instruction to rejoice over insults because of him, and read again of the great heavenly reward, she wondered whether she had instead missed something. Maybe she *was* hiding her faith, or maybe she was restricting her community and fellowship in ways that she should not. She didn't exactly want to go looking for insults simply to rejoice and gain a heavenly reward, but maybe, just maybe, God wanted her in habits and places where people took sufficient notice of her faith, and reacted to her faith even with insults, that the reward would be hers.

Flee persecution. Matthew 10:23.

As often as Jesus instructed and exhorted to love, bless, and pray for enemies, and to rejoice when they insult you for following him, he separately instructed that believers would find times to flee persecution. As the following recount of one gospel account shows, Jesus specifically instructed the disciples to flee persecution as they moved from town to town on their gospel mission. Turning the other cheek, giving the shirt off one's back, and going the extra mile, are all appropriate actions when responding to opponents who demand and take things from you. So, too, is rejoicing over insults to faith. We encounter enemies, perhaps co-workers, neighbors, and even fellow congregants, from whom we cannot and should not flee but to whom we should instead respond in love. Yet Jesus does not insist that we remain in a place that has rejected the gospel message and is persecuting the messenger. He instead counsels in that setting to flee persecution. Persecution can be very uncomfortable and of course very dangerous, and flight seems an obvious solution at least for self-preservation. But Jesus's instruction to flee persecution only implies that the purpose is self-preservation, when flight also has other purposes including to spread the gospel message. Flee persecution, and in doing so, spread the gospel message.

When Jesus sent the twelve disciples out on their first mission alone, giving them elaborate instructions, he spoke to them about the enemies that they would encounter. Indeed, he warned the disciples that everyone would hate them because of him. They should expect complete rejection in towns that they visited along their way. Jesus had already instructed the disciples to leave those towns that rejected them, shaking the dust off their feet as they left. They need not worry about those towns, which God would judge severely. Jesus told them that they would be like sheep among wolves but that he would protect them and the Spirit of their Father would give them what to say. Jesus concluded his instructions about how to deal with enemies as they traveled from town to town on their gospel mission, saying, "When you are persecuted in one place, flee to another." Jesus wanted the disciples moving away from persecution, out of godless towns, to other towns where they might share the gospel message.

He had not expected persecution. He also recognized that the persecution that he sensed was persecution only on a very limited level, certainly not what would qualify as persecution in many other settings. He was never in physical danger and probably did not even face the job loss, career damage, and other harms that he feared might occur if he did not take the right action. What was clear, though, was that the faith message that he carried was not at all welcome, indeed, was vigorously rejected, and that he would not be heard on any sacred *or* secular matter related in any way to it. He thus pondered the appropriate response. How should one behave when one's very identity in faith the community of which one is a part so thoroughly rejects? He felt as if he were a non-entity, not even a person any longer within that community, as if it would no longer even acknowledge that he existed. Oddly, though, even as he felt isolated, ostracized, and condemned within that community that previously had meant so much to him, he also felt freed, released of responsibility for it. Then, he remembered Jesus's instruction to flee persecution, leave the place, and shake the dust off one's feet. Now *that* was the right approach.

Forgive those who sin against you. Matthew 6:14.

Whatever relationship we assume with respect to enemies, meaning in this instance those who sin against us, we should be forgiving them those sins. No matter whether one flees or stays in response to enemies and persecution, Jesus still instructs to forgive those who sin against you. Sin is disobedience to God. Thus those who sin against us are those who violate God's commands in ways that affect us adversely. Some sins by others do not affect us, while other sins affect us deeply, bringing about substantial harm and loss. One might think that we would have little responsibility to forgive another's sins especially when those sins harm us. When God forgives sins, why should we also do so, particularly when the other's disobedience has harmed us directly? Yet forgiving others who sin against us is exactly what Jesus instructs. He also tells us why we must do so, which is that God will not forgive us without our forgiving those others. Again, one might wonder why God would withhold our forgiveness when we withhold forgiveness of others. But anyone who assumes that they do not sin and that their sins, if any, hurt no one, makes a false assumption. How could God forgive us when we are so like those others whom we hesitate to forgive because they have harmed us? When we forgive others who sin against us, we are only doing what we ask God to do for us. Do for others what you would have God do for you.

As he continued to speak at length to the crowd that had followed him up the mountainside, Jesus reached the subject of prayer, in the middle of the Sermon on the Mount. After addressing the crowd with how they should pray, not for show but in secret to their Father, Jesus gave them a specific example in the form of what many call the Lord's Prayer. The prayer, of course, included a request that the Father forgive the debts of the one who prays as the one who prays forgives the debts of others. That part of the prayer established a condition for forgiveness, one that might have surprised some in the crowd, which was that the one who prays must forgive others in order to expect God's forgiveness. After concluding the prayer, Jesus explained that the debts that the crowd was to forgive had to do with sins against them. He said, "For if you forgive other people when they sin against you, your heavenly Father will also forgive you." Spelling out the condition for forgiveness even further, Jesus continued that if the crowd's members did not forgive others who sin against them, then their Father would not forgive their sins. Jesus wanted the crowd to forgive others who sin against them.

Her head told her to forgive, but her heart was having a harder time going along with it. She had long known and mostly practiced Jesus's command to forgive others. She knew quite well the consequence of not forgiving others, which was to deny herself God's forgiveness. The thought of God denying her forgiveness was of course scary to her, for she knew that she needed God's forgiveness. She would have obeyed the command without the incentive, but the incentive was a remarkably powerful reminder. Even so, when others hurt her deeply enough, depriving her of some respect or right, and did so because of their evident corruption, her head said forgive, but her heart said no. She kept returning, though, to the way that Jesus had stated the incentive. She would have no forgiveness if she gave none. She knew that her heart desired forgiveness, in fact badly needed it. So she decided that what she needed to do, consistent with Jesus's command and its incentive, was to connect her heart's need for forgiveness with her heart's reluctance to forgive others. She needed her heart to feel for others in the way that her heart felt for herself. As she reflected more on the hearts of others, and how those hearts must cry out for forgiveness like her own heart cried out, her own heart began to soften into forgiveness for others. She had a way yet to go, but Jesus's command had gotten her started.

Be merciful. Luke 6:36.

Jesus addresses one other command, a summary sort of command, toward our relationship with enemies. Jesus commands us to be merciful. Judgment reflects due consequences for bad actions. Mercy reflects the withholding of full judgment when judgment is due, the withdrawal or limiting of just consequences for bad action, when the wrong does not merit that limitation. Mercy, a misunderstood attribute and action, is not a weakness in God or others who have the right and responsibility to judge. Rather, extending mercy reflects the expectation that mercy will do more to rehabilitate the wrongdoer than would full judgment. God wants us to pull up short of demanding everything that we are due from others who have harmed us. In doing so, we change the equation, leaving the one who sins against us owing regard for the one who withholds judgment. Through mercy, we build bridges to and for others, bridges of sacrificial love that reach to God, just as God built a bridge for us through the merciful sacrifice of his Son. Mercy is God's attribute, a prime attribute of his deepest love. God wants us to reflect his attributes to others, just as he wants us to know and continue to benefit from his attributes. We must be merciful, must show mercy, to be like our Father on whose mercy we so greatly depend.

Jesus concluded that part of his message on the plain in which he addressed loving enemies, with an admonition to be merciful. He had already said to love, bless, and pray for enemies. He had already said to turn the other cheek, give the shirt off one's back, and walk the extra mile. Jesus then explained how different following his commands would make his hearers than those who did not know and follow his commands. He told the crowd that even sinners love their friends, so how would they be any different loving only friends and not enemies? If they lent only to those who could repay, how would they be any different than sinners who do so? The only way that they could distinguish themselves in their love, and reap the great reward of children in God's kingdom, would be to follow Jesus's commands to love enemies, do them good, and lend without expecting payment. Jesus then connected the extraordinary actions that he was commanding with a concept that his hearers may have known well, that of mercy. Jesus concluded, "Be merciful, just as your Father is merciful." To love and bless enemies is to be merciful, as God is merciful.

He loved the thought, concept, and attribute of mercy, even loved to extend mercy in the relatively few instances where he had the right and responsibility of judgment. He knew justice well, had justice at his core, as a prime attribute of love. He knew too, though, that mercy must balance justice, without which neither could be any part of love. Justice without mercy becomes retribution, while mercy without justice becomes lawlessness, disconnecting cause from consequences. He had received mercy, more times than he could count. As often as he received mercy, he nevertheless never demanded it, indeed hardly ever even expected it. The moment one expects mercy, he believed, one has tipped the balance against it. Judgment should instead result. Mercy must remain in the hands and discretion of the judge, for the moment one compels mercy, it is no longer mercy but tolerance and indulgence. He did not want to be indulged and tolerated but instead held to account, only yet with God's great mercy. He knew that he owed God everything and that God had every right to take everything from him but also that God had extended him mercy through his glorious Son. Although he had long ago accepted God's offer of mercy, that which he had not earned and did not deserve, its value to him continued to grow each day. That gift of God was why he loved mercy so much and was so willing to extend it.

509

Conclusion

We are *always* doing or not doing one or more of the many things that Jesus said to do or not do, or said how to do them. We tend to refer to Jesus's statements, instructions, and admonitions when a question arises, a crisis arises, or a new situation or other special stimulus presents itself. We might even think that *what Jesus would do and have us do* are only concerns in those special situations, sort of like a code of ethics meant only to set boundaries beyond which we should not go, leaving a wide arena for us in which to do as we please to do.

That approach, though, is not the way to think about Jesus's instructions. Jesus said enough about what to do and not do, and how to do it, to apply to *everything* that we do. We could at any moment evaluate our current activity or relationship to see whether we are right then obedient. What are you doing now, and why? Can you identify one of the hundreds of things that Jesus said to do or not do that would justify your thoughts and actions? To live in this fashion would be to follow Jesus's instructions, to obey God.

Yet doing so mechanically, in a formula-like manner, would of course turn us into something we are not and turn our relationship with Jesus into something that it isn't. What our intent might best be instead would be to dwell in Christ, to accept that the Holy Spirit residing in us wants to bring to our mind, perspective, and spirit the words of Christ addressing all actions and relationships. Attending to Christ's commands, instructions, statements, and examples constantly, consistently, and in personally welcoming fashion, might be more like what it means to walk with Christ, dwell in Christ, and know Christ, just as he invites and warrants. That might be how one

511

lives presently in God's kingdom. Think of how rich life would be if at every moment we were living through Jesus's words.

Epilogue

They walked and talked together as they strolled through the glorious kingdom in their resurrected bodies. The realm, though spectacular in an unblemished way that their former abode did not approach, still looked so familiar to them. They had known the kingdom in their earthly life, although they had hardly realized it, had seen it only through a dark lens, not nearly as they knew it fully now, basking in its fruitful splendor. They had in their earthly life barely trusted that the kingdom was theirs then in part as it was in full now. Yet in the little that they did trust and believe, they had then already had partial access to it, with more of it theirs to grasp in faith and obedience. They had even then in their earthly lives lived at times and in part in the kingdom through knowing its King as their Lord and Savior. Now, having finished their earthly terms, first he and then she sometime later, they lived in the kingdom's fullness, lacking nothing, having everything because they had the King and the King had them.

In the realm, they had finally realized the obedience that they had so long desired but so poorly fulfilled in their earthly lives. While on earth, they had struggled to focus on the words and commands of the King in their naturally corrupt state, here they were constantly and naturally aware of the King's desires, in fact always doing as he wished. Of course, they couldn't explain their newfound obedience, even if they had thought to question it, which they had no need for doing. Their resurrected bodies, while preserving their prior identities, never hungered or thirsted, never craved, never caused them any fatigue, anxiety, or insecurity. Their new minds, while preserving their personality and memory, never doubted, never worried, never obsessed. Most of all, their new hearts had nothing

513

but love for everyone because of the all-powerful and complete love of the King within and around them, no longer mediated by the evil that had been within and around them on earth. They walked and talked in perfect obedience to every word and desire of the King, which was after all that which sustained the realm in its glorious and perfect condition.

Their talk was of the delight that they took in knowing that their child and many of their friends and ones that they had then regarded as their enemies would soon join them in the kingdom. They felt no loss or loneliness at not having those for whom they waited patiently with them already in the kingdom, for the kingdom admitted of nothing anything like loss. Talking of those to come was pure pleasure, pure delight in knowing that more would join them to celebrate the King and that the King was drawing them now and would welcome them then. They thought back to their own full entry into the kingdom, the bliss and joy that they had felt, fed by the ecstasy that came finally and fully from their now-complete submission to the King's utter and enduringly benign authority. They had on earth long sensed that they would in heaven feel such joy for the King, although on earth they could hardly appreciate how rich kingdom joy was or how perfectly the King's unmitigated proximity sustained it, having had only rare glimpses of it on earth. Those glimpses, though, had led them forward in confidence and anticipation to the kingdom. Now, all was obedience, all was complete, with eternity to enjoy Him.

Table of Citations